Anonymous

The Medical chronicle

Vol. 2

Anonymous

The Medical chronicle
Vol. 2

ISBN/EAN: 9783337731137

Printed in Europe, USA, Canada, Australia, Japan

Cover: Foto ©ninafisch / pixelio.de

More available books at **www.hansebooks.com**

THE MEDICAL CHRONICLE.

A Monthly Journal for the Practitioner.

GEORGE H. ROHÉ, M. D., Editor.

Vol. 2.

[*AUGUST* 1883 *TO JULY* 1884.]

BALTIMORE:
Press of Thomas & Evans.

INDEX.

ORIGINAL ARTICLES:—

ARNOLD, A. B.—Neurasthenia	97
ARNOLD, J. D.—Œdema of the Glottis in a case of Syphilitic Ulceration of the Larynx	43
BRANHAM, J. H.—Fetal Auscultation	181
CATHELL, D. W.—Fly Blister on a Young Child and its Sequelæ	124
CHAMBERS, J. W.—The Etiology and Pathology of Croupous Pneumonia	117
COSKERY, O. J.—A Case of Basedow's Disease	1
COSKERY, O. J.—The Value of Dry Lint as a Dressing in Compound Fractures	83
COSKERY, O. J.—Three Cases of Spindle-Celled Sarcoma	219
CUDDY, J. W. C.—Treatment of Catarrhal Pneumonia	140
FRIEDENWALD, A.—Recent Progress in Ophthalmology	2
GUNDRY, RICHARD.—The Relations of the Powers of the Individual in Matters Concerning the Public Health	77
HILL, J. HARVEY.—Indigestion in Young Children	199
HILL, W. N.—Infant Mortality	206
LEONARD, B. F.—Acquired Amenorrhœa, with Complete Uterine Atresia, etc.	160
LEONARD, B. F.—On the Treatment of Dysmenorrhœa and Abortion	41
LEONARD, B. F.—Operation by Galvano-Cautery on Internal Hemorrhoids; Cure	179
LYNCH, J. S.—Hemorrhagic Malarial Fever	182
LYNCH, J. S.—The Qualifications Necessary for the Successful Study of Medicine	61
McINTOSH, W. PAGE.—Vaccination in the New-Born	44
McINTOSH, W. PAGE.—Strangulated Hernia.—Intermeningeal Hemorrhage.—Tubercular Peritonitis	6
NORRIS, WM. H.—Biliary Calculi	222
PERCIVAL, CHAS. FREDERICK.—The Pathology of Pneumonic Inflammations in the Lower animals	121
PILGRIM, C. W.—Abortion	21
REID, E. M.—Symptomatology of Catarrhal Pneumonia	139
ROHÉ, GEORGE H.—Epithelioma of the Hand.—Simple Ulcer of Forearm	98
ROHÉ, GEORGE H.—Non-Parasitic Sycosis	157
ROHÉ, GEORGE H.—A Trip to West Virginia	208
SANFORD, A.—Two Cases of Extirpation of the Ovaries	161
SCARFF, J. H.—A Hairpin in the Bladder	162
STEWART, J. G.—The Treatment of Chronic Ulcers	85
WHEATON, C. A.—Amputation at the Hip-Joint.—Arrest of Hemorrhage by a New Method	137
WINSEY, WHITFIELD.—A Case of Placenta Previa; Shoulder Presentation and Spontaneous Evolution	24

INDEX.

CORRESPONDENCE:—

Clinical Instruction in London.—M. H. Atter	45
Clinical Teaching in Vienna.—Wilmer Brinton	142
Does Borax Cause Psoriasis?—E. Wigglesworth	214
Kaposi, Neumann and Rosenthal.—Wilmer Brinton	101
Medical Education in Turkey.—T. W. Kay	144
Prag as a Medical Centre.—Wilmer Brinton	8
Railroad Surgery.—J. D. Mulhane	189
The Contagiousness of Croupous Pneumonia.—C. M. Pool	162
The Report of the Maryland State Board of Health.—J. S. Conrad	163
The Vienna Lying-In Hospital.—Wilmer Brinton	46
Vacation Gossip.—Wilmer Brinton	86

ANALECTS:—

Acute Rheumatism in Childhood	14
A Formula for Irregular Heart Action	104
Alcohol in Trichinosis	108
Albumen in Healthy Urine	107
Alleged Increase of Insanity in the United States	108
A Lure for Trout and Black Bass	73
A Method of Rendering the Skin Insensible	194
An Infant Fifty-six Years of Age	110
Apomorphia as an Emetic	15
A Sensitive Reflex Area in the Posterior Nares	31
Average Health of Miners	57
Bacteria; their Mutability	150
Ball of Hair in the Stomach	56
Bismuth Treatment of Wounds	23
Boracic Acid in Cervical Endometritis	90
Bromide Salts for Abdominal Neuroses	129
Bromide of Sodium	57
Bromide Ulcers	30
Carbonic Oxide in the Air	108
Cascara Sagrado in Internal Hemorrhoids	150
Cancer of the Rectum Relieved by Scraping	149
Castor Oil and Glycerine	74
Carbolized Iodoform	30
Chloral Hydrate as a Vesicant	108
Clinical Study of the Action and Uses of Caffein and Convallaria Majalis as Cardiac Tonics	130
Corrosive Sublimate in Gonorrhœa	138
Co-existence of Chancre and Chancroid	131
Coca	169
Constant Crying of an Infant from Hunger	105
Concentrated Solution of Saline Cathartics	106
Coffee in Strangulated Hernia	72
Convergent Squint	15
Determination of Sex	150
Diabetes	190
Diagnosis of Diseases of the Stomach	193
Diagnosis of Diabetes	150
Divulsion of the Internal Os for Dysmenorrhœal Headache	147
Diagnostic Value of Uterine Hemorrhages after the Menopause	111
Diphtheria and Infected Milk	88
Disinfection of the Stools in Enteric Fever	28
Dyspeptic and Uterine Headaches	34
Effect of Strychnine upon Dilatation of the Heart	31
Effects of Quinine on the Ear	29
Electricity in Skin Diseases	74
Emetics in Croup and Suffocative Bronchitis	54
Envious of Hunter	36
Ether Spray as an Immediate Cure for Neuralgia	150
Examination per Rectum in Coxitis	232
Extirpation of Goitre	74
Fœtus in Fœtu	169
Fresh Paint	172

INDEX.

Fruits of Compulsory Vaccination	33
Funnel Drainage in Anasarca	30
Gallic Acid in Hemorrhage from Urinary Organs	227
Goodell's Mixture	31
Headaches and Kerosene Lamps	73
Hemorrhoids	74
Hints on the Treatment of Constipation	148
Hot Water Vaginal Injections	110
Hot Water for Inflamed Mucous Surfaces	92
How to Remove a Tight Ring	73
How to Prevent Loss of Alcohol from Specimen Jars	57
How Celluloid is Made	55
Influence of Syphilis upon the Progress of Cancer	131
Influence of Diphtheria upon Pregnancy	109
Intestinal Occlusion Due to a Biliary Calculus Impacted in the Rectum	104
Intestinal Concretions	73
Influence of Fowler's Solution upon the Hemoglobin	36
Inherited Syphilis of the Mammary Glands	32
Infectious Pneumonia	15
Iodine as a Gastric Sedative	72
Knee-Chest Posture for Dislodging Twins	104
Let Nature Remove the Placenta	127
Longevity of Males and Females	75
Losing his Memory	75
Local Treatment of Erysipelas	74
Malignant Disease of the Testicle Tapped for Hydrocele	229
Mercuric Bichloride as an Antiseptic	90
Nasal Catarrh	33
Neuralgia of the Second Branch of the Trigeminus	192
Non-Vesicating Croton Oil	173
Observations on Hydrocele	125
Oil of Wintergreen in Rheumatism	57
Oral Pathology	169
Painless Treatment of Condylomata	180
Panaritium	170
Pathology of Old Age	131
Perspiration in Albuminuria	194
Prevention of Sea Sickness	132
Prevention and Cure of Sea Sickness	167
Prolapse of the Transverse Colon	111
Proper Method of Trephining	228
Punctured Wounds of the Skull	165
Puerperal Eclampsia	109
Rectal Alimentation	57
Resection of the Knee	229
Resorcin as a Remedy in Cystitis	75
Remedies in Neuralgia	53
Results of Medical Legislation in Illinois	16
Rectal Antiseptics in Typhoid Fever	14
Researches on the Physiology of the Bile	10
Rheumatism—Three Types	105
Rules for Reducing Dislocations of the Hip Joint	109
Sea Bathing	16
School Hygiene	109
Semmola on the Pathogenesis of Bright's Disease	35
Small Doses	56
Sore-Throat in Children	214
Steam after Tracheotomy Operations	230
Substitute for Mercurial Ointment	36
Successful Abdominal Surgery	132
Surgical Expedients in Emergencies	50
Surgical Use of Collodion	228
Surprising the Urethra	75
Symptoms of Iodoform Poisoning	215
Syphilitic Neuralgia	149
Syphilis and Rachitis	72

INDEX. 239

Tears of Blood.. 112
The Management of Chorea 164
The Cadaveric Poisons.. 113
The Causation of Nervous Disease... 224
The Conversion of Malignant Tumors into Innocent Growths......................... 112
The Cotton Pellet as an Artificial Drum-head..................................... 28
The Diatetic Treatment of Diabetes Mellitus...................................... 226
The Proper Feeding of Infants.. 91
The Statistics of Paracentosis Pericardii.. 71
The Erysipelas Germ.. 56
The Nature and Treatment of Scrofula, from the Standpoint of Recent Investigations Concerning the Influence of Bacilli.............................. 231
The New Indian Cure for Syphilis... 82
The Relationship existing between Physicians and Druggists....................... 12
The Ophthalmia of Small-pox.. 10
The Radical Cure of Exomphalos... 128
Three Infectious Diseases in the same Individual................................. 107
Thomsen's Disease.. 30
Thoracic Diseases.. 29
To Abort a Stye.. 74
Treatment of Hay Fever and Allied Disorders..................................... 191
Treatment of After Pains... 169
Treatment of Diabetes with Bromide of Potassium.................................. 151
Treatment of Whooping Cough.. 92
Treatment of Warts and Condylomata by Carbonic Acid.............................. 56
Treatment of Typhoid by Ergot.. 15
Treatment of Hemorrhoids... 12
Treatment of Acute Abscess... 230
Trichiniasis in Illinois... 147
Tuberculosis One Hundred Years Ago... 146
Tuberculosis, Scrofula and Lupus... 25
Vaccination in India... 150
Veratria in Muscular Tremor.. 215
Vesication in Diphtheria... 151
Winter Eczema.. 103
Why Phosphorus should not be given to Red Haired People.......................... 157

SOCIETY PROCEEDINGS:—

Michigan State Board of Health... 188
The American Public Health Association... 88
The Michigan State Board of Health... 123
Transactions of the American Dermatological Association. *Supplement*.......

EDITORIAL:—

A Fabrication.. 17
A Cowardly Attack.. 133
Annual Report of the City Health Department...................................... 153
Anti-Vivisectionism.. 93
Another Step in Advance.. 75
An Unsuccessful Suit for a Diploma... 38
Our New Volume... 17
Quinan's Medical Annals of Baltimore... 176
The Administration of Ether by the Rectum.. 233
The American Public Health Association... 233
The Annual Message of Mayor Latrobe.. 133
The American Medical Association.. 195, 216
The Meeting of the Medical and Chirurgical Faculty of Maryland................... 195
The Twelfth Annual Commencement of the Baltimore College of Physicians
 and Surgeons... 173
The Medical Service at Bay View Charity Hospital and the Medical Colleges
 of Baltimore... 174
The Report of the State Board of Health.. 153
The National Board of Health... 113
The Baltimore Polyclinic... 155
The Index Medicus.. 93
The Alumni Prize... 76

INDEX

The Coming Lecture Session.. 58
The Prospect of an Epidemic of Cholera....................................... 37
The Necessity of a Law to Regulate the Practice of Medicine in Maryland... 17
The American Public Health Association....................................... 58
Tweedledum and Tweedledee.. 38

CURRENT LITERATURE :—

Annual Report of the Supervising Surgeon-General of the Marine Hospital Service for 1883.. 115
Butler's Daily Pocket Record.. 95
Bulkley's Eczema and its Management.. 217
Courty's Treatise on the Diseases of the Uterus............................. 39
Chesney's Shakespeare as a Physician....................................... 197
Dulles' What to Do First in Emergencies..................................... 94
Gibney's the Hip and its Diseases... 177
Hammond's Sexual Impotence in the Male..................................... 59
Hamilton's Health Aphorisms... 95
Hamilton's Manual of Medical Jurisprudence................................. 155
Hamilton's Dialogues on Medical Ethics..................................... 197
Howe's Excessive Venery, Masturbation and Continence....................... 155
Health Hints for Travelers.. 234
Lindsay & Blakiston's Visiting List... 95
Otis' Clinical Lessons on Syphilis and the Genito-Urinary Diseases......... 114
One Hundredth Anniversary of Harvard University............................ 217
Quinan's History of the Introduction of Inoculation and Vaccination into Maryland... 19
Report of the Connecticut State Board of Health............................. 59
Rosse's Medical and Anthropological Notes on Alaska........................ 94
Registration Report of Rhode Island for 1882............................... 155
Report of the State Board of Health of West Virginia for 1881-3............ 196
Sanitary Conventions at Pontiac and Muskegon, Mich., 1883.................. 134
Sanitary and Statistical Report of the Surgeon-General of the Navy for 1881 94
Semple's Diseases of Children... 196
Sexual Neurasthenia... 234
Transactions of the Medical Society of West Virginia....................... 59
Ziegler's Text-book of Pathological Anatomy................................ 18

FLOTSAM :—

..........................19, 40, 60, 76, 96, 115, 135, 156, 177, 198, 217, 234

The Medical Chronicle.

BALTIMORE, AUGUST, 1883.

ORIGINAL ARTICLES.

ARTICLE I.
A CASE OF BASEDOW'S DISEASE.

By OSCAR J. COSKERY, M. D.,
Professor of Surgery, College of Physicians and Surgeons, Baltimore.

Morris S———, aged 28 years, was admitted into St. Joseph's Hospital March 19th, 1883. He had been in several institutions before, among which may be mentioned St. Luke's Hospital in New York, the "Jewish" in this city, Providence in Washington, D. C.; from the latter he came to St. Joseph's.

His family and personal history up to the time of entry into hospital, furnished by himself, is as follows:

Father died at 38, his widowed mother at 37, of cancer of the breast(?). Had two brothers, both healthy. No sisters.

His disease had commenced twenty-two months ago. He first noticed that his eyelids itched and pained him, he was constantly rubbing and winking them. His brother one night first noticed a staring condition of the eye-balls; this followed rapidly upon the first symptom. Soon palpitation of the heart came on. After all these symptoms had continued for three or four weeks, the throat began to enlarge, and in a few weeks reached a size much greater than now. In despite of various plans of treatment, local and constitutional, (among others may be mentioned the tapping and injection of the goitre) the size of the gland remained about the same for two months, then commenced to diminish and continued to do so until the present size was reached, about fifteen months ago. Since then very slight fluctuations in its size have been noticed. All this time he has been losing flesh and growing weak, but most especially so for the last three months. Nearly all through his sickness he has suffered from repeated attacks of diarrhœa, but about three months ago this symptom increased in severity and became constant. He would often have twenty stools in twelve hours. Six weeks ago œdema of legs and scrotum came on, with cough and expectoration, loss of appetite and frequent attacks of pyrosis Suffered also from pain in the abdomen, loins and head, and had found that his temperature was always above the normal (99° to 101°.)

On admission into hospital his condition was as follows:

An extreme state of emaciation; the eye-balls revealing nearly half their circumference; a swelling of the thyroid gland to such an extent that the tape line carried over its most prominent part and the apex of the seventh cervical vertebra (which it was exactly opposite) showed $13\frac{1}{2}$ inches.

The complexion was muddy, the eyebrows drawn together, hair and beard scanty, and a persistent cough with moderately profuse expectoration racked the patient. Upon examining the chest, in places tubular breathing was noticed with very coarse rales, but no cavities could be positively made out. The pulse was rapid; indeed, during his entire residence in hospital it ranged from 100 to 120. Diarrhœa was constant. Urine passed frequently and in large quantities. An examination of the latter showed that it was acid in reaction, clear, and with no traces of albumen or sugar. A distinct blowing sound over the heart and over the thyroid gland. The arteries and veins of the head, face and neck stand out and pulsate visibly. The legs and scrotum are œdematous. Appetite enormous, but, as he says, "it is not a healthy one." Respiration 30 per minute. No enlargement of the liver or spleen was noticed. From the temperature chart, while in hospital, which was most carefully kept by the then house-surgeon, Dr. Hoopman, and extended over nearly three weeks, the fluctuation morning to evening was found to be almost uniformly about one and a half degrees; in the morning 99°, in the evening 100.5° to 101°. The patient having run the gamut of the pharmacopœia with the exception of tinct. ferri. chlor. and cod liver oil, was put upon that treatment. It seemed to do well for a few days but he again fell off and the changes were rung upon the different tonics. He rapidly grew weaker and died of exhaustion at 10.35 P. M., April 10th, 1883. He had asked the sister in charge of him to give him some milk; she propped him up with her left arm, the feeding-cup being in her right hand, when, before he commenced to take the milk, his head dropped upon her breast, and respiration ceased. She immediately called for assistance, but he was dead. The immediate cause was syncope. Thirteen hours after death the eyes were as staring as in life, and, by the same measurement as before, over the vertebral prominence, the neck was fourteen inches in circumference. The usual hypostatic congestion of the body was present, while rigor mortis was very slightly marked. No post-mortem was obtained.

Basedow's or Graves' disease is not so common but that the history of each individual case may prove of interest to medical practitioners. It was my intention to have added to the above notes of this case some quotations from the modern, accepted, text books, but upon consulting Reynolds' system, Bristowe's practice, Niemeyer and others, I have thought it better to give my own "unvarnished" case, and to refer the reader to such books if he wishes to observe the numerous discrepancies and resemblances. One remark I would like to make: Do not the many catarrhs in the above case point to a subparalytic condition of the sympathetic system of nerves and a consequent hyperemia of the parts?

ARTICLE II.
RECENT PROGRESS IN OPHTHALMOLOGY.
BY A. FRIEDENWALD, M. D.,
Prof. of Diseases of the Eye and Ear, College of Physicians and Surgeons, Baltimore.

Jequirity Ophthalmia. Wecker, (*Annal d'ocul.*, 1882,) has called attention to a peculiar purulent ophthalmia which is established by the application of an infusion of jequirity (abrus precatorius). This agent is extensively employed in Brazil for trachoma, and, it is said, with excellent results. He obtained the information regarding the remedy, from a gentleman who had used it in his own case for granular ophthalmia, with success. Wecker has availed himself of this remedy in diphtheria, granulations and pannus, with satisfactory results. M. Terrier, at the meeting of the Société de Chirurgie read a report on a memoir of M. José Cardoza of Rio Janeiro, on the employment of this drug. An infusion made of the seed, and applied to the conjunctiva in granular ophthalmia, sets up an acute inflammation, and may when an intense effect is produced, cause severe accidents. It should, therefore, be used with caution. M. Terrier availed himself of the remedy in one case of trachoma, producing an intense purulent ophthalmia, which disappeared without favorably influencing the previous granulations.

Dr. U. H. Brown, of Syracuse, N. Y., in an article in the *Med. News* (April 14, 1883, p. 412) publishes a very satisfactory experience with the jequirity in four cases of inveterate trachoma with pannus. He gives the following formula which is used in Brazil: "Triturate 32 well-pulverized seeds, and macerate them twenty-four hours in 500 grammes of cold water. The following day add 500 grammes of hot water. Filter the liquid immediately after cooling." We copy from this article the conclusions which Wecker has reached in the employment of this lotion.

"*First.*—That the lotion of the infusion of the seeds of jequirity produces a purulent ophthalmia of a croupous nature, of which one can regulate the intensity according to the number of applications made and the strength of the remedy which is employed.

"*Second.*— That the cornea does not run the least risk during the development of the purulent condition, as it is only when the ophthalmia is pushed to the point of a veritable diphtheria that this membrane shows a passing circumscribed desquamation.

"*Third.*—That jequirity ophthalmia rapidly cures granulations and with infinitely less danger and trouble to the patient than inoculations with gonorrhœal pus, for the ophthalmia produced by jequirity disappears of itself in from eight to twelve days, without the intervention of any treatment, by simply confining the patient to a darkened room."

Dr. S. Pollack of St. Louis, read a paper before the Missouri State Medical Asssociation at Jefferson city, in May, 1883, on "Jequirity in Ophthalmia," in which he makes a statement of his personal experience with the drug, in which he fully endorses the favorable reports which have been published by others.

In the *Boston Med. and Surg. Journal*, June 28, 1883, Dr. Myles Standish reports thirteen cases in which the drug was used with very favorable results.

Iodoform in Eye Diseases.—Brettauer, in a report to the 13th meeting of the Ophthal. Society of Heidelberg, publishes his experience with the local application of iodoform. He finds that this remedy does not cause any irritation in diseases of the conjunctiva and cornea, that it diminishes the conjunctival secretion; furthermore, that it brings about retrogressive changes in granulations, and acts beneficially in sclerosing keratitis. He uses it in the form of powder, or ointment with equal parts of vaseline.

Lange (*Petersburg Med. Wochenschrift*, 1882, No. 10) advises adversely to the use of iodoform in ophthalmia neonatorum. He found it to act injuriously in favoring the development of granulations, which finally become so extensive as to injure the nutrition of the cornea, and thus favor the occurrence of corneal lesions.

Deutschmann has found the application of iodoform as a powder, also in the form of ointment to exert a salutary influence in injuries of the cornea, causing them to heal rapidly. He has also made use of the remedy, with great satisfaction, in operative wounds. He does not report favorably for it in ordinary conjunctival catarrh, blenorrhœic affections, and granular conjunctivitis but recommends it in the serpent ulcer of Saemisch. (*Archiv. f. Ophthalm.* vol. xxviii, p. 214.)

Mooren saw trachoma disappear after the use of iodoform, which was rubbed on the lids in the form of collodion, or applied to the conjunctiva in a salve.

Grossman (*Ophthal. Review*, vol. 1 pp. 141, 214) recommends iodoform in purulent conjunctivitis. It must be reduced to an impalpable powder, otherwise it irritates the cornea mechanically, a precaution, the importance of which the writer has had opportunity to verify.

Vossius, in an article in *Archiv. f. Ophthal.* vol. xxix part 1 p. 297, contributes an article in which he records his experience with this new remedy. He does not speak well of it either in gonorrhœal ophthalmia, trachoma or pannus; but praises it without stint in corneal ulcer.

Hirschberg, in *Central Blatt fuer. Augenheilkunde*, March No., 1882, has had an opportunity to observe a very singular effect of this agent on the eye. A case in which resection of the hip joint was performed, and where iodoform was freely applied, was attended by central amblyopia, which disappeared when the remedy was withdrawn.

Deutschmann has supplemented in vol. xxix, *Arch. Ophthal.*, his article on iodoform which appeared in a previous number, and which has been referred to above. His further experience confirms his previous conclusions; and he therefore rejects it as a remedy in ophthal. neonatorum and granular conjunctivitis. In ulcus serpens it continues to give him great satisfaction. He found it to act so satisfactorily in traumatic and operative lesions that he was induced to apply it to the eye after operations, and he has been so well pleased with his first experience in this direction, that he does not hesitate to employ it after cataract operations, and he speaks very flatteringly of it in this connection.

Priestly Smith,(*Ophthal. Rev.* May 1, 1882) treated a case of gonorrhœic ophthalmia with iodoform. The effect was so favorable that the patient was discharged after a week. It was from the report of this case that Vossius tried it in the same affection; but gave an unfavorable report of it, as was stated above. It will be found, on refering to his paper, that he abandoned the remedy after a day's trial. The writer reported a few months ago, to the Balto. Med. Asso., two cases of gonorrhœic ophthalmia, in which the happiest results were attained from the use of iodoform freely dusted in the eye. He at the time thought that this treatment was original with him; but he subsequently learned that Dr. Harlan of Baltimore had reported three cases of purulent ophthalmia, (*Md. Med. Journ.*, Nov. 1882.) one of which undoubtedly was of gonorrhœal origin, in which this treatment had been extremely satisfactory. More recently Priestly Smith's case came to the writer's knowledge. Since then another case of gonorrhœal ophthalmia presented itself in his practice, in which the remedy has again fully sustained its good reputation.

Antiseptic Solution of Atropine and Eserine.—Kromer (*Correspondenzblatt f. Schweizer Aerzte*, 1881, No. 79.) finds that by boiling sol. of atropine and eserine, and then adding thereto either boracic acid 4:100 or carbolic acid 1:1000, the solution remains clear and perfectly free from bacteria. This, undoubtedly, is a valuable contribution, for all who employ these collyria extensively can bear witness to the change which soon makes its appearance; and since it has been established that it is important that the eye in disease should be kept free from micro-organisms, we should be careful to employ the means indicated by Kromer, to protect the diseased organ from infection.

Blepharitis due to the presence of pediculi pubis in the eye lashes of children.—Bleicher, (*Wiener Med. Wochenschrift*, No. 32, 1882,) and Leviste, (*Jour. des connais. Med.* No. 32, 1882,) call attention to this condition, and intimate that it exists more frequently than is generally supposed. The writer demonstrated a case of this kind to the class of the College of Physicians and Surgeons, during the past winter. Why are children especially exposed to this condition? The pediculi pubis, like other pediculi, as all will remember, who have listened to Hebra's lecture on the subject, strictly maintain their rights to their natural territory, viz.; the hairy parts of the body, beard and eye lashes. Where else can they domicile in children?

Nerve Stretching in Ophthalmic practice.—The stretching of nerves employed in general surgery, has been introduced by Wecker in ophthalmic practice. The optic nerve was the first upon which the stretching was done. No very favorable results have as yet been reported. Of late other nerves have been treated in this manner.

Panas (*Semaine. Med.* March 2 1882,) has been enabled to relieve hysterical blepharospasm by stretching the infra-orbital nerve.

Badal, (*Gazette d' Ophthal*. No. 5 1882) stretched the supra-orbital, and infra-orbital nerves in the cases of two women suffering with neuralgia of the fifth nerve, paralysis of the oculomotor, and atrophy of the optic nerve. The success was very moderate.

Alexandroff, (*Archiv. d' Ophthal.* vol. 4 No. 4,) stretched the supra-orbital nerve in a man who suffered from severe blepharospasm on both sides, tic douloureux, and hyperæsthesia of the skin of the face. On the right side complete success was obtained, on the left marked improvement.

Ophthalmoscopic Optometry in the inverted image.—Parent. (*Rec. d' Ophthal.* 1881, Sept.) Refraction can be determined in the inverted image in two ways: (1.) By gradually moving the object lens to and from the eye, and noticing the size of the image. In emmetropia it remains the same whether the lens is held nearer to or farther from the eye. In hypermetropia the image decreases when the object lens is removed from the eye examined. In myopia it increases under the same conditions. (2.) By observing the parallactic displacement in comparison to a certain amount of upward motion of the object lens. If we move the lens in the vertical plane, the image changes as follows: in emmetropia to an equal extent, in myopia to a lesser extent, in hypermetropia to a greater extent. If certain glasses be placed before the eye examined, and these experiments be made, the amount of anomaly of refraction can almost be fixed by trying until the motions shall correspond to what they should be in emmetropia.

Disease of the lachrymal passages. Galezowski (*Rec. d'oph.*, 1882, No. 8) has devised an instrument which corresponds in thickness to a number 4 of Bowman's probes, which is introduced in the lachrymal canal, and by pressure at its outer end, the two blades of which it consists are forcibly separated.

Mooren treats catarrh of the lachrymal sac and duct with lukewarm solutions. He resorts to this treatment after the acute symptoms have somewhat subsided. He recommends solutions of boracic acid, salicylic or carbolic acid. In only a few cases is the introduction of probes required.

Chilret (*Rec. d' ophth.*, 1882, No. 6) is adverse to the dilatation of strictures of the lachrymal canal by means of probes, and recommends incision according to a modification of Stilling's method.

Treatment of Glaucoma.—Snell has found eserine not only useful in the treatment of acute glaucoma, but also in the chronic form of this disease, although to a minor degree. He records a case of acute glaucoma where iridectomy was declined; not having any eserine at hand, pilocarpine discs were used, with the effect of soon relieving pain; and in a few days the attack passed off entirely.

Streatfield (*Brit. Med. Jour.*, July 27, 1882) recommends the introduction, into the British Pharmacopœia, of a much weaker solution of atropia, with a view of curtailing the danger of superinducing glaucoma when there is a predisposition. He thinks the danger of causing glaucoma in this way is much exaggerated; but it should be more generally known that a very weak solution of atropia suffices for the production of mydriasis.

Cataract. Hodges (*Brit. Med. Jour.* Sep. 2, 1882) has, during the past six years, invariably performed a preliminary iridectomy in his cataract operations. He is well satisfied with his results. He regards it as a great advantage that the anterior chamber can be kept free of blood by this method when the lens is removed; and that it is an additional advantage for the operator to know how the patient will bear narcosis. All will have to agree that the removal of the lens is rendered both simpler and safer where an iridectomy has previously been performed. How an anesthetic will be borne, can, however, not always be predicted on the basis of a previous narcosis. Prof. W. T. Howard of this city, had the misfortune of losing a patient from chloroform, who had borne the anesthetic admirably well on a previous occasion.

Schmeidle (*Wiener Med. Wochenschrift*, No. 16 and 18, 1881) has prepared the statistics of the cataract operations performed at von Arlt's clinic from 1874 to 1881. 1,547 peripheric extractions were performed in 1,460 persons. Good results were obtained in 91.2 per cent. dubious in 6.44 per cent. and loss in 2 per cent.

Knapp (*Archives of Ophthalmol.* Vol. XII, No. 1,) publishes a report of the eighth series of one hundred consecutive cataract operations. He obtained 90 per cent. of good results, 8 per cent. of moderate results, 2 per cent. of failures. His method of operation has undergone some alterations. The corneal section gradually shifted from the peripheric-linear of v. Graefe into the circular-marginal of de Wecker. The excision of the iris has been less extensive, and the capsule has been opened peripherically, along the corneal section with a sharp needle cystotome. He attaches great importance to his method of opening the capsule. The utmost care was taken to prevent any foreign substance—conjunctiva, blood, iris, capsule and portions of lens tissue—from remaining in the wound. Antisepsis was used in every alternate case without demonstrating that it was of any advantage. Usually a subsequent central division of the capsule was required to secure permanently good results. Thus far, he has not seen this operation do harm in any case.

A NUMBER of young doctors in Cincinnati have organized a "Drake Medical Society." More *quackery* in the profession.

ARTICLE III.

HOSPITAL REPORTS.

BALTIMORE CITY HOSPITAL.
[REPORTED BY W. PAGE McINTOSH, M. D.]

CASE I.—*Strangulated Hernia*—Michael R———, white, male, aged 50 years, was admitted to City Hospital June 29, 1883.

History as far as gleaned was as follows: Three years ago while doing some heavy work, he suffered a rupture on left side, at which time the gut was returned with very little trouble; since that time the gut has frequently come down, but was always returned without difficulty. Suffered no pain, bowels generally regular. On Monday, June 25th, while getting out barrel hoops, the gut came down. Being unable to return it, he took train for the city; upon arrival he went to his home but not feeling very badly did not call a physician. Patient tried cold applications and rest in bed, but continued to get worse. On 27th, vomiting set in and kept up to such an extent that the patient was unable to retain anything he drank. Took nothing solid, had no appetite. At 11 o'clock A. M., a physician was called, who immediately tried to reduce by taxis (no chloroform used,) but failed. During day of 28th, vomiting became stercoraceous and the patient states that the pain was so intense that he was delirious a large portion of the time. On evening of 28th, had a dose of salts which was immediately ejected. Pain intense, vomiting continued. On morning of 29th, the same physician who had failed on 27th, tried again to reduce the bowel with the same result as before. I should state that up to this time the patient says he had not been able to pass anything from the bowels, not even wind. On the evening of 29th, five days from time of rupture patient was brought to the City Hospital for treatment. He presented most pitiable appearance; the intens physical suffering he had undergone coupled with the mental anxiety, loss of sleep and inability to retain nourishment gave him a generally collapsed appearance. Upon examination I found a complete indirect hernia of medium size on the left side. The parts were very painful and tense. I determined to try taxis, and with the assistance of Drs. Branham and Bowers, the patient was thoroughly chloroformed, placed on his back with his thighs flexed and slightly abducted. Grasping the tumor firmly I made pressure directly in the line of descent, at the same time using a slight kneading motion; in about twenty minutes I had the satisfaction of feeling the gut slip in. The patient, who as before stated had passed absolutely nothing from the bowels for four and a half days, had an operation within two hours after the reduction of the hernia. One-fourth of a grain of morphia was administered and the patient kept perfectly quiet. Slight diarrhœa supervened, but soon subsided as did all pain and tenderness, and the patient made a good recovery. The interesting points are: 1—The great length of time the gut remained constricted without a fatal result; possibly the constriction was of a *passive* nature at first, but that it assumed an *active* type is evidenced by the excessive pain with stercoraceous vomiting. 2—The amount of manipulation practiced without hastening or precipitating a fatal termination.

A not uninteresting point about this patient was, that on the right side there existed a cystic hematocele of the cord, which very much resembled a supernumerary testicle, and therefore gave rise to considerable difference of opinion as to its nature. Aspiration and microscopic examination settled the question.

CASE II.—*Inter-meningeal Hemorrhage.* B. D———, aged about 30 years, was brought to the City Hospital July 1st. Examination revealed the presence of four scalp wounds over the right parietal bone, three of which gaped open exposing the bone.

The symptoms presented at this time were: A comatose condition, shallow, stertorous breathing, left pupil very much contracted, right one slightly so. Rigid contractured condition of left side with occasional spasmodic twitchings of limbs.

The rapidity with which the symptoms supervened, there being no prodromata, precluded the idea of rupture of aneurism of middle cerebral artery though the age of the patient would lead us to suspect such a condition. Fracture of base of skull was quite probable, but there was no facial paralysis or hemorrhage from ear, nose or eye. The twitchings of extremities were strongly indicative of inter-meningeal hemorrhage. This condition, according to Virchow, only occurs from traumatism or pachy-meningitis hemorrhagica, the latter in old persons. Accordingly the diagnosis was made of inter-meningeal hemorrhage on right side involving parts posterior to the anterior lobe.

Autopsy: Rupture of one of the arteries of the pia-mater, with clot sticking firmly in it, extensive hemorrhage covering whole motor area of right side. No fracture of base or other part of the cranial case. All the other organs normal.

CASE III.— *Tubercular Peritonitis.* Joseph S———, colored, aged about 28 years, was brought to City Hospital, July 4th. At time of admission the patient stated that he had been suffering from dropsy and that a physician had tapped him. An examination revealed the fact that patient was suffering from an extensive peritonitis.

His condition at this time was such as to justify the prognosis of a fatal termination in a short time. The usual plan of treatment was pursued but the patient died 18 hours after entering hospital.

Autopsy: Thoracic cavity contained about 2 quarts of serous fluid. Posterior portion of lower lobe of right lung very much congested, lower lobe of left lung hepatized. Heart normal but contained ante-mortem clot filling and occluding tricuspid valves and extending into the pulmonary artery. Pericardium contained about one ounce of serous fluid. Pleura adherent to chest walls. Brain and membranes normal except a few drachms of serous fluid in ventricular space.

Abdominal cavity contained about three quarts of serous fluid mixed with lymph.

Strong adhesions of peritoneum covering different parts of intestines, and literally studded with tubercles, intestines matted and adherent; mucous surface normal. Omentum infiltrated with tubercle and in places three-fourths of an inch thick. Pancreas was a tubercular mass. Spleen slightly contracted, the peritoneum covering it was firmly adhesive and covered with tubercles; substance of organ healthy.

Liver and kidneys normal.

A recent inflammation marked the point of entrance of trocar.

ARTICLE IV.

FOREIGN CORRESPONDENCE.

A Practitioner's Vacation.—Bremen.— Customs of the Fatherland.—Prag.— Professors Gussenbauer and Chiari.— Prag as a Medical Centre.

PRAG, June 2nd, 1883.

Throwing aside the cares of "practice," I left Baltimore on the 11th of last month for my first voyage across the big pond, and a year's holiday on the continent. As I intend to spend the greater portion of my vacation in Germany, I purposely took passage in a German vessel—the steamship *Braunschweig* of the Baltimore and Bremen line. I would advise all who come over here with no better knowledge of the language than I had at the start, to follow my example. It is surprising how soon one 'catches on' to the ordinary colloquial expressions in a foreign language when one is restricted to it entirely. I became quite well acquainted with Dr. Freitag, the clever young medical officer of the *Braunschweig*. As he understood no English and I very little German, we both derived considerable amusement from our attempts at making ourselves understood.

I stopped a few days in Bremen, which is a very delightful city of about 100,000 inhabitants, with a general well-to-do air about it. Some of the customs are rather amusing at first to a practical American. Men kiss each other at meeting, although there seems to be no dearth of ladies here; they also kiss the ladies' hands, although their faces are not uncomely. Dogs, singly or in teams, are used as beasts of burden; women are engaged in some of the laborious occupations that are with us reserved for the sterner sex. Theatres open at seven and close at or before ten; the ushers being (in Bremen, at all events) young ladies, who sell the programmes; these useful adjuncts to a performance not being distributed gratis. Among other peculiarities I noticed were the profound bowing of gentlemen acquainted with each other when meeting on the street, the quantities of beer consumed, and the very long time it takes a German to dispose of his *Mittagessen*.

Prag, the ancient capital of the kingdom of Bohemia is the second city in size of the Austrian empire. Its population is about 250,000, nearly equally divided into German speaking and Bohemian. The city has many points of historical interest, the most prominent of which is the palace of the Freiherr Von Waldstein, the hero of the thirty years war, whose tragic end is familiar through Schiller's sublime drama of "Wallenstein." To me, however, and probably to the readers of THE CHRONICLE, the most interest centered in the venerable university which has been in existence since 1348; hence antedates all other similar institutions in Germany. The medical department comprises the following buildings; anatomical, pathological, chemical, zoological and physiological institutes,—as a rule fine three or four story structures.

The hospital accommodations may be called ample for a city only two-thirds the size of Baltimore. There is a general hospital with 1300 beds, a lying-in hospital with 300 beds, a child's hospital with 200 beds, an insane asylum with a capacity of 500 and a foundling asylum with accomodations for 200 inmates. At the out-patient department of the hospitals about 20,000 patients are treated annually. The autopsies made at the pathological institute average 125 a month. About 500 medical students are in attendance in the medical department. Among the Americans here are Drs. Mitchell, Councilman and Morison of Baltimore, who have all been attracted here probably by the fame of Chiari the professor of pathological anatomy.

The majority of the students in attendance are Bohemians, who are unable to understand German. Hence, a number of the chairs are filled by two incumbents, one lecturing in Bohemian, the other in German. This arrangement does not seem to work very harmoniously, and there is an impression that in the near future there will be two distinct faculties teaching in the two languages.

The term of medical instruction in this university is five years, each year being divided into two sessions or "semester." Doubtless the *methods* of medical education here are more thorough than in our own country, but it is not at all settled that they make better doctors. The German student never burns his midnight oil over his books; he prefers to spend his nights in the "Kneipe," where he enters into beer drinking contests, or else in other places of amusement. He also has the reputation of never studying very hard until the last semester. It may be that in the end the average German student when he gets his degree is no better qualified to practice medicine than an intelligent, honest and diligent American student after his three years of hard study. This is my opinion at present; I may, of course, change it when I know more of Germany and German students.

The German professor of surgery here is Gussenbauer, formerly an assistant to Billroth, and not unknown in medical literature. He is comparatively young, not over 37, a rapid and neat operator, a clear and fluent lecturer. At his clinic a few days ago there were two cases of fistula in ano, the actual cautery being used in both cases. A third case was a plastic operation for the relief of an extensive cicatrix on the neck resulting from a burn. Listerism is not used, but instruments, hands of operator and assistants, and the parts operated are washed with carbolized water. Carbolic and iodoform gauze are used as dressings. One thing that struck me very forcibly was the large number of assistants present. I counted ten, besides two men servants, and all seemed to be busy. It seems to me however that so many were unnecessary.

At Prof. Chiari's pathological demonstration, which I attended a day or two ago, there were specimens of tuberculous brain, cancer of the liver, cancer of the nares and contracted kidneys, all obtained from the autopsy room during the previous 24 hours. Such a demonstration is held every day from 12 to 1 o'clock, and there seems to be always plenty of material to interest the student of pathology. So far as my knowledge goes, Prag at the present time furnishes exceptional inducements for the study of pathology. The teacher, Chiari, is one of the best anywhere; living is cheap, and the fees are almost ridiculously low: for example, the ticket to Prof. Chiari's demonstrations and lectures during a semester of four months duration, is a little less than five dollars in our money.

I leave in a few days for Vienna.

W. B.

Now is the time to Subscribe!

ANALECTS.

New Researches on the Physiology of the Bile.

[Translated for the MEDICAL CHRONICLE.]

Prof. C. von Voit has recently published the results of a series of experiments to determine the influence of the bile on the absorption of alimentary substances in the intestinal canal. The experiments were made upon dogs with biliary fistulæ. The absorption of albumen, carbo-hydrates and fat were determined both before and after the establishment of the fistulæ. The following results were obtained:

1. The digestion and absorption of albumen, taken into the body in the form of meat is not affected by the withdrawal of the bile through a fistula. The proportion of nitrogen in the feces is not increased and the excretion of urea is as large as before the operation when the same quantity of meat is given. The amount of flesh food which can be digested without producing digestive disturbances is as large after as before the establishment of the fistula. Gelatin added to the meat is absorbed with equal facility as before.

2. The loss of the bile through the fistula does not retard the absorption of carbo-hydrates added to the meat in the form of bread or grape sugar. The excretion of urea is not diminished. A diet limited exclusively to bread is equally well digested and suffices to sustain the body weight as before the withdrawal of the bile.

3. On the other hand the absorption of fat is retarded to a very marked degree, by the establishment of a biliary fistula. While in the normal condition, from 4-8 ounces of fat can be ingested, of which 99 per cent. is absorbed, only 40 per cent. of a smaller quantity is absorbed after a biliary fistula is established. Even small quantities of fat regularly cause digestive disturbances, and bloody intestinal discharges result when larger quantities of fat are added to the food. Much unchanged fat is contained in the feces, which take on a clay or grayish-white color and ointment-like consistence. The grayish-white color of icteric stools, is said by von Voit to be due to the excess of fat present in the feces and not to the absence of biliary coloring matter.

The failure to absorb such large quantities of fat naturally interferes with nutrition. An animal which before the establishment of a biliary fistula maintained a balance between the income and outgo of proteids, on a mixed meat and fat diet, rapidly loses weight on the same diet after the operation and finally dies. The ravenous hunger of dogs with biliary fistula, is explained by the non-assimilation of the fat when they are fed on a mixed diet. Dogs fed on a bread and meat diet on the other hand, keep in good condition and do not manifest the ravenousness of those fed on meat and fat.

Although the bile is of the greatest importance in promoting the absorption of fat it possesses no antiseptic properties. The function of the bile is principally to saturate the intestinal villi, and so promote the absorption of the emulsified fat. The fat is principally absorbed unchanged; the decomposition caused by the pancreatic secretion only taking place to a very limited extent.

The Ophthalmia of Small-pox.

In a paper read as an admission thesis to the Baltimore Academy of Medicine. (*Md. Med. Journal,* June 16, 1883) Dr. Herbert Harlan gives the following account of the symptoms and treatment of this serious complication.

Occasionally we find ordinary hyperæmic conjunctivitis of a chronic character, frequently blepharitis marginalis and trichiasis, where eruption pustules attacked the margin of the lid, and stillicidium where the puncta or lachrymal passages were interfered with. But the most serious of the complications accompanying or following small-pox, as far as the eyes are concerned, are the lesions of the cornea. These are of the character of ulcers and appear in a variety of forms. Sometimes we find the cornea involved as soon as the swelling of the lids permits an examination. Again, sometimes the eyes are healthy until the fifth or sixth week. Most frequently the eye is attacked at the second week, from the twelfth to the fifteenth day. The depth, extent and situation of the ulcer varies in almost every case, though the most common location seems to be between the nasal border and the centre.

Those ulcerations which take the acute form run a more rapid course, and are accompanied with pain and intolerance of light. In fact the symptoms are identical with the phlyctenular keratitis so common in strumous children, where the photophobia is such that it is impossible to examine the cornea without the aid of an anæsthetic, and any attempt to open the lids is followed by a gush of tears, and their involuntary and spasmodic closure. The lids are greatly swollen, the palpebral and orbital conjunctiva is much congested and the sclerotic zone of vessels around the cornea deeply injected.

The appearance of the ulcer itself varies with the case and the stage of the disease. It usually begins with a whitish patch raised above the surrounding surface. The centre of this sloughs with well defined but rugged and irregular edges.

In the milder cases one or two vessels make their appearance over the surface of the cornea, carrying material for repair and the phlycten heals kindly and leaves only the slightest nebula behind. In the more serious cases two or more ulcers may form and run together, or a single one may extend in breadth and depth, attacking layer after layer of the cornea until perforation follows with escape of aqueous, staphyloma and sometimes panophthalmitis

When the inflammation stops short of this point, and the process of repair goes on, opacities of the cornea are left and these interfere with vision in accordance with their size and location. When the ulceration takes the subacute form, it is not characterized by any of the more urgent symptoms of the acute variety. The pain, photophobia and congestion, are all less. The ulceration is a very tedious process, but fortunately does not often involve the deeper layers of the cornea. Perforation rarely takes place, and the opacities left behind though not very dense are apt to be lasting.

Vaccination of course lessens the number and severity of the cases of variola, but seems to exert no influence on the severity of the corneal ulceration following an attack. Two of my worst cases, one of which lost an eye, had been vaccinated and had only mild cases of varioloid, while on the other hand, in several who suffered from confluent smallpox, the eye trouble following it was of a very mild type.

The treatment of secondary variolous ophthalmia resolves itself into the treatment of the various forms of corneal ulceration. First and most important of all, the physical condition of the patient must be improved in every way possible. He should have tonics, and the best are probably iron and quinine. He should have good food, cleanliness and fresh air.

Some preparation of opium is valuable where the pain is great.

Locally, a strong solution of atropia should be dropped into the eye and the lids kept closed with a light pad and bandage. In many cases finely powdered iodoform dusted into the eye gives great relief.

In certain cases where the ulcers are asthenic in character, a good rubbing with the yellow oxide of mercury ointment does much good. This treatment should supplement the atropine drops, and is especially applicable where blepharitis is a complication.

When the ulcer is rapidly and plainly progressing, and there is danger that the cornea may be perforated, it is sometimes advisable to perform paracentesis, and this may be done directly through the floor of the ulcer. By this means the aqueous is evacuated, intra-ocular tension lessened, the pupil dilated from the atropia, and after a single tapping the ulcer goes on to heal kindly. The edges of the ulcer may, with advantage, sometimes be touched with the actual cautery by means of a needle heated in the flame of a spirt lamp.

The Relationship existing between Physicians and Druggists.

In a paper read before the Baltimore Medical and Surgical Society, (*Gaillard's Med. Journal*) Dr. J. W. C. Cuddy gives forcible expression to his views of the relationship between physicians and druggists. He says: The habit which druggists have of giving to their customers copies of prescriptions is a very pernicious one. They commit a moral wrong in so doing, for the prescription is simply an order from the physician to supply what, in his opinion, is needed at that time. If a copy is needed to be taken out of the city, or for any other purpose, the physician is the proper one to give it, he alone being responsible for ordering what is needed, the druggist being simply the dispenser of such medicines ordered.

As regards the custom of repeating prescriptions without the request of the physician, it is one which has been mooted long and seriously. In my own mind there is no doubt concerning it. I believe it to be injudicious on the part of the druggist to renew any prescription without an order from the physician who wrote it. After a given quantity of a mixture is taken, or a given number of pills used, the physician alone is competent to say whether the same remedy be re-demanded or not. The patient and his friends are not supposed to be able to know, and the apothecary is certainly in no position to decide. I know the argument about the patient having got the prescription and paid for it, that then it is his, and the druggist assumes the right to act on his order, but such reasoning is fallacious in the extreme. The question of the order and the supply is between the physician and the druggist, and the relationship existing between them is too close, and the dependence of one upon the other too great for one to act independently of or to the detriment of the other. This can be finally and fully settled only by an amicable conference between the physicians and the druggists. As it is, it will go on interminably with bickerings and misunderstandings.

Prof. Henry Smith, of Philadelphia, had printed on his prescription papers, in large letters the words, "Do not repeat this prescription without my order." In speaking of this to a druggist he told me that he would not obey such an order. Such a druggist ought not to be patronized. I am in the habit frequently of giving an order for the renewal of a prescription as follows:

Repeat No.—, Date,—, and signing my initials just the same as I do in an original prescription. I intend to do it universally hereafter, hoping that this view will come to be known, and then respected accordingly.

The Treatment of Hemorrhoids,

At a recent meeting of the Louisville Medical Society (*Med. Herald*, June, 1883), Dr. D. W Yandell read an abstract of an elaborate paper on the treatment of hemorrhoidal tumors by two methods: 1. By dilation of the sphincter ani muscle. This method applies to all internal hemorrhoids which are so high up as to prevent extrusion. He has treated nine cases in this way, with uniformly prompt success; six cases were acute and three chronic. 2. By injection with carbolic acid, the crystals being liquefied by the least amount of fluid possible. He takes equal parts of glycerine and water, and adds just enough to make a liquid which may easily be forced through the needle of an ordinary hypodermic syringe. This method to be used only in cases of *external* hemorrhoids, or such as may be extruded at the anus. He had treated 22 cases of this kind by injection, and obtained the same universal success as by dilatation of the sphincter in internal piles. In a few only did much pain occur. The injected tumors disappeared without, in his opinion, any sloughing, and without coagulation of the contents. He thinks pain does not now so often follow injection as formerly. He had known a fatal case of pyemia follow the use of the ligature, and no good ever attended suppositories, salves, and other forms of medication.

Professor J. M. Matthews said: "After an experience of seven years in the special practice and after having tried the injection plan upon a number of cases, I can but object to it, and that for several reasons: 1. To throw an acid into a tumor that is being constantly fed by a large vessel, is, in my opinion, fraught with much danger. A piece of clotted blood or fibrin may be carried into the circulation, constituting an embolus from which death may occur. 2. I do not think there can be any doubt but that the throwing of an acid into the pile coagulates the blood. Indeed, I am sure this has been the case in my experience. In this event, the tumor sloughs, and supposing we have a number of tumors, the ulcerated surfaces left would be quite sufficient to cause a stricture of the gut. I am now treating a case of this kind caused in this manner. 3. As to the matter of pain, if the pile is injected sufficiently near to the *base*, it must result in more pain than the ligature, and if you do not inject to the base you fail to cure the pile. In other words, you can inject, say, the upper third of the pile and slough it away without much pain, but is the inflammatory action sufficient to cause the reabsorption of the other *two thirds* of the tumor? I do not think so. 4. The sloughing of the tumor or tumors may cause extensive hemorrhage." Upon the whole, Dr. Matthews concluded that inasmuch as the ligature was so simple of execution and free from danger, he would prefer it, in the majority of cases, to the acid treatment.

As to the method by dilatation referred to by Dr. Yandell, and advocated by the French, he could not think it of any use save in an acute attack of piles or rather *incipient* piles, which is but a varicose condition of the blood-vessels or a mere strangulation. If a deposition of fibrin had taken place, and a tumor formed in consequence, he did not believe that the dilatation of the muscle would effect a cure.

Dr. Ed. Von Donhoff was entirely in accord with the views of Dr. Matthews. The very mechanism by which piles are formed from the strangulation of loops of blood-vessels, causes inflammation which makes a fibro-plastic tumor out of the coats of the incarcerated vessels, and after this has occurred, no amount of dilatation of the sphincter-ani muscle could bring about resolution.

If dilatation be practiced at the very onset, the strangulated vessels may be liberated by dilatation of the sphincter, in the interlacement of the fibers of which the vessels were caught. In all cases of fissure, and generally before operating on internal piles, it is found necessary to practice forcible dilatation of the sphincter-ani. This is a well-known and long-established proceeding. He has witnessed extensive sloughing of the rectum from injecting carbolic acid, and never practices it now.

Dr. W. O. Roberts has great faith in the treatment by injection of equal parts of carbolic acid, glycerine, and water. He knew a case of death from pyemia, induced by ligating hemorrhoidal tumors.

FELLOW'S Hypophosphites is very highly recommended in all debilitating diseases especially tuberculosis and depressing nervous disorders.

Acute Rheumatism in Childhood.

Dr. Vohsen, (*Jahrb. f. Kinderh.* XIX. I.) summarises the present knowledge on this subject as follows:

1. In almost half the cases of rheumatism of the joints there occur endocarditis, and later valvular defects.

2. The mitral valve and pericardium appear to suffer most frequently, and endocarditis is usually developed in the first week of the disease.

3. Whilst salicylate of soda exerts a most beneficial effect in relieving the affections of the joints, it has no influence on the course of the heart-complications.

4. The mildest form of rheumatism of the joints, as shown by slight fever, little swelling, and very transient pain, seems especially to predispose to heart-complication, and hence indicates the necessity for careful examination in the mildest cases.

What determines heart-complications in acute rheumatism still remains most uncertain. No reason can be assigned on anatomical or physiological grounds for the only peculiarities of the infantile heart, viz., the nodules of Albinus situated at the cardiac orifices of the veins and the relative narrowness of the aorta at the opening of the ductus Botalli. These are most marked during the first year of life, when acute rheumatism and endocarditis are of most exceptional occurrence. Bouchut, from an experience of 200 necropsies, concludes that nine-tenths of children dying with febrile affections have endocarditis.

A possible explanation of the problem may be found in looking at acute rheumatism as an infectious disease, and regarding the infantile heart as possessed of slight resisting power to the virus of the infection; and the figures of Von Dusch lend some support to this view; for out of every forty-five cases of endocarditis fifteen were idiopathic, twenty were associated with acute rheumatism, and the remainder with distinct infectious diseases. The fundamental similarity in structure of endocardium and the synovial membranes, may account for the frequency of both being the sites of the structural manifestation of the virus.

Dr. Vohsen, in favoring this view, dwells on the frequent semi-epidemic character of rheumatism, and the well ascertained relationship between endocarditis and the recognized acute infectious diseases.—*London Medical Record*.

Rectal Antiseptics in Typhoid Fever.

Dr. Gallois, in a communication to the *Journal de Medicine*, relates his experience in the use of antiseptics in typhoid fever. For the past five years he has employed in typhoid fever, rectal injections of phenic acid, and has never observed any toxic effect. In benign cases it is his custom to order an injection each morning to which is added from ten to twelve drops of phenic acid dissolved in alcohol. In graver cases he advises a second injection in the evening. These injections have always been well borne. He admits the antipyretic action of the drug, but employs it for its antiseptic action. He also employs, in cases where fever is high, sulphate of quinine. The mortality is said to be very low.

Treatment of Typhoid by Ergot,

Amongst the novelties of medical practice with which we are now surfeited, is the proposed employment of ergot in the treatment of typhoid. The results of this practice amply justify its introduction if we may rely on the published evidence. M. Débove administers in certain cases of typhoid one gramme (15 1-2 grs.) of ergot in two doses. Of twenty-four cases, eight were very grave, eleven were serious, and five were of moderate severity, and of these but one proved fatal. In a former series of six cases, one was very grave and five were of moderate severity, and all recovered. In still another series of six cases, three being very grave, two serious, and one of moderate severity, all recovered but one.—*Med. News*.

Infectious Pneumonia.

Attention is drawn in a report presented by Mr. Harold Palmer to the Newtown and Llanllwchaiarn urban sanitary district, to a prevalence of pneumonia, which strongly resembles similar outbreaks which have been regarded as of an infectious character. (The Lancet.) A strong and healthy male adult was, in June last year, suddenly seized with a severe form of pneumonia, which rapidly assumed a so-called typhoid character. The general symptoms raised a suspicion that the disease was of a septic nature, and due to faulty sanitary conditions; a view which was confirmed as the result of an inspection of the house. Having regard to these facts, prompt measures were taken to do away with the unwholesome drain conditions which had been found, but the medical practitioner in attendance, as also two other persons were seized with the same disease, and two of the cases, including that of the medical man, proved fatal within a few days. In all the four cases the pneumonia was double, and the patients were male adults. This is by no means the first instance in which a similar result has followed on a first case of this disease. Indeed, a single visit to a house where this form of pneumonia has prevailed has been attended by the occurrence of urgent lung inflammation within a few days, death speedily resulting. It is always possible that the disease may, as regards causation, be similar to enteric fever, and that the pneumonic condition, which as a rule supervenes at a later stage, may, when it takes precedence of the bowel and and others lesions, assume a specially virulent character, masking the more ordinary symptoms, and having, as a rule, a rapidly fatal termination Further experience, however, as to the disease is needed before any decided opinion can be expressed on this point.—*Louisville Med. News.*

Subscribe for the MEDICAL CHRONICLE.

Convergent Squint.

The development of squint always progresses *pari-passu* with the continued effort to overcome deficient refractive power, or from lack of power to fix the two eyes at the same time upon an object. The want of sufficient power of refraction may be compensated by extra use of the accommodation, or focusing power ; and as soon as this exertion begins to bring on fatigue the optical axes of the eyes deviate in the direction of the overtaxed muscle. It is common to all excesses of muscular effort that spasm follows. The irritation causing the spasm may be kept up until structural changes may occur in the muscular substance, and the contraction becomes permanent. Suspending the accommodation has long been practiced to relieve temporary squint by doing away with the necessity for converging power. Dr. C. A. Bucklin, of New York, has used eserine, half a grain to three drams of water, instilled morning and evening, with very favorable results. He reports a case of squint of several weeks' standing cured by the use of eserine, and the correction of the hypermetropia with glasses. His paper is somewhat sensational, but it contains at least a grain of scientific truth. If the treatment be preceded by correction of the deficient refraction, eserine may be used in time to prevent the necessity of tenotomy.—*Med. Herald.*

Apomorphia as an Emetic.

A writer in the *British Medical Journal*, cites a number of cases to show the benefits of apomorphia as an emetic. The principal feature is the speedy evacuation of the contens of the stomach without nausea or bad after effects, and this is truly a very valuable point gained. The writer claims that by the hypodermic administration of one-half gr. of apomorphia, the stomach ejects its contents within from one to seven minutes—no nausea—no depression, but a prompt vomit.

Sea Bathing.

At the present time, when the sea-bathing season is about to commence, it may be useful to recall the chief general indications and contraindications which respectively sanction and forbid bathing in the sea. "Shall I bathe?" This is a question which thousands of health-seekers will be asking of their doctors during the next few weeks. While the stimulus of a fresher air, of change of scene, and of new occupations, together with rest from accustomed work, are the elements from which the weakly, the worn, and the worried reap physical and mental restoration in a sojourn on the sea-coast, it is unquestionable that bathing in the open sea is, in itself, a powerful restorative agency, which many persons may employ with very great advantage. The universal experience of our race, through unnumbered ages, has shown the value of sea-bathing in both preventive and curative medicine. A good rule laid down by an experienced physician, is this: in all cases showing impaired functional powers, without any manifestation of inflammatory symptoms—in short, in those cases in which the exhibition of alteratives and tonics is indicated—sea-bathing, may, with proper precautions, be resorted to; it is contraindicated in persons of plethoric habit of body, in cerebral congestion, in organic disease of the heart, in aneurism, and in all persons who have the inability safely to encounter a comparatively severe shock; while it is also to be forbidden at certain periods in which the female constitution is not prepared for the application of powerful remedies. Because it tends, in certain conditions of impaired health, to cause determination of blood to the viscera, bathing in the open sea is generally unsuitable for persons disposed to congestive disorders of the lungs, kidneys, liver, and brain. Albuminuria, advanced anæmia, and a liability to hæmoptysis, are also conditions which are usually accepted as contraindicating sea-bathing. It is hurtful to bathe babies in the sea; children under two years of age are too young to bear with advantage the comparatively severe shock of a cold sea-bath. In old age, when the bodily powers are unequal to a vigorous reaction, sea-bathing may do much harm, especially in the subjects of extreme arterial degeneration. In suitable cases, and under proper precautions as to time of bathing and duration of exposure, a daily bath in the open sea is a valuable restorative. In individuals who are fairly robust, it is a stimulant, alterative and tonic, promoting appetite, tissue-change, and excretion, and bracing up the nervous, vascular, and muscular systems. Sea-bathing is especially useful as a powerful and unsurpassed tonic in delayed convalescence from acute diseases, in many chronic affections, and in persons whose strength has become enfeebled by injurious excesses, by mental strain, or by unhealthy occupations.—*British Medical Journal.*

Results of Medical Legislation in Illinois.

According to the official report of the Illinois State Board of Health, which has control of the issuing of licenses to practice under the existing law, "there are now only about 650 non-graduates left in the State, as compared with about 3800 at the time when the law went into effect." The change has been brought about in part by non-graduates leaving the state in search of a more salubrious climate or in part by many resuming their studies and finally graduating at medical schools. The same effect has followed similar legislation in California and other states which have adopted similar laws. The average status of practitioners in such States has derived a well-marked elevation and the standard of medical education has been correspondingly raised. This should disarm hostility to the law.—*Pacific M. & S. Journal.*

The Medical Chronicle.

A Monthly Journal for the Practitioner.

GEORGE H. ROHÉ, M. D., Editor.

☞ It is requested that all literary and business communications, books for review, exchanges, etc., be addressed to, and all checks, drafts and post-office orders drawn to the order of
DR. GEORGE H. ROHÉ,
95 Park Avenue, - - - - Baltimore, Md.

BALTIMORE, AUGUST, 1883.

EDITORIAL.

OUR NEW VOLUME.

We take pleasure in calling the attention of our readers to the improved appearance of this issue of the MEDICAL CHRONICLE.

By adopting the double columned page and omitting the leads between the lines we have been enabled to increase very considerably the amount of reading matter. The subscription price will remain as heretofore, ONE DOLLAR PER YEAR.

The Necessity of a Law to Regulate the Practice of Medicine in Maryland.

Maryland was one of the first, if not the very first state in the Union which passed a law to regulate the practice of medicine.* After remaining in force for nearly half a century this law was repealed through the efforts of the Thompsonians, who possessed for a time considerable popular influence. In 1867, a new Medical Practice Act was passed by the General Assembly, which was however repealed at the session of 1868. Since that time the inhabitants of the state have been at the mercy of, and fleeced by, a horde of the most shameless quacks that ever infested a community.

During the last few years, several other states have followed the example so early initiated by Maryland, and have passed laws for the protection of the public against incompetent persons engaging in the practice of medicine. The most notable, as well as the most successful of these attempts were made in the states of Illinois and West Virginia. According to the testimony of the authorities charged with the execution of the law in those states, the best results have followed. The example of Illinois and West Virginia has been followed by Wisconsin, Missouri and Nebraska; while Pennsylvania, New York and Michigan have also passed laws somewhat different from those in the first-named states, but designed to accomplish the same object, viz : the protection of the public against quackery.

A movement is now on foot, which it is hoped may gather sufficient strength to succeed in convincing the General Assembly next winter of the necessity of enacting measures to place this state on a level with her younger sisters in the West. The Illinois law which has been productive of so much good under the energetic administration of the state board of health seems to us a good model to imitate.

We believe this to be a Fabrication.

The *New England Medical Monthly* for July, publishes the following item : " In Germantown, Pa., recently a lady was sent to the pest house for small-pox, when it was found that she only had the measles. While in the hospital she took varioloid. Five similar cases were reported in Baltimore during one week. They must have curious health authorities in both of these places.'

So far as Baltimore is concerned we have authority for stating that it is not true that " five similar cases " of mistaken diagnosis occurred " during one week."

THE honorary degree of M. A., was worthily bestowed upon Dr. Chas. Frederick Percivall of this city by William and Mary College at its last commencement.

---

*Act of 1801, conferring additional powers upon the medical and chirurgical faculty of Maryland.

CURRENT LITERATURE.

A Text-book of Pathological Anatomy and Pathogenesis. By Ernst Ziegler, Prof. of Pathological Anatomy in the University of Tubingen. Translated and edited for English students by Donald Macallister, M. A. M. B., etc. Part 1. General Pathological Anatomy, London, MacMillan and Co., 1883.

Several excellences distinguish the first volume of the above work, chief among which is a succinct statement of the theory of teratology. Most manuals on pathology omit mention of this topic altogether, and the special treatises besides being very voluminous are in a foreign language and inaccessible to a large number of students who read English alone. Prof. Macallister's translation has thus supplied a long felt desideratum.

The author has expurgated old erroneous doctrines, and has brought the subject into accord with the modern and enlightened tenets of experimental biology.

The word mesoblastic is introduced, qualifying tumors, and designating those which arise from the tissues of the middle layer of the blastoderm; the upper and lower layers (epiblast and hypoblast) should be likewise, and have been so used by us during the past three years in our public lectures. There should be some uniform basis of classification under which all tumors could be arranged; the most simple is a quasi Linnæan one which we apologize for introducing, somewhat out of place, in this connexion.

Class: Tumor.
Order: Recurrent, non-recurrent, malignant.
Genus: Epiblastic, mesoblastic, hypoblastic.
Species: Carcinoma, sarcoma, *histic*, (i. e. tissue growth.)
Variety: This trivial designative may be such terms as encephaloid, scirrhus, lymphoma, granuloma, lymphadenoid, myxoma, myoma, neuroma, teratoma, or whatever appellative may strike the fancy of the observer or describer. Cysts and teratological inclusions are not in strictu sensu tumors, and are so classed only because it is expedient rather than lawful.

The final of the several excellences to which we shall refer in Professor Ziegler's work is the chapter on the etiology of tumors. The author takes a rational, philosophical, scientific view of the matter, and makes little or no mention of those dogmas of pathological superstition; "force of disease," "specific product of diseases," "morbid morphology," "embryonic buds," etc.

Having previously defined pathology to be physiology working under abnormal, inhibitory or disturbing conditions, he finds a sufficient explanation of the appearance of tumors in perversion of the function of tissue-reproduction, on the one hand in the direction of excess and temporary exuberance; on the other in diminished resistance of the surrounding tissues. If constitution be defined as mode of function peculiar to the individual, and diathesis be taken to mark the prominent dormant peculiarity, then there are those who have a peculiar tissue constitution, either local or general, hereditary or acquired, which restricts the force and so perverts the function of ultimate normal tissue-assimilation as to result in a tumor-diathesis.

In the foregoing we have not used the author's language, but have endeavored to preserve its sense, which is also that of others prominent among the best authorities of the present day.

The chapters upon the bacteria, moulds and animal parasites set forth the recent theories upon these topics, are abreast of the times, profusely and well illustrated, as is also the entire work. The type is good, the size and *heft* of the book is literally manual, not bimanual nor requiring both hands and arms to wield it, from which exercise the tired practitioner of medicine shrinks.

We predict that the profession will find the present volume acceptible, will welcome it, and await impatiently the publication of the second, concluding part of the work in which the doctrines laid down in the volume before us shall receive special exemplification.

We have a single suggestion to add, and this is that the translator might with advantage have added a definition of such technical terms used as may be with difficulty understood by those readers who are not classical scholars.

N. G. K.

The Introduction of Inoculation and Vaccination into Maryland, Historically Considered. By J. R. Quinan, M. D. Reprinted from *Maryland Medical Journal*, June 23, 1883. Pp. 12.

In this excellent paper, Dr. Quinan has given a true account of the introduction of inoculation and vaccination into the state of Maryland. The researches of the author have shown that inoculation was practiced in this state very soon after its first introduction into England. Dr. Quinan also shows conclusively that vaccination was performed as early in Maryland as in any other state in the Union. It appears probable that its introduction into this state antedates, or is at least contemporaneous with the experiments of Dr. Waterhouse in Massachusetts, heretofore credited with being the first vaccinator in the country. The paper deserves a careful perusal by every one interested in the early history of the medical profession in Maryland.

The Ophthalmia of Small-pox. By Herbert Harlan, M. D., Surgeon and Lecturer on Ophthalmic Surgery at the Presbyterian Eye and Ear Charity Hospital, Baltimore, etc. Reprinted from *Maryland Medical Journal*, June 16, 1883. Pp 4.

A practical paper on one of the more serious accidents of small-pox.

FLOTSAM.

THE degree of L. L. D., has been conferred on Dr. H. C. Wood by Lafayette College, Pa.

A warning to Emma Abbott: Gruber reports a rupture of the membrana tympani from kissing.

IT is said that a few drops of tincture of belladonna will prevent the nausea from quinine if taken before the latter.

THE *Independent Practitioner* will hereafter be exclusively devoted to dentistry under the editorship of Dr. W. C. Barrett of Buffalo.

A Sanitary Convention will be held at Muskegon, Mich., on August 23 and 24, under the auspices of the Michigan State Board of Health.

Those of our readers wanting medical or other books and stationery, can find a large stock at Cushings & Bailey's, 262 W Baltimore Street.

RESORCINE, dissolved in twice its weight of water is claimed to be an efficient and inodorous substitute for iodoform in the treatment of chancroid.

IF YOU WANT anything in the line of surgical instruments, from a needle to a galvano-cautery battery, address Chas. Willms & Co., 79 N. Howard Street.

ACCORDING to Dr. Coelho seasickness is promply controlled by subcutaneous injection of morphine in the epigastric region, in doses of one-eight to one-sixth grain.

THE POLYCLINIC is the name of a new journal edited by the faculty of the Philadelphia Polyclinic, and published by P. Blakiston, Son & Co. It succeeds the *Medical Register.*

THE Seventh annual meeting of the American Dermatological Association will be held at Lake George, on the 29, 30 and 31 of August. A full report of the proceedings will appear in the CHRONICLE.

THE *New England Medical Monthly* for June contains a fine portrait and sketch of Dr. N. S. Davis, the Editor of the *Journal of the American Medical Association.*

MR. BUTLIN reccommends a ten grain solution of chromic acid in cases of chronic superficial glossitis, and in ulcerative affections, including those of syphilitic origin.

COL, GEO. E. WARING, JR., the eminent authority in Sanitary engineering has been elected Secretary of the National Board of Health in the place of Dr. Charles Smart, U. S. A.

PROF. BARTHOLOW has been elected dean of the Jefferson Medical College as the successor to Dr. Ellerslie Wallace, who has resigned from the Faculty on account of ill health.

DUGONG oil is said to be an efficient substitute for cod liver oil, being free from the unpleasant odor and taste which characterize the latter, and much less liable to undergo change in keeping.

WISCONSIN has also passed a medical practice law, somewhat similar to that of Illinois. Maryland which had, we believe the first law of the kind in the country, is now without regulation of any kind.

THE Philadelphia Hospital for skin diseases has a new official on its staff. He is called a *balneologist*, and his duty is to superintend the giving of baths to patients sent there for the purpose by physicians.

THE Physician's supply agency, No. 358 N. Gay St., is a new institution established for the convenience of the members of the profession. Any article needed by the physician from a prescription blank to a buggy, will be furnished at the lowest cash prices.

SIR HENRY THOMPSON thinks that if cigarettes are not "smoked more than half way through" they are the least injurious form of tobacco smoking. The *N. Y. Med. Journal* endorses this opinion in a sensible editorial in its issue of June 23.

WINIWARTER has been using, with astonishing success, parenchymatous injections of hyperosmic acid in sarcoma, lymphoma and strumous adenoma. It fails to do good in carcinoma. Three drops of a one-per-cent solution are injected daily.

THE oil of yellow sandal wood is being lauded again in the journals as a specific against gonorrhœa. The dose is 15 drops three times a day, on sugar or in capsules. It is said to stop the discharge within two days, but requires to be continued two weeks or longer to prevent relapse.

THE *Detroit Lancet* says "In recent discussions of ethical questions some seem to forget that the code of ethics has nothing to do with the rights of individuals as free American citizens. The code is no part of any state or national laws. The code is simply a social arrangement of a purely voluntary character."

A CORRESPONDENT of the *British Medical Journal* states tnat he has found the application of a strong solution of chromic acid, three or four times, by means of a camel's hair pencil, to be the most efficient and easy method of removing warts. They become black and soon fall off.

AT a recent meeting of antivivisectionists in Manchester, Prof. Gamgee, the professor of physiology in Owens' College, addressed the meeting explaining the methods used in the experiments, and the results obtained. Resolutions which had been prepared, protesting against scientific research, were rejected by a large majority.

FOR several years past the pharmaceutical preparations of Messrs. Sharp & Dohme and John F. Hancock have been winning high praise from the profession here for their purity and excellence of manufacture. We refer our readers to their advertisments in the CHRONICLE.

The Medical Chronicle.

BALTIMORE, SEPTEMBER, 1883.

ORIGINAL ARTICLES.

ARTICLE I.

ABORTION.

With the Histories of Two Cases—One Preventable and One Inevitable.
By CHARLES W. PILGRIM, M. D.,
Late House Physician, Bellevue Hospital, N. Y.

Abortion, in its medical sense, is the term applied to the expulsion of the fœtus from the womb at any time between the commencement of pregnancy and the beginning of the seventh month, or, in other words, before the product of conception is yet viable. It is true that there are a few cases on record where fœtuses born at six, five, or even at four months, have lived, but such cases are too rare to affect the general law.

When labor occurs after viability but before full term it is called *Premature*. The ancients used the term *Effluxio* when the expulsion of the ovum occurred at a very early period, while the term *Miscarriage* is used by women to embrace all these divisions. In law, also, the medical distinctions are disregarded and the term *Abortion* is applied indiscriminately to the expulsion of the fœtus at any period before the completion of gestation.

Abortions are most apt to occur during the early months of pregnancy, that is, between the second and the third, when the union between the chorion and decidua is slight, and happily it is just at that period that they are almost free from danger. Premature labor is also comparatively safe and requires but little special treatment as it differs but slightly from the normal process. But abortions occurring between the third and fifth months are fraught with extreme danger on account of the vascular relations between the maternal and fœtal systems resulting from the formation of the placenta, and often require prompt treatment at the hands of the physician to avert death from hemorrhage.

The causes of abortion are very numerous and often obscure. According to Mr. Whitehead's observation, of 2,000 pregnancies one in seven terminated in abortion. It is a habit which is very easily established, and a woman who has aborted once is very apt to do so again. Any serious disease, either acute or chronic, is apt to cause it, such as small-pox, relapsing fever, scarlatina, syphilis, etc. Reflex irritation is a very frequent cause, and it may arise from the intestinal tract, the nipple, the vagina or the ovaries; a dead or diseased ovum acts in the same way by irritating the uterus, and it is to this knowledge of reflex action that we owe the valuable practice of plugging the vagina when we wish to induce uterine action. The custom of placing the child to the breast at an early period has its origin in the same physiological law. Diseases of the uterus and its appendages, and of the ovum as well, are prolific causes, as for instance, congestion of the womb which occurs in plethoric women at the menstrual period, excessive uterine irritability found in nervous females, tumors, ulcerations, displacements, adhesions of the appendages, fatty degeneration of the chorion and placenta, apoplexy of the placenta, etc. The surrounding atmosphere exerts considerable influence over this accident and the epidemics of miscarriages spoken of by some authors were undoubtedly due to this same cause.

Cazeaux says: "According to the report of Lancerotte, the women inhabiting the summit of the Vosges are very subject to abortion, and they are in the constant habit of descending into the adjacent plains to avoid this accident;" and Leishman says: "Of the five hundred Arabs who were suffocated in the caves of Dohra, in 1845—as is said by the orders of Duc de Malakoff—a considerable proportion were women, and of these, many who were pregnant, aborted." The fact that abortions occur before death from asphyxia bears out Brown-Sequard's theory that the irritation of the uterine fibres by the carbonic acid in the venous blood is the direct cause of labor at full term. Other oxytocics are ergot, borax, savin, rue, etc. Their action is not thoroughly understood, but, ergot certainly, and the others probably, act through their influence upon the spinal cord. The last causes which I shall refer to are excessive mental emotions, such as fright, anger, joy and grief, and mechanical violence such as blows, falls and kicks. I am aware that the importance of these causes is greatly overrated, and that many pregnant women suffer from the most violent mental emotions and physical shocks without the least unfavorable result. Cazeaux tells us of a young girl in the fifth month of pregnancy, who, being rendered desperate by the desertion of her lover cast herself from the Pont Neuf into the Seine, but was rescued and taken to the Hotel Dieu where gestation pursued its regular course. M. Gendrin speaks of a young lady, in the same stage of pregnancy, who was thrown from her chaise over the horse's head by the stumbling of the animal, and Dr. Pogan relates an instance in which his coachman drove over and seriously injured a woman eight months pregnant, and in neither case was the natural course of pregnancy in any way altered. But notwithstanding these notable cases the histories which I give below show, without a doubt, that fright and violence may be classed among the causes.

Case 1 is that of a young woman, aged eighteen, who had been married six months. She was admitted into Bellevue Hospital Saturday, November 19th, 1881, and gave the following history. Previous to her marriage and up to Tuesday, the 15th, she had been perfectly well. She began to menstruate at fourteen, and was always regular up to the time of her marriage, since which date she has not menstruated. Two and a half months ago she noticed that her abdomen commenced to enlarge and it has increased in size continuously up to the present time. On Tuesday evening last she received such a severe fright that she fainted and afterward had what appeared to be an hysterical convulsion. Wednesday morning she noticed that blood was flowing from the vulva. This bleeding soon stopped but was in a little while followed by pains which started from the back and passed forward through the abdomen. These pains were intermittent in character and recurred at short intervals up to the last two days, but since then they have been pretty constant. She has not bled any since Wednesday.

An examination gave the following result: Abdomen a good deal enlarged, and umbilicus almost effaced; vagina somewhat livid in hue and covered by a copious secretion; cervix high up, softened superficially and carried towards the sacrum; os almost closed; uterus very much enlarged, reaching almost up to the umbilicus; breasts enlarged and tense and areola well-marked.

The treatment consisted merely of complete rest in bed and the administration of 30 minims of Tr. opii deodorata every 3 hours.

On the 21st, two days after admission, she bled a little but the pain was not very marked.

On the 29th, she still complained

of slight pain, but there was no discharge of blood after the 21st.

On the 5th of December she was discharged, as she had been free from pain and all other unfavorable symptoms since the last entry.

The above case is a fair example of threatened and preventable abortion, and the treatment is both simple and satisfactory; but the following case which was admitted in the afternoon of Tuesday, December 27th, 1881, was quite different in symptoms, treatment and result. The patient, who was 23 years of age, and, as was supposed, in the sixth month of pregnancy, stated that on Saturday morning, the 24th of December, she fell and struck the lower part of her abdomen with great violence against a low chair. This was immediately followed by a profuse hemorrhage from the vagina, together with a severe pain in the small of the back, and some pain radiating down the thighs. She was faint from the loss of blood and from the severity of the pain.

On the next day she still had pain, and hemorrhage at times.

The day after, which was the day preceding her admission, she had a chill, was feverish, had severe lumbar pain and vomited twice. An examination at the time of admission showed profuse bleeding, cervix softened and os externum dilated enough to readily admit the finger. The membranes had ruptured. The breasts, abdomen, etc., were corroborative of pregnancy. There were no signs of fœtal life. As preventive treatment was considered useless, a vaginal douche of hot water was gently given, a drachm of the fluid extract of ergot administered, and tamponing, according to the method recommended by Dr. Fordyce Barker, resorted to. It was done as follows: A piece of compressed sponge of proper size, was placed in the os uteri, after which the vagina was loosely packed with the ordinary "kite-tail" tampon. The hemorrhage was checked, and at 4.30 the next morning, about twelve hours after admission, severe pains began, and when I reached the bedside I found the tampon forced out and the head of the child presenting at the vulva. The child was delivered in about fifteen minutes. The placenta came away, without interference, soon after, and it was found that decomposition had begun. The day after delivery her temperature rose to $101\tfrac{1}{2}°$ F., but it fell to normal after the administration of twenty grains of quinine followed by a vaginal douche. There were no more unfavorable symptoms and she was discharged January 11th, 1882.

The above histories, which are typical of the two classes, that is those which are merely threatened and preventable under proper treatment, and those which are inevitable no matter what treatment is adopted, show that the most prominent symptoms are pain and hemorrhage, while the physical signs are softening of the cervix and more or less dilatation of the os. The condition of the os is our chief diagnostic point in determining whether the abortion is preventable or inevitable, and the examination should be very carefully made before treatment is begun, for, to tampon in a "preventable" case would be criminal, while to adopt preventive treatment in an "inevitable" one would be worse than useless and might result in the death of the patient.

THE *Journal of the American Medical Association*, has made its appearance under the chief editorship of Dr. N. S. Davis, of Chicago. While the typography is somewhat disappointing to connoisseurs of the 'art preservative,' the contents of the journal give promise of securing for it a high position in the ranks of medical journalism. We trust it may always be a faithful exponent of the highest aspirations of the profession in America.

ARTICLE II.

A Case of Placenta Prævia; Shoulder Presentation and Spontaneous Evolution.

BY WHITFIELD WINSEY, M. D., BALTIMORE.

I was called Sunday evening, June 10th, to see S. F., colored, a strong, healthy looking woman, aged 39, who, I was told had been having labor pains since 10 o'clock the previous evening. She said she had been losing blood, though at first in moderate quantities, from the beginning of the labor. When I arrived at her bedside she was losing blood quite freely—had saturated two pads and was then using a third. I immediately made an examination and found that I had my first case of placenta prævia, and that the placenta covered the os uteri centre for centre, that the os was dilated to about the size of a silver half dollar, and was quite rigid—the pains were of moderate strength and frequency, and with each recurring one there was a gush of blood. I could not make out a presentation. I determined to use the rubber tampon, but upon trial of one I had in my bag I found it useless. I did the next best thing I could, saturated a piece of sponge with some vinegar, carried it up to the os with difficulty, it being very high, and packed the vagina with raw cotton saturated with the same material. I remained with the woman long enough to see that the hemorrhage was at least temporarily checked and then left the patient in charge of the midwife who had preceded me in the case and went for my friend Dr. B. F. Leonard, to obtain of him, a rubber tampon which I knew he had, and, if possible, also his assistance. I was fortunate in securing both.

He returned with me to the woman about 5 a. m., and it was found that the pains were about the same, and that there had been no further hemorrhage. We therefore determined to wait and watch the progress of the labor for a time without interference, which we did until 5.30 a. m., when the pains being stronger I removed the cotton and sponge and we both examined her by conjoined manipulation (which as a matter of course, started the hemorrhage afresh), and arrived at the following conclusions: That the placenta covered the os centre for centre, that the shoulder was presenting, probably the right anterior dorsal position, and that the os was neither dilated nor sufficiently dilatable to admit of the performance of version—it was therefore agreed to insert the rubber tampon and wait, which we did, waiting until eight o'clock. The pains then being much stronger and more frequent (owing largely to the tampon), we examined and found the os still too small for the performance of version, the uterus still above the brim, but Dr. Leonard having quite long fingers succeeded in feeling an elbow. It was agreed to retampon, give the woman one-half grain morphia subcutaneously to modify the pains and perhaps thereby facilitate dilitation, and leave the woman until 9.30 o'clock in charge of the midwife unless sooner summoned (I being quite near). We then left her. At 9 o'clock I was summoned and in ten minutes was at the woman's side, when I found both child and placenta in the world. The midwife said she sent for me because, being informed by the woman that something had come, she raised the bedclothes and found the tampon had been forced out and that a hand was protruding through the vulva—there were a few more strong and rapid pains and the head was forced through the vulva followed immediately by the placenta as in a normal labor. The child was still-born, as was expected, we having several times unsuccessfully ausculted for the fœtal heart. The woman stated that the movements of the child ceased shortly after the beginning of the labor.

I have reported this case because of its presenting three abnormal features: placenta prævia and shoulder presentation, in a vast majority of cases requiring the resources of our art; and a spontaneous evolution, which, though known as among the possibilities in nature never should be relied upon to take the place of art.

ARTICLE III.

Tuberculosis, Scrofula and Lupus.

[The first part of the long delayed volume on Skin Diseases in Ziemssen's Cyclopedia, has at last appeared in the original. It deviates very markedly in its treatment of the subject from the hitherto recognized authorities in dermatology in Europe and in this country. The most advanced opinions on the parasitic origin of skin diseases are adopted. The section on "Chronic Infectious diseases of the Skin," is from the pen of Prof. A. Neisser, of Breslau. From this section we translate and condense the following paragraphs on Tuberculosis, Scrofula and Lupus, which diseases the author considers identical in their origin.—Ed. CHRONICLE.]

Although but a short time ago the parasitic nature of this group of diseases was denied by many authorities, tuberculosis, and with it scrofula, is now the best known, and the sole objectively demonstrated chronic infectious disease of man.

Villemin, Cohnheim, Tappeiner, Schuchhardt, Deutschmann, Baumgarten, Toussaint, Ziegler, Martin, Fehleisen, Damsch and others showed experimentally that tuberculosis could be communicated by inoculation, by feeding, by inhalation of vaporized tuberculous matter, etc., to healthy animals. It was also shown in these experiments that certain species of animals, rabbits, guinea pigs, etc., presented a particular predisposition to the tuberculous process, while others, such as dogs and cats offered more or less resistance to the effects of the inoculated matter.

The nature of the infectious agent was investigated by a number of experimenters, prominent among whom are Klebs, Schuller, Deutschmann, Damsch, Aufrecht, Baumgarten and others, but it remained for Robert Koch to demonstrate, beyond doubt, that a specific bacillus is the cause of tuberculosis and scrofula.

The proof furnished by Koch, consisted in the demonstration of a parasitic micro-organism (bacillus) in tuberculous new formations. The bacilli are always found in large numbers in those localities where the tuberculous process is beginning, or rapidly progressing. Koch has further shown that the tubercle bacilli, freed from the diseased tissue, cultivated in coagulated blood-serum, and afterward inoculated, produced tuberculosis in the inoculated animals. The inoculations were followed by the disease in dogs, cats and rats as well as in the more susceptible rabbits and guinea-pigs.

The rapidity with which the morbid process took place, as well as the extent of organs involved, depends upon the amount of infectious material inoculated. Acute miliary tuberculosis only occurred when a large quantity of the infectious material was introduced at once in a great number of places.

The conclusion follows from Koch's discovery that, while tuberculosis may be hereditary, in consequence of intra-uterine infection, the disease is as a rule acquired. Koch's researches have furthermore shown that a large portion of the affections termed scrofulous, are veritable tuberculosis.

While Virchow, and afterward Auspitz, called attention to the similarity in the histological structure of tubercle and lupus, Friedlander first considered lupus to be a local tuberculosis of the skin. He demonstrated the constant presence of giant cells and nests of epithelioid cells in the lupus tissue as in tubercle, and concluded that the pathological process was identical in the two affections. Schuller and Hueter have successfully inoculated lupus tissue upon healthy animals, and the former has cultivated micro-organisms which, when inoculated into the lungs of healthy animals produced general miliary tuberculosis, and when injected into a joint produced characteristic tnbercular inflammation of the joint and secondary general tuberculosis.

These results of experimental research appear to the author to justify the classification of these three affections under one head, and to treat them as simply modifications of one morbid process due to the same cause, *i. e.*, infection by the bacillus tuberculosis.

ANALECTS.

Bismuth Treatment of Wounds.

The use of bismuth in antiseptic surgery has yielded good results in Germany, especially in the hands of Kocher, of Berne, who has used it more extensively than any other surgeon. From experiments made by Schuler, Kocher's student, he concluded that the antiseptic qualities of bismuth were due to its preventing the development of micro-organisms of putrefaction, and Kocher has shown that, in the treatment of wounds, less depends upon disinfection—annihilation of micro-organisms, than upon antisepsis—preventing the development of the bacteria.

In view of the ill effects sometimes following its use, it is better not to apply the bismuth in the form of powder in unlimited quantities. One per cent. of bismuth suspended in water has fulfilled all the requirements of thorough antisepsis. Owing to the insolubility of bismuth, it should be most thoroughly triturated in water in order that no grittiness should be present, and the emulsion thus formed should be shaken until the salt is equally diffused throughout the fluid before using. Kocher applies it in the following manner:

From an ordinary squirting bottle the wound surface is moistened at intervals in the course of an operation, so that the loose cellular tissues in particular are covered by a thin film of bismuth; at each dressing this procedure is repeated, but when the edges of the wound have been brought into apposition, bismuth made into a thick paste, is spread upon the line of suture and allowed to dry into a crust. This method has been followed by the happiest results. The dressings of Kocher then consist of (1) strips of absorptive material covered by (2) a layer of gauze—both of these having been dipped in a ten per cent. solution of bismuth, and the moisture thoroughly wrung out before application—and over these is laid (3) a piece of India rubber cloth, (4) cotton wadding, and (5) a dry roller bandage finishes the dressing.

Having in view the fact that, with favorable external surroundings, the open treatment of wounds is not inferior to the antiseptic method, he adopted a plan which he calls the "secondary suture" in which he claims to have retained all the advantages of the open treatment without interfering with the success of antiseptic methods. In all cases where it did not seem advisable to rapidly complete the dressing, as after a prolonged operation or because of the exhausted condition of the patient, the sutures were not tied, but bismuth was applied in various ways. If hemorrhage was present, bismuth-gauze was introduced into the wound, —when, however, hemorrhage had ceased, the bismuth dressing was applied only to the surface, the edges of the wound having been brought into contact. After twenty-four or even twelve hours, but when secondary hemorrhage had supervened, after thirty-six or forty-eight hours, the wound was finally closed by the sutures, no opening being allowed to remain. For this "secondary suture," catgut cannot be used because of its weakness, and strong silk thread should be provided, since, because of the plastic swelling of the lips of the wound, some force is required to bring them into apposition—especially when the wound has been permitted to gape. The secondary suture was employed in a number of operations of widely varying character and situation, and, as a result of this experience, Kocher asserts boldly that the formation of wound secretion after twelve to twenty-four hours is not a necessary consequence of simple traumatism.

Bismuth possesses, to an eminent degree, the property of reducing the amount of wound secretions; it has long been successfully used as an astringeut in case of abnormal secretions of the intestinal canal. In its dessicating and astringent qualities are found a considerable part of its value. It is, therefore, of double value in the treatment of wounds in that (1) it secures perfect asepsis of the surface, and (2) it limits secretions in the cavity of the wound.

To obtain the advantage which bismuth offers for securing union by first intention, certain other points must receive attention. The collection of a quantity of blood in the cavity of the wound must be prevented. This may be obtained by the forci-pressure forceps of Pean, Billroth, or by Kocher's modification of the latter. The advantages of these forceps consist in the fact that they grasp firmly when applied, take up a limited amount of space, and are absolutely aseptic. Hemorrhage therefore, can be promptly controlled. Since extravasation from blood and lymph vessels cannot be absolutely prevented by ligature, a uniform compression of the edges and surface of the wound throughout its whole extent is necessary.

In cases where the great irregularity of the surrounding conditions did not admit of the application of sufficient pressure, the secondary suture was substituted.

In Kocher's experience with bismuth, usually within twenty-four hours, but varying from twelve to thirty-six hours, secretion from the cavity of the wound ceased. Small superficial granulations along the lines of sutures sometimes delayed healing for days; these are simply treated by the application of bismuth paste, when healing by scab will ensue.

With the rapid healing of wounds following the use of these methods, care must be taken against too early exertions upon the part of patients, subjecting them to the possible detachment of emboli, from imperfectly organized thrombi in the several vessels. Experience shows that there is particular danger of this in wounds of the neck and other parts, where the ligature of a large vein may have been necessary.

The perfect asepsis secured by bismuth is the chief point in its favor. For instance, in a case of knee-joint disease with fungous degeneration, where the joint was opened and the diseased tissue removed, then dressed with bismuth and the secondary suture, without the use of drainage-tubes, rapid and uncomplicated recovery ensued.

Another advantage of bismuth, if used according to this method, is the entire absence of direct systemic effects. The great simplicity of the method, and the absence of cumbersome details and apparatus, is of great advantage to the surgeon. The convenience and freedom from annoyance to the patient as well is greatly in its favor. The application of the salt upon a fresh wound surface causes, momentarily, a smart burning sensation. On the second day, when the secondary suture is applied the patient no longer complains when the bismuth irrigation is used.

As an antiseptic, bismuth is of greater use than iodoform on account of its insolubility. If it is desired to disinfect hands or instruments, or if an infected wound and the integument surrounding it must be disinfected, *i. e.*, if pathogenic organisms, which have found entrance to the wound, are to be destroyed, soluble antiseptics, like carbolic acid or corrosive sublimate, should be used.—*Annals of Anatomy and Surgery, June, 1883.*

Disinfection of the Stools in Enteric Fever.

The importance of the thorough disinfection of the stools in enteric fever is, to those who believe in it at all, so great, and its practical results in the control of the extension of the disease are so manifest and direct, that any additional data as to the best methods of employing disinfection cannot fail to be of interest. On the other hand, there are quite as many other physicians to whom the subject appears to have no importance whatever. These latter either do not believe in the necessity of the disinfection of enteric fever stools, or else they regard it as of so slight moment that it matters not practically whether it be attended to or not, or, finally, whilst professing to recognize its importance, they adopt in practice imperfect or incomplete measures to accomplish it. Indeed, it may be regarded as the exception to the rule, rather than the rule, both in private practice and in hospitals, to systematically and thoroughly disinfect every stool, even in well-characterized cases of enteric fever. To both of these classes of physicians it cannot but prove of advantage to read the excellent paper on this subject published by Dr. James C. Wilson, in the *American Journal of the Medical Sciences* for April, 1883.

He shows that although the nature of the germ that gives rise to enteric fever is unknown, many facts in its natural history are established by abundant proof. Of these, the following have a direct bearing upon this subject:

1. It is invariably derived from a previous case of enteric fever.

2. It is eliminated with the fæcal discharges.

3. It is not capable of producing enteric fever at once in susceptible persons exposed to it, but must undergo changes outside the body before it acquires that power.

4. It retains its activity in favorable situations for a lengthened period, the requirements to this end being decomposing animal matter, especially fæcal discharges, and moisture.

5. In such situations it is capable of reproducing itself.

These are the facts which indicate with singular directness the true measures necessary to prevent the spread of the disease, the efficient prophylaxis.—*Medical Gazette.*

The Cotton Pellet as an Artificial Drumhead.

Prof. Knapp, of New York, advocates the use of a pellet of cotton wet with glycerine as an aid to hearing in cases of defective membrana tympani. He sums up his experience as follows:

1. Cotton pellets, moistened with glycerine and water (1 : 4) and worn as artificial drum heads, are a great aid to many cases of partial or total defect of the natural drum-head with or without otorrhœa.

2. Their therapeutical action in arresting profuse discharge on the one hand; and in preventing the mucous membrane of the drum-cavity from drying up on the other, is most valuable.

3. They protect, like the natural drum heads, the deeper parts of the ear against injurious influences of the atmosphere, etc.

4. In some cases they are quite indispensable, and may be worn for a lifetime with permanent comfort and benefit.

5. In other cases they are needed only periodically, according as the copiousness of the discharge, or the exsiccation of the mucous membrane requires their action in the one or the other direction,

6. The period during which a pellet may be left in the ear varies with the condition of the parts. They should be changed frequently, *i. e.*, every day, or every few days, so long as the discharge is considerable. They should not be worn at all when the discharge is abundant or offensive. When there is no discharge, they may be left as long as they are comfortable (to the patient) and the hearing is good. So far as my experience goes, they are apt to become unclean in a week or two. They ought then to be removed, the ear cleansed either with dry cotton, or cotton steeped in warm soap suds, and new pellets introduced.

7. The management of the ear disease should remain in the hands of a physician until a stationary condition, either of slight, or no discharge, has been reached. During the time the patient is under treatment, he can be taught how to cleanse his ears and remove and replace the pellets.—*Archives of Otology.*

Thoracic Diseases—Some Points in Diagnosis.

J. Milner Fothergill, of England, in the *Medical Times and Gazette*, offers the following suggestions:

In all cases of thoracic disease it is well to count the pulse and respiration, and take the ratio.

When the ratio is preserved, yet both accelerated, it is well to take the temperature. When, however, the temperature is normal, and both are not accelerated, then look for the reason why the one is.

When the pulse rises in rapidity while the respiration is normal, the condition of the left ventricle and the mitral orifice must be carefully examined.

But when the opposite condition is found—when the breathing is accelerated and there exists no obvious lung condition to account for it—then, depend upon it, the thoracic space is diminished from some cause, whether it can be discovered or not.

Not uncommonly it is correct to suspect some damming of the blood at the mitral orifice, which leads to an overfull condition of the pulmonic circulation, and the excess of blood limits the thoracic space. Then listen to the closure of the pulmonic valves; hear what they have to say. Your suspicions may be confirmed, and perhaps after awhile a mitral whiff develops to settle the matter. Conversely, when you catch a mitral murmur, and the respiration is not accelerated nor the pulmonic valve sound accentuated, the lesion is small, no matter how loud the murmur.

Finally, it is quite possible at times to apprehend mitral stenosis before a murmur is audible. Often the murmur is to be heard only when carefully sought for.—*New York Medical Times.*

Effects of Quinine on the Ear.

The investigations of Dr. Roosa in regard to the action of quinine upon the ears have recently been corroborated by J. Orne Greene (*Boston Med. and Surg. Journal*), who formulates the following conclusions:

"(1.) Clinical experience the world over is, that quinine occasionally produces serious injury to the ears. (2.) From our present knowledge, both clinical and experimental, we are justified in asserting that the action of quinine upon the ears is to produce congestion of the labyrinth and tympanum, and sometimes distinct inflammation with permanent tissue changes. (3.) That the action of the drug upon the ears should always be considered in prescribing it, and changes in the ears, due to existing or previous inflammation of those organs, constitute a contra-indication to the medicine in large doses or for a long time except under urgent circumstances. (4.) That where large and continuous doses are absolutely necessary an occasional intermission of the administration is desirable, if possible, to diminish the risks to the ears."—*Miss. V. Med. Monthly.*

Funnel Drainage in Anasarca.

This is a method of removing large quantities of fluid, devised (*Glasgow Medical Journal*) by Dr. Straub, Tubingen. It is similar and affords more relief in equal time than Southey's. The apparatus consists of an ordinary glass funnel, of two inches diameter, attached to the end of which is an India rubber tube one-eighth inch in diameter, and long enough to reach to the floor. If the apparatus is filled with water, and the mouth of the funnel firmly applied to the skin of a patient lying in bed, while the end of the tube is immersed in a vessel on the floor containing a little water, it will be found to adhere quickly and act as a sucker; and when the funnel is applied over several small incisions or punctures in a case of œdema, the tube acting as a siphon will keep up a continuous drainage of serum into the vessel. The force of the suction can, of course, be regulated by altering the level of the vessel, and the flow of fluid can be watched by a piece of glass tubing let into the India-rubber tube. The apparatus, if protected by a small cage or cradle, can be left on for any length of time, and is not displaced by movements of the patient if ordinary care is taken. Enormous quantities of serum have been drained off in this way. In one case of chronic Bright's disease, there were drawn off in two and a quarter hours, over seventy-eight ounces; in seven hours, over ninety-six ounces; and in twenty-four hours, two hundred and seventy-eight ounces; and in another case of extreme general dropsy from Bright's disease, nearly forty-three pints were removed in seventy-nine hours.

Bromide Ulcers.

Dr. E. C. Seguin, reports two instances of ulcers on the legs resulting from the bromide treatment. These ulcers were large, and were elevated quite uniformly above the skin. Their edges were abrupt, almost vertical, with no signs of cicatricial action. The floors were firm and grayish-red, with here and there an adherent crust. The secretions were fetid, sanious and puriform, and the ulcers bled upon being touched with moderate violence. So firm was the tissue of these ulcers that it did not look like ordinary granulation tissue; it was composed of large masses, and at several points presented a slightly villous, or rather papillomatous appearance. These ulcers looked like epitheliomata; but in each case they were symmetrical, and the microscope proved that they offered no evidence of malignancy. They began as papules, became boils, and after discharging, degenerated into ulcers.— *New York Medical Times.*

Thomsen's Disease.

There is a curious kind of disorder known as Thomsen's disease, which is, fortunately, very rare. It was first so called, by Dr. Thomsen, of Schleswig, who suffered from it all his life, and who described it in 1876. The disease consists in a contraction or rigidity of the voluntary muscles, which comes on suddenly during their movement. If a person with this complaint throws his arm forward, as when casting a stone, the arm does not come back to the side, but remains extended. So with other movements, such as walking and running. It is a disease of the nerves, and is considered incurable.—*Med. Record.*

Carbolized Iodoform.

According to Carl Scher (Berl. Klin. Wochensch., No. 48, 1882), carbolic acid is an excellent corrigent for disguising the odor of iodoform. Add 0.05 carbolic acid to 10 grm. iodoform, and the odor is entirely covered, and it does not return even at the highest temperature. Two drops of ol. menth. pip., added to the powder, increases the pleasantness of the odor.

A Sensitive Reflex Area in the Posterior Nares.

Dr. John N. Mackenzie (*Am. Journ. Med. Sci.*, July, 1883), describes a sensitive reflex area in the posterior nasal region heretofore not recognized. He details a number of cases and sums up his conclusions as follows:

(1) That in the nose there exists a definite, well defined sensitive area, whose stimulation, either through a local pathological process, or through the action of an irritant introduced from without, is capable of producing an excitation, which finds its expression in a reflex act, or in a series of reflected phenomena.

(2) That this sensitive area corresponds, in all probability, with that portion of the nasal mucous membrane which covers the turbinated corpora cavernosa.

(3) That reflex cough is produced only by stimulation of this area, and is only exceptionally evoked when the irritant is applied to other portions of the nasal mucous membrane.

(4) That all parts of this area are not equally capable of generating the reflex act, the most sensitive spot being probably represented by that portion of the membrane which clothes the posterior extremities of the inferior turbinated body and that of the septum immediately opposite.

(5) That the tendency to reflex action varies in different individuals, and is probably dependent upon the varying degree of excitability of the erectile tissue. In some, the slightest touch is sufficient to excite it, in others, chronic hyperemia or hypertrophy of the cavernous bodies seems to evoke it by constant irritation of the reflex centres, as occurs in similar conditions of other erectile organs, as, for example, the clitoris.

(6) That this exaggerated or disordered functional activity of the area may possibly throw some light on the physiological destiny of the erectile bodies. Among other properties which they possess, may they not act as sentinels to guard the lower air-passages and pharynx against the entrance of foreign bodies, noxious exhalations, and other injurious agents to which they might otherwise be exposed?

Apart from their physiological interest, the practical importance of the above facts in a diagnostic and therapeutic point of view is sufficiently obvious. Therein lies the explanation of many obscure cases of cough which heretofore have received no satisfactory solution, and their recognition is the key to their successful treatment.

Effect of Strychnine Upon Dilatation of the Heart.

Professor Maragliano formulates the results of the exhibition of strychnine in cardiac dilatation as follows: 1. In one or two days the size of the heart was reduced, and in five or six days very considerable dilatations were caused to disappear. 2. If, immediately upon reduction in size of the heart, the strychnine were withheld, the dilatation was frequently reproduced. 3. The daily dose of sulphate of strychnine required was from 1-32 to 1-20 of a grain.—*Memorabilien.—N. Y. Med. Times.*

Goodell's "four chlorides mixture" is composed as follows:

℞ Hydrarg. bichlor . . . . gr. j-ij
Liq. arsen. chlor, ... ℨj
Acidi. hydrochlor. dil.
Tr. ferri. chlor., of each, . ℨij
Syr. Zingib, ... ℨij
Aquæ ad., ... ℥vj

M. Sig.—Two teaspoonfuls three times daily in water, after meals.

This is prescribed by Prof. Goodell as an alterative tonic.

Dr. P. A. Carrington, a graduate of the College of Physicians and Surgeons (class of 1883), has been appointed hospital steward in the Marine Hospital service and assigned to duty in Baltimore.

Inherited Syphilis of the Mammary Glands.

Dr. C. C. F. Gay, of Buffalo, reports (*Med. Record*, July 28, 1883), a case of syphilitic disease of the mammary gland in a female patient 19 years of age. The symptoms were as follows: About four years ago the patient began to have pain in both mammæ, especially the left, which became so sensitive that the weight of the bedclothes upon it could not be borne. Menstruation regular and without influence upon the mammary pain. No evidence of acquired syphilis in the patient. The left breast was hard and nodular, conveying the sensation of schirrus; it was excessively tender; nipples retracted. A small tumor was also noted in the right breast. A diagnosis of non-malignant growth was made, and the right breast removed by Thomas' method. The edges of the wound were united and antiseptically dressed. No union followed, and, as after three weeks, the wound presented an appearance recalling a syphilitic ulcer, the patient was put upon the iodides of mercury and potash, and rapidly improved. The enlargement in the right breast disappeared.

It was afterward discovered that the father of the patient, had been treated for constitutional syphilis about the time the patient was born.

[It must be confessed that the conclusion reached in this case is not unimpeachable.—ED.]

The New Indian Cure for Syphilis.

This is introduced to the profession by Dr. J. Marion Sims, through the *British Medical Journal.*

For many years it had been employed by the Creek Indians of Alabama. Of its good results Dr. Sims was an interested witness during his early professional career in Alabama. From the Indians the remedy passed into the hands of the slaves. The matter was finally studied by an intelligent physician Dr. McDade. From this study Dr. Sims obtains his facts. Eliminated of the inert remedies that entered into its composition, the formula for the remedy is as follows: " Fluid ext. smilax sarsaparilla ; fluid ext. stillingia sylvatica ; fluid ext. lappa minor ; fluid ext. phytolacca decandra, āā ʒ ij; tinct. xanthoxylum Carolinianum, ʒ j. Take a teaspoonful in water three times a day. The fluid extracts should be made from freshly gathered roots in order that their strength may be retained. The illustrative cases given of the effects of combination of drugs are quite striking and as convincing as such an amount of such evidence can ever be.

McDade has used the remedy with satisfaction in cases of scrofula and thinks it would be worth trying in cancer. This may or may not prove useful when tried under different circumstances than those of the first observers, but it will certainly have an extended trial after the advertisement given it by Dr. Sims. Large numbers will use it simply because an eminent man has commended it. Others will use it because they have learned of it. Others because they have failed to relieve some cases by the use of ordinary remedies. The course pursued by McDade and Sims in this matter is certainly commendable. The former had his mind open to consider the availability of any remedy from any source that had an appearance of affording relief to any form of disease. In humble ways start very many of the best means for combating disease. Having satisfied his own mind of the value of a certain remedy he communicates it to others. Among these is Dr. Sims. Being convinced that the remedy is worthy of a wider field of study he lends the use of his great name to bring it before a proper audience. Now we hope that it may be fairly studied and the results made evident to the world.—*Detroit Lancet.*

Diphtheria and Infected Milk.

Dr. Paine, in his last report on Cardiff, refers to the diffusion of diphtheria in that town by a contaminated milk supply. On inquiring into the causes of a fatal outbreak of diphtheria at a farm house, Dr. Paine found that milk for town distribution was obtained from this source, and, believing that the well-water was at fault, he caused it to be examined, and found that it contained an excessive amount of sewage contamination. The use of the well for drinking purposes was prohibited by the sanitary authority, but it was not forbidden for other general use. Sometime afterward several deaths from diphtheria happened in the town, and it was ascertained that the milk used by the patients had been obtained from this farm. The tin vessels used for conveying the milk were rinsed night and morning with water obtained from this well. The well was afterward permanently closed, and no other fatal cases of diphtheria occurred in the town.—*British Med. Journal.*

Treatment of Soft Chancres and of Buboes by Salicylic Acid.

The efficacy of *salicylic acid* in the the treatment of soft chancres and of buboes appears to us to be unquestionable. While not an absolute specific, it is, in our opinion, capable of being most advantageously employed.

Odorless, only slightly painful in its application, soluble in alcohol and in glycerine, and leaving no stain on linen, it is preferable, in these important respects, to most other agents employed for the cure of the above named affections, while perhaps inferior in certain other particulars to some among its rivals.

It may be resorted to in all cases, and is equally available in private and in hospital practice.—AUTIER; *Th. de Paris (Jour. of Cut. and Ven. Dis.)*

IODOFORM in doses of one grain is said to be a good vermifuge.

Cure of Squint without Operation.

In the early stages of convergent strabismus, before the internal rectus muscle is permanently contracted, Dr. Boucheron (*Schmidt's Jahrbucher*, January 17, 1883), claims that a cure is possible without operation. He states that as convergence is caused by efforts of accommodation for near objects, if we take away the power of accommodation squint will not occur. He maintains a constant mydriasis by the instillation of atropine night and morning. A cure is usually obtained in two or three weeks. If atropine is not well borne, other mydriatics, such as duboisia, may be used. In nine cases of intermittent strabismus the author obtained eight cures by this method.—*Med. Record.*

Nasal Catarrh.

Cubeb is the remedy most relied on in the Throat room, for constitutional impression in the ordinary form of the complaint. Fifteen or more drops of the oleo resin, on sugar, after meals; or a few grains of the recently prepared powder, with two or three grains of salicylate of cinchonidia, in pill or capsule, are the forms in which it is usually prescribed. Cleanliness, by douche or spray, is essential in giving the parts a chance to get well, which they often do by cleanliness alone, without any topical medication. — *The Polyclinic.*

Fruits of Compulsory Vaccination.

Statistics reported in the *Union Medicale* give the number of deaths in the French army from small-pox at 1,037. In the German army during the same period there was not a single death from the same cause. Vaccination and re-vaccination upon entering another army corps are compulsory in Germany.

IN the gouty diathesis, one of the most useful remedies is iodide of lithium.

Dyspeptic and Uterine Headaches.

Dr. H. Thomson, Prof. of Mat. Med. and Nervous Diseases in the University of New York, discourses as follows upon this practical subject:

The cause of gastric headache is acidity of the stomach, but the acidity here means the absence and not the presence, of gastric juice. A mixture of acetic and butyric acid determines the acidity of gastric dyspepsia. The gastric juice is odorless *per se*. The acetic acid is produced by the decomposition of starch and the nitrogenous element of the food, while the fermentation of the fats produces butyric acid.

Gastric headache usually begins at night. The headache of Bright's disease, due to gastritis and to the fermentation of food, comes on very soon after its ingestion, so that patients have a headache and sour stomach within an hour or two after eating. Patients with dyspeptic headache wake up with a dull sensation in the head, or "sick headache." This variety of headache is ordinarily frontal, involving also the eyes. The head feels hot all over,—in the occiput, vertex and forehead. The headache increases during the day, becoming very violent, and with it the face turns pale. The patients frequently suffer from nausea and vomiting. The tears run, and the nose, mouth and throat feel as if burned, from the exceedingly caustic or acrid nature of the fermented contents of the stomach. By thorough emesis, the patient is relieved.

Lime water allays the irritability of the stomach. A glass of vichy or a little alkali for the time being will counteract the acidity, but the use of alkaline drinks should be reserved until after the patient has vomited. They are of no use before vomiting, as the food in the stomach is not fit to be digested, and, if attempted, will only cause more suffering and inconvenience.

This headache may be habitual, and might be mistaken for migraine. Such patients are uniformly dyspeptic. They have weak stomachs, and are subject to heartburn, and complain of a sensation of soreness at the sternum. You notice in the case before us redness of the pharynx, which is one of the signs tending to sour stomach. Palpitation and intermittent action of the heart are exceedingly common with these patients.

Pepsin and muriatic acid are the best preventives of sick headaches arising from dyspepsia. Vegetable bitters, with carbonate of ammonia, and a little iron, should be taken regularly for about two or three weeks. Pepsin and muriatic acid are frequently serviceable in preventing these headaches. Fatty food is most likely to cause headaches, and beer among the drinks. Smoking tobacco at night should be avoided by dyspeptics. Should the sufferer be one who is obliged to eat his meals by railroad time, he must stop this mode of life if he wishes to be relieved of his headaches.

Uterine headaches are to be divided into those which belong to the early menstrual period, and those which belong to the menopause. We have, then, chlorotic or amenorrheal headaches, including hysterical headaches and the headaches of the menopause. Chlorotic headaches are very common. The headaches of the menopause are violent, but there is a tendency at this time on the part of patients to exaggerate their trouble. They are full of all sorts of fears. If you listen to such a patient, you will hear a catalogue of symptoms which will puzzle you and lead you to suppose that you have an exceedingly serious case.

The chlorotic form of headache is peculiar. The eyes become affected and are weak. The pain is at first frontal, accompanied with throbbing of the temporal arteries and with some flushing of the forehead and face, while the hands and feet are ice-cold. The bones ache, and there is severe pain in the small of the back and very frequently at the nape of the neck. Where there is curvature of the spine the headache is always worse. Curvature of the spine, due to general debility of the muscular system, of itself causes pain in the occiput.

This form of headache is relieved by treatment by aloetic purgatives.

The following combination is a good one, as the soap prevents the griping effects of the aloes:

℞ Pulv. aloes,
" nucis vom. āā gr. j.
" saponis gr. v.

Make up into a capsule. Aloin and strychnine make a very good pill. But I prefer the above. Then give iron. The feet may be kept warm by applying to them a bag of hot salt or bottles of hot water.

The headaches of the menopause are characteized by a flushed face and excited pulse. The patients complain of buzzing in the ear. Warm water applications relieve these headaches. Febrile headaches are relieved, on the other hand, by cold water. The patients should be given 30 grain doses of sodium bromide. Gentle laxatives, as the compound liquorice powder, should also be administered. Diuretics are good agents in the treatment of the manifold troubles of the menopause. There is, at this time of life, a considerable vaso-motor disturbance, as the system is adjusting itself to an entire change in the vascular balance. The condition of a woman at the menopause is very much like a man who has had an habitual discharge suddenly healed up. Sometimes there is derangement of the functions of the kidneys. Should you ask the question, "Are you passing the same quantity of water that you usually do?" they will say "no." The specific gravity of the urine is rather low. and here we have an explanation of a good deal of the derangement of the head. Diuretics have often, in my hands, relieved the headaches that resisted every other kind of treatment. Sweet spirits of nitre, 3 j., mixed with a little tincture of nux vomica, taken three times a day, will make a good diuretic.

Ergot is indicated where there is throbbing when the ear is laid on the pillow. This remedy has a special control over the innervation of the sympathetic of the neck. The artery that supplies the middle ear is supplied by the sympathetic. The artery that supplies the cochlea and the labyrinth comes from the vertebral and not from the carotid. The ergot may be given in drachm doses of fluid extract.

Semmola on the Pathogenesis of Albuminuria.

Semmola, in a recent paper read at the Académie de Médicine (*Le Progrès Méd.*, Nov. 24, 1883), states that he first, in 1850, pointed out the dependence of albuminuria on the quality of ingesta, and that the increase after nitrogenous diet led him to adopt the view that the renal disease was secondary, and that the primary departure from health was the failure to utilize the albuminoids in the economy. Later, in 1861, he proved that a healthy kidney could excrete albumen, but that, if prolonged, this led to anatomical changes.

His principal arguments for the hematogenous origin of albuminuria are:—1. the diminution of the excretion of urea from the commencement of the albuminuria, without its accumulation anywhere; 2. identity of the albumen excreted in Bright's disease with the serum of the blood; this is not the case in other forms of albuminuria; 3. the bilateral affection of the kidneys; 4. the confusion resulting from the anatomical point of view.

During the past few years, he has become convinced that differences in diffusion power lie at the bottom of this question. He has found—1. that the albuminoids in the blood of Bright's disease diffuse more than the albuminoids of the blood in other forms of albuminuria; 2. that, in early stages of Bright's disease, if the blood be examined before and after the cure, the diffusibility of the albuminoids of the blood augments, diminishes, or stops in relation with the quantity of albumen in the urine; 3. that this physico-molecular constitution of the albuminoids of the blood produced by more or less considerable default in the functions of the skin. He found that the blood of animals with varnished skins always contained diffusible albuminoids when the varnishing involved at least one-half of their cutaneous surface. In these circumstances there was albuminuria, and the bile also contained albumen. He has collected a certain number of cases of chronic eczema and psoriasis, which alternated with albuminuria, and were finally cured by prolonged hydro-sudopathic treatment. He relates a curious case of seborrhœa, which produced effects like those of varnishing the skin. The patient felt the least breath of air, was always cold, looked very cachectic, and had albuminuria. He was cured perfectly by similar active treatment directed to his skin, and the albuminuria, has never reappeared.

Dr. Semmola thinks the causes of the diminished activity of the skin are generally cold and damp. These act insidiously, producing by degrees an increase in the diffusibility of the albuminoids, a diminution in the urea excreted, and finally the forced elimination of albumen by all the depurative channels of the body. The saliva and sweat, as well as the bile, may be shown to contain albumen. This is the explanation of the albuminuria of Bright's disease, as distinguished from other forms having a purely local cause, congestion, inflammation, etc. By injecting egg-albumen under the skin, he has been able to produce all the phenomena of nephritis; thus proving that the continuance of this abnormal secretion may bring about inflammatory changes in the kidneys. —*London Medical Record.*

Dr. E. Gover Cox, of Baltimore, died on the 20th of August.

Influence of Fowler's Solution upon the Hæmoglobin in the blood.

From an investigation made to determine the effects of the medicinal administration of some remedies upon the proportion of hæmoglobin in the blood, Dr. Fenoglio, of Turin, concludes that the iron preparations vary considerably in their effects; Fowler's solution increases the hæmoglobin, and this becomes more marked the longer it is given. In spite of the general opinion to the contrary, the administration of Fowler's solution is indicated in anæmia, chlorosis, and in general in all conditions in which there is a decrease in the hæmoglobin, for the influence of this agent is very evident in increasing the proportion of the hæmoglobin; and, furthermore, its use increases the appetite and produces a general improvement in the bodily appearance and condition.—*Southern Clinic.*

Substitute for Mercurial Ointment.

A French physician, Dr. R. Vizier, recommends 4 or 5 per cent. solution of corrosive sublimate in glycerine in place of mercurial ointment for parasites of the skin. Glycerine is not absorbed by the skin and to a great extent prevents the absorption of medicines. Therefore, on account of its greater cleanliness and greater security from the absorption of mercurials, this solution is to be preferred to blue ointment.—*Pacific Med. and Surg. Journal.*

Envious of Hunter.

The *Medical Press* records that Dr. Cery, of St. Thomas' Hospital, London, disbelieving in the inoculability of the Hunterian chancre, submitted himself to inoculation, and after three or four failures succeeded in producing true chancre on the arm, which was followed by secondary and tertiary symptoms severe enough to incapacitate him from work.

The Medical Chronicle.

A Monthly Journal for the Practitioner.

GEORGE H. ROHÉ, M. D., Editor.

☞ It is requested that all literary and business communications, books for review, exchanges, etc., be addressed to, and all checks, drafts and post-office orders drawn to the order of
Dr. GEORGE H. ROHÉ,
95 Park Avenue, - - - - Baltimore, Md.

BALTIMORE, SEPTEMBER, 1883.

EDITORIAL.

The Prospect of An Epidemic of Cholera.

The more than probable invasion of this country by Asiatic cholera within the next twelve months, may render some comments upon the conditions which favor the spread of this disease not irrelevant. It is well known, that cholera is propagated along lines of human travel, especially water courses; that it usually prevails most in low-lying districts, and that it rages with especial violence in such localities where the sanitary surroundings are bad. It is also known that local physical conditions of soil, differences of moisture or porosity have a decided influence in determining the epidemic prevalence of the disease.

These facts being unquestionable, it behooves us to take the necessary precautions to prevent the introduction of the cholera poison from abroad, and, what is still more important, to take such measures as will prevent its spread if once introduced. The relative importance of quarantine and local sanitation in preventing epidemic cholera is well characterized by von Pettenkofer, who compares cholera epidemics to powder explosions. The virus of cholera, he says, is the spark which evades the strictest quarantine. The powder is the *ensemble* of local conditions which predispose to the outbreak. "It is, therefore, wiser to seek out and remove the powder than to run after and try to extinguish each individual spark before it drops on a mass of powder, and igniting it, causes an explosion which blows us into the air with our extinguishers in our hands."

Although the effect of local predisposing causes upon the spread of cholera has been most clearly demonstrated by von Pettenkofer and his disciples from the history of numerous local epidemics, the theory which requires, besides the introduction of the cholera poison, the contemporary action of certain local and temporary dispositions in the soil or atmosphere and in the individual attacked, is not universally accepted. The opposition to the theory comes mainly from authorities who hold to the contagiousness of cholera, its conveyance through drinking water infected by cholera discharges, and its excludability by quarantine and sanitary *cordons*. The inefficiency of the latter measures, and the importance of local sanitation were long ago stated in the admirable report of the College of Physicians of Philadelphia, published in 1832. Still more clearly, however, was the question stated in a little pamphlet published in this city by Dr. Thomas H. Buckler, in 1851.* Dr. Buckler says: "Epidemic cholera would seem to depend, not on a single, but two concurrent causes. The first is probably general, and widely diffused over a vast extent of country, but requiring in every instance some local influence to ignite the epidemic poison and bring it into action." In another place Dr. B. writes: "It would seem that the disease depended on some wide-spread influence, which required in every instance the operation of miasmatic or malarious exhalations to bring it into action. It is only at the cross-roads of the general

* A History of Epidemic Cholera, as it appeared at the Baltimore City and County Almshouse, in the summer of 1849. By Th. H. Buckler, Physician to the Baltimore City and County Almshouse; Baltimore, 1851.

and local causes, if it may be so expressed, that the disease is found, and nowhere else." In the "miasmatic and malarious exhalations," Dr. Buckler clearly recognizes the effects of a poisoned ground-atmosphere, which is the basis of von Pettenkofer's theory of the spread of cholera, first formulated by him in 1854, and more fully developed afterward.

It may be thought by some that the discussion of this matter is premature, but as the chances are more than even that cholera will be introduced into this country before another year, every community should be prepared to act rationally and understandingly. It must be obvious to every observer, that our cities are in a fit condition to offer to the cholera poison a favorite breeding place. A watchful quarantine, thorough local sanitation and such other measures as reason and experience indicate should be adopted before the epidemic is upon us.

An Unsuccessful Suit for a Diploma.

The case of Jacob M. Davis, against the College of Physicians and Surgeons, has attracted considerable attention on the part of both the medical and legal professions. The case in brief was this: Jacob M. Davis was a student at the College of Physicians and Surgeons for the past two sessions. At the end of the last session he was entered as a candidate for graduation. The Faculty, after examining him, decided that he was not qualified for graduation, and hence, refused to grant him a diploma. Nine others of the class met the same fate, and gracefully accepted the situation, but Davis claimed that the diploma had been refused not on account of personal unfitness, but on account of the character of his parents, which, it appears, was in in ill-repute. He then, upon the advice of counsel, applied to the Superior Court of this city for a mandamus to compel the College to issue the diploma. The Court (Judge Phelps), decided that the issuing of a mandamus to compel an institution of learning to confer a degree upon any person considered incompetent by the institution in question, was beyond the power of the Court.

It is said the plaintiff will invoke the judgment of the Court of Appeal.

The decision of Judge Phelps appears so entirely just, that it looks absurd for any one with common sense, to expect its reversal by the higher court.

"Strange, all this difference should be, 'Twixt tweedledum and tweedledee!"

From the recent action of the Louisiana state board of health, it appears very clearly that the attacks on the national board of health emanating from that body were altogether inspired by petty, personal spite. Since the marine hospital service has taken charge of the quarantine at Ship Island, the Louisiana board seems to be anxious to have all quarantine service performed at that station. While the national board of health had charge of the Ship Island establishment, it was repeatedly and solemnly asserted by Dr. Jones, the president of the Louisiana state board, that to send vessels to Ship Island to perform quarantine, would destroy the commerce of New Orleans. Have the conditions of existence of New Orleans commerce changed within the last year?

DR. DANIEL R. BROWER, Prof. Mental and Nervous Diseases and Medical Jurisprudence. Woman's Medical College, and Editor *Chicago Medical Journal and Examiner*, says: " I have been using BROMIDIA in my practice for several months and find it to be a *very valuable hypnotic*. The disagreeable taste of the chloral and the bromide are quite effectually concealed, and the depressive influence of the drugs on the circulation admirably counteracted by the cannabis indica and hyoscyamus."

CURRENT LITERATURE.

A Practical Treatise on the Diseases of the Uterus, Ovaries and Fallopian Tubes. By A. Courty, Professor of Clinical Surgery, Montpellier, France. Translated by Dr. Agnes M'Laren, with a preface by Dr. J. Matthews Duncan. Philadelphia: P. Blakiston, Son & Co. 1883. Baltimore: Henry C. Erich agent, 358 N. Gay Street. Price, cloth, $6.00; sheep, $7.00.

In the last ten years several classes of books upon the diseases of women have been written. Some of these are from the pens of young men of little practice and much reading; others, from the pens of older men of little reading and considerable practical experience, while a third class emanated from the minds of physicians richly stocked with learning and the results of personal observation. The first class of books are of no use to the student whatever; they consist in the majority of cases simply of a crude mass of undigested material, gathered together from note books. The second class are valuable as records of personal experience, but to the student or physician just beginning the study of the specialty, they are apt to be misleading on account of failure to recognize and properly appreciate the work of other laborers in the same field.

The third class of books, on the other hand, comprise those of most value, and they are the only ones, with which the student should begin his studies. Of this class, the work of Prof. Courty stands easily among the very first. For clear and concise descriptions, accurate notions of pathology and rational methods of treatment, Prof. Courty has no rivals among systematic writers on gynecology. His knowledge of the literature of his subject appears to be thorough and discriminating, while his large practical experience and observation are manifest on every page. In the words of Professor Duncan, Courty's book is "the carefully elaborated and repeatedly revised work of a man at once imbued with the science and immersed in the practice of gynecology, of one who has long lived in a centre of general science and learning, amidst an abounding population, and who enjoys the great advantage of combining in his sphere of practical activity both hospital and private patients—two classes which differ in their circumstances and in their aspects for observation, favorable and unfavorable to the student."

Fifth Annual Report of the State Board of Health of Rhode Island. Providence, R. I., 1883. C. H. Fisher, M. D. Secretary

This volume contains, in addition to a general health report of the state, an exhaustive article upon "the composition and properties of milk," by Mr. Edwin E. Calder, and an address on "parks and open places in cities," by Dr. Franklin C. Clark.

On Nasal Cough, and the Existence of a Sensitive Reflex Area in the Nose. By John N. Mackenzie, M. D., etc. Baltimore. Reprint. Pp. 11.

An excellent paper, detailing the circumstances of the author's discovery of a sensitive reflex area in the posterior nasal region, and calling attention to the great frequency of cough as a symptom of nasal disease. The pamphlet will well repay study.

A Contribution to the Study of Neglected Lacerations of the Cervix Uteri and Perineum. By T. A. Ashby, M. D., Prof. of Obstetrics, Womans' Medical College, etc. Reprint from *Maryland Med. Journal.* Pp. 11.

An excellent paper, based upon a thorough study of the literature of the subject, and upon personal experience.

FLOTSAM.

Dr. J. GILMAN died in this city on the 1st of August. He was 64 years of age, and was a prominent member and for a number of years treasurer of the Medical and Chirurgical Faculty of Maryland.

DR. ROSWELL PARK, of Chicago, has been elected Professor of Surgery in the Buffalo College of Physicians and Surgeons. Although quite a young man, Prof. Park is not unknown to the readers of the medical journals.

THE *New Orleans Medical and Surgical Journal* for August, 1883, comes to hand beautifully attired in a new suit of type. It has now no superior in the country as a well-conducted and handsomely printed journal.

DR. L. S. MCMURTRY, who has been for about a year one of the editors of our excellent contemporary, the *Louisville Medical News*, has retired from that journal and has been succeeded by Dr. H. A. Cottell, who was formerly conected with the *News* in the same capacity.

Dr. T. W. KAY, a graduate and Cathell-medalist of the College of Physicians and Surgeons (class of 1879), has been appointed lecturer on materia medica and zoology in the Syrian Protestant College in Beirut, Syria. Dr. Kay will also lecture on geology in the preparatory department.

IN the pamphlet of Dr. Buckler, quoted in our editorial in this issue, the opinion is expressed that "quarantine ought to be just as much under the direction of the general government as the collection of revenues or any other function which it has to perform. Laws regulating emigration and a system of quarantine are so intimately connected, that neither can be perfect so long as they are separated:" Many who have given the subject much thought in recent years have arrived at similar conclusions.

DR. J. BERRIEN LINDSLEY, the treasurer of the American Public Health Association, is engaged in the preparation of a work of much interest to Tennesseeans and all others interested in local American history. The work is entitled "The Military Annals of Tennessee," and will comprise a complete military history of that state from 1812 to 1865, compiled from original and official records. Dr. Lindsley has been engaged in collecting the materials for his history for over twenty years, and will doubtless produce an interesting and valuable work.

WE publish the following as of interest to our readers :

Philadelphia, Dec. 22, 1882.

An analysis of seven samples Quinine Pills, obtained without knowledge of the manufacturers, was made and published in the American Journal of Pharmacy by me, and those made by WILLIAM R. WARNER & Co., were found correct as to quantity and purity of Quinine.

HENRY TRIMBLE.
Analytical Chemist.

THE *Cincinnati Lancet and Clinic* has begun an active war upon the porkopolitan board of health, which is composed of "five saloon keepers and one quack doctor." Of " Dr." Beck, the medical member of the board, one of the judges of Cincinnati, said in the course of a decision in a case tried before him: "This Dr. Beck, who perpetrated this swindle, and who was on the stand, I cannot help saying, seems to be the most infamous scoundrel that it was ever my fortune to hear of." Nice man to be on a health board! It seems that no respectable member of the profession would consent to be a candidate for the position of health officer to this board. An ex-temperance orator with "faith cure" proclivities, has been elected to the position.

The Medical Chronicle.

BALTIMORE, OCTOBER, 1883.

ORIGINAL ARTICLES.

ARTICLE I.

On the Treatment of Dysmenorrhœa and Abortion.

BY B. F. LEONARD, M. D., BALTIMORE.

As the treatment of dysmenorrhœa is confessed to be unsatisfactory, the profession will welcome the advent of any remedy which promises to be useful in this often distressing affection.

Classification is extremely useful, but the limitation of the varieties of dysmenorrhœa is not so exact in nature as in the text-books, several factors often being present in the same case. Even in cases where we are accorded the fullest liberty of examination for a diagnosis, we often fail to give satisfactory and continued relief. Besides these, we meet many cases, as in young virgins and others, where it is undesirable to subject the patient to a physical examination. In these, our diagnosis is presumptive and our treatment must be tentative. After having run the gamut of suitable remedies, my attention was attracted to an abstract in the *New York Medical Record* (vol. xxii, p. 613), of Dr. Purdy's article in the *N. Y. Med. Journal and Obstetrical Review*, on the use of viburnum opulus in dysmenorrhœa. Not being able to procure the remedy in town, Messrs. Parke, Davis & Co., kindly sent me a lot of their fluid extract to experiment with. (It can now be had of Mr. John F. Hancock.) The results of its use have been so decided, after nearly a year's trial of the remedy, that it has been determined to make them public.

I have selected a few typical cases from an extensive series, to show to what conditions the drug is applicable, and when it is futile to expect relief from other than mechanical means.

Case 1. Mrs. Ellen B., 35, nullipara: has moderate pain for two days before the flow and after it sets in the pain is violent and spasmodic. She is confined to bed during every menstrual period—latterly her sufferings are more intense. An examination revealed a marked cervical constriction from anteflexion. A prolonged attempt was made to introduce a probe, but failing in this, a small tupelo tent was passed into the internal os by seizing the cervix with a vulsellum and making traction to straighten the canal as much as possible.

In a few hours violent pains set in, accompanied by a premature free menstrual flow. The tent was withdrawn and the viburnum opulus ordered, but its only effect was to somewhat modify the pains and the quantity of the flow; as she was clamorous for relief I was compelled to give her decided doses of sod. bromide and morphia. In three weeks, after a tent treatment, she menstruated again, almost painlessly, without taking any drugs. In this case the drug was a comparative failure from cervical constriction due to anteflexion.

Case 2. Mrs. J., primipara: this is a case of what Duncan calls "one-child sterility," having been pregnant only once, and that in the first year of wedded life, sixteen years ago. Had always, even when single, suffered from disordered menstruation, usually a spasmodic dysmenorrhœa, with menorrhagia—the latter usually profuse enough to cause marked anemia. She has had several attacks of cellulitis, terminating by resolution. Examination showed a hyperplastic uterus slightly retroverted, but with a free uterine canal. Cannabis Indica had given the best results in her case, but there was yet something wanting to make her comfortable during her periods. This desideratum the viburnum opulus supplied. Her menstruation became absolutely painless, with a moderate normal flow. She has now passed five periods in perfect comfort, by taking daily three 20 drop doses during the first few days of menstruation.

Case III. Mrs. D. C., 3 para : had spontaneously aborted in August, '82. Became pregnant again in Feb., '83. Her local condition was normal, except a large slit in the left side of the cervix, with a profuse vaginal discharge. During and after a critical illness from gastric ulcer, during March and April she had symptoms of imminent abortion, but by rest and medication the miscarriage was prevented, the alarming pains, however, frequently recurring. In May, the exhibition of this drug was followed by complete subsidence of the pains, and she is happily now near her accouchement.

Case IV. Mrs. A., a young married woman, who had a premature still-birth, followed by a miscarriage in the third month ; has nearly completed her third gestation, her condition being decidedly influenced by the use of the viburnum opulus. In her case all the usual medication, including the v. prunifolium had previously been tried in vain.

Case V. Miss Emma, 22 : dysmenorrhœa during all her menstrual life : sufferings were so great as to induce her to permit an examination, after the failure of viburnum opulus to give relief. She was cured by dilatation of a flexed canal, with stenosis.

Case VI. Miss Hester, 19, but rather immature : has menstruated since 16 ; always with pain during the day before the flow sets in and during the first two days. Latterly, her pain became so violent that she had convulsive attacks, with cold extremities and skin. In her case it was desirable to succeed without recourse to a local examination. Her treatment extended nearly one year ; nothing but a decided narcotism giving her even a moderate relief. She was placed on the viburnum opulus, 15 drops every 15 minutes during the violent attacks ; otherwise the drug was taken regularly four times daily in 25 drop doses, its use beginning two days before the flow set in. The result was brilliant ; she has now menstruated painlessly for months, with a normal flow in place of a formerly scanty one. She has developed, and is now a hearty woman.

It will be seen by a perusal of these cases, that, aside from threatened abortion, this drug is most useful in spasmodic dysnemorrhœa ; abolishing pain and regulating a scanty or excessive flow. My experience agrees with that of Hale and Meyer (l. c.)—it is a direct uterine sedative. To carry this deduction to its logical conclusion, the drug should be useful in menorrhagia, due to fibroids or other causes. I have had but one experience of this sort—a profuse and exhausting menorrhagia due to subinvolution (the uterine canal being 5 inches long). The viburnum op. was of positive use in limiting the flow, but, of course, other suitable treatment was required. In cases where an examination is not permitted, this drug may be expected to give relief, where the pain does not last throughout the flow ; where the pain ceases after a few days, although the flow continues. Where the pain and flow are conterminous there is probably a local condition not amenable to drugs, but only to local treatment.

I conclude, therefore, that in viburnum opulus we have a remedy valuable in neuralgic, congestive or spasmodic dysmenorrhœa, besides being of extreme use in threatened abortion.

314 East Baltimore Street.

TRY THE MEDICAL CHRONICLE for one year.

ARTICLE II.

Œdema of the Glottis in a case of Syphilitic Ulceration of the Larynx.—Tracheotomy avoided by the use of the Catheter.

BY J. D. ARNOLD, M. D. BALTIMORE.

Œdema of the laryngeal investment, whether chronic or acute, is perhaps the most formidable complication to be met with in the treatment of throat affections. The chronic form is an ordinary concomitant of cancerous, typhoid, syphilitic and tubercular infiltration; indeed, in phthisis of the larynx, the slowly established œdematous swelling of the arytenoid bodies is almost pathognomonic, and constitutes one of the earliest symptoms of this disease. On the other hand, acute œdema of the structures surrounding the glottis is of rare occurrence save when due to some traumatic cause, such as the inpaction of foreign bodies, or wounds from incautious use of instruments in the larynx, etc.

In very exceptional cases it is witnessed as a symptom of catarrhal and syphilitic inflammation. The instance about to be related belongs to the latter class, and its history is as follows:

An unmarried man, age 37, applied for treatment in January of this year. He stated that nearly two years ago he had a chancre which healed without pronounced induration of the inguinal glands, but was promptly followed by a well-marked roseola, upon the appearance of which he sought medical advice. His physician ordered inunctions of ung. hyd-arg. ʒ i twice daily. Salivation occurred after two weeks use of the ointment, which was then discontinued, and a mixture (nature unknown) prescribed, of which he took seven bottles. After this he appeared free from all symptoms of disease, and remained well until a month ago, when, for the first time, his throat became sore. At this time his physician prescribed large doses of Pot. iodide, and shortly after sent him to me for examination and treatment of the throat trouble. Upon examining with the mirror I found a broad, shallow ulcer upon the base of the tongue, and the anterior face of the epiglottis. The whole laryngeal mucus membrane was intensely red, but intact. To the ulcer I applied Tinct. iodini, et. glycerini, partes aequales, and wrote for Hydr. protoiodid. grs. 1½, to be taken daily.

On the 4th day after his first visit to me, I was summoned in haste to patient's home, and found him with alarming dyspnea, which he said came on about three hours before and had been increasing ever since. A hurried laryngoscopic examination discovered enormous swelling of both arytenoids and ventricular bands, whilst the epiglottis (which I really expected to find œdematous) was normal in contour. The glottis was nearly obliterated, and death from suffocation imminent. I put an ice poultice to the throat, ordered continuous swallowing of crushed ice and hastened off for tracheotomy instruments. I brought with me, however, a laryngeal bistouri and catheters. On my return, I found the patient excitedly pacing the room, and it was with much difficulty that I could prevail upon him to sit quietly enough for the introduction of the mirror. Whilst in the midst of an effort to scarify the arytenoids, he sprang from his chair and fell to the floor, unconscious. Kneeling at his side I thrust my left fore-finger into his mouth, drew forward the epiglottis and succeeded in passing a catheter (No. 1) into the glottis; holding the instrument in place, I dashed a pitcher full of ice water over his head, and happily, breathing—which had been suspended—recommenced. With the catheter still in situ, he was lifted into bed, and the ice-bag again applied to his throat. When the lamp had been arranged at the bedside, I withdrew the catheter and succeeded in freely scarifying both arytenoids. A large quantity of bloody serum was immediately coughed up, and when the patient became somewhat quieted, I introduced catheter No. 3 with the aid of the mirror.

I remained with the patient all night, passing the catheter every hour and gave ice during the intervals. At six o'clock the following morning the mirror showed that the swelling of the arytenoids had in great measure subsided, both cords being visible; patient complained of intense pain in the larynx. I gave him Tinct. opii acetatis gtts. xxx, in whiskey, and left him still swallowing ice pills. At my next visit, four hours later, he was sleeping calmly and with noiseless respiration. One week thereafter, patient was able to resume his occupation.

The ulcers upon the tongue and epiglottis soon yielded to combined constitutional and topical treatment, and the functions of the larynx remained unimpaired. This case is specially instructive in two particulars: first, as showing the possibility that occlusion of the glottis by œdema may suddenly occur in the course of syphilitic inflammation of the throat; second, the catheter is an invaluable aid, in case of such accident, for the avoidance of tracheotomy.

The catheters used were of hard rubber, which are easy of introduction, even without the aid of the mirror. The method of this procedure is briefly as follows: The fore-finger of the left hand is passed over the back of the tongue until it touches the epiglottis, which is caught with the tip of the finger and drawn forward, gently, but firmly; the retching thereby produced is a help and not a hindrance to the operation. The catheter is grasped in the right hand (pen fashion) at a little distance in front of its curve, and its tip carried along the finger until it presses upon the posterior surface of the epiglottis; the finger is then removed and the catheter pushed quickly down upon the cords, which, in their next outward inspiratory excursion, allow the instrument to slip into the chink of the glottis. Of course in œdemas of a high grade, considerable force may have to be used. Special care must be taken to hug the epiglottis closely with the tip of the catheter, lest it slip over the arytenoids into the œsophagus. At the first introduction it is best that the operator retain the instrument in place with his own hand until the convulsive efforts of the laryngeal constrictors to expel it be quieted, when it may safely be left to the patient himself, except, as in the above case, when suffocation is imminent. The catheter should be retained only a few minutes at first, the period of retention being increased at each introduction.

ARTICLE III.

VACCINATION IN THE NEW BORN.

BY W. PAGE McINTOSH, M. D.,
Resident Physician, Maryland Maternite Hospital.

As being a propos to the much discussed question of vaccination, I wish to give the result of some observations made at the Maternité Hospital during the late small-pox epidemic. On November 19th, 1883, Mrs. D. W. was admitted to the Maternité for confinement. When patient entered hospital she was well advanced in the first stage of labor. Labor normal. Did well up to 26th, when she had slight exacerbation of temperature, but complained of no pain. 27th, same as on previous day. 28th, complains of pain in back and limbs, slight chilliness, etc. On morning of 29th, symptoms were such as to justify the diagnosis of variola, eruption just making its appearance. The infant, which had been previously vaccinated, was sent with its mother to quarantine hospital, where both died. All the other patients had been vaccinated, and all new patients were vaccinated on entering.

Observations made on a series of thirty odd cases were as follows: The women were vaccinated two weeks previous to confinement, (this being the ordinary time of admission) and in nearly all the virus took well, showing a well-marked vaccine vesicle, some of the patients suffering from slight fever. The infants of these women were vaccinated when *one day old*, and I do not call to mind a *single instance* in which the vaccinations failed to take.

This would seem to show that vaccination of the pregnant woman *does not* protect her offspring. Lusk, of New York, says: "The healthy child of a mother affected with variola, or of one vaccinated during pregnancy, may be insusceptible to vaccination for some time after birth."

The cases just cited would seem to lead to a different conclusion. Another point which I wish to discuss is, at what age should an infant be vaccinated? Dr. Smith in his "Diseases of Infancy and Childhood," says, that the most suitable time for vaccinating an infant is when it is about four months of age, that is to say, not under that age. The reason he assigns for not vaccinating earlier, is the danger from erysipelas—a child four or five months of age being better able to successfully combat an attack of this trouble than one younger. This point is well taken, but I am confident that with care in the selection of the virus, and cleanliness in all the details, the danger from this trouble is reduced to a minimum: at any rate the child runs less risk of taking erysipelas, than it does of contracting small-pox, allowing that the necessity for vaccination exists. In the series of thirty-two or three cases noted, erysipelas developed in only two, both of which made a good recovery. In conclusion it may be stated that not a single case of variola or varioloid developed in the hospital after the first case was sent away.

Professor Parrot, an eminent French physician, whose valuable contributions to our knowledge of infantile syphilis have made him famous, recently died in Paris at the age of 53 years.

FOREIGN CORRESPONDENCE.

A Stroll to the London Hospital—Methods of Clinical Instruction.

London, July 17th, 1883.

Yesterday, in company with another medical man, I started for the East London Hospital. Passing through Fenchurch street and Aldgate, we came into the broad thoroughfare of Whitechapel. There were so many objects of interest on all sides, that our progress was slow. We stopped to see a monstrosity, in shape of a man, without legs, supported on feet that extended out from his hips; his arms consisted of a very short stump on the left side, and a longer one on the right, that resembled an arm to the wrist. He was indulging in the pastime of top-spinning; he would wind the top rapidly between the right stump and his lips, then holding it there he would, by violently jerking his head around, land the top on a board eight feet away; not only that, but on our tossing a penny on the board he spun the top on it, to the great joy of the crowd of urchins that surrounded him—a feat of dexterity under difficulties, that commanded the admiration of older children, ourselves included.

We got past him, however, and past moral monstrosities in shape of drunken women; business monstrosities in shape of gloved and chimney-pot-hatted men, peddling meat for cats; past architectural monstrosities in shape of long piles of bricks and boards, where alleged improvements were going forward; till, finally, we espied across the street a long, solid building, whose lower windows seemed on a level with the street, and surrounded by a high wall. On arriving at the open gate, we found ourselves at the London Hospital. We began discussing the best way of getting inside, when we saw a small crowd of students gathered near the door. We quickly assimilated ourselves with them and went in. Hanging our hats in a little room beside the entrance, we traversed a long corridor; the foremost gentleman opened a door to one side, and in a moment we were in the presence of the clinic of one of the professors of surgery. He is a good-looking gentleman of about 35; round face and full figure; he reminded me very strongly of Professor Bevan, of Baltimore, even to the sound of his voice, but he has that peculiar roll in the accent of the last syllables of a sentence common to even the cultured Englishman. He was seated at a desk in the middle of the room; the lever-handles of three bells were at his elbow; paper, pens and ink were before him; the patients were ranged from the door of the room beyond, like Dundreary's night shirts, in a "wow," each held in his hand a paper, giving the name and other characteristics of the applicant; and if he had been there before, his disease and treatment; if not, it contained an order from the proper person authorizing him to present himself at this time and place. The professor asks a few questions, and then turning on his revolving chair, toward the dozen or so students collected around him ("the very cream of the class," it is whispered me), and asks one of them: "What do you think of this?" The gentleman is sitting near him, and he grasps the arm of the patient and turns it around, asks a few questions, and guesses it is erysipelas. "And what do you think of it?" to another, farther off. Well, for certain reasons, he thought it was erythema. These answers were repeated with more or less confidence by a half dozen. Some said they had not examined the case; others made no reply. He looked at me, but said nothing; either he saw that I was not a regular attendant, or else knew by my appearance that I understood the case thoroughly, and asked no farther. He then began the regular clinical instruction—told why it was not erythema, nor erysipelas, and why it was lymphadenitis; dwelling on the distinguishing characteristics of each in a very clear and succinct manner,—made a few scratches with his nail on the arm of the patient, to illustrate the appearance of the redness that distinguished it from the other diseases. He then wrote a prescription, which he read to the class,—it was lead lotion—turned one of the levers, a servant appears and he directs him to "show this patient the way, if you please," and the process is repeated till the hour is past. I believe they stick more to simple remedies than we do; he prescribed lead lotion for three different patients in the half hour I staid, and yet the conditions were not identical.

When you take into consideration that the established fee for a single visit in London is five dollars, you see why the hospitals are so much more extensively patronized than ours; this one, in particular, which is surrounded by the very misery of London. M. A.

The Vienna Maternite.—What May be Learned There. — Some Interesting Observations.

VIENNA, August 5, 1883.

In the obstetrical department of the Vienna University, there are 10,000 children born every year, and by far the majority are born out of wedlock. The department is divided into what are termed 1st, 2d and 3d clinics; each having a professor, with two assistants. Prof. Carl V. Braun has charge of the 1st clinic; Prof. Joseph Spaeth, of the 2d, and Prof. Gustav Braun of the 3d. The third clinic is devoted entirely to the education in obstetrics of midwives. No medical men are admitted to this clinic.

Besides the two assistants, each clinic has five "hebammen," (midwives), who take charge of all cases of midwifery not under the care of the medical men, practicing in the wards. Although they are women of education in their branch, and of experience far greater than the average medical man, yet in any case presenting difficulties, either the 1st or 2d assistant must be notified at once; and I have understood that in the third clinic, where women are educated, they are instructed when in practice, if they have a case requiring instrumental delivery, or turning, or of retained placenta or eclampsia, to send for a doctor.

These clinics take turns in receiving their lying-in patients; for instance, the 1st clinic will take in patients from, say 8 o'clock a. m., to-day until 6 p. m.; then the 2d clinic will receive them for a certain number of hours, etc. In this manner all the clinics are supplied with subjects (if I may so term them), for the students and doctors who are practicing in the two clinics. By taking out the professor's ticket, costing 10½ gulden, ($4.20), you have the privilege of practicing in his clinic for a whole semester. The men are divided into groups of four, two groups coming on duty every 24 hours. At the present time, most of the students being away, in Prof. Carl Braun's clinic, we have only about 4 groups; therefore, we are kept going most of the time, if we desire it, it being entirely optional with the doctor if he wishes to work or not. You are assigned to a patient, make your own examination, and watch the case to the end; if it is required you apply the forceps, one of the assistants being with you. Each patient has a blackboard along side of her bed, and your name is marked on it; under it is placed the name of the midwife who assisted you, so that in case of sepsis the source may be traced. After you have been assigned to a patient, no one else is allowed to make a vaginal examination without being requested to do so by one of the assistants. The majority of women who are confined here are of the lowest classes. Sometimes you find one who has the appearance of some refinement, but it is the exception to the rule. The protection of the perineum during labor, is laid great stress on here, and in this, the midwives show remarkable skill. I have seen often since I have been here, heads of children delivered (in primipara) by these women without the slightest rent in the perineum, which I am satisfied would have taken place, with the methods we use in our country, and found, if the doctor would only look for it. All women, with their first child, are delivered on their side. The same position is assumed by multipara, if there is indication of rupture of the perineum. The midwife supports the perineum from below,—the woman is instructed when the head is about being born, to restrain her pains, keep her mouth open, etc.; then the midwife as it were gradually teazes the head out, at the same time gradually slipping the perineum over the head, face, and so on. During this time if a severe pain comes on, the head is really kept apparently from coming through by main force. The process has to be seen to be appreciated. When rupture does take place, in spite of all care, the rent is sewed up at once. The antiseptic precautions are wonderfully complete. You are compelled to wash your hands in a solution of carbolic acid and permanganate of potash, and scrub your nails thoroughly after each vaginal examination, and before making another. The patient's uterus and vagina is washed out with three or four quarts of cold water (carbolized) immediately after the placenta has been removed, if the case has been any way tedious, or an instrumental one. Ergot is not used here at all, except in cases where the patients have some hemorrhage, then the powdered ergot is given internally, or the fluid extract given hypodermically over the uterus. The forceps used are Carl Braun's, a modification of Simpson's, of Edinburg. For the application of forceps the usual anesthetic used here, consisting of three parts of chloroform, one each of ether and alcohol, is used. Morphia hypodermically and hydrate of chloral by the rectum is the treatment for convulsions.

During the past two weeks, in clinic number 1, we have had three cases of convulsions, all occurring in young women with their first child; in all these cases the urine was heavily loaded with albumen; two of these were delivered with forceps. One of the three died, the morphia and chloral treatment being used. In private practice, in this case, individually, I would have taken about a quart or less blood from her arm, but such treatment would be censured here.

After the birth of the child, it is weighed and measured, and the results placed in grammes and centimetres, on the blackboard at the mother's bed. Ten minutes after the birth of the child the placenta is expressed by Credé's method exclusively, no traction being allowed on the cord whatever. In several cases of retained placenta that have occurred since I have been in the wards, the patient was given the usual anesthetic mixture and the placenta removed by passing the hand into the uterus and detaching the placenta—the hand and arm being first thoroughly washed and scrubbed and anointed with carbolized vaseline.

The women are all confined in one large room, having about twenty beds. Everything is as clean as it could possible be; the amount of clean linen used every day is astonishing. The room has a great many large windows and is well ventilated, being even pleasant there on a hot July day. The exposure during the process of labor is such that our negro women in Baltimore would not submit to it. On the day when our clinic is full, you can visit there and see from morning to night, women having their babies, and watch the process from the foot of their bed. Sometimes you can find a crowd of students and doctors doing the same.

The women do not seem to mind the exposure much. After the birth of the child and extraction of placenta, the woman is changed and made comfortable at once. Then she is allowed to remain in this bed (in the room where they are confined) for three hours, at the end of which time two porters (men) come in with an apparatus somewhat similar to a small lounge, on which she is placed and carried to another room where there are about twelve or fifteen other patients, who have been recently delivered. She remains in bed until the eighth day, with rather light diet, soup (German style), being the major portion of the food. If everything goes right, she leaves the hospital with her baby on the tenth day. The temperature of the patient is taken before the birth of the child, immediately after, and then for some days to come, morning and night. If there is an increased temperature immediately after the birth, the doctor and midwife are not allowed to attend any more cases until the case is watched a little longer. The assistants visit the wards of the convalescent patients every morning. I have had the pleasure of accompanying one of them two or three times recently. It was to me quite a novelty to go from room to room and see from 100 to 150 women, who had been confined within the last four, five or six days. The assistant would be met at the door of each room by the nurse in charge, and she would accompany him around her room. The doctor would look at the temperature marked on the board, examine the condition of the patient's uterus through the abdominal walls, throw the clothing down, examine the external genitals, discharge, etc., give what directions were necessary in each individual case, and pass rapidly along. One of the notable cases, pointed out during one of these visits, was a woman, age 52 years, who had been recently delivered of a child; the case being one of placenta previa. The child was dead. The mother recovered. The woman looked to be fully as old as was stated.

The women when they come in the hospital always bring their own and the new-comer's clothing. On going into the clinic recently I witnessed a sight that probably could not be seen elsewhere. Fifteen babies, who had been born during the night, were laid out in two beds, done up in swaddling clothes of various colors and kinds, preparatory to being carried into the chapel for baptism.

The mortality among the women is not very great; in 1000 cases during the last month, they claim to have lost only two mothers, one from eclampsia, and one who had placenta previa.

The assistants of these obstetrical clinics are young men from 28 to 33 years of age, and are qualified by education and vast experience to give special courses on their branch; and most medical men who come here to qualify themselves for general practice, besides those coming especially for obstetrics, avail themselves of these courses. One of these courses on operative obstetrics, viz: "Curs ueber operative Geburtshilfe," is a most excellent one, lasting six weeks, two hours a day, five days a week, costing 20 guldens ($8.00). To show the cosmopolitan character of the Vienna school, I would mention that in a recent class of ten of us, three were from the United States, two from South America, one each from France, Holland, Germany, and two from Austria. Besides having thorough instructions in recognizing the various positions of the child, all of the obstetrical operations were performed, such as the application of forceps, craniotomy, decapitation, etc. The cadaver is used, and a dead baby in the pelvis, the examination for positions, turning, etc., being done through the vagina of the subject. The weather being warm, it required a fresh subject every day or two, and I should judge that during the six weeks course not less than twenty bodies were used for demonstration. Sometimes during the hot days of July this kind of work on a dead body was not pleasant, but it certainly was a practical way of teaching the subject. One method of application of the forceps here, is to apply them in the oblique diameters of the mother's pelvis in cases of what they term here, "abnormal rotation," and rotate the child's head in the pelvis, a procedure which, I believe would be a very dangerous one, both to mother and child, in the hands of any one who has not had vast experience. In teaching the positions of the child, they somewhat simplify the American method; for instance, taking the vertex presentation, what we term "left occipito-iliac anterior," they term first position, the opposite side the second position, and all other vertex presentations they class as abnormal rotation. There is another course given, called the "touch"-course, class limited to four men, costing 50 guldens, ($20.00), for 20 lessons of 2 hours each; this being the costliest of any of the private courses here.

Each of us examine a patient, first externally, finding, if possible, the position of the child, counting the fœtal heart-beats, and where best heard, finding the feet of the child; then we measure the pelvis externally.

After the examination externally, we then make a vaginal examination, and note the condition of the vagina; of cervix, if first child; if there be laceration from former labors; if the woman is in labor; if so, what position is the child? What stage of labor? if the bag of waters is ruptured or not; approximate to the time of labor, etc.; and, finally, measure the pelvis internally, which is done by running two fingers in the vagina and touching the promontory of the sacrum, then marking the hand, withdraw your fingers, wash, and measure, allowing one to one and-a-half centimetres for the pubic bone and soft parts, and then, the examiner is interviewed by the teacher, and if wrong, is corrected. In the course, each man will have the opportunity of examining over 100 different women. The probabilities are that there is no place in the medical world where a man can obtain instruction similar to that obtained from these two courses, and if he cannot master the art here, he had better throw his diploma into the fire, sell his books, and take a position as street-car driver.

WILMER BRINTON.

ANALECTS.

Surgical Expedients in Emergencies.

The necessity for *evacuating an over-distended bladder* is liable to become immediately urgent on occasions when a catheter is not quickly attainable. It is remarkable how often the condition is overlooked by practitioners, until it becomes one of suffering and danger, demanding instant relief. The continued dribbling that often occurs from an almost bursting bladder may mislead or blind one to the grave danger. The absence of a catheter on one such pressing occasion led me to contrive a ready means of evacuating the urine. The recourse was to a piece of iron bell wire, bent double on itself, and the blunt double end passed readily through the urethral tract to the bladder. The distention of the urethra by the double wire allowed the urine to freely pass between the wires.

A female catheter may be extemporized from a short piece of rye straw, the end of which is to be closely wrapped for a short distance with thread; or the end of the straw may have its sharpness removed by dipping into melted sealing wax. The stem of the ordinary clay tobacco pipe is also efficient for the purpose, Such crude substitutes, when oiled, are readily introduced.

The operation of venesection would probably be more frequently resorted to when needed, if a proper lancet, in perfect order, were at hand; but the critical time for relief of an actively congested or inflamed lung or brain is sometimes allowed to pass, for want of a ready and certain method of opening a vein. I once, on a pressing occasion, bled a patient at the bend of the elbow, with perfect ease and precision, with but a blunt-pointed and dull knife, by resorting to a simple, convenient expedient. Having put on the usual constricting bandage to distend the veins, I first transfixed the most prominent vein with a fine needle. Thus held securely, it was very easy, with even the dull knife to cut a valvular incision into the vein, and the blood flowed freely.

For the arrest of nasal hemorrhage I know of no device so good as one that may be readily extemporized with a strong piece of cord and some small pieces of sponge. The cord is tied securely to a piece of sponge, cut rounded, and just large enough to be forced backward through the nostril. Then a number of similar pieces of sponge, with a hole through the centre of each, are threaded successively on the cord. The sponge on the end of the cord is then pushed, with a probe or dressing forceps, through the nostrils, quite back to the faucial orifice; and the rest of the threaded pieces of sponge are slid back, one at a time, until the nares is tightly filled. When the patient becomes secure against a repetition of hemorrhage, the plugging is readily removed, one piece of sponge being withdrawn at a time, with the dressing forceps. The posterior nares may also be easily plugged by introducing either a slender gum bougie or a piece of thick cat gut string, with a cord attached, through the nares, catching one end of it in the fauces with forceps, and drawing it forward through the mouth. To the cord which follows, a piece of sponge or pledget of lint is tied, to be drawn up into the posterior nares.

A method of making unirritating

and painless pressure within the nares, in cases of obstinate epistaxis, is by a piece of the intestine of a chicken or other small animal, about twelve inches long, partially filled with either air or water. One end of the intestine is, while empty and collapsed, pushed backward through the nares; when thus lodged the air or water in the end is forced, by compression with the hand from the pendulous portion, into the part lodged in the nares. Strong, equable compression can be made rendering hemorrhage impossible.

In a case of *hemorrhage from the intercostal artery*, from homicidal stabbing, I arrested the flow immediately by making pressure within the pleural cavity, directly on the vessel, by introducing into the wound the handle of a door-key. The key was then turned transversely, so as to make direct pressure, and maintained in that position for some hours, until there was no more tendency to hemorrhage. The same mechanical action might be effected by the similar use of the handle of an ordinary gimlet.

As a very efficient *substitute for Esmarch's elastic bandage*, I suggested, some years ago, in an article in the *Philadelphia Medical Times*, the use of a bandage made from ordinary flannel, cut bias, so as to increase its elasticity. Such an elastic bandage, from a material almost everywhere at hand, is, I know from experience, perfectly effective.

The hemostatic action of hot water does not seem to be sufficiently known and appreciated among practitioners. It is so effective, and can be so readily applied, that it may well displace from practice all other hemostatics. Water at a temperature not beyond tolerance of the immersion of the hand in it, which is a temperature of from one hundred and fifteen to one hundred and twenty degrees, is ordinarily all that is necessary; but in some cases not amenable to treatment by the ligature, a temperature above 160° F., the coagulating point of albumen, may be necessary.

The absence of a tenaculum may be well replaced by a small fish-hook secured to a pen-holder.

For *dislodging a foreign body in the œsophagus* by forcing it downward, an ordinary carriage or riding whip, knotted far enough from the end to insure the proper degree of flexibility, may be an efficient expedient in an emergency.

Materials for splints for the temporary dressing of fractures can be at almost all times extemporized from the materials of wooden boxes and binders' boards. To dress fracture of the forearm and of the leg, in a case required to be removed to a distance from the scene of the accident, I once improvised an efficient dressing by breaking into strips some ordinary palm-leaf fans, which were at hand, and bound them on the limbs. I commend the material for its merits of being elastic and comfortable to the shape of the limb. Good temporary dressings can also be made from common straw cut to proper length and bound in layers on the limb.

For a readily made fixed dressing, a plan I have resorted to is with ordinary sand-paper as the material. The sand-paper is dipped into warm water to soften the glue, and is then applied and retained with a bandage. The glue of the sand-paper soon gives rigidity; body and firmness are produced by the sand and paper. Strong fixed dressings, it should be remembered, can be readily prepared with the familiar domestic commodities of starch, or with the combination of eggs and flour.

In removing a patient with a fractured thigh or leg, the uninjured limb can be made to temporarily act as a splint and take care of the injured one, by simply bandaging the limbs together. It should be borne in mind that many fractures of the long bones can be well treated without splints. Fractures of the femur are not now generally treated with splints. After coaptation is effected, simple extension, by means of weights, is the only essential. Fractures of the clavicle are, I am convinced, from practical experience and much attention to the subject, the most effectively treated by keeping the patient in the supine position of the body, with the head alone slightly elevated to relax the sterno-mastoid muscle, one of the factors of displacement of the fragments. If this position, on a level mattress, is maintained for a week or ten days, the tendency to displacement is so overcome that a mere sling for support of the arm and shoulder, or other simple dressing, is all that is necessary.

The simple postural method of treatment, without splints, is applicable to most fractures in the vicinity of joints. In fractures of the upper end of the humerus, splints are usually of no real practical advantage, and the injury can be well treated by position of the arm, and by support against the thorax, maintained by adhesive strips, or bandages, occasionally aided by an axillary pad.

The usual fracture of the lower end of the radius, transverse in direction and produced by a fall on the extended palm of the hand, if properly reduced by longitudinal traction and forced flexion of the wrist and hand, has rarely a tendency to displacement if the wrist and hand are maintained in a state of moderate flexion, without the use of any splint.

The ordinary splint, applied on the outside of a fractured jaw, is mechanically inefficient for the object, and has no advantage over an ordinary bandage or handkerchief, applied to keep the part at rest.

Many surgical instruments are made after traditionally complicated forms. Scalpels, bistouries and needles should not be crooked. I know of no use for curved knives, and the occasions for the use of curved needles may be limited to a few plastic procedures in cavities. The ordinary surgical needle, with its absurd and inconvenient curve, I long ago discarded in favor of the more efficient, simple, and cheap glovers' needles. A good surgical needle can be readily made from an ordinary sewing needle, broken off above its point and ground to such an oblique point as is given to the hollow needle of the hypodermic syringe.

A common gimlet is an *efficient instrument for opening the mastoid cells*, in cases of abscess, when there is grave threatening of cerebral complication, demanding prompt action.

The patient use of a carpenter's rasp may safely substitute the trephine, in cases of fractured skull, by cutting away an angle or edge of bone at the point of fracture, and allowing an elevator, such as a small screw driver, to be inserted beneath a depressed fragment.

In regard to the traditional forms given to instruments, I have inquired of different instrument makers why the sharp, triangular point is made on the ordinary silver probe, but it remains unexplained. I have never seen any surgeon use this bayonet-point of a probe, and know of no possible use for it.

The facility with which rectal injection can be performed with large quantities of fluids, by hydrostatic pressure, renders not essential the use of a syringe, if a piece of india-rubber tubing long enough can be obtained. The lower bowels may also be distended, in case of intussusception, by injecting water and carbonic acid gas, forced from the ordinary mineral water bottle or syphon, fitted to the rectal tube.

In cases of violent inflammation and traumatic injuries of the eye, needing immediate use of a mydriatic, the universally present stramonium may well substitute belladonna or atropia.

For antiseptic use many readily procured substances may well replace carbolic acid. None is so cheap and efficient as that most neglected preventer of putrefaction, sulphurous acid, made simply by exposing water to the fumes of burning sulphur in a close chamber. The antiseptic action of a saturated watery solution of turpentine has also the advantage of convenience of procurement and cheapness. For this purpose turpentine should be kept continually in water and exposed to warmth, and frequently agitated. Diluted alcohol has merits as an antiseptic which have not received proper attention.

Recent investigations have proved that the bichloride of mercury is the most powerful of all germicides, and that it can be used effectively in unirritating dilutions of one part to two thousand or more of water. These readily obtainable substances prevent the decomposition of animal matters, and, without disputing over the germinal, chemical or other theories of their action, all surgeons must admit that putrefaction is the most common factor in preventing the healing of wounds, and that it should be avoided.—*R. J. Levis in The Polyclinic.*

Remedies in Neuralgia.

Dr. Charles R. Francis, in a series of articles in the *Medical Press and Circular*, discusses the etiology, pathology and therapeutics of neuralgia. The latter division of his subject is particularly interesting, his discussion of it being extremely rational, regarding the pain as but a symptom of a pathological condition. The remedies which he advises have reference to a permanent relief of those conditions and to palliation. There are probably few diseases which are more empirically treated by the profession than is neuralgia. The necessity for immediate relief of the great pain frequently endured, seems, in the majority of instances, to blind the practitioner to the necessity of attention to the fundamental cause. This empiricism is not at all times traceable to the fault of the practitioner, for the demand for palliation is so pressing that there will be found few patients who will submit to the endurance of pain during the tedious means frequently necessary to unseat the disease in its citadel, with a view to its permanent eradication. An intelligent treatment of neuralgia must regard it as a prayer of the nerve for healthy blood, and the great desideratum of treatment must be the elimination of morbid matters to which these symptoms may be due, or the supply to the system of material, the absence of which manifests itself in the pain.

Dr. Francis, in discussing these permanent remedies mentions the benefit to be derived from electricity, from galvanism, quinine and arsenic. As medicinal agents, more particularly quinine and arsenic demand his attention. Quinine is beneficial in neuralgia in two ways: 1st, as a nerve tonic, and 2d, as an antiperiodic. As a nerve tonic it is valuable in depraved conditions of the system characterized by anemia. In the second place it is valuable in those forms of neuralgia which are characterized by regularity of intermissions. For the first of these purposes it must be given in tonic doses; for the second in large or antiperiodic doses. Probably very great mistakes are made in the exhibition of quinine in large doses for neuralgia. It may be laid down as a rule that quinine in antiperiodic doses is absolutely useless in all neuralgias which are not characterized by regularity in intermission. The only exception to this rule is in the case of neuralgia of the cerebral nerves, quinine being beneficial here, without any reference to intermittency.

Arsenic is valuable not only in neuralgia of an intermittent type, but also as a nerve tonic, given with a view to adding tone to the nerve fibre. The rules which regulate its administration are practically the same as those which obtain in the case of quinine, the only exception being in the case of the cerebral nerves, large doses of arsenic not being beneficial in neuralgia of these.

Dr. Francis found great benefit from counter-irritation in the form of flying blisters, and particularly in the neuralgic pains common to nervous, sensitive women. These flying blisters, he however, found to be most beneficial where there is effusion between a nerve and its sheath, or a thickening of the latter. This condition generally obtains in sciatica in which complaint blisters applied above and along the course of the seat of pain are very valuable adjuvants. They are also decidedly useful in the intercostal neuralgia, which remains as a sequel of shingles.

Dr. Francis places great stress upon the necessity of hygiene and abstinence from alcoholic drinks and excesses in the matter of diet. The patient who refuses to give the most scrupulous attention to these particulars will take medicine in vain, neuralgia being a symptom of weakness, and the tendency of those excesses is to aggravate this condition and to this extent militate against the success of medicinal agents. Great patience and perseverance are necessary in the treatment of obstinate neuralgia, and the patient must be admonished of the necessity of these virtues.

In this connection we also call attention to an article in a recent number of the *Medical Record*, by Dr. D. N. Camman, in which he extols the value of menthol as an external application in neuralgia, regardless of the nerve or nerve-trunk attacked—facial neuralgia, lumbago, fugitive pains in the chest, intercostal neuralgia, pleurodynia and gastralgia. Dr. Camman's testimony is very strongly corroborative of that of Dr. F. E. Stewart, whose reports as to the value of a solution of menthol in the bromide of ethyl as an external application in neuralgia, are doubtless familiar to our readers.—*Therapeutic Gazette.*

THE introductory lecture at the Woman's Medical College will be delivered by Prof. Cordell on Oct. 1, at noon.

The Use of Emetics in Croup and Suffocative Bronchitis.

Dr. C. J. Hare, in an address,(*Brit. Med. Journ.*) speaks as follows concerning the use of emetics in certain diseases :

In former times, it was not unusual to commence the treatment of many diseases with the administration of a dose to procure vomiting; although the remedy might then be given sometimes indiscriminately and according to routine, only those who have seen the effects of emetics, properly and judiciously given, can conceive the beneficial effects they sometimes produce. In the early stage of an attack of croup, it was by no means unusual to give an emetic of tartarized antimony or of ipecacuanha ; and it is in accordance with the recorded experienc of some of the best authorities and most practical men, and quite consonant with my own experience too, that symptoms which presented the most certain augury of a severe attack were by these means cut short, the hoarse voice resumed its natural character, and the feverish symptoms were in a few hours relieved. I know quite well that a great fear is entertained by some as to the depressing effects of emetics; but the fear is theoretical, and not practical, and those who have had most experience in the administration of them best know how groundless the fear is. In diphtheria, too, I have seen the false membranes which are out of the reach of local remedies, and which the patients cough and cough in vain, and utterly exhaust themselves to get quit of, readily brought up by the action of vomiting, to the immense relief of the sufferer.

In suffocating bronchitis, the effect of emetics is sometimes magical, and by their administration in such cases not only is immense relief given, but I verily believe—I am certain—that lives are saved. You are called to a patient who has been ill a few days, with increasing dispnœa ; she is sitting up in bed (I draw from nature), for to lie down is impossible; she is restless, and tossing about; the lips, and indeed the whole face, blue; the eyes watery and staring; the pulse quick and small; the cough constant; the expectoration semi-transparent and tenacious; over every square inch of the chest, front and back, from apex to base, you find abundance of rhonchi; moist, sonorous and sibilant ones in the upper part of the lungs, and muco-crepitant or mucous *rales* towards the bases. Ammonia and stimulants, right and good in their way, perhaps, in such a case are too slow in their action; the patient is, in fact, more or less slowly, more or less rapidly suffocating. An emetic of twenty-two grains of ipecacuanha in an ounce of water is given; in ten or fifteen minutes the patient vomits and brings up a huge quantity of that tenacious mucus, and the whole aspect of the case is altered; the distressed countenance is relieved; the breathing is at once quieter; and the patient is able for the first time for the past twenty-four hours to lie moderately low in bed, and to get some sweet refreshing sleep. The patient is, in fact, rescued from the extremest peril, and in this case, and many similar ones too, I believe, from otherwise most certain death. Of course, in such cases the emetic is not given for its effect on the stomach, but for its collateral effect in mechanically clearing out the enormous amount of secretion which accumulates in the bronchial tubes, and which the patient is otherwise quite incapable of getting quit of; and thus the half-choking, almost asphyxiated, condition is changed for one of comparative comfort, and time is gained for the action of other remedies. No doubt the secretion may, and often will, accumulate again; and I have not hesitated again in bad cases to repeat the same good remdy; but it is a fact, and a very positive one too, that, quite contrary to what those who have had no experience in the plan suppose, the system rallies instead of being more depressed under the action of the remedy.

How Celluloid is Made.

While about everybody has heard of, seen or used celluloid, only a few know what it is composed of, or how made. The following is a description of the process carried out at a factory near Paris for the production of celluloid: A roll of paper is slowly unwound, and is at the same time saturated with a mixture of five parts of sulphuric acid and two of nitric, which falls upon the paper in a fine spray. This changes the cellulose of the paper into pyroxyline (gun cotton.) The excess of acid having been expelled by pressure, the paper is washed with plenty of water until all traces of acid have been removed; it is then reduced to a pulp, and passes on to the bleaching trough. Most of the water having been got rid of by means of a strainer, the pulp is mixed with 20 to 40 per cent. of its weight of camphor, and the mixture thoroughly triturated under millstones. The necessary coloring matter having been added in the form of a powder, a second mixing and grinding foliows. The finely divided pulp is then spread out in thin layers on slabs, and from twenty to twenty-five of these layers are placed in a hydraulic press, separated from one another by sheets of thick blotting paper, and are subjected to a pressure of 150 atmospheres until all traces of moisture have been got rid of. The plates thus obtained are broken up and soaked for twenty-four hours in alcohol. The matter is then passed between rollers heated to between 140° and 150° F., whence it issues in the form of elastic sheets. Celluloid is made to imitate amber, tortoise shell, coral, malachite, ebony, ivory, etc., and besides its employment in dentistry, is used to make mouthpieces to pipes and cigar-holders, handles for table knives and umbrellas, combs, shirt fronts and collars, and a number of fancy articles.—*Nat. Drug Jour.*

Treatment of Warts and Condylomata by Carbolic Acid.

M. Jullien has described in the *Annales de Dermatologie* the treatment used by Tommaso de Amicis and himself in cases of warts and condylomata. It consists in repeated cauterizations by means of pure carbolic acid, and is best adapted to large sessile growths, or to fungating cauliflower-like vegetations. The *modus operandi* is very simple. Crystals of pure carbolic acid are kept in a small bottle; the warts having been washed, the bottle is warmed in a flame or in nearly boiling water and the crystals touching the glass melt. The fluid is supplied with a brush or cotton-wool to the whole surface of the warts, which assume at once a shiny white appearence. The white layer soon fall off, and on the next day the operation can be repeated. Pure carbolic acid causes much less pain than either chromic or acetic acid. It has been noted that when the cauterizations are repeated, the last are more painful than the first. The number of cauterizations necessary for curing the patient is, of course, variable. In a case of vegetations on the glans and prepuce, the cure was complete after two applications.

The Erysipelas Germ.

At the recent congress of German surgeons, Fehleisen demonstrated the micrococci of erysipelas. A patient had been inoculated forty-five hours previously, and when shown displayed a typical erysipelas. The micrococci which had been implanted, were the product of more than thirty generations, cultivated on gelatine, and could be considered entirely free from extraneous matter or germs. Of eight thus inoculated, only one failed to show typical results. The last trial in April was just as successful as the first during the previous August, and with the same culture. The one person on whom the experiment failed, had suffered from an idiopathic attack but a short time before.—*Annals Anatomy and Surgery.*

Ball of Hair in the Stomach.

Schœnborn exhibited a specimen removed from the stomach of a girl who had suffered for two years. A tumor of the size of the fist could be felt in the gastric region, the same being painful on pressure. The diagnosis as between a tumor of the spleen of the omentum was uncertain. Upon operation, it was found to lie in the stomach, whence it was removed. Incision of the tumor showed it to consist of short hairs matted together. It afterward transpired that this girl, with a number of schoolmates, "in order to gain a clear voice," was in the habit of biting off her hair and swallowing the ends thus bitten off. The case is not unique. Seven similar cases are recorded, one of which was complicated by a second similar mass in the intestine; but all the others ended fatally—one from hemorrhage from the stomach, the others from peritonitis, or incurable vomiting. Some of these patients had swallowed the hairs in their full length.—*Annals Anatomy and Surgery.*

Small Doses.

Dr. Thorowgood says, regarding the use of small doses:—"I have come to the conviction that the doses of many medicines as set forth in books, are often needlessly large, when we seek not an eliminant or evacuant effect, but a gradual alterative or specific action of the remedy. There is probably no medicine regarding the definite action of which physicians agree better than iron; but is it necessary for the cure of facial neuralgia to give an insoluble powder like the hydrated oxide of iron in a dose ranging from thirty grains up to three or four drams?" He has found one-third of a grain of calomel, two drops of tincture of aconite, one-fiftieth of a grain of strychnia, and similar small doses of other medicines to act much more satisfactorily than when larger doses were given.

How to Prevent Loss of Alcohol from Specimen Jars.

At the last meeting of the American Association for the Advancement of Science (*New York Med. Journal*) Prof. Burt G. Wilder and Dr. S. H. Gage of Cornell University, advocated the use of vaseline to prevent evaporation of alcohol from specimen jars. Experiments tried last spring indicated that during three months, at ordinary spring and summer temperatures there was no appreciable loss of 95 per cent. alcohol from glass phials or jars, whether upright or inverted, or on the side, provided the corks were smeared with the vaseline on the bottom as well as on the side. Ground-glass stoppers were anointed and firmly inserted, and the rubber rings of fruit-jars and the specimen jars made by Whitall, Tatum & Co., were coated on both sides and the covers well screwed down. The authors had also used the vaseline for preventing the loss of other liquids, including chloroform and oil of turpentine; as a lubricator of drawers and to prevent the sticking of the covers or stoppers of cement phials; and for the prevention of rust upon steel instruments.

Oil of Wintergreen in Rheumatism.

In thirteen cases in which this remedy was used by Dr. Flint in Bellevue Hospital, the results were better than ordinarily obtained from salicylic acid. The oil is administered in doses of 10 drops several times a day in flaxseed tea, or in milk. When taken in this manner it is less disagreeable than salicylic acid or salicylate of sodium. —*N. Y. Med. Jour.*

Bromide of Sodium,

Which was first highly recommended by the late Dr. George M. Beard, as a prophylatic of seasickness, has recently received the fullest endorsement of Mr. T. M. Kendall, who reports the results of treatment in two hundred cases. The dose is 10 grains, 3 times a day.

Average Health of Miners.

The opinion is expressed by Dr. Carpenter, of Pottsville, Pa., formed from long personal acquaintance with the subject, and sustained by the almost unanimous testimony of practicing physicians, mining engineers, colliery owners, and miners themselves, that were it not for accidental injuries and deaths, the mining class would show as good average health, as fair a percentage of longevity, and as low a death-rate as any other class of manual laborers; and that the hygienic condition of American mines are receiving more attention and consequent improvement year by year. No comparative statistics of the average length of miners' lives, or of their liability to disease, have officially appeared, but old men are common among them, and are still hale and hearty for their age. Their principal diseases, according to a statement in the *Scientific Press*, are miners' asthma, consumption and rheumatism, and, among those who have worked long in badly ventilated places, dyspepsia, tremors, vertigo, and other ailments arising from blood-poisoning. The two principal causes are dampness and bad air-pumps, precaution obviating the one, and proper ventilation the other.—*Med. Gazette.*

Rectal Alimentation.

Prof. James Tyson gave the following directions for preparing food for rectal alimentation: Take one-half pound of fresh pancreas, the so-called sweet-bread of the market house; mince it well and pulpify it in a mortar at 100° Farh.: then strain through a cloth, and mix it thoroughly with one and one-half pounds of minced beef (without fat,) and the yolk of an egg. Stand this aside for two hours. Use one-half of this for one enema, and use it in one day, as it will not keep longer. It ought to be prepared daily.—*Med. Digest.*

The Medical Chronicle.

A Monthly Journal for the Practitioner.

GEORGE H. ROHÉ, M. D., Editor.

☞ It is requested that all literary and business communications, books for review, exchanges, etc., be addressed to, and all checks, drafts and post-office orders drawn to the order of

Dr. GEORGE H. ROHÉ,
95 Park Avenue, - - - - Baltimore, Md

BALTIMORE, OCTOBER, 1883.

EDITORIAL.

The American Public Health Association.

The eleventh annual meeting of the American Public Health Association will be held at Detroit, Michigan, from November 13th to 16th, inclusive. A preliminary schedule of subjects to be discussed at the meeting has been published. The topics upon which contributions of facts and experiences are desired, are as follows:

I. *Malaria.*—Its etiology and the methods for its prevention in localities or in persons; its American history; its specific particles; its origin; the conditions of its pervasion; its laws of extension, etc.

II. *Foods.*—Their adulteration; healthy or deleterious modes of preservation and the function of legislation in regard to them. Ascertained facts as to adulterations in this country. Facts as to canned goods, condensed milk, artificial butter and cheese, prepared meats, etc.

III. *Vital Statistics.*—Methods and results; defects apparent. How far foreign modes of tabulation are to be followed. Systems of collection and classification. Race vitality and the care of population as indicated by statistics.

IV. *The Control and Removal of all Decomposable Material from Households.*—The mechanical laws, constructions and appliances relative thereto. The construction of all inside pipes and their connections, their traps and syphonage, flushing, ventilation. How they shall be connected with out-door receptacles, and yet be free from ill effect.

It is needless to urge upon our readers the importance of correct knowledge upon the above subjects. Every physician is under obligations to the public to inform himself as thoroughly as possible upon the methods of prevention or restriction of disease. In the CHRONICLE, we have from the beginning, endeavored to keep our readers informed of the progress of public hygiene, and have taken occasion several times to call attention to the valuable work that is done in this cause by the above association.

A large attendance of members is expected at the coming meeting, and interesting and valuable discussions are anticipated. We shall publish a summary of the proceedings, but urge all those who take an interest in preventive medicine to become members of the association and attend the meetings in person.

The Coming Lecture Session.

The prospects for a large class in the College of Physicians and Surgeons during the coming session, are excellent. A considerable number of students have already arrived and matriculated, and it seems probable that by the first of October, when the regular session begins, the halls will be well-filled. Prof. Lynch will deliver the introductory lecture in the lower hall, on Saturday, September 29, at 8 P. M.

THE Faculty of the Minnesota College Hospital has invited the editor of the CHRONICLE to deliver a course of lectures on hygiene in that institution during the coming session. We shall leave for the North West, to fulfill the engagement, about the middle of October. The CHRONICLE will appear on time as usual.

CURRENT LITERATURE.

Sexual Impotence in the Male. By William A. Hammond, M. D., Surgeon-General, U. S. Army (retired list); President of the American Neurological Association, etc. N. Y., Bermingham & Co., 1883. Price, cloth, $2.50.

The mere announcement of a new book by Prof. Hammond is sufficient to attract the notice of all the reading members of the profession. He has such stores of learning, and is withal such a thorough master of literary expression that every one of his works is, as the saying goes, 'as interesting as a novel." The book, whose title stands at the head of this notice is perhaps the most interesting of all his works, treating as it does of a class of affections of which next to nothing is known by the great mass of practitioners. The author's immense experience and his extensive reading have enabled him to give the details of many most curious cases, which add greatly to the value and interest of the book.

A friend at our elbow suggests that the book will prove a formidable competitor to the novels of Paul de Kock and similar works, which occupy so large a space in the *private* libraries of young physicians. It certainly cannot be recommended as proper Sunday reading for very young men.

The Physician's Supply Agency, 358 N. Gay St., Baltimore, will furnish the book on receipt of price.

Fifth Annual Report of the Connecticut State Board of Health. C. W. Chamberlain, M. D., Secretary. Hartford, Conn., 1883.

This volume contains, besides the general reports of the board and executive officers, the following practical articles: Hatting as Affecting the Health of Operatives, by L. Dennis, M. D. Sanitary Arrangements of the new Hospital buildings at Middletown, by A. M. Shew, M. D. Syllabus of a Course of Lectures on Sanitary Science, by Prof. W. H. Brewer, M. D. Uncertainties and Risks in the Use of Proprietary Articles, by Prof. C. A. Lindsley, M. D. How Can we Escape Insanity?, by Charles W. Page, M. D. Epidemic Intermittent Fever in Connecticut and parts of New England, by G. H. Wilson, M. D. Microscopical Examination of Potable Waters in the State of Connecticut, by Wm. J. Lewis, M. D. Milk as a Medium for the Transmission of Disease; Some of the Organic Impurities of Drinking Water, and Impure Ice, by C. W. Chamberlain, M. D. Heating and Ventilation of the Hartford High School, by Geo. Keller, and Protective Inoculation, by Noah Cressy, M. D., V. S. Appended to the volume is the report of the Bureau of Vital Statistics. The report as a whole is a credit to the board and to the State of Connecticut.

Transactions of the Medical Society of the State of West Virginia. S. L. Jepson, M. D., Secretary. Wheeling, 1883.

This is a small volume of less than 100 pages, but which contains some good, practical papers. Among these are, The Germ Theory of Disease, by Dr. E. C. Myers; The Abuse of Ergot in Obstetric Practice, by Dr. D. P. Morgan; Insanity as a Disease, by Dr. George H. Carpenter; Puerperal Fever, with Special Reference to its Treatment by Intra-uterine Antiseptic Irrigation, by S. L. Jepson, M. D.; A Case of Intra-peritoneal Hematocele, by Dr. R. W. Hall, and some Anomalous Obstetrical Cases, by C. F. Ulrich, M. D. The volume lacks both index and table of contents.

PAMPHLETS.

A Tracheotomy Tube for Gradual Withdrawal, and report of a case in which it was used. By H. F. Hendrix, M. D. Reprint, pp. 4. From St. Louis Med. and Surg. Journal,

August, 1883.——The Annual Announcement of the Department of Medicine and Surgery of the University of Michigan, for 1883-4.——Announcement of the Polyclinical and Laboratory Course of Instruction for Students and Practitioners, University of Louisville.——Electricity in the Treatment of Diseases of the Skin. By W. A. Hardaway, M. D. Reprint, pp. 9. From St. Louis Courier of Medicine, June, 1883.——Observations on the management of Enteric Fever, according to a plan based upon the so-called specific treatment, by Jas. C. Wilson, M. D., Physician to the Jefferson Medical College Hospital, and to the Philadelphia Hospital. Reprint, pp. 13.——Some Remarks on Naso-aural Catarrh and its Rational Treatment. By John N. Mackenzie, M. D., Surgeon to the Baltimore Eye, Ear and Throat Charity Hospital, etc. Reprinted from Transactions of the Medical and Chirurgical Faculty of Maryland, for 1883, pp. 22.——The Classification, Training and Education of the Feeble-minded, Imbecile and Idiotic. By Chas. H. Stanley Davis, M. D. Meriden, Conn., pp. 46.

FLOTSAM.

THE cholera epidemic in Egypt has come to an end.

CANNABIS indica, in doses of 5 minims of the tincture every 3 hours, is recommended in menorrhagia.

THE next annual meeting of the American Academy of Medicine will be held in New York on October 9 and 10.

DR. H. P. BOWDITCH has been elected dean of Harvard Medical School, as the successor of Dr. Calvin Ellis, resigned.

DR. R. B. MORISON has returned to Baltimore from abroad, where he has been pursuing the study of dermatology for the past year.

THE official report of the Transactions of the American Dermatological Association will appear in the next number of the CHRONICLE.

PROFESSOR H. NEWELL MARTIN of the Johns Hopkins University has been appointed Croonian Lecturer of the Royal Society for the current year.

THE new building of the Harvard medical school will be dedicated on the 15th of October Dr. Oliver Wendell Holmes will deliver the address.

THE transactions of the Medical and Chirurgical Faculty of Maryland for 1883 have been printed and are ready for distribution at the library.

MILK drawn from a woman who sits indoors and drinks whiskey and beer, is certainly as unwholesome as milk from a distillery-fed cow.—*Hamilton's Health Aphorisms.*

TYPHOID fever seems to be epidemic in New York. In August there were 244 cases reported, against 96 in the corresponding month of last year. The board of health has issued an address to the public urging increased attention to distinfection.

A colored man, 52 years of age, died in Baltimore on August 29, of *hysteritis*, according to the medical attendant's certificate. The same "doctor" recently certified that a woman, 45 years old, died of *cholera infantum!* And yet there are reputable physicians here who oppose a law to regulate the practice of medicine in this State.

DR. REEVES of the West Virginia state board of health continues to "keep it up." Another travelling quack passing under the name of " Dr. Johnson" was forced to leave the state in a hurry a few weeks ago, under a threat of prosecution for violating the law regulating medical practice. Let "Dr. Johnson" come to Baltimore. Here he can pursue his calling without interference from state board of health officials.

The Medical Chronicle.

BALTIMORE, NOVEMBER, 1883.

ORIGINAL ARTICLES.

The Qualifications Necessary for the Successful Study of Medicine.

The Introductory Address before the Class at the College of Physicians and Surgeons, Baltimore.
By PROF. JOHN S. LYNCH, M. D.

Gentlemen of the Faculty and Gentlemen of the Class.

I frankly avow to you my belief that in selecting me to deliver the first, or introductory lecture of the course for 1883-4, my colleagues have not been influenced so much by their belief that I possess any special qualifications or fitness for the task, but because each one of them desired to shift the labor of preparing such a lecture from his own shoulders to those of some one else; and as I have not had the honor of filling the role for eight years, they have elected me with an unanimity that was beautiful if not surprising to witness.

You will understand then that it is not of my own volition that I appear before you to-night, and I sincerely regret that one better qualified for the task has not been selected.

In entering, as many of you are now, upon the study of the noble science of medicine, there are three questions which should receive your most careful preliminary consideration; otherwise you may discover after spending much time, labor and money that you have wasted your youth in the acquisition of knowledge that is useless, and wedded yourselves to an occupation for which you have neither taste nor fitness.

These questions are:

1st. What is the nature of this science whose details you are about to attempt to master?

2nd. What are your own personal qualifications and fitness to acquire and practice this science? and,

3rd. What are the best means which will enable you to acquire and practice it?

And it is to a brief discussion of these questions that I propose to devote this hour.

The science of medicine, like every other science, consists of an accurate knowledge of facts duly systematized. But the facts in medicine differ somewhat from the facts of other sciences, in the fact that they are purely empirical. While many other branches of knowledge have been enlarged by purely inductive reasoning and scientific theorizing, no single fact in medicine can be said to have been thus discovered or established, but has only been discovered and established by long continued and oft-repeated observation. It may then be said to be "the accumulated experience of successive generations of persons who have practiced the art of medicine."

But I think I hear some of you exclaiming: What! does theory then hold no place in the true science of medicine? And are all the beautiful theories which we heard from the professor of pathology last winter mere brutum fulmen, or as the lawyers put it, ultra vires, and signify nothing? I answer, no. Theory or speculation are always admissible to explain facts whose causes we do not understand, or as Humboldt expresses it, "speculation is always admissible in the absence of accurate knowledge." And so in addition to our knowledge of our store of empirical facts, we have many theories which have been mostly invented to explain those facts. But while our facts are solid and unchangeable, our theories are ever changing from generation to generation, as some newly discovered fact proves a former theory to be untenable. Scarcely a generation ago the medical world was about equally divided into two schools of pathology—"humoralists" and the "solidists"—and the battle between these parties was hot and fierce until about twenty-five ago, when Rudolf Virchow smashed both theories by the enunciation of his cellular pathology.

Theories in medicine then, are not and should not, be taught or accepted as absolutely true, but only conditionally so, as affording the best explanation within our reach, of observed facts, and they should always be announced and accepted with this reservation. Many of the theories which are to-day accepted as true, will doubtless be exploded in a subsequent age as we have exploded many of those of our predecessors.

But you may ask, is there then no true theory of medicine? I answer, Yes, there is, there must be. But as medical science deals especially with that unknown, and possibly unknowable quantity—life, we are necessarily in many cases still groping in the dark and anxiously looking for the dawn of that purer and better light which will ultimately guide us through the intricate mazes of obscurity and doubt which still beset us. I have full faith in the ultimate mission of our noble profession, and an abiding confidence in the final success which must meet the strong minds and brave hearts that are now everywhere wrestling with the problems of life both in health and disease.

But when I tell you that many of our theories in medicine are possibly false, I must also tell you that they are sometimes so because many of the so-called medical facts upon which they are constructed are also false. Medical facts—or at least those which we are in the habit of receiving and accepting as such, differ, as I have already said, from the facts of other sciences, because they are not always susceptible of physical or mathematical demonstration. We cannot reduce them to a formula and say, as in geometry, because A is equal to B and B equals C, A and C are also equal.

To illustrate my meaning more clearly, and to show you at the same time the difficulty of establishing absolutely a medical fact, let us suppose a man comes to you suffering from a fever or a diarrhœa, or any other one of the thousands of bodily ills from which we suffer. You introduce into his stomach a certain quantity of some substance we are in the habit of using as medicine, whereupon the man recovers. Now, you cannot positively assert that the medicine cured him, because you can never prove that he would have died had he not taken it, or that he would not have gotten well all the same if he had not taken it. But if you repeat this experiment many hundreds of times with the same unvarying result, then only are you at liberty to accept as absolutely true, what was in the first instance only possibly, or at most, probably so. Now the oldest and wisest of practitioners of medicine will tell you that there is scarcely a single article of our materia medica that thus acts uniformly and unfailingly in all cases; that even quinine sometimes fails to cure ague, and occasionally syphilis is not cured or even improved by mercury. It is an unfortunate tendency of the human mind to form conclusions and even to attempt to formulate laws from imperfect and insufficient observation, and it is this that has led to so many errors and vagaries in medicine. It is this habit or tendency which gives to every old woman, and old man too, a sovereign remedy for every disease under the sun and it was upon such observations imperfectly made and comprehended that the accomplished but shallow Hahnemann built up his preposterous system of medicine.

You will do well therefore to remember that the amount of credence to be yielded to an asserted fact in medicine, depends upon the ability and credit of the observer, since it is *only* by observation and not by demonstration that medical facts are to be established.

With so many sources of error it is not surprising that medical science is still imperfect and that its *solid* growth has been slow.

A brief reference to its history will show you *how* slow this growth has been in the past; under what difficulties and disasters it has laboriously worked its way upward from the realm of barbarous superstition into the bright light of science; and it will also show you what have been its solid and useful achievements, and under what obligations it has placed and is still placing humanity in the past and in the present.

The earliest records of the human race prove that men even in the first dawn of civilization sought to find out means of relieving and curing the diseases to which they were liable. This fact is established not only in the history but even in the mythology of the Greeks, Phœnicians, Egyptians and other ancient races. Indeed if Darwin's theory of the descent of man be true, there probably lived at one time a race of doctors, with hairy skins, pendulous tails and long and pointed ears; and I may remark in parenthesis, that the fact that an occasional specimen possessing the last of these characteristics is found even in our own day, lends great probability to the correctness of Darwin's theory.

But it is only since about 200 years before the Christian era that medicine could make any claim to be considered a rational science, at which time Hippocrates—to this day styled the father of medicine—gathered the scattered fragments of knowledge then extant, enriched them by his own acute observation, and transmitted them to posterity in his writings. Patronized and encouraged subsequently by the Ptolemies, to one of whom is due the credit of legalizing human dissections, hitherto forbidden, the science attained a dignity and importance before unknown, and reached its highest cultivation and perfection in the celebrated school of Alexandria, which up to the time of its alleged destruction by the Mahommedans, continued to be the centre of medical knowledge. To their great credit be it said, the succeeding caliphs atoned in some measure for the barbarism of their predecessor; for it should not be forgotten, that encouraged by a succession of enlightened caliphs, the Nestorians and Jews not only preserved by translating them into Arabic, the works of Hippocrates, Areteus, Galen and Dioscorides, but also fostered medical literature by founding the College of Djondassabour and the University of Bagdad, in which were raised up such men as Rhazes, Avicenna, Albucasis, Avenzoar and Averroes, each of whom added important original contributions to medicine. And this too, at a time when Christian Europe was shrouded in the gloom of popular ignorance and priestly superstition; when ecclesiasticism in medicine ruled supreme, and diseases were cured (?) by the laying on of hands by stupid monks while mumbling prayers in barbarous latin, by the invocation of saints, or the application of their relics; and epileptics and insane persons were supposed to be possessed by devils, which were only to be exorcised by the invocation of the names of St. Peter and St. Paul, with such extraneous aid as might be derived from bell, book and candle.

The Mahommedan power broken, their great scholars no more, the patronage of the illustrious caliphs no longer enjoyed, dreary centuries of ignorance, superstition and priestcraft succeed. To the shrines of saints, crowds repaired as they had at one time to the temple of Aesculapius, the worshippers remaining, the divinity only changed.

Here was a paradise for quacks; for fetishes said to be the relics of saints, were believed to cure every disease and were worth a hundred times their weight in gold. As an evidence of the medical progress of these dreary centuries, it is said that for nearly fourteen hundred years Galen and Dioscorides were the only medical authorities of Europe. In the meantime, plague and pestilence, revelling in death, stalked unrebuked among the nations and untold millions descended into premature graves.

Light at last beams upon this Cimmerian darkness, and glorious old Padua begins to shine out, a single star "glittering upon the brow of night," and soon, under the patronage of Frederick Barbarossa becomes the acknowledged source of medical knowledge throughout the world. Succeeding German emperors continued his enlightened policy; archiators or chief physicians were appointed in every town of a certain size throughout the empire, whose duty it was to examine and license practitioners of medicine; and in a number of the principal cities medical schools were established, whose professors and lecturers were paid a regular salary by the state. And now for the first time, other names besides those of Greeks and Arabians, find a place in medical history. Vesalius, Fallopius, Spigelius and Sanctorius perfected at Padua those anatomical discoveries which have forever connected their names with the nomenclature of our art. Ambrose Paré laid the foundation of surgery; Servetus discovered the pulmonary circulation, which Harvey soon after supplemented with the systemic; Asellius discovered the lacteals; Malpighi demonstrated with the microscope the capillary circulation, and showed the minute anatomy of the glandular structures; Willis traced the course of the nerves and localized the functions of the brain; Von Graaf investigated the generative organs; and Ruysch, perfecting the art of injecting, pushed his investigations into minute anatomy. In a word, medical inquiry and physiological investigations were excited and sustained by able and enthusiastic minds, and medicine in Europe, redeemed from ignorant empiricism, was elevated into the dignity of a rational science, and placed upon a sure philosophic foundation.

This is a brief history of the past. What are the glories of the present day, the triumphs of the 19th century? These far transcend in importance all previous advances. The last sixty years have shown more advance toward a perfect science and bestowed more boons upon suffering humanity than all the previous years of medical history and discovery.

Medical chemistry by isolating the active principles of medicines and discovering new combinations of inorganic substances, has furnished us with nicer and more pointed weapons with which to wage warfare against disease. The discovery of quinine alone has on the Western continent rendered habitable the fertile valleys and broad savannahs which, now teeming with the wealth of luxuriant harvest, would otherwise have remained the home of savage beasts alone, or have proved the charnel house of the brave adventurers who sought to reduce it to subjection.

Anesthetics have lifted the primeval curse from woman, and deprived the surgeon's knife of all its dreaded horrors.

The operation of ovariotomy, invented by our countryman McDowell, has redeemed thousands of women from certain death; while the invention of the metallic ligature by Le Vert has enabled Sims and his followers to rescue and to restore to society and usefulness other thousands from abject wretchedness and loathsomeness by the cure of vesico and rectovaginal fistules.

Auscultation and percussion have by opening up to us a new method of investigating diseased organs, added to man another sense; and by the application of their principles, the merest tyro of to-day, can pronounce with certainty upon diseased actions that would have baffled Sydenham or Cullen in the full meridian of their powers.

The thermometer has again been called into aid in the correction of diagnosis, and by its help we can often now pronounce at once upon the nature of diseases when formerly we were compelled to wait many days for the slow, perhaps fatal development of symptoms.

The ophthalmoscope and laryngoscope have opened to our inspection, living organs never before revealed to human vision; and the treatment of those organs, thanks to the aid thus furnished, has become as exact and scientific as it was before uncertain and empirical.

The hypodermic injection of medicines has enabled us to bid defiance to a rebellious stomach, and relieved us of all doubt as to the action of our remedies.

The microscope has revealed to us the secret of many physiological processes, and brought to light the heretofore unknown causes of many pathological actions. But above all it has made possible the cellular pathology of Virchow which has taught us how we live and grow, and how and why we are sick, and brought us very near to the real secret of diseased action. All these, with the sphygmograph, the atomization of medicines, and the improved methods of treatment with the products of chemical research, are some of the achievements of the present century and speak in trumpet tones the rapid strides of progressive medicine. This list of the solid advances of our science and of the obligations under which it is placing the human family, might be almost indefinitely lengthened, for every day is adding some new claim founded upon some new gift of science, some new boon conferred; but I have already said enough to redeem the boast I have made that this century has transcended all previous time in medical discoveries and advancement.

When I recall the noble aims and purposes of our glorious science; when I see its faithful votaries searching nature's arcana for truths and treasures to add to its store; when I remember the long line of brilliant names emblazoned on the pages of its history, from the sage of Cos down to its trusty sons of the present, whose names lend dignity to the science, and give assurance to the world that the accumulated wisdom of ages will receive fresh accessions from their labors; when I see its monuments in all the civilized world, its temples adding beauty and grandeur to every landscape, I feel that I can smile at all the malevolence of its enemies and—harder still to bear—all the misconstruction of its friends.

What though quackery and empiricism flourish for the hour? Why heed the puny efforts of homœopathy and its kindred delusions to direct the stream of science from its accustomed channels, or to stem the mighty current of its perennial spring and accumulated waters? True science rears its column high above the creeping things that crawl about its base. The names carved upon its monumental granite, stand out as sharply as ever across the centuries, defying all the puny efforts of sciolists and isms and pathies and self-styled reformers to deface them. Their mad flight against the imposing column of true medicine but insures their destruction, as like,

The feeble sea birds, blinded in the storms,
On some tall light-house dash their little forms,
And the rude granite scatters for their pains
Those small deposits that were meant for brains.
Yet the proud fabric in the morning sun
Shines all unconscious of the mischief done.
Still the red beacon pours its evening rays
For the lost pilot, with as full a blaze;
Nay, shines all radiant o'er the scattered fleet
Of gulls and boobies brainless at its feet.

And now let us briefly inquire what are the personal qualifications requisite to enable you to study and practice the science whose history I have briefly outlined. This is a subject of the utmost importance to you, since it will depend upon your possession of the necessary personal qualifications whether your life in the future will be a success or failure in this, your chosen profession. A quaint, but observant philosopher has said that too often in the union of men with occupations in life, he was reminded of a board containing a number of holes, some of which were round and some square; and into these holes were inserted pegs—round ones into the square, and square ones into the round holes, resulting of course in a general misfit. Such an error as this inevitably results in great individual discomfort and—what is of greater importance—a very great diminution of individual achievement in all that goes to make up the aggregate progress in the arts of civilization as well as intellectual advancement. In this way it often happens too, that one-half of many of our lives are wasted in endeavors to correct the mistake of the other half; while the great majority have neither the discernment nor ability to discover and repair sufficiently early in life the blunder into which thoughtlessness or enforcing circumstances may have driven them.

Unfortunately the choice of a profession is far oftener determined by whim and caprice, or by the influence of parents, guardians or friends, or fortuitous circumstances, than by any clear and philosophical analysis of character or qualification. The medical profession, I am afraid, is no exception to this observation, for we certainly find many in it who have no special, or indeed ordinary adaptation to it. A cynical friend of mine once remarked to me that when a man has a son who is too stupid to be a lawyer, too lazy to become a mechanic or a farmer, and too vicious to be a priest, he made him a doctor. I sincerely hope, gentlemen, that none of you come within either of these categories.

But let us suppose that each one of you has made, or is about to make that careful self-examination requisite to test your fitness for the noble profession upon which you are about to enter; let us inquire what are the qualities you have or should discover which fit you specially for it.

A sound mind in a sound body is of course requisite to achieve greatness in any avocation of life. It is true that some men have attained high fame in many purely intellectual pursuits, with feeble bodies and imperfect physical senses. In our profession however this can never be accomplished, because the *practice* of medicine requires a large amount of physical labor as well as intelligent thought. And even apart from this; besides the robust physique which is essential to enable you to labor and bear up against fatigue, the intelligent and successful practice of physic is based entirely upon your power of observing and appreciating external facts and phenomena, and deducing from them those conclusions which experience and established laws have shown logically to flow from them. A physician must therefore not only have all his natural senses in perfection, but he must also have brains enough to reason correctly upon the facts which these senses may bring to his consciousness. A deficiency, or even any notable impairment then, of any of these senses, will disable you pro tanto for the efficient discharge of your duties as physicians; and in the sharp competition with which you will meet hereafter you will assuredly be driven to the wall by the operation of Darwin's inexorable law of the survival of the fittest.

But you must not only have all your physical senses in perfection—a perfection that can only exist in connection with a sound nervous organization—you must also live so as to keep them so. You must indulge in no habits that will impair your nervous system, blunt your senses, or diminish that intellectual force that should lie behind and above these senses. An immoderate indulgence therefore in narcotics and stimulants is included among the circumstances which should and *do* disqualify for the study or practice of medicine and should therefore be sedulously avoided.

But gentlemen there is in addition to these, still something else that demands our consideration before we can conclude that you are properly prepared to enter upon the study of medicine. You may have a sound physical organization; possess all the senses in the highest perfection; have a good brain capable of high intellectual achievement; an emotional system not liable to sudden or causeless excitation or depression, and perfectly under the control of your will; you may be devoid of habits which are calculated to impair or in any way injure your nervous system; yet there may be wanting an important factor in preparing you for this study. This is a certain amount of acquired knowledge and intellectual culture. An honored member of our profession who has reaped abundant laurels in the fields of literature—I allude to Dr. Oliver Wendell Holmes—has asserted that the medical profession in this country is the least cultivated and most ignorant of all the learned professions; and although there are found in history the names of many individual members of our profession who have attained immortality in the highest intellectual achievements, candor compels me to admit the justice of that assertion.

A physician, gentleman, whose duty it is to minister to the physical sufferings of mankind has often another and—I had almost said a higher duty to perform. He often has also to deal with the mental emotions, and to mitigate and console the moral pangs of his patients—to cheer the despondent, to encourage the weak and downhearted; to instruct the ignorant; to warn and improve the vicious, and finally to point out to the dying such hopes and consolation as he may be able to deduce from reason or extract from revelation.

To do all this *well* requires a large insight of man's nature, both intellectual, moral and emotional. He cannot do this if his own mind is steeped in boorish ignorance, or if he is deficient in a knowledge of the laws of reasoning and above all that vast sum of accumulated knowledge which constitutes our professional and worldly wisdom.

But while intellectual culture is so essential to the *practice* of medicine, it is not less so to an easy and complete mastery of the science itself. To a medical student who is not already prepared by long training in the various mental processes, and above all if he does not have some knowledge of those languages which constituted for so many centuries the repository of all scientific knowledge, and to which scientists still repair to obtain an elegant nomenclature—the mastery of technicalities alone present an amount of labor appalling.

Do not understand me, gentleman, to assert that a knowledge of Latin and Greek is absolutely necessary to the study of medicine; for some of the brightest luminaries of medical science were at the beginning of their careers deficient in this and many other useful accomplishments. But there are very few, I apprehend, to whom are given the large brains and strong wills that will enable them to surmount the enormous difficulties attending such an achievement.

The technology and terminology of medical science have always been and still are derived mostly from the Greek and Latin languages; and to any one entirely ignorant of these, an ordinary medical treatise of to-day is almost as unintelligible as if written in Chinese.

Studying the theory of medicine therefore, to such an one is like trying at one and the same time to master a science and the language in which it is written. An entire lack of this knowledge therefore, must enormously increase the difficulties which will beset you, as well as prevent you from possessing and exhibiting that air of polish and finished culture which every physician ought to possess, and which a classical education usually bestows upon its possessor.

These then, gentlemen, briefly, are some of the subjective or possessive qualifications for the study upon which you are about to enter; and the responsibility of deciding the question of your fitness for this study, rests alone with you and your advisors—your parents' friends and medical preceptors. For I wish to say here, once for all, that I regard the clamor against medical colleges for turning out graduates, sometimes of small intellect and less culture exceedingly unjust. It is the medical profession at large who ought, and who have the power to deal with this question, since all colleges require as a prerequisite to graduation in addition to two full courses of lectures, a year of preliminary study. If preceptors therefore would frankly place before young men of inferior parts and acquirements, the difficulties in the way of their becoming competent physicians, dissuade them from the undertaking, and failing in this, refuse to take them into their offices or aid them any way in prosecuting the undertaking, the problem would be solved at once.

There is a great deal said and written in our country at this time about the necessity for a higher education in medicine, and the excessive, and as is alleged, unnecessary number of medical graduates in the U. S.; and the number of annual graduates in some of the older and more densely populated countries of Europe is quoted in what I may call an "odious comparison." But it should be remembered that the conditions are very different in all the countries of the old world except possibly some parts of Russia, from those existing here. The total area of Europe is 3,627,000 square miles, with a population of 350,000,000; or about 96.5 to the square mile; while the total area of the United States, exclusive of Alaska, is 3,026,494.89 miles, with a population of only 50,000,00, or 16.5 to the square mile. In a densely populated country, one physician can minister to the wants of thousands. While in a sparsely inhabited country like the United States, he can minister only to a very few hundreds, because they are so widely scattered. Judged by this criterion, I do not believe the colleges of the United States are turning out too many doctors, and I think I can safely promise every one of you—although you will probably constitute not more than one-thirtieth of the total number who will graduate in the next two years—that you will find a place in which to do your chosen work, and by which you will win your bread.

In regard to the question of "higher education" too, I am afraid that our medical journals contain a good deal of twaddle and nonsense. While I advise you and all others always to aim high and to strive for the best medical education attainable, I cannot ignore the fact that there is not only room but an absolute necessity for doctors in some parts of our vast country, who have not received such a costly education—costly both in time, in labor and in money, Let us suppose that a young man has fulfilled all the requirements of the higher education advocates; that after going through a preparatory school, he has gone to a college, and after four years of study has taken his degree of A. B. or A. M.; that he has then attended a medical school for four years more (for that is the demand); and taken the degree of M. D., and then spent two years more in attendance upon some one or more of the great hospitals of Europe or of the United States. He has now spent about sixteen years in study, at an expenditure of something like $4,000 in money, and ought certainly to be thoroughly equipped for his work. But what kind of work? Is it, or can it be expected that this young man will now go and locate himself at—we will say—Brown's cross roads, away out in the wilds of Colorado or New Mexico, and spend his days in galloping weary miles over a rugged country, and curing cow boys and backwoodsmen of the ague and fever, or sewing up the wounds inflicted upon each other in drunken brawls? The idea is preposterous! And yet the poor people around Brown's cross roads need a doctor, and if they can't obtain the services of such an elaborately educated one as I have described, they will be glad to get one, and will gladly pay one who has *not* been so expensively educated, and who, after all, will, in a very few years of experience, learn to treat them perhaps as successfully as the other man. There is then a demand in many parts of the United States for physicians of moderate ability and inferior education, and wherever there is a demand for anything, there will always be a supply. The law is as fixed as truth itself.

But I would not have you believe from this that I am in favor of an inferior and slipshod education of any kind, and last of all of a medical education; and if any of you have come here with the belief that you can get a diploma cheaply, cheap either in the pecuniary or intellectual sense, I must disabuse your minds of that error, and tell you that you have come to the wrong shop.

Unquestionably, a great deal has been done and is still doing, to render education more thorough in our medical schools than it was a few years ago. The number of professors has been enlarged in all schools; and far more attention is now paid to practical clinical instruction, by which alone, the student can acquire the *art* as distinguished from the theory of medicine; and I am decidedly of the opinion that the average medical graduate of to-day is more thoroughly grounded in the theory of medicine, has better opportunities for becoming acquainted with the practice, and is generally better armed for the conflict with disease and death, than was the graduate of 15 or 20 years ago.

And now gentlemen, a few words as to the means by which you can best attain a knowledge of this science, such a knowledge as will qualify you to take your place in the noble army of toilers, whose mission is one of strength and mercy, and whose sole aim is to relieve mankind of pain and suffering, and to prolong, as far as possible, the short space of life allotted to us upon this sphere.

You will have inferred, if you do not already know, that medicine is viewed under two aspects, that is, theoretical and practical; or more exactly the scientific knowledge of medicine, which includes all that has been learned by ages of experience; and the practical application of this knowledge to the curing of disease.

The first of these is to be acquired from books and oral teaching or lecturing; the other can only be learned by observation at the bed-side, or as it is commonly called, clinical or experimental teaching. By the one, you may learn all that has been definitely settled or established by the labors and experience of your predecessors; by the other, only can you acquire the art or knack—like that of the handicraftsman—of recognizing or diagnosing disease and applying the appropriate remedy. Without the latter, you may know all that has been learned of the history of disease; of anatomy, physiology, pathology and therapeutics, and yet be almost entirely inefficient as a practitioner; because you will be unable to recognize a disease when you see it. But with this knowledge alone you may at last attain a tolerable degree of success though totally unacquainted with text-books, and even though you have never heard of Neimeyer, Flint or Watson; just as an ignorant carpenter may learn to construct a very good house, though he may never have heard of Sir Christopher Wren, and knows nothing whatever of the science of architecture.

But if this be so you may ask, "what is the utility of poring over text-books, and listening to lectures?" Why not begin at once as a practitioner and acquire at once, that practical skill which is at last the only thing that can insure your success?

The answer is plain enough. The student that begins at once as a practitioner, begins just where the earliest member of the art began, and each one will have to learn over and over again for himself, the same lessons of experience and at the same cost of failure and disaster, and the science of medicine would stand still. But by first learning either by reading or lectures the accumulated experience of the past, each succeeding generation begins where the former ended, and thus there is a continual advancement. A celebrated oculist once declared thus he had ruined "a hat full of eggs" before he perfected the operation for extraction of cataract, an operation which now—thanks to his experience—almost any surgeon can perform as well as he.

And so you too, gentlemen, may at last attain a fair degree of skill as practitioners by the experimental method alone, but you will do so at a fearful cost of human life and suffering.

Sir Thomas Watson, whose admirable system of lectures constitutes the finest contribution to medical literature in any language, treats this question in the following felicitous manner: "One man," says he, "shall travel into a foreign land, knowing nothing beforehand of its scenery or its climate, of its natural productions, its manufactures or its works of art, and ignorant alike of the manners, customs, history, laws and language of its inhabitants; another shall visit it after having furnished his mind with information upon these subjects, by reading and by conversing with men who have already passed over the same ground. Supposing the visit to be limited in each to a certain, but not long period of time, and I need not ask your opinion as to which of these travellers will reap the greatest harvest of enjoyment and profitable knowledge from his journey."

The main object and utility then, of text-books and systematic lectures explanatory of the principles and descriptive of the practice of medicine, is to prepare the reader or hearer for observing to the best advantage, the actual phenomena of disease and the power of remedies over it. They are intended to fit him for seeing with intelligence, to enable him to read and understand and interpret the book of nature when it is laid open before him, in short, to qualify him for clinical study; for it is only by clinical study in the hospital, or the sick chamber, and among dying, where you can either thoroughly or safely learn the practice of medicine.

It is in medical colleges alone that both these methods of teaching are to be found blended, and where both the science and the *art* of medicine are to be acquired; and while I neither underrate the importance of a careful study of well selected text-books, nor depreciate the value of practice, even without the experience of instructed minds to guide you, I can assure you that it is only by a judicious combination of didactic lectures and clinical instruction that both the art and the science can be mastered quickly, pleasantly and safely.

Read your text-books then by all means, diligently and faithfully; listen to both didactic and clinical lectures, patiently, absorbently, and understandingly; but observe the phenomena of disease in the hospital, the clinical lecture room, or the domestic sick chamber, carefully, observantly and profitably. Do all these diligently and constantly, for the amount of success that will crown your efforts depends absolutely upon the amount of labor you perform.

And now in conclusion, permit me to congratulate you upon your choice of a school in which you are to prosecute the studies which are to prepare you to discharge the high and honorable and holy duties of a physician. For without undue assumption, I can say that I think you will find no institution in our land which blends more judiciously the two modes of instruction I have pointed out, or that has equipped itself with more or better facilities for enabling you to learn those practical clinical lessons which I have told you are absolutely essential to enable you understand and practice the art of medicine.

ANALECTS.

The Statistics of Paracentesis Pericardii.

The history of the operation was briefly related from its first suggestion by Riolan in 1649. Its practical introduction was traced to Dr. Rovers, of Barcelona, who operated successfully in two cases in 1819. In 1841 there was a remarkable series of cases in an outbreak of scurvy in Russia, in which the pericardial effusion was composed mostly of blood. Nine were operated upon and six recovered. In 1854 Trousseau's essay was published upon some cases of his own and of M. Aran, which revived interest in the subject. In 1866, Dr. Clifford Allbutt introduced the operation to this country, and it was performed by Mr. Wheelhouse and Mr. Teale.

Rosenstein, in 1871, made a great practical advance in operating by free incision with drainage. A complete list of the recorded cases up to date was given in a tabular form, with the addition of several cases hitherto unpublished, making seventy-nine cases in all. Of these, fifty-six had been in males, for which no reason could be assigned, and they had been uniformly distributed over the early ages of life. Phthisis and pleurisy had been associated with twenty-three cases, rheumatism with eleven, scurvy with nine, general dropsy with five, injury with three; in twelve cases there had been no associated disease. The fluid had been in fifty-eight cases serous, in twelve purulent, in nine bloody. The amount evacuated had been in forty-six cases less, in thirty-three cases more, than a pint. It was not rare to evacuate as much as two or three pints. The largest quantities had been found in the scorbutic cases, and from one of these about ten pints had been evacuated. It had been sometimes observed that great relief was given by the withdrawal of one or two ounces, and that this had been followed by the absorption of the rest of the fluid. Dieulafoy's careful experiments had led to the selection of a place in the fifth left space, about an inch from the sternum, as the safest point for puncture. The following conclusions were drawn:

(1.) Paracentesis pericardii is not only justifiable, but an operation which may be safely undertaken with ordinary precaution, for only one case is recorded in which the operation was in itself fatal, and, with this exception, all the patients were greatly relieved by the removal even of small amounts of fluid, and many recovered completely who would probably have died had the operation not been performed. (2.) The most suitable place for puncture is, in ordinary cases, in the fifth left intercostal space, one inch from the edge of the sternum; but if the pleura be adherent, the puncture may be made safely much further out, and even in the sixth space. (3.) The instrument employed should be a trocar and canula, with or without aspiration. (4.) The operation may be performed with advantage, not only in the pericardial effusion of rheumatic or primary origin, but also in those which occur in the later stages of general dropsy, if it should appear that the fluid in the pericardium is adding to the difficulties under which the heart is placed. (5.) Purulent pericarditis is best treated on general principles, like empyema. (6.) The pericardial sac may be safely opened and drained. (7.) This treatment, moreover, appears to be the only one which offers the slightest hope of recovery. (8.) The results do not seem to be as unfavorable as those of empyema, for the walls of the cavity are better able to contract rapidly, and thus permit its complete obliteration.—*British Med. Jour.*

Iodine as a Gastric Sedative.

The employment of iodine for the relief of the vomiting of pregnancy has been somewhat in vogue for a number of years. And while the success attending its use has been pointed out with more or less enthusiasm, its exact value has never been established. Dr. T. T. Gaunt has for a number of years been employing the compound tincture of iodine in drop doses in nearly all forms of emesis, and reports thirteen cases of the most varied character, in all of which vomiting was promptly arrested by the use of this drug.—*Am. Journ Med. Sciences, St. Louis, M., and S. Journ.*

Coffee in Strangulated Hernia.

Dr. Antonia Sarra relates (*Med. Record*), that he was called one evening to attend a man 63 years of age, suffering from a strangulated femoral hernia. The patient was nearly moribund, there was no appreciable radial pulse, the face was pinched, the extremities were cold, and the attempts to vomit were almost incessant. Happening to remember the report of a similar case relieved by coffee, Dr. Sarra ordered an infusion of this substance to be employed as a drink and also externally, and then took leave of the patient, warning the family that death was inevitable unless a prompt amelioration ensued. Upon returning early next morning, he was surprised to find his patient in perfect health. The man stated that soon after taking the coffee he experienced a feeling of warmth and returning strength, then a large quantity of gas was expelled above and below, and when he put his hands upon the tumor it at once slipped back into the abdominal cavity, much to his astonishment as well as joy.—*Weekly Med. Review.*

Syphilis and Rachitis.

M. Parrot read before the Académie de Médicine his researches upon this subject, and he has come to the conclusion that rachitis is the special lesion which hereditary syphilis produces in the bones. He further states that in all cases of hereditary syphilis there are found, from the last months of intra-uterine life to a period near the second dentition, systematic, polymorphous alterations of the skeleton, and all of them resemble lesions of rachitis. Several patients were presented by M. Parrot to the Society, affected with syphilitic osseous lesions, varying in degree, all of which would have been formerly considered rachitic lesions.

At a later meeting of the Society, M. Cazin presented a communication upon this subject, in which he opposed the views of Parrot, and mentioned numerous cases in which rachitis was manifest without it being possible to discover any trace of a syphilitic history. The writer ended his paper by saying, that if we did not accurately know the nature of rachitis, this affection is certainly not a metamorphosis of syphilis. M. Lucas-Championniere supported the views of M. Cazin, and said he had never considered syphilis as a cause of rachitis. M. Despres did not accept the opinion of M. Parrot, as to the relation of rachitis and syphilis; the latter, he said, had been able to base his opinion, up to a certain point, upon the pathological anatomy of the affections, but their clinical nature absolutely opposed the idea of their identity.—*Gazette Med., de Paris.—The Polyclinic.*

A Lure for Trout and Black Bass.

The following "trick" comes rather late in the season, but if our sporting readers will bear it in mind, it may save them money and disappointment when next year's fishing days arrive:

A lure for trout and black bass is suggested by one of the writers to a sporting periodical that is somewhat novel. He says that he has used it for thirty years, and never saw its equal as a bait. The skin of the neck and the head of a fowl, with speckled and red feathers, cut into narrow strips with the feathers on, makes a most enticing bait and it may be used fresh, or be kept pickled in salt brine from fall to spring. He says: "When on the hook it is a most enticing bait, and being tough hangs on well and looks bright. I have caught a basket of trout with one bait. Sometimes you may want a bait like a bug or grasshopper, or a large miller; this you can closely imitate by leaving one or two feathers. Sometimes by cutting from the wattles near the bill with a feather or two, or a piece of the comb and a piece of the little feathers attached, will lure a trout when nothing else will."

Headaches and Kerosene Lamps.

The *Boston Journal of Chemistry* thinks that the headaches that many thousands wake up with every morning, are brought about by kerosene lamps "turned down low." A small flame in a lamp chimney does not cause enough draft to insure complete combustion, and slumberers breathe carbon and carbonic acid gas as literally as if they stood over the chimney of a petroleum refinery. A little light may be supplied in a bedchamber, if any indeed is required, by a specially prepared taper, by a candle, or by a wick floated in animal or vegetable oil, but the "turned down" kerosene lamp cannot be used except to one's disadvantage. — *Southern Clinic.*

How to Remove a Tight Ring.

A novel method of effecting the removal of a ring which has become constricted around a swollen finger, or in any other similar situation, consists simply in enveloping the afflicted member, after the manner of a circular bandage, in a length of flat India rubber braid, such as ladies make use of to keep their hats on the top of their heads. This should be accurately applied—beginning, not close to the ring, but at the top of the finger, and leaving no intervals between the successive turns, so as to exert its elastic force gradually and gently upon the tissues underneath. When the binding is completed, the hand should be held aloft in a vertical position, and in a few minutes the swelling will be perceptibly diminished. The braid is then taken off and immediately reapplied in the same manner, when, after another five minutes, the finger, if rapidly uncovered, will be small enough for the ring to be removed with ease.—*Langdon, Gaz. des Hop.*

Intestinal Concretions.

Dr. Schuberg (*Virchow's Archiv.*) considers that the chief seat of intestinal concretions is the cæcum. They may also occur in the colon. They are of two kinds, either regular fæcal calculi or concretions. The latter are consequent upon the former, with the exception of those due to the copious use of grain or of magnesia, etc. All other concretions are fæcal calculi impregnated with inorganic salts, and in the centre fæcal residues or foreign bodies can almost invariably be found. Foreign bodies generally form the starting point of concretions; the most common are the seeds of fruit and hairs. In man it is probable that hair often gets into the intestinal canal from the habit of biting the beard, and this is perhaps the cause why 80 per cent. of intestinal calculi occur in man and only 20 in women.

Electricity in Skin Diseases.

Both in the acute stage of herpes zoster and in the chronic neuralgic condition which often follows, the constant current is of especial value. I can fully endorse Duhring's statement that the pain and eruption may often be arrested by its timely application. The moistened sponge electrodes should be directly applied to the neighborhood of the eruption, and over the course of the implicated nerves. A descending current of about ten cells should be employed; each sitting should last ten minutes or more, to be repeated once or twice daily.

All varieties of baldness are helped by electricity, notably in the form of faradism.

I am well convinced that alopecia areata is greatly benefitted by a moderately strong current applied directly to the seat of the disease.—*W. A. Hardaway, in Courier of Medicine.*

Castor Oil and Glycerine.

A mixture which is of an agreeable flavor and in which the nauseous smell of the oil is efficiently disguised, can be made thus:

℞ Ol. ricini, . ℨj,
Glycerini, . . ℨj,
Tr. aurantii, . . m xx,
Tr. senegæ, . . m v,
Aquæ cinnam, . ad. ℥ss.

This forms a beautiful emulsion, is easily taken, even by children, and if administered at bedtime will produce a gentle motion the following morning.—*N. Y. Med. Journal.*

The Local Treatment of Erysipelas.

Phenic acid, 1 part.
Alcohol, 1 part.
Essence of turpentine, 2 parts.
Tincture of iodine, 1 part.
Glycerine, 5 parts.

With this moisten all superficial erysipelatous patches every two hours. Rothe, *Revista Farmaceutica.—Therap. Gazette.*

For Hemorrhoids.

Dr. Benj. Lee, of Philadelphia, recommends the following (*Medical Times*):

Pulv. rhei, ℨiv;
Pulv. aloes, . . ℨiij,
Pulv. myrrh, . ℨij
Sapon. Hisp., ℨiiss,
Ol. cajeput., . . ℨj.

The powders are to be rubbed together and the soap then worked in, afterwards the oil. The well-mixed mass is kept in tight bottles. The fresher it is, the better. Three grains of this mass makes an effective pill, which is non-irritating, and may be used a long while without diminishing the susceptibility of the intestines, and often with positive benefit to the hemorrhoidal affection. Cascara sagrada in two-grain doses is also beneficial.

To Abort a Stye.

Dr. Louis Fitzpatrick writes to the *Lancet* that he has never seen a single instance in which the stye continued to develop after the following treatment had been resorted to: The lids should be held apart by the thumb and index finger of the left hand or a lid-retractor, if such be at hand, while the tincture of iodine is painted over the inflamed papilla with a fine camel's hair pencil. The lids should not be allowed to come in contact until the part touched is dry. A few such applications in the twenty-four hours are sufficient.

Extirpation of Goitre.

Prof. Kocher has extirpated goitrous thyroid glands 101 times, with a mortality of 25 per cent. in malignant cases, and 5.1 per cent. in non-malignant. The tissues should not be ligated *en masse*, but all the vessels carefully isolated and divided between two ligatures. Tracheotomy should be avoided unless specially indicated. Billroth extirpated the gland in 68 cases with a mortality of 73 per cent. Seven of the cases were attacked by tetanus after the operation.

Surprising the Urethra.

"In urethral stricture I have," says M. Diday, "in order to avoid confounding it with a spasm and to overcome this, if it exists, an infallible method. When the end of the sound is in contact with the coarctated portion of the canal I suddenly put the following question to the patient: 'How long is it since you have been with a woman?' If it is a simple spasm the sound immediately enters."

Resorcin as a Remedy for Cystitis.

Dr. J. Andeer, reports extensive use of resorcin in acute and chronic cystitis, and claims for it almost specific curative power. He reports one hundred and fifty-six cases where, either by him or to his personal knowledge, it was injected into the human bladder with the best results in vesical catarrh. Acute cases have been entirely cured by the injection of a five per cent. solution.

Losing His Memory.

M. Chevreul, now 97 years of age, has commenced a new course of lectures on organic chemistry, at the museum of natural history. Speaking of some slight phenomenon, he said, the other day: "This fact was first mentioned to me in 1802, by a Leipsic student named Schamberger or Schomberger, I am not sure which; it is curious, but I am beginning to lose the memory of names."

Longevity of Males and Females.

Dr. P. V. Schenck (*St. Louis Courier Med.*) says that out of 102,831 individuals who have passed the age of ninety years, 60,303 are women and only 44,523 are men. In Italy 241 centenarian women are found for 141 men of the same age. During ten yea 72 deaths of centenarian women were recorded in the New York statistical tables and only 19 males. In Sweden the number of old women who exceed 80 years is to that of the old men as 33 to 19. The last United States census shows that of those over 80 years the females exceed the males by 22,000.--*Lancet.*

The Medical Chronicle.

A Monthly Journal for the Practitioner.

GEORGE H. ROHÉ, M. D., Editor.

☞ It is requested that all literary and business communications, books for review, exchanges, etc., be addressed to, and all checks, drafts and post-office orders drawn to the order of

Dr. GEORGE H. ROHÉ,

95 Park Avenue, - - - - Baltimore, Md.

BALTIMORE, NOVEMBER, 1883.

EDITORIAL.

Another Step in Advance.

The Faculty of the College of Physicians and Surgeons, of Baltimore, has recently adopted a resolution requiring all students to sign the matriculation register a second time, at the end of the course, when their tickets will be countersigned by the Dean. This will prevent students from leaving in the middle of the session and offer their tickets as evidence of attendance on a full course of lectures. The tickets will state distinctly, that, unless countersigned by the dean, they will not be considered—in this school at all events—as showing that the holder of the ticket has attended a full course. It is only after the student has registered again at the end of the session that he can obtain this endorsement of the dean. It is believed that this requirement will put a stop here to the custom so largely prevalent among first-course students everywhere, of leaving college before the end of the session. The authorities of the College of Physicians and Surgeons are determined to do everything in their power to render every matriculation ticket issued by them valid evidence of attendance on a full course of lectures. Another rule in force in this college, is that the tickets of those schools which hold their regular session in the summer-time, are not recognized as evidence of a full course of lectures. While the enforcement of these requirements will necessarily subject the college to some pecuniary loss, it is believed by the faculty that the profession will properly recognize and appreciate this movement in the direction of a more thorough medical education.

The Alumni Prize.

We call attention to the announcement which appears in our advertising pages of the prize offered to the members of the Alumni Association of the College of Physicians and Surgeons of Baltimore. We are confident that an essay worthy of the prize will be submitted, and we trust that the competition will be active, and render the securing of the prize an honor worth struggling for.

FLOTSAM.

DR. L. D. BULKLEY will give a course of free lectures on diseases of the skin in the New York Hospital, beginning October 17.

THE first popular Sanitary Convention under the auspices of the Maryland State Board of Health, will be held in Baltimore on the last Tuesday in November.

WE have used Packer's Tar Soap largely in hospital and private practice, and can recommend it highly as an excellent antiseptic and detergent soap. It has proved especially useful in seborrhœa and parasitic affections.

THE *Atlantic Journal of Medicine*, is a new claimant for professional favor, coming to us from Richmond, Va. Drs. R. B. Stover and H. G. Houston, are the editors. The subscription price is $3.00 per year. We wish it success.

THE *Medical World* is a new weekly, published in Philadelphia. Price $2.00 per year. The first number has a fair lithographic portrait of Prof. Austin Flint, Sr., as a supplement.

THE commercial bodies of New Orleans have combined with the auxiliary Sanitary Association for the purpose of suppressing the small-pox epidemic in that city. Meanwhile the Louisiana Board of Health listens complacently to historical accounts of quarantine and intramural interments by the president of that body, and neglects its obvious duties.

DR. HORATIO C. WOOD, who has had editorial charge of the *Philadelphia Medical Times*, since its establishment, has retired, and is succeeded by Dr. Frank Woodbury, who has been assistant editor of the *Times* for the past year. Dr. Woodbury has had considerable experience in journalism, and will doubtless make the *Times* a better journal even than it has been in the past.

SURGEON-GENERAL C. H. CRANE, of the army, died October 10, in his 58th year. He occupied the office only fifteen months, having been appointed upon the retirement of Surgeon-General Barnes. Surgeon D. L. Huntington has been directed to take charge of the office until further notice. Dr. J. H. Baxter, chief medical purveyor, is the most prominent candidate for the vacancy.

"THE best buggy for the money," is the verdict of those who have bought their phætons of R. F. Briggs & Co., No. 53 W. Fayette street. Mr. A. W. Hawks, the energetic and courteous manager for the firm, discourses learnedly of the comparative advantages of Brewster, and various other double-back-action springs, tops, axles and hubs. If you want a comfortable, durable, stylish and cheap buggy call on, or write to him.

The Medical Chronicle.

BALTIMORE, DECEMBER, 1883.

ORIGINAL ARTICLES.

ARTICLE I.

The Relations of the Powers of the State to the Rights of the Individual in Matters Concerning the Public Health.

An Address Delivered Before the First Sanitary Convention of Maryland, Held at Baltimore, November 27th and 28th, 1883.

BY RICHARD GUNDRY, M. D., Professor of Materia Medica, Therapeutics and Mental Diseases, College of Physicians and Surgeons, Baltimore; Superintendent of Maryland Hospital for the Insane, etc.

The objects of this convention I take to be, to arrive at such agreement as may be possible as to the essential needs of the community in a sanitary point of view. Some, perhaps, would add that the main object is to formulate a *law* which, approved by us as a convention, should be presented to the legislature and passed by them to enforce certain practices and regulations for the improvement of public health. Now, the discussion of the sanitary wrongs suffered by the community, and suggestions for their remedy is an excellent thing if it shall open the eyes and understanding of the community in general to the importance of the subject—to the magnitude and constant increase of the sources of disease and degeneration—to the full recognition of the dangerous character of many of these things which people too often think to be of trivial weight and harmless, or at least only harmful to other people; if, I say, we can do anything to arouse public opinion to recognize and remedy these things, our convention will be a great success; but if we take for granted that as the self-elected instructors of the people it needs only our imprimatur to seal the success of a law—if the formulating of such a law be the do-all and be-all of this meeting we shall find that we will only confirm the definition of the grammarian, who defined the word convention as a "noun of multitude, signifying many but not always signifying *much*." To have upon the statute book a good law for sanitary purposes is a good thing, provided you have a strong healthy popular opinion to sustain it—not otherwise. Better far, that the law be deficient in some detail, with an enlightened and aroused public opinion upon the subject, than the most perfectly devised law with an apathetic or hostile sentiment in the community where it is to be enforced. There is in reality no law so inefficient as that which is not fully supported by public opinion. If enforced it is regarded as tyrannical, and constant jarrings and frictions occur which increase the original dislike for it, and ultimately cause its disregard or repeal, or if they cannot be effected, revolt and anarchy. For it is fallacy to suppose that because our laws are made by persons freely chosen by us (by the counting of noses) and therefore are the formulated expression of our will, and must be obeyed, and really are generally obeyed,—laws are necessarily the expression of popular opinion. In reality they sometimes are; as often not. Public opinion is constantly changing from day to day, as the light of knowledge increases; its movements are oscillatory, but with a direction usually slowly determined. Not always is that direction ascertained. The eddies of the current often draw us out of the main stream, and that legislation as a rule is the most successful which keeps within sight, but just a little ahead of the wave—abreast or a little more—which discerning the shape popular opinion is assuming, has the apparel ready to clothe it with.

Generally legislation follows in the wake of popular opinion, which has loudly demanded it, and when obtained, it is viewed with somewhat of distrust as extorted by force.

If the legislation should be too much ahead of the "popular bark," neglect and dislike follow. We are too apt to think that majorities, however obtained, are all that is needed to determine a question. Sir Robert Peel said most philosophically to Mr. Cobden, when he heard of the overthrow of Louis Phillippe by the French Revolution of 1848, "That comes of trying to carry on a government by means of a mere majority of a chamber, without regard to the opinion out of doors." From what I have heard, Maryland has had upon her statute books, several good laws for sanitary purposes. Her law for Boards of Health and other sanitary purposes is good. How much of it is in operation, thoroughly and smoothly working with the support of the people? In how large a portion of the State are its operations felt or attempted? So long as no epidemic is present, the law lies dormant, and the evils it was created to suppress are fostered by its neglect. The question itself is a subject of cheap wit and derision. When an epidemic breaks out in a community unprepared, then the strong arm of the law is evoked, its ministers censured, and with all the hurry and confusion of a panic, the provisions of the law hurriedly, and harshly, and expensively carried out. In proportion as the danger fades away, reaction sets in; the extent of the evil fought is contracted in the memory, the expense and harshness are only remembered and exaggerated, and thus sullen indifference succeeds to recrimination. But as a rule, all is not lost, some step has been gained and held, and thus gradually and slowly, step by step, is a system of law and regulation built up, and efficiency of its administration secured. Let us hope that the panic and terror of the late epidemic of small-pox will lead to the more general practice of vaccination *when there is no epidemic*, instead of waiting till the enemy is at our doors. Let me illustrate the results of attempts to enforce sanitary laws in neighborhoods not enlightened upon the subject of their purport.

Two instances occur to me, drawn from very different states of society, but illustrating how the popular bias towards mistrusting sanitary doctrines and methods influences juries to give undue weight to adverse testimony. In the life of Lord Abinger, an instance is given of his astuteness in cross-examination, in the case of a nuisance fully proven—with expert testimony as to its deleterious effects upon the health of the community—and the case looked conclusive. The last witness put on the stand to prove the nuisance, or something connected with it, and who loudly complained of it, was a healthy looking matron, who gave her testimony clearly. Scarlett commenced his cross-examination as to her own history, who she was, how long she had been married, and how many children she had had, how she raised them, rousing her pride to describe them—a mother would naturally—he was stopped by the opposing counsel, who objected to the scope of his examination as irrelevant; and the judge saying he really did not see how they bore upon the matter, he merely said he would like to continue and it would soon appear. Going on, he got from the witness that she had been healthy as the average; had raised a large family of healthy children, and then closed, saying: that is my case, a cause could not be unhealthy, and produce such results, and triumphantly defeated the opposite side, dispelling all the positive evidence of the ill effect of the complained nuisance by the negative testimony of one whom it had failed to effect. As well deny in a time of universal bankruptcy that there is a prostration of business because Astor and Vanderbilt had their millions in safety. Allowing for the acts and power of the lawyer, effective in making the worse the better cause appear, and yet there is much due to the mistrust with which juries naturally approach such subjects on which their information is limited.

The other incident occurred about 16 years ago, in a rich and intelligent county. A case was on trial where the nuisance complained of was a large distillery, with its enormous hog styes, contaminating the air and streams adjacent, making the lives of those in the adjacent village uncomfortable by reason of the bad smell, and some *few* cases of fever had been traced to its influence. The facts were made out to the jury. Expert testimony showed the probable effect from the continuance of such a state of things, and everything looked conclusive, when the defence put in the witness box a respectable looking farmer, who had succeeded in life, and was well-to-do. He testified that the nuisance complained of was nothing at all to be feared; rather an advantage, giving the extraordinary reason that he owned a very bad smelling privy himself. He admitted it was terrible, and added he was subject to headaches, which he always cured by inhaling the odor from that privy (placing his face over the seat). The man was honest, and in ordinary things, intelligent; and his practical knowledge outweighed the positive testimony of the other side, and all the theories of the experts, in the view of the jury. A year or two after, that neighborhood was scourged by an epidemic of fever, resulting from the state of things unredressed.

Juries only represent the average intelligence of the communities, they are drawn from, and go into the jury box, impartial enough, but impartial as the personal equation of each limits him, that is to say, biased more or less by his association, habits of thought and extent of cultivation. A community thoroughly aroused to the importance of sanitary questions, will furnish jurymen capable of investigating such questions in an enlarged and enlightened manner, and less liable to be swerved by secondary considerations or legal sophistries. It is to juries that the question will naturally come; or if to magistrates, will the result differ materially?

Gradually as occasion has been developed, there has sprung up a class of men who have given these subjects of sanitation their earnest study, and this class will gradually increase. Among them have been lawyers, engineers, clergymen, physicians, and scientists. Of course, the larger portion come from the medical profession, whose training should fit them for such investigations; but the study of state medicine, or the prevention of disease, is only in its infancy in our land. Wherever boards of health have been established, there should be, and generally is, a nucleus of organization for all workers in this direction. At first the power confided to them may be small, but gradually as the knowledge is disseminated, popular opinion, organized by intellect, influenced by morality, and devoted to high and noble aims, presses to their assistance either by encouraging voluntary efforts or by the authority of law, which then can be enforced. But these transactions in law to be safe, should be the gradual product of popular opinion, so as to secure the practical well-being of the community, and to allow its social and industrial forces to develope, unimpeded by unnecessary restrictions. Thereby carefully avoiding the exciting of violent passions, provoking reaction, offending large classes and generating enduring discontent among the people of any class.

It is to the voluntary efforts of this class, that all success hitherto achieved is due; that laws in certain directions have been enacted and carried out successfully as the expression of the will of the State. Agitate, constantly agitate, must be the sanitarian's cry. When we point reproachfully to what is done in other countries, and contrast the clean streets of European cities every day of the year, with the general condition of our cities in this respect—except, perhaps for a few days before an election—we may perhaps sigh and wish for more direct power to enforce this law in these respects, but we must remember our limitation, and that the efficiency of such work here must be regulated by the standard our intelligence demands; but we also can reflect how rapidly that intelligence once aroused has redressed many errors, and hope for the future revives. Until it can be impressed upon our people generally, that these questions are really questions of life and death, of wealth and poverty, our laws simply encumber our books of statutes and ordinances.

The word State is not used in any specified sense. I have nothing to do with state rights or wrongs, but I use the word to imply the personification of what Cicero described: "Multitudo juris consensio et utilitatis communione sociata," whether embodied in a general government, state government, municipality or township, making and enforcing laws, ordinances or regulations. In order to the promotion of general health or the health of each, what have all a right to demand from each? It will be found that practically the amount of the individual's surrender of his self-acting power is guaged by the proximity and number of the community he is a member of. A man dwelling apart with his family, forms a law unto himself practically—because his evil practices, if any, effect no one but himself and family—the rest of the community can only take cognizance of very grave practices whereby the health of members of his family may be vitiated. The other extreme is found in the crowded city, where practically every man's act affects every other man's health and comfort in a greater or less degree, and where, if he does not care for his neighbor's condition, that condition may re-act upon himself directly or indirectly with fearful effects. Between these two extremes of personal contact are intervals of every extent, modifying more or less inter-personal relations and reactions. It is from city life, therefore, that we must draw most of our illustrations of the conflict of state power and individual rights, and they are then brought close to the light and more generally recognized. In the country on a broader scale, may be the same evils, but these effects are not so immediate, and are therefore ignored with less resulting evil. But unfortunately the tendency of modern life is towards the cities, and this is rapidly increasing, especially among the poorer classes.

In the East, 35 per cent.; in the West, 15 per cent.; in the South, 7 per cent. are within the city limits. They are drawn by the gravitating force of city life. The hope of finding work, the fascination of city sights and sounds holds them. And when here, what then? There is a disturbance of the social equilibrium. They are, a part of the time, out of work. They live from hand to mouth. They can learn no provident habit, since they never have enough to save. They cannot maintain regular work habits. They cannot afford to pay rent enough to live apart from other families. They crowd into small rooms, which have no adequate provision for sewerage, pure air or pure water. They come under the infection of imitation from other families. There are few open spaces for children to play in Neatness and order disappear. The man frequents the corner or the saloon. The woman finds no companionship, save that of dirty, dishevelled women.

It was discovered by George Combe that when the rabbit warren was not properly cleaned, the female killed her young, and the male became quarrelsome. The organism of the animal was injured and rendered miserable by dirt, and nervous irritability akin to insanity was the result, and he adds, "The deleterious physical condition in which many of the human poor habitually live, is the cause of some of their sufferings and crimes."

The steps of descent from self-help to crime and idleness, voluntary or involuntary; discouragement, crowded condition; evil association impossible of avoidance; uncleanness; doles of food or money; increasing dependance; demand for public aid—crime. Thus many a hard working man and honest woman has broken under the social pressure, and become pauperized, or criminal, or both. Now as the State has at last to provide for this class of persons, and their provision entails trouble and expense, it is decidedly preferable to interfere before the last step is reached, and arrest this degeneration, and in one respect, at least, this interference regards points of sanitation. If lack of cleanliness leads to crime, clearly the State has a right to say the individual shall be required to be clean. To be clean again includes several factors, pure air, pure water, ventilated houses, means of disposing of filth excreted or made by necessary contamination. Without these, efforts at cleanliness are spasmodic and exceptional. Now if the State insists on this cleanliness, it must see that these necessary agencies for it are provided. First—water, as free as possible to the poor, not as a question of charity but as a question of economy, for cleanliness is cheaper than pauperism or crime. Then not only the freedom of supply, but the purity of that supplied. That this is a matter of economy may also be urged as the result of experiments and investigations. The epidemic of cholera in London in 1848-9, and 1853-4, showed the effects of water distribution—by a comparison of areas supplied by two water companies. The Southwark and Vauxhall, and the Lambeth. Each of these companies during the epidemic of 1848-9 and one of them (Southwark and Vauxhall) during the epidemic of 1853-4, had supplied its customers with sewage-polluted water of the Thames—and the miscellaneous sewage with which the water was polluted, had of course included choleraic discharges. The statistics of the two outbreaks in relation to the two quantities of local population were as nearly as could be estimated these. The quantity of population supplied by the Southwark and Vauxhall company suffered in the epidemic of 1848-9 at the rate of 118 cholera deaths for every 10,000 of population, and in the epidemic of 1853-4, at the rate of 130 for each 10,000. The quantity of population supplied by the Lambeth company, suffered in the epidemic of 1848-9 at the rate of 125 for each 10,000 of population, but in the epidemic of 1853-4 only at the rate of 37. And what was the single discoverable difference of condition in favor of the one quantity of population which suffered comparatively so little when the second epidemic befell? The company which supplied it with water had in the interval since the first epidemic, improved its supply to comparative excellence; whereas the other company were distributing water of even filthier quality than before. Dr. Simon adds: "It is in the highest degree probable, that of the 3476 tenants of the Southwark and Vauxhall Co., who died of cholera in 1853-4, two-thirds would have escaped if their water supply had been like that of their neighbors."

The necessity of baths brought within the reach of the poorest as an auxiliary in the work of cleanliness needs no lengthened argument. The spread of baths for the poor is due very much to the work of one poor woman, and illustrates the inception of popular opinion. In 1832, when the cholera first appeared in England, there was a poor woman named Catherine Wilkinson, who was so impressed with the necessity of cleanliness as a preventative of the disease, that she encouraged her neighbors to come to her comparatively better house, which comprised a kitchen, parlor, three small bed chambers and a yard, for the purpose of washing and drying their clothes. The good that was manifested, induced some benevolent persons to aid her in extending her operations. The large amount of washing done in one week in a cellar, under the superintendence of this excellent woman represented the amount of disease and discomfort kept down by her energetic desire to do good without pecuniary reward. Such was the origin of public baths and wash-houses in England, which Catherine Wilkinson had the satisfaction of seeing matured in Liverpool in 1846 in a large establishment under the corporation, to the superintendence of which she and her husband were appointed. The system has spread so that for a few cents all over the larger cities, baths are within reach of the poor. Plenty of water for drinking, washing and bathing of a proper quality, means diminution of all epidemic diseases and an increased self-respect, with decrease of pauperism and crime.

Then it is clearly impossible to have the full benefit of this increased supply without the power of carrying it off when used without doing harm to the rest of the population. For this a proper system of sewerage must be devised. A system which will not contaminate either the air of dwelling houses or the stream from which potable water is supplied. Both the supply of water to dwellings and the discharge of excreta, requires skilled operatives to arrange and put in the necessary pipes and apparatus. This, if deficient, is not only detrimental to the parties, but to other innocent parties, producing disease and death by introduction of sewage gas, and requires that it should be supervised by competent persons, for the work of the plumber is hidden to a great extent, and the damages are great but insidiously produced when the work is imperfect. Has not the State the right to determine upon what conditions the work shall be done? Moreover the State claims the right also to supervise dwellings where large numbers congregate (tenement houses), first for the protection of the poor against wealth, but principally as a police right to keep down pauperism, disease and crime. When these tenement houses have been properly supervised, their ventilation looked after—cleanliness enforced and proper sanitary arrangements introduced (as far as possible) the death rate has been very materially lowered. In New York from 1868 to 1873, the percentage of the death-rate among the tenement-house population, fell from 75 to 64 per cent.—11 per cent.—in consequence of such supervision, while in private houses where no such supervision was exercised, the death-rate increased in these years. "May I not do what I please with my own," is the historical exclamation of a ducal owner of rotten boroughs when reform was threatened. The limitation of this liberty is now believed in more largely when it conflicts with the interests of others; and this limitation seems to be in proportion as any harm results to a large or helpless portion of the community. In time I hope it will be thought a crime to take advantage of the necessities of the poor, to rent houses with wet cellars, damp walls, ill ventilation, dark rooms, imperfect supplies of water or means of sewage removal.

The adulteration of food has always claimed the attention of the State, and thus butchers, bakers and others are brought into the class which may require supervision. This supervision has existed from ancient times in nearly all states.

No great industry arises, conferring employment to vast multitudes of people and benefitting very materally the community in which it is situated, without in time also developing attendant evils peculiar to it. Sometimes, but rarely, these evils are detected and corrected as they are discovered, but too often it requires special press of public opinion or its embodiment, law, to enforce the proper remedy. The large canning establishments, slaughter houses, almost every industrial pursuit carried on by large numbers associated together, has at some time engaged special attention on account of some evil introduced or increased by them. The restriction of the hours of labor of children, the sanitary arrangements of the work places, the use of antidotes against poisonous substances employed in manufactures, the security of the neighborhood against contamination depends upon the right of the State to protect itself against wrong-doing.

The universality of the election franchise has brought with it the duty of placing the means of enlightenment within the reach of all; but if we expect our future citizens and voters to be intelligent and instructed, we must also see that the places provided for their instruction are suitable for such purposes in a sanitary point of view and not detrimental to their physical and mental health. School hygiene should be the study, not only of every teacher, but the anxious object of solicitude to every supervising officer connected with the schools.

To another point popular opinion should be earnestly aroused: the arrest of causes of preventable disease. If scarlet fever springs from animal contamination; if typhoid fever is disseminated from fecal sources; if typhus from excessive overcrowding, the immense loss occasioned to the State by sickness and death in the diminution of its resources, should lead it to seek out means of curtailment of these evils. Take one instance alone: the planting of the eucalyptus tree has comparatively banished ague from some of the places where it most prevailed, in Algiers and Italy. Where it is adapted to our climate, why should not its planting be urged and tried? If successful, laws encouraging and enforcing such culture would speedily follow until it would be considered wrong in certain places for malaria to exist. The owner of the soil would be forced to put a stop to the evil.

In all these, the conflict of the State on behalf of the many is constant against the claims of some individual, but as he is not exempt from the good or the evil flowing from all the conditions of society, he too, in another way receives his portion of the benefit. As time advances, practically greater enlightenment will reveal more and more points of contact with each other in our duties to each other and in the benefits flowing from these performances. We shall more readily assent to their embodiment in laws and customs, systematic enforcement against the refractory, and then, and not till then, realize the correctness of judicious Hooker's description when he exclaims: "Of Law, there can be no less acknowledged than that her seat is the bosom of God, her voice the harmony of the world. All things in heaven and on earth do her homage, the very least as feeling her care, and the greatest as not exempt from her power."

ARTICLE II.

THE VALUE OF DRY LINT AS A DRESSING IN COMPOUND FRACTURES.

BY O. J. COSKERY, M. D.,

Prof. of Surgery, College of Physicians and Surgeons, Baltimore.

On September 26th, 1881, Mr. B., a master workman, had his shirt-sleeve caught by a revolving shaft, and before the machinery could be stopped, had been bodily carried around the shaft a number of times. The injuries he received were a comminuted fracture of the left upper arm, and a compound comminuted fracture of both bones of the forearm on the same side. The opening in the skin through which the radius projected, had to be enlarged, in order to return the bone. A piece of dry lint was put on over the wound, and a rectangular splint along the inner side of the whole limb, with pasteboard cap to outer side of upper arm and shoulder. No great swelling or pain coming on in forearm, the piece of dry lint was allowed to remain until it fell off, which was in the third week when the wound was found to be perfectly healed. Not one drop of pus was ever seen. I would only mention here, that the upper arm did also well, and the patient was at work in about three months.

Elizabeth H., aged 71, on October 3rd, 1881, fell upon her hand. She received a compound comminuted fracture of both bones of the forearm. When first seen by me on the next day, the ulna was found stuck through the skin for nearly one-quarter of an inch. The opening was large enough, however, to allow of its easy reduction. A piece of dry rag was put over the wound, and as no swelling or pain came on, was allowed to remain. Between three and four weeks after, it came off itself, and the wound was found completely closed. The union of the fractured bones was also good.

James S., aged 27, had his right leg broken by a rock falling upon it. When admitted into St. Joseph's Hospital, on June 28th, 1883, three hours after injury, there were several small openings in the skin leading down to the fractured point, which was a few inches below the head of the tibia, and through which wound blood was oozing pretty freely. The mark of a rope, which had been applied above the knee-joint to arrest the hemorrhage, which was reported to have been free, was plainly discernible. The fluffy side of a piece of dry lint being applied over the wound with moderate pressure, seeming to arrest the flow of blood, a padded splint was put upon the outer side of the limb. During the night, rather profuse venous hemorrhage came on, which was controlled by applying the bandage more tightly over the pad of lint. No great swelling or pain coming on in the neighborhood of the wound, the temperature of the patient never rising above 100.5 the dressing was not disturbed until July 8th, when from one of the original wounds a very small amount of discharge took place. On July 11th, this had closed. July 26th, patient was walking on crutches, with the limb in plaster of Paris splints. September 19th, patient discharged well, but still wearing plaster "splints."

These cases have not been selected because they were favorable ones for such treatment, but exactly for an opposite reason. They were all very seriously handicapped. The first by the complication of a comminuted fracture of the humerus; the second by the age (71) of the patient, and the third by the profuse venous hemorrhage. Still, in spite of these disadvantages, they did perfectly well. My principal object in this paper is to call attention, first, to the importance of rapid conversion of a compound fracture into a simple one, if possible, and second, to the very convenient and easy method by the use of dry lint. I do not think that we need to use any germicide in order to prevent the changes that will take place in a wound if such germs are introduced, so much as we do to not allow of their introduction. If we can bring about a consummation so "devoutly to be wished" by the simple laying on of a piece of lint, is it not better and nicer to do so thus, than to cover our patient over with wet, foul smelling applications? One other point; how will we know that our dry lint is going to succeed? By the absence of any signs of inflammation in the neighborhood of the wounded part. If swelling and pain do not come on, then the lint should be allowed to remain. But if these symptoms make their appearance, and especially if the pain is of the throbbing character, the dressing must be removed at once, and all idea of converting the compound into a simple fracture, abandoned.

Now is the time to subscribe!

ARTICLE III.
THE TREATMENT OF CHRONIC ULCERS.

BY J. GORDON STEWART, M. D., MARKLE, PA.

To discuss ulcers in all of their details, as to etiology, nosology, pathology, etc., would be to write a book, hence, in this article I will confine myself to the consideration of the treatment of ulcers. Chronic ulcers have been in years past, the *opprobrium medicorum*. In every community you will find persons suffering from chronic ulcers. These ulcers have been treated by Dr. A. and Dr. B. They have been anointed with ung. zinci oxidi, ung. tabaci, ung. stramonii, ung. plumbi comp., *ad infinitum*, and finally after months and years of fruitless effort to cure them, the owners of the ulcers have been told by these grave and learned M. D.'s, not to heal them, for "as sure as you do, it will go to your lungs." I have often wondered what the antecedent of that pronoun "it," is.

In learned works on ulcers, they have been divided into many classes: the varicose ulcers, the eczematous ulcer, etc. Now while I admit there are many causes of ulcers, I believe with Prof. Rohé, of Baltimore, that there is only one kind of ulcer.

An ulcer may be defined: a solution of continuity with formation and destruction of normal elements. When the destructive action is in preponderance, the ulcer is spreading; when the formative, the ulcer is healing.

In order to give my treatment, I shall describe a few representative cases:

Case 1.—Mrs. A., aged 67, large ulcer of three months standing, caused by cellulo-cutaneous erysipelas, on back of hand and wrist, five inches long by about two wide; deep, edges ragged and undermined, and pouring forth a great amount of pus. As the patient was anemic, ordered iron and quinine, internally. Ulcer to be dressed morning and evening with a solution of carbolic acid (1 to 30 or 40), to be used with a hand-ball atomizer (Delano's or Richardson's generally used); the spray to be blown strongly *under the edges of the ulcer* and all over its surface until thoroughly cleansed. *No sponge or cloth to be used on the surface of the ulcer.*

A cloth oiled with an ointment of vaseline and carbolic acid to be applied to the ulcer and then lightly bandaged. Hand and arm to be kept at perfect rest. In twenty-seven days ulcer entirely healed.

Case 2.—Mr. B., aged 51, unmarried, farmer. Two ulcers about 4½ by 2½ inches, *of 17 years* standing. situated, one on the outer, one on the inner side of the leg, lower third. Ulcers deep, edges callous and ragged, surface partly covered with pale, unhealthy looking granulations, exuding a thin and sanious pus; whole foot and leg greatly swollen, and having a dark mottled appearance. Ordered tr. ferri chl. and Fowler's solution internally, after meals; same local treatment as in case 1, with the addition of applying a domette flannel roller tightly from the toes to above the ulcers, and then lightly to the knee.

The ulcer on the outer side of the leg healed readily, the one on the inner side healed until it came to a point over the tibia, then it came to a stand still, when I burnt the whole surface and edges with solid nit. silver, and applied poultices for twenty-four hours, and resumed former treatment. In six months from commencement of treatment, ulcers were well, swelling nearly all gone from foot and leg,—and I had my fee.

Case 3.—Mr. C., aged 77, farmer and mechanic. *Forty-three years ago*, after an attack of typhoid fever, an ulcer formed just above the ankle joint. When first seen by me, it presented this appearance: Ulcer extending two-thirds of the way around the leg; for an inch around the ulcer there were warty looking excrescences, ulcer about three-fourths of an inch deep. No signs of granulations; great amount of pus exuding from the dark surface, emitting a sickening odor. This case looked hopeless, but as Emerson says: "The knowledge of having done the thing before, increases courage." Prescribed the same local treatment as in case 2, and gave internally, ext. stillingiæ flu. 30 m., three times a day. The ulcer healed for a time, but slowly. I then painted the ulcer and the parts surrounding it with an ethereal solution of cantharides, poulticed it, and then proceeded as before, except that I substituted for the carbolic acid ointment, the following:

℞ Ext. eucalypti glob. flu. . ℨij,
   Vaselini . . . ℨiij,
   M. ung. . . . .

I directed the ulcer to be filled with this, night and morning. Ulcer well in five months, but foot still remains swollen.

The points I wish to insist upon in the treatment of chronic ulcers are these:

1.—Rest to the affected part.
2.—The use of the atomizer with an antiseptic solution to stimulate and cleanse, thus avoiding breaking down the weak granulations in dressing.
3.—When practicable, the use of well regulated pressure with elastic bandages.
4.—The occasional use of strong stimulants to the surface of the ulcer.
5.—Such internal treatment as may be indicated.
6.—To quote from the Westminster shorter catechism, "perseverance therein to the end."

FOREIGN CORRESPONDENCE.

Vacation Gossip.

VIENNA, September 26, 1883.

I returned to this city a few days ago after a rambling trip through Germany. Among other places visited were Munich, Nurnberg, Leipzig, Berlin and Dresden. Munich and Dresden are the great art centres of Europe and in the latter one meets almost as many English and Americans as one does natives. Berlin ranks next in size to London and Paris, and the river Spree which flows through it reminded me in some places of our own Jones' Falls. There are large universities in Munich, Leipzig and Berlin, the medical departments of which are well attended.

As I visited all these institutions during the holiday season I am sorry to say I had not the pleasure of seeing some of the medical and surgical celebrities which have made these institutes of learning so famous over the civilized world. Yet I saw enough to convince me that none of them offer the same advantage to a medical man that Vienna does. Munich is a cheaper city to live in, and in Berlin for some time past they have had clinical courses, somewhat similar to those in Vienna; but I take it for granted that when you find the graduates of these universities coming to Vienna by scores that they recognize that the clinical instruction here is superior to what they can receive at home.

Just at the present time we are having in this part of the world quite an exhibition mania. The Electrical exhibition is in progress here in the Rotunda, the building where the great exhibition of 1873 was held. The exhibition there of the medical electrical apparatus is sufficient to tempt even a non-specialist to make a purchase of a battery. The International Pharmaceutical exhibition held in this city came to a close a few weeks ago. A great many countries were represented, among them the United States, by WM. R. WARNER & Co., of Philadelphia, and PARKE, DAVIS & Co. of Detroit, who had quite a large exhibit. WM. WOOD & Co., of New York, had an exhibit of pharmaceutical literature. From a critical examination of the exhibits of some of the German countries and that of Austria, I am satisfied that for elegance and palatability, their pharmaceutical preparations will compare very favorably with those of our own country.

In the International Art exhibition in Munich, one of the pictures which attracts general attention is by Arthur Quartly, formerly of Baltimore. The subject is New York Harbor. In Berlin, the hygienic exhibition is attracting considerable attention. The exhibition proper is held in an immense building, consisting of iron and glass, with several small annexes, in the centre of a good sized park or square. I found a great many things there to interest medical men. The display of surgical instruments was very great, also of rubber goods, antiseptic bandages and surgical requisites in general. A Dr. Feust, of Leipzig has on exhibition there the model of a calf (life size) showing the condition of the animal after inoculation—the most life-like thing that I have ever seen. Two forms of apparatus for reducing the temperature of the body, one of metal, one of rubber, made in coils for the head, face, arms, breast, etc., yet all being connected and forming one apparatus. The coil being hollow, water was forced through the whole apparatus with an arrangement somewhat similar to a syphon. Two large laboratories of which Dr. Koch is the director, and fitted up in a nice manner with microscopes, specimens, etc., and one of Dr. Koch's assistants three times a week demonstrates what is to be seen in the microscopical world.

While I was away from the city an unfortunate event occurred here. Dr. Nathan Weiss, docent for practice of medicine and nervous diseases in the university of Vienna, committed suicide by hanging. He was quite a young man, (35) only married a month, had a good income from practice and his class at the university on disease of the nervous system was always well attended, and he was looked upon as the most prominent man of his age in the city. The cause of suicide is unknown. Prof.

Carl Braun of the 1st obstetrical clinic, was in charge of the Crown Prince's wife during her recent confinement. It was probably an unfortunate thing for the distinguished professor that the child was a daughter, for in this part of the world they generally give a title to the fortunate medical man who assists in the birth of a future king. This has been rather an unfortunate week in the 1st obstetrical clinic, one death from puerperal eclampsia ; treatment, hypodermic injections of morphia and chloral by the bowels. The second death was a very unfortunate case: a woman over thirty, third confinement, was brought into the wards on a stretcher, with the history of placenta praevia. She had been in charge of a midwife and doctor in the town, who attempted to turn without success, and as the hemorrhage was great they sent her immediately to the hospital. As soon as she arrived the 1st assistant turned and delivered a dead child ; he also diagnosed rupture of the uterus ; the placenta came away ten minutes later. As the woman was evidently dying, transfusion was attempted, the vein was opened in the arm, but she died before the act of transfusion was consummated. A post-mortem made later in the day showed an immense rent beginning in the vagina and extending up the left side of the uterus to the fundus. The cause of the same is thought by some to have been efforts made to deliver the child before the woman was brought into the hospital. This, of course, is purely conjectural.

WILMER BRINTON.

———◆———

THE name of that excellent technical journal, *The Electrician*, will be changed with the beginning of the new volume to the *Electrician and Electrical Engineer*. It will be edited by Mr. Frank L. Pope, an old time telegrapher and writer upon electrical science.

SOCIETY PROCEEDINGS.

American Public Health Association.
Philadelphia Medical Times Report.

The eleventh annual meeting of the American Public Health Association, held at Detroit, Michigan, which closed November 16, was one of the most successful in the history of the Association. The subjects discussed were practical, and the majority of the papers read were of more than average value. Business was dispatched with commendable speed, owing to an efficient executive committee, and the duties of presiding officer were performed with dignity and grace by Dr. E. M. Hunt.

The proceedings of the first day comprised papers on the Texas Cattle-Fever, by Dr. Salmon, of the Agricultural Department; on Swine-Plague, by Dr. J. M. Partridge, of Indiana; and a report on Actinomycosis in cattle at the Chicago stockyard, by Dr. Wm. T. Belfield which was accompanied by microscopic specimens of the appearance of the diseased tissues, and of the fungus *actinomyces*,—the cause of the disease. Dr. Salmon's paper was very elaborate, and considered the question very fully, whether the disease called "Texas Fever" was really a specific disease of cattle, or whether a number of widely-different affections were included under this name. The conclusion arrived at, after a thorough sifting of the evidence, was that Texas fever is an acute, contagious, specific disease of cattle, that it is endemic in Texas and other parts of the Southern United States, and that it may be, and is frequently spread by contagion, to other parts of the country. The paper deserves the careful study of all sanitary officers and stock-raisers. The report of Dr. Belfield on actinomycosis is of especial interest as being the first exact contribution to our knowledge of the disease made in America. As actinomycosis is communicable to man, and is invariably fatal in the latter, the value of his observations is apparent. The common name for the disease in cattle is "swell-head," or "lumpy-mouth," from the characteristic lesion, a series of tumors of the upper jaw, which on examination with a microscope shows a fungus consisting of club-shaped rods radiating from a common centre. The affected animals lose flesh, and eventually die with symptoms resembling pyemia.

The discussion on malaria was opened with a paper on its etiology by Dr. G. M. Sternberg, U. S. A. This paper was followed by equally elaborate ones from Surgeons A. A. Woodhull and Charles Smart, also of the army. Dr. Sternberg's researches, statistical and otherwise, showed that the cause of malarial fevers was not produced in the absence of heat, moisture and vegetable decomposition. The intimate nature of the cause he did not attempt to elucidate. Dr. Woodhull's views were nearly similar to those arrived at by Dr. Sternberg, while Dr. Smart struck a more practical chord by showing that malarial diseases could be caused by polluted drinking-water, and urging the necessity of more frequent and thorough analysis of drinking-waters, in order that the immediate cause of malaria might be discovered.

The discussion revealed a singular want of definiteness of opinion as to the nature and cause of malaria among those taking part in the debate. Several members, however,—among them Dr. Rohé, of Baltimore, Col. G. E. Waring, of Newport, and Dr. Wight of Detroit,—pointed out the relation of the motions of the ground-air and ground-water to the spread of malarial diseases.

In the evening a brief address of welcome, full of good sense and good humor, was delivered by the Governor of the State, who was followed by Dr. Brodie, of Detroit, and Dr. John Avery, President of the Michigan State Board of Health. The President, Dr. Hunt, then delivered his annual address. Dr. Hunt sketched briefly the origin and progress of the Association, giving a concise account of the advancement of sanitary science since its organization, and the Association's share in producing the advancement. The address was scholarly in matter, eloquent in manner, and gracefully delivered. Although occupying over an hour in delivery, it was listened to with close attention by the large audience present.

The inevitable paper on Yellow Fever appeared on the second day's programme, but was quickly disposed of, and the Association proceeded to the discussion of more profitable matters. The Adulteration of Foods was discussed by Drs. W. K. Newton, of Paterson, New Jersey, Prof. A. R. Leeds, of Hoboken, and Profs. Kedzie and Vaughn, of Michigan. The only thing clearly brought out was that laws against adulteration were of comparatively little use, because they were not properly enforced.

An excellent paper was read on the Hygiene of Schools, by Dr. C. J. Lundy, of Detroit. It was discussed by Dr. A. N. Bell, of Brooklyn, and Dr. Jones, of Massachusetts.

In the evening, addresses on Physical Training were made by Prof. Madison Watson, of N. J., and Prof. Sargent, of Cambridge, Mass. The advantages of the various systems of physical culture were clearly explained, and its importance as a part of the school curriculum was strongly urged.

Dr. James E. Reeves, Secretary of the West Virginia Board of Health, delivered an excellent address on the Usefulness of State Boards of Health in Guarding the Public Welfare. It presented in a clear light the importance of sanitary organizations, and a becoming pride was expressed by the speaker in the advanced position held by his own State. The feature of the West Virginia law regulating the practice of medicine was explained, and an exposure of what looks like a bit of very sharp practice on the part of one of the medical schools of the Southwest was made to give spice to the entertainment. Dr. Reeves apparently has little hope for reform on the part of those States lying in proximity to the borders of his own State, for he says, "Little West Virginia, nestled in the mountains, and looking into the near future for the coming time when her inexhaustible stores of native wealth shall be unlocked to hundreds of thousands of busy laborers, has proudly acknowledged allegiance to the goddess Hygeia, under whose health-inspiring banner she has already won substantial victories and benefits for the saving of her citizens. But, while flushed with the stimulus of her triumphs, she turns in sadness and with outstretched arms and pleading voice to her elder sisters by whom she is immediately surrounded,—Ohio, Pennsylvania, Maryland, and the dear old Mother State,—and says to them, "How long, oh, how long shall the land which the Lord thy God giveth thee be the *Paradsie* of quacks?"

The questions of sewage removal and final disposal, the ventilation and proper construction of sewers and water-closets, were discussed by Drs. J. H. Raymond and Bell, of Brooklyn, Mr. R. Hering, C. E., of New York, Dr. Oldright, of Canada, Col. Waring, and others who by study and experience were able to contribute to a more thorough knowledge of the subjects under discussion.

The Increase of Insanity in the United States was the subject of an able paper by Dr. Foster Pratt, of the Michigan State Board of Health, read as the closing paper of the meeting. The author showed that the percentage of insane of foreign birth in this country largely exceeded the percentage of the native insane. He advocated the passage of laws to prevent the immigration of insane persons, paupers, and criminals from foreign countries. Resolutions praying Congress to pass such laws were adopted by the Association.

The officers elected for the current year are—

President, Dr. A. L. Gihon, Medical Director, U. S. Navy.

First Vice-President, Dr. James E. Reeves, of West Virginia.

Second Vice-President, Hon. Erastus Brooks, of New York.

Secretary, Dr. Irving A. Watson, of New Hampshire.

Treasurer, Dr. J. B. Lindsley, of Tennessee.

The next meeting of the Association will be held in St. Louis in October, 1884.

The local committee, under the chairmanship of Dr. Wm. Brodie, made it pleasant for every one by their attention to the comforts of the visitors.

ANALECTS.

Boracic Acid in Cervical Endometritis.

Boracic acid is highly recommended by Dr. W. H. DeWitt in the treatment of cervical endometritis (Cinn. Lancet and Clinic). He cites a case in which, after going through the entire list of remedies used in such cases, he determined to test the value of boracic acid. Moistening a camel's hair pencil and covering it with the powder, it was carried as high up as possible; at the same time the convexity of the neck was also covered with the acid on account of excoriation. Four days later there was very decided improvement, and the acid was then applied by packing the cervix with it as firmly as admissible. The patient was directed to elevate the hips and remain in that position fo two or three hours, in hopes that some of the acid would find its way to the parts above the cervix. In one week another examination was made, when it was found that all inflammation had disappeared. — *Weekly Med. Review*.

Mercuric Bichloride as an Antiseptic.

Bichloride of mercury has long been known to possess superior antiputrefactive properties, but its toxic effects have prevented its general use among surgeons. It has been found that in solution varying in strength from 1 to 1,000 to 1 to 20,000, bacteria were killed, or their further development checked. The bacillus of splenic fever which resists the action of all antiseptic agents, was destroyed in a solution of strength 1 to 1,000; in a solution of 1 to 5,000, its growth was markedly retarded. Kummell was the first to attempt practical tests of the bichloride as an antiseptic wound dressing, using a 1 to 5,000 solution. He then increased the irrigating fluid to 1 to 1,000, and even to a one per cent. solution without dangerous symptoms supervening. On account of the action of the bichloride upon instruments, and the danger of the atomization of even a dilute solution it cannot be used as a spray.

Kummell deprecates the use of sponges except when required in the operation itself; the cheapness of the bichloride justifying its free use in cleansing the parts. The floor and walls of his operating room are scoured and scrubbed with the solution and no accident has yet occurred to either attendants or patients. In persons with sensitive skin the bichloride may give rise to an eczematous condition of the parts surrounding the wound. In wounds in which putrefactive changes have already occurred, the mercuric bichloride solution quickly banishes the odor and arrests the septic processes.

The dressings devised by Kummell consist of sublimated gauze and cotton, silk, catgut, oil and inorganic materials. These latter comprise powdered glass, sand, coal ashes, asbestos, lint made from spun glass, and, for the purpose of drainage, capillary threads of spun glass.

In order to have a powder dressing he takes common white sand, sifts it well, and then heats it in a covered vessel over a coal fire; upon cooling it is mixed with an ethereal solution of the bichloride and kept for use in glass stoppered bottles. To make the preparation, 10 grms. of the bichloride is dissolved in 100 grms. of ether; this quantity is amply sufficient to perfectly impregnate 10 kilo. of previously heated sand. This sand dressing can be used in many ways, as, for instance, filling in previously disinfected and bloodless wound cavities where primary union cannot be hoped for. The under dressing is not to be disturbed for several weeks, or until healing has taken place. The outer portions are removed from time to time as the secretions find their way through and dry thereon, and new pieces are supplied in their stead. When irrigation of the parts is required the solution of the bichloride is used, and new sand applied where the old has been washed away. Wounds thus treated are found to be aseptic and odorless. Large cavities can be kept filled with the sand for a week without the appearance of a single drop of pus. The rapidly forming granulations push the sand outward from the bottom of the cavity, and when removed, disclose the wound firmly cicatrized as under a scab. A great advantage of this dressing will be found in its applicability to compound fractures, and other injuries requiring the use of a plaster of Paris dressing. Here, on account of the scantiness of the discharge under this dressing, the fixed apparatus may be left *in situ* for several weeks without being disturbed.

In four cases of Pirogoff's amputation, where this antiseptic dressing was used, healing took place without reaction of any kind, bony consolidation and absolutely dry linear cicatrices being present in from ten to fourteen days. The record is the same in degree in the treatment of ulcers, suppurating joint cavities, old fistulous openings and sinuses, which had previously resisted iodoform treatment.

Another feature of Kummell's antiseptic method consists in the employment of glass wool or wadding. This material is derived from annealed glass rods, which are capable, when heated, of being drawn into long delicate fibres, having a diameter of from 0.01 mm, to 0.006 mm. These can be compressed into masses for convenient use. These masses can be rendered antiseptic by immersing them in the bichloride solution. A dry dressing thus prepared will absorb secretions very rapidly.—*Annals of Anat. and Surgery.*

The Proper Feeding of Infants.

The conclusions presented by the Committee to the Eleventh German Physicians' Association in regard to the alimentation of young children are (Med. News): 1. The natural food of children, mothers' milk, is to be preferred above all others. 2. Only in case of positive contra-indication, or non-appearance of the milk, should a wet-nurse be employed. 3. Only in cases of impossibility of obtaining a wet-nurse should artificial food be employed. 4. The contra-indication against the mother nursing, is actual disease or a predisposition to disease. 5. Hereditary syphilis demands the milk of the mother; that of the wet nurse should only be used with great caution. 6. Examination of a given specimen of milk furnishes no clue as to its value in a given case. 7. Good cow's milk alone is fit to take the place of woman's milk as food for the child. 8. The quality of good, sweet cow's milk for a child which must be artificially fed is one of the most important essentials in the hygiene of young children. 9. All children's foods, including Liebig's soup(food), on account of the large quantity of starch contained in them, are unfit for children during the first month.—*Weekly Med. Review.*

Subscribe now

Treatment of Whooping Cough.

Croton-chloral in whooping cough is spoken of by Dr. Webb in the *American Practitioner*. He relates an experience of two hundred cases. It was found to be well borne by children, with rare exceptions. To get its full value it must be given in large enough doses to produce quite a marked effect. A child a year old will bear a grain every four hours, and it should be kept up for the first week, after which the cough is usually so much relieved that the dose may be lessened. It seldom fails to bring the cough under entire control within a fort-night. Children from ten to twelve years old require two grains, while an adult will not often bear more than four grains. An eligible mixture is a drachm dissolved in two ounces each of comp. tr. cardamon and glycerine. Sometimes good results have attended its combination with tr. belladonna. No appreciable benefit was derived from a combination with the bromides.

Hot Water For Inflamed Mucous Surfaces.

Dr. George R. Shepherd, Hartford, Conn., says in the *Medical Record*: "I have used hot water as a gargle for the past six or eight years, having been led to do so from seeing its beneficial effects in gynecology. In acute pharyngitis and tonsillitis, if properly used at the commencement of the attack, it constitutes one of our most effective remedies, being frequently promptly curative. To be of service it should be used in considerable quantity (a half pint or pint) at a time, and just as hot as the throat will tolerate. I have seen many cases of acute diseases thus aborted and can commend the method with great confidence. I believe it may be taken as an established fact that in the treatment of inflammation generally, and those of the mucous membranes in particular, moist heat is of service, and in most cases hot water is preferable to steam. All are familiar with its use in ophthalmia and conjunctivitis, as also in inflammation of the external and middle ear, and I feel confident that those who employ it for that most annoying of all slight troubles to prescribe for, viz., a cold in the head, or acute coryza, will seldom think of using the irritating drugs mentioned in the books, nor of inducing complete anesthesia with chloroform in preference to the hot water douche.

IN an article upon the administration of quinine, by Dr. David Young, in the Practitioner, the following conclusions are drawn: 1. Never give quinine in antipyretic doses in cases where the bowels are confined and the secretion of urine is scanty. 2. In cases where it is being administered, and an increase of dose is desirable, this may be safely done if the skin, bowels and kidneys maintain their normal functional activity. 5. In many cases of remittent and intermittent fevers, the combination of the drug with chloride of ammonium, or a salt of potash or soda, is likely to be more easily tolerated as well as more useful than if it be administered in a pure form. 4. During the administration of quinine, should a headache come on or increase in intensity, the case requires the most careful attention.— *Weekly Med. Rev.*

Drs. Chas. A. Cooke and Ralph B. Watkins, resident physicians at Bay View Asylum, Baltimore, Md., have some observations on picric acid as a test for albumen. They found that in malarial cases in which quinine and cinchonidine were being used in large doses, these alkaloids were excreted in the urine, and gave, with picric acid, a reaction simulating albumen. Solutions of the alkaloids were found to give similar precipitates.— *Medical News.—Polyclinic.*

Subscribe to the MEDICAL CHRONICLE. $1.00 in advance.

The Medical Chronicle.

A Monthly Journal for the Practitioner.

GEORGE H. ROHÉ, M. D., Editor.

☞ It is requested that all literary and business communications, books for review, exchanges, etc., be addressed to, and all checks, drafts and post-office orders drawn to the order of

DR. GEORGE H. ROHÉ,
95 Park Avenue, - - - - Baltimore, Md.

BALTIMORE, DECEMBER, 1883.

EDITORIAL.

Anti-Vivisectionism.

For several years past the discussion of the vivisection question has occupied a large share of the time of the more intelligent classes in England and Germany, and recently a mild outbreak occurred in France, where an excitable female savagely assaulted Dr. Brown Séquard with an umbrella, just as the distinguished physiologist was demonstrating an experiment upon a living animal before a popular audience. We had hoped that the practical American mind would resist this craze, but it seems we were mistaken. An American anti-vivisection society has been organized with headquarters in Philadelphia. We have received from the society a number of tracts, consisting of articles and extracts from speeches of Dr. H. J. Bigelow of Boston, Mr. Lawson Tait, Dr. Chas. Bell Taylor and others of Great Britain, strongly denouncing the practice of vivisection. According to these authors experimental investigations in physiology are objectionable for three reasons: 1, the great cruelty involved; 2, the demoralizing influence of the practice upon the pupil and experimenter; and 3, the barrenness of the results obtained.

If it were necessary to convince any of our readers of the baselessness of these charges, and if we had the space to devote to the purpose, facts could be given in abundance in opposition to the arguments of the anti-vivisectionists. Our reason for taking notice of the society at all is merely to call attention to its evident object, which is to endeavor to restrict the liberty of scientific investigation by obtaining the enactment of laws in the several states against physiological experiments upon living animals.

We trust that physicians will be watchful and prevent any tampering with legislatures, which may tend to restrict the liberty of teaching. Allow this first step to be gained, and soon post-mortem examinations and dissections will be likewise prohibited, on the ground that the human body is too sacred a thing to be subjected to the indignity of the anatomist's knife.

The Index Medicus.

It is a matter for sincere regret that less than *one per cent.* of the regular physicians in this country, are sufficiently interested in medical literature to give active support to such an important publication as the *Index Medicus*. We have on several occasions called attention to the very great value of this publication to every physician who cares for the scientific and practical advancement of his profession.

The publisher has just issued a circular to the subscribers of the *Index* stating that owing to the lack of patronage received from the profession an increase of the subscription price would be necessary, or, that its publication would be discontinued. The latter event would be a serious loss to medical literature in this country, and we trust there will be found sufficient national and professional pride among American physicians to prevent such a misfortune.

Mr. F. Leypoldt, 31 and 32 Park

Row, New York, will give all desired information concerning the future prospects and subscription price of the *Index*. All who propose sustaining the publication, should write to him at once.

CURRENT LITERATURE.

Sanitary and Statistical Report of the Surgeon-General of the Navy, for the year 1881.

The appointment of Dr. Philip S. Wales as Surgeon-General of the Navy, four years ago, signalized the beginning of a new era in the history of the naval medical service. In the naval laboratory established by the present Surgeon-General, sanitary investigations into the organic constituents of the air and of the soil have been made by Surgeon J. H. Kidder and his successor, Past Assistant Surgeon T. H. Streets. The reports for 1880 and 1881 give excellent evidence of the thorough manner in which these observations were conducted. A very full statistical report of the morbidity rate in the entire navy, and on each vessel in commission, is also contained in the volume. The sanitary report for each vessel is accompanied by a chart showing the percentage of carbon dioxide, relative humidity, average monthly temperature on both spar and berth decks, days of snow or rain, number of days on which the berth-deck was wet, and the percentage of sick to total strength. It is of course evident that statistical tables based upon such a thorough method must yield much more accurate results than the old systems of "vital statistics" so-called.

Concluding the volume is a report on the "Pharmacopœias of all Nations," by Surgeon J. M. Flint, which has already been noticed in the CHRONICLE.

The volume reflects the highest credit upon Surgeon-General Wales and the department of which he is the head.

Notes and Memoranda. Medical and Anthropological. Botanical and Ornithological. Made during the cruise of the Revenue Steamer Corwin in Alaska and the N. W. Arctic Ocean in 1881. By Irving C. Rosse, M. D., John Muir, E. W. Nelson and T. H. Bean. 4 to pp. 120.

The "notes" of Dr. Rosse are the most interesting contribution to our knowledge of the habits and customs of the natives of the extreme north-western appendix to the United States made since the publication of De Chamisso's fascinating "Reise um die Welt." The remarks on the diseases peculiar to the natives, the effects of alcohol, of climate, general anthropological notes, and a brief account of Arctic mosquitoes are exceedingly interesting. Mr. Muir's Botanical Notes on Alaska, and Mr. Nelson's report on the birds of Behring sea and the Arctic Ocean, add to the value of the volume.

What to Do First in Emergencies. By C. W. Dulles, M. D. P. Blakiston, Son & Co., Philadelphia.

This little book is written for the general public, and will prove to such of the laity as can understand it, a useful manual.

A number of important suggestions are made in the "Preliminary Remarks," the first of which is that the by-standers should be prevented from crowding around the injured, and thus cutting off the supply of fresh air. Another very important suggestion is that the surgeon should be notified as to the nature of the injury so that he can bring suitable instruments.

The laity are very properly cautioned against giving large doses of alcohol. The usual method of artificial respiration is given for drowning and suffocation by gases.

Some of the methods given for the removal of foreign bodies from the throat, such as the use of scissors as forceps, and a bent hair pin as a blunt hook, would appear to be dangerous in the hands of an inexperienced person, and should only be advised when it is impossible to get a surgeon, and the sufferer is in imminent danger of suffocation.

The great danger of attempting to remove foreign bodies from the ear by means of hard instruments, is very properly cautioned against. Different forms of unconsciousness are very accurately described, and the indications for their treatment clearly and correctly given.

The treatment recommended for ordinary burns is very judicious; but for burns with acids, washing and ordinary treatment for burns are recommended, and the application of alkalies is omitted.

Directions are given for the reduction of several important dislocations. Among them those of the humerus and inferior maxilla. Persons ignorant of anatomy would be likely to do harm in attempting to reduce dislocations of so important a joint as the shoulder. No special directions are given as to the after-treatment. This is an important omission, as great harm may be done by using a joint too early after dislocation.

Very explicit directions are given for the treatment of various forms of hemorrhage, and the more common cases of poisoning. On the whole, this manual gives a clear description of the more common surgical emergencies, with the best and simplest methods of treatment, given in plain English and with few technicalities. Its directions will be readily understood by the general reader, and if carefully studied by the laity, many harmful procedures so commonly witnessed in medical and surgical emergencies, will be avoided.

Lindsay and Blckiston's Visiting List. Thirty-third year of publication.

This old favorite comes to us again improved in many points. In addition to the posological tables which have been revised to accord with the new Pharmacopœia, a diagram of the chest to aid in the diagnosis of thoracic diseases, and illustrations of Sylvester's method of artificial respiration are given. For compactness, neatness and durability, it is not exceeded by any similar publication, and its price makes it perhaps the most desirable of all.

Health Aphorisms; and an essay on the Struggle for Life against Civilization, Luxury and Æstheticism. By Frank H Hamilton, A. M., M. D. Late Professor of Surgery in Bellevue Hospital Medical College and Surgeon to Bellevue Hospital, etc. Bermingham & Co., New York, 1882. Price 50 cents.

This little book is directed to lay, rather than professional, readers. Its object is to disseminate a knowledge of the laws of health among the people.

Many popular errors regarding these subjects are pointed out. Many practical suggestions are made, which, if adopted, would in a short time improve the health and physique of the present generation.

The second part embraces an essay on "The Struggle for Life against Civilization, Luxury and Æstheticism," which was read before the New York Academy of Medicine, and abounds with hints regarding house sanitation and its relation to disease. Although primarily intended for popular use, we know many physicians who would be benefited by a careful perusal of these terse aphorisms.

The Physicians' Daily Pocket Record. By S. W. Butler, M. D., Eighteenth year. Philadelphia, D. G. Brinton. Price, $1.50.

This excellent visiting list contains a number of new features which make it a very desirable daily companion for the physician. The very full posological table gives the doses both in the old and in the metric systems, so that the relation of the two can be seen at a glance. The daily record is without printed dates, so that the use of the book can be commenced at any time.

PAMPHLETS.

The Sanitary Control of Epidemic Diseases. By John B. Hamilton, M. D., Surgeon-General U. S. M. Hospital Service. Reprint from Appleton's Annual Cyclopedia, 1882. Woman as a Physician. The Introductory address to the class of the Woman's Medical College of Baltimore. By Prof. E. F. Cordell, M. D., etc. Relation of Eye and Spinal Diseases. By A. Friedenwald, M. D., Prof. of Eye and Ear Diseases, College of Physicians and Surgeons, Baltimore. Reprint from Transactions of Med. and Chir. Faculty of Md. The Work of Health Officers, and of Local Boards of Health in Michigan, including Duties under Laws amended and passed in 1883. Circular from Michigan State Board of Health. Diagnosis of Ovarian Tumors. Lectures by Edw. Borck, A. M., M. D., etc., St. Louis, Mo. Report of Proceedings of the Illinois State Board of Health. Quarterly meeting held at Chicago, October 18-19, 1883. Proceedings of Michigan State Board of Health meeting of October 19, 1883. The Uselessness of Vivisection upon Animals as a method of Scientific Research. By Lawson Tait, F. R. C. S., etc. Extracts from the Evidence given before the Royal Commission on the Practice of Subjecting Live Animals to Experiments for Scientific Purposes. Dr. Bell Taylor on Vivisection. Cottage Hospitals. By L. W. Baker, M. D. Medical Supervision of the Public Schools. By L. W. Baker, M. D., Baldwinville, Mass.

THE President has appointed Dr. Robert Murray as Surgeon-General of the army.

FLOTSAM.

THE first Sanitary Convention of Maryland, held in Baltimore on November 27th and 28th, was a decided success.

WITH the beginning of the new year the *Sanitarian*, which is now published weekly, will return to its monthly form. The subscription price will remain at $4.00 per year.

WE desire to return thanks to our editorial brethren, Owens of the *Northwestern Lancet*, and Connor of the *Detroit Lancet*, for fraternal courtesies extended during our recent Western trip.

THE name of *New Remedies* will be changed to *The American Druggist* with the new volume to begin in January. The subscription price is reduced to $1.00 per year, and the reading matter will be increased.

DR. DUDLEY S. REYNOLDS has resigned the editorship of the *Medical Herald*, and will be succeeded by Drs. Edward Miller and W. H. Galt. Bro. Reynolds in his valedictory, promises to "complete an *undertaking* of authorship in the near future." Does he mean that he will attend to the burial of medical writers? If so, let Mulheron look out!

A JOINT committee of the Board of Trade and Cotton Exchange of Mobile has prepared for distribution a well-written and neatly printed and illustrated pamphlet giving an account of the business and other attractions of the beautiful old city by the Gulf. The brochure, which is the production of Mr. Erwin Craighead, an experienced journalist, is crammed full of facts and figures grouped in an interesting manner. We would advise those of our readers who propose going South, either for business or pleasure, to send for a copy of the publication and familiarize themselves with the social, business or climatic advantages of the Gulf City.

The Medical Chronicle.

BALTIMORE, JANUARY, 1884.

ORIGINAL LECTURES.

ARTICLE I.

NEURASTHENIA.

A Lecture delivered at the College of Physicians and Surgeons, Baltimore.

BY A. B. ARNOLD, M. D.,

Professor of Clinical Medicine and Diseases of the Nervous System.

[Reported for the MEDICAL CHRONICLE.]

The late Dr. Beard of New York described under the name of neurasthenia, a functional affection of the nervous system, which he alleged to be extremely common among the adult male population of the United States. He says, "One reason why neurasthenia has been so long neglected, is that the symptoms are in some instances so subtle and difficult of analysis and classification. One who has never seen and carefully examined a large number of cases of this disease would not believe it possible that it could manifest itself in so many different ways." Prof. Erb* adopts the nomenclature of Dr. Beard, and devotes a short chapter to the discussion of the disorder which it implies, although he does not claim for it the multiplicity of symptoms which Dr. Beard has enumerated. Nearly all the morbid phenomena which are said

*Ziemssen's Cyclopedia.

to characterize neurasthenia are usually classified under different affections, chiefly hysteria, spinal irritation and hypochondriasis. It will hardly be disputed that many vague and ill-defined symptoms come frequently under notice, which cannot be satisfactorily referred to maladies of such uncertain pathology and inconstant clinical features. Experience fully sustains what physiological teachings leads us to expect, that numerous and diversified disturbances of the nervous system can be directly traced to the depressing influences of physical over-exertion and mental strain and worry. Whatever other causes may be assumed to favor their occurrence, and among these seminal losses and neuropathic diathesis stand pre-eminent, it is but fair to consider nervous exhaustion a fruitful source of manifold disorders. The practical importance of recognizing such a condition, under the many disguises it may assume is apparent.

CLINICAL HISTORY.

Among the great array of subjective symptoms, variable and fluctuating in character, even in the same patient, there is none more constant and conspicuous than a feeling of muscular weakness and unusual tiredness. Of hardly less frequency is the existence of lumbar and dorsal pain, which is apt to extend to the occiput and vertex. Sometimes patients complain of a distressing feeling of constriction around the chest, or of a choky sensation, dyspnœa and cardiac excitement. This is occasionally associated with epigastric uneasiness and annoying eructation. The hyperesthetic condition causes shifting pains of a neuralgic character in different parts of the body. Micturition and defecation produce considerable discomfort, and the sexual function seems to be enfeebled. Young men in whom some of these symptoms are associated with spermatorhœa or nocturnal emissions evince much apprehension of becoming victims of serious spinal disease, or of being threatened with impotency or paralysis. The latter event particularly suggests itself by the sensations of numbness, formication and coldness in the lower extremities. Real paralysis does, however, not occur, although neurasthenic persons are incapable of sustained muscular efforts, and may be somewhat unsteady in their gait. Under these circumstances, a hypochondriacal disposition is not seldom developed.

Neurasthenia is sometimes rapidly established in persons of an hereditary tendency to neurotic diseases, but generally its progress is slow and of variable intensity.

DIAGNOSIS.

It is above all necessary in the diagnosis of this disorder, to inquire into the previous history of the patient, his habits and present pursuits. A thorough examination and sifting of the symptoms must be instituted, as they may be easily mistaken for those of organic disease of the spinal cord. The beginning of *chronic myelitis* is distinguished by paresis or paralysis of the lower extremities, the anesthesia, and enfeeblement of the sphincters. The early stage of *ataxia* is characterized by the fulgurant pains in the limbs, the ocular disturbances, the dullness of the patient when his eyes are closed, and the absence of the patellar knee reflex.

TREATMENT.

Hygienic measures are of the first importance in the management of every case of neurasthenia. It is necessary that the patient change that mode of life which led to brain exhaustion, spinal irritability, and enfeeblement of the general nervous system. He may require absolute rest and quiet, or be benefited by exercise that does not cause fatigue. The recuperative influence of mountain air, or a visit to the sea shore, should not be neglected; of sleep; substantial, but easily digested food, and a judicious course of tonic remedies, especially iron, quinia and strychnia complete the constitutional treatment.

Much benefit is sometimes derived from the frequent sponging of the spine with sea-salt water and friction with a rough towel. The restoration of the muscular vigor may be assisted by massage and general faradisation.

Among the empirical remedies which have been used in the treatment of neurasthenia, it appears that phosphorus, arsenic and zinc are favorably spoken of by some observers. Monobromate of camphor in doses of from 2 to 4 grains, occasionally relieves the headache. The sedative action of cannabis indica is said to be of special service in this neurosis. My own experience induces me to prefer small doses of chlorate hydrate and morphia in combination. Decided relief of the spinal pain is sometimes obtained from the application of ether spray.

ARTICLE II.
EPITHELIOMA (RODENT ULCER) OF THE HAND. SIMPLE ULCER OF THE FOREARM.
A Clinical Lecture
By GEORGE H. ROHÉ, M. D.,
Professor of Hygiene and Clinical Dermatology, College of Physicians and Surgeons, Baltimore.

GENTLEMEN:—The first case I show you to-day is one which has been under observation of myself and Dr. Huck, the chief of the clinic, for nearly two weeks. The patient is a man about 60 years of age, and for the past four months has had upon the back of his left hand, over the fourth and fifth metacarpal bone, a circular ulcer which has gradually become larger and deeper until it is now as large as a silver half-dollar, and about a quarter of an inch in depth. The ulcer is not painful or sensitive, and as you see, I can squeeze it and touch its surface without causing any complaint. The patch is perfectly dry, and those of you who are near enough, can see that it is studded with small papillary elevations, giving it an irregular surface. The border of the ulcer is somewhat elevated and sloping down to the mamillated base, which, as you can see, is about a quarter of an inch below the surface of the normal skin. The border and base feel hard and infiltrated. At first I thought this infiltration might be inflammatory, and for that reason kept the patient under observation, applying merely a mild, soothing, ointment, and occasionally painting with a solution of nitrate of silver (3 i to ℥ i). Under this treatment, I expected this induration to disappear if it was merely inflammatory thickening, but anticipated no change if, as was probable, the hardness was dependent upon epithelial infiltration. The treatment has had no effect, and the spot appears to be a little larger than it was two weeks ago.

The patient says that the growth first appeared as a little pimple which gradually became larger until it has arrived at its present size; there has never been any pain in it, but it has never shown any tendency to heal, although various ointments had been used by the advice of apothecaries, and other persons equally competent to treat the affection. He finally, seeing that his hand "got rapidly no better," came to the dispensary for proper treatment.

The history of the case as I have given it to you, taking into consideration the patient's age, his apparent good physical condition, the steady enlargement of the ulcer in size, and its unresponsiveness to mild treatment, point to the diagnosis of epithelioma. On examination, I find no lymphatic enlargement present, nor did I expect to find any.

The occurrence of cancer is so thoroughly associated in the minds of the laity and of many practitioners and students, with *pain* as a symptom, that I desire to state here that destructive epitheliomatous ulceration not infrequently occurs, where there is no pain whatever. I recall a case that I saw last spring, of epithelioma beginning in the right nipple and in the course of four years destroying a surface fully fifty square inches in extent, with numerous secondary nodules of the skin of the trunk, in which the only subjective symptom complained of was a slight itching. Another case was that of a man of 38, who had an epitheliomatous ulcer about six inches square on his back, just above the sacrum. This patient also had never complained of pain in the ulcer. The absence of pain, then, is not of sufficient importance to enter into consideration in making a diagnosis.

The lesion on this patient's hand is what is termed in most English textbooks *rodent ulcer;* but the researches of Thiersch, Waldeyer, Moore, Billroth, Jonathan Hutchinson and Dr. J. Collins Warren, have shown that the disease is pathologically the same as epithelial cancer, although clinically it is not so malignant, progressing more slowly, not involving the system generally, and being less likely to return if removed by operation.

All forms of cancer are characterized by the presence of epithelial cells in abnormal arrangement in places where they do not normally belong. In fact, anatomically, cancer may be roughly defined as: a morbid growth, the essential feature of which is epithelium out of place. In the mild forms of epithelioma, such as the so-called rodent ulcer, the epithelial infiltration progresses superficially, rather than downwards into the deeper tissues and vessels; as Mr. Moore expresses it, "rodent cancer is eminently local and centrifugal." Why one form of epithelioma should destroy the deeper tissues and infect the system, and another prove merely locally destructive is not explicable at present, but Waldeyer has made an ingenious suggestion which may help to a solution of the problem. He says that in the form of cancer known as rodent ulcer there is always found an unusually profuse development of small granulation cells in the connective-tissue substratum of the ulcer, that is, in the corium. He suggests that perhaps this cellular infiltration prevents the penetration of the proliferating epithelia into the deeper tissues, and that the progressive ulceration gets rid of both the epithelial and granulation cells.

In view of these facts, rodent ulcer may be said to be potentially malignant, that is to say, although it does not ordinarily tend to destroy deeper structures, infect the system, or recur when removed by operation, yet at times it does become a very malignant growth, one that may with truth be termed a cancer.

In the treatment of all malignant or semi-malignant growths, such as cancer, sarcoma, lupus or tuberculosis, it is of the first importance to remove the morbid tissue *thoroughly*. An inefficient use of the knife, curette, scissors or cautery is generally worse than letting the growth entirely alone.

Probably excision, if it can be thoroughly performed, gives the best results in removing malignant growths. The extent to which the tissue is to be removed can be distinctly marked out, and in many cases the edges of the wound can be brought together by suture, and primary union obtained; thus avoiding prolonged suppuration, and perhaps an unsightly scar. But, in this case, where the area occupied by the morbid process is already considerable, and where the use of the knife would result in the waste of normal tissue that can ill be spared, I think it would be more advisable to resort to another method.

That which I propose to use is one which has given me satisfactory results in other similar cases, and above all in cases of lupus, of which disease I shall have more to say at some other time. This method is known as erasion, or scraping. By means of a small, spoon-shaped instrument with sharp edges—called a curette—all the morbid tissue is scraped away. Considerable pressure is used, in order to dig out any epithelial plugs which may have penetrated deeper than the general base of the growth. The patient is stout-hearted and is willing to undergo the operation without an anesthetic, although I have told him it would be pretty painful.

As I begin digging out the morbid tissue, you see the instrument meets with hardly any resistance until the healthy fibrous tissue of the border and base of the growth is reached. Here, in spite of considerable force, I can detach nothing. I continue scraping until I have removed all the tissue from a space about an inch and a half in diameter and one quarter of an inch deep. The bleeding, as you see, is pretty free, but will presently cease spontaneously. Having removed all the morbid tissue I could scrape away, I now take a piece of fused nitrate of silver and thoroughly cauterize the surface in order that I may not leave any particle of the growth behind to infect the healthy structures. The dressing for a few days will be simply dry cotton and after the eschar comes off, the wound will be dressed with iodoform ointment. I believe I have seen good effects from the use of arsenic internally in cases of cancer, and I shall therefore direct this patient to have three drops of Fowler's solution, gradually increased to six drops, three times a day.

[In three weeks the wound had entirely healed, the spot being covered with a flat, soft, pliable, healthy-looking scar.]

I now show you another case of ulcer on the forearm of this little girl of twelve. She has had it about two months. It is about an inch and a quarter in diameter, and of an oval shape, the long diameter being parallel with the axis of the arm. Contrary to what we observed in the preceding case, the surface of this ulcer projects above the normal skin, and the florid looking granulations with which it is covered, are bathed in pus. The patient looks somewhat anemic and broken down in health.

The history is that about two months ago, a small boil appeared on the arm, which was poulticed until it opened, and was then dressed with an ointment procured at the apothecary's,

Upon inquiry, I find that this ointment produced a free suppuration, and the sore became larger instead of smaller. You will generally find that apothecaries and most other amateur doctors, whether male or female, use irritant applications where soothing ones should be used, and in this way they unintentionally make a good deal of practice for you, for the patients getting no better, or perhaps worse, will eventually in most cases seek relief at the hands of a properly qualified physician. This is a simple ulcer occurring in an anemic individual, and under proper treatment ought to heal rapidly. The ulcer will be painted with a solution of nitrate of silver (3 i to ℥ i) to repress the exuberant granulations, and dressed with freshly prepared oxide of zinc ointment. Internally the patient will take 15 drops of tincture of the chloride of iron, three times a day.

FOREIGN CORRESPONDENCE.

VIENNA, Nov. 1st, 1883.

Since about the middle of October the courts, yards, etc., of the Vienna General Hospital have presented quite a busy appearance, owing to the return of the students to the lectures, clinics, etc. Most of the professors delivered their introductories on the 15th. Prof. Kaposi began on the 12th in his preliminary remarks on diseases of the skin; he dwelt for some time on the thorough knowledge of the physiological anatomy of the skin and its appendages as being necessary for a thorough understanding of the many forms of skin disease. He made a great many divisions of skin diseases, viz.: Diseases of the epidermis, of the blood vessels, of the nerves, etc., and made two divisions of all skin diseases in general, viz.: One leaving scars on the patient, the other not. His lectures are purely of a clinical character, each one being illustrated by from one to twenty cases of the disease on which he is lecturing.

Twice a week the lectures are delivered in the wards of the hospital, and in two hours he has before you in rapid succession 50 to 75 patients with all forms of skin disease. One can not help being impressed with the fact that very little medicine is given internally, except when the patient is very debilitated, or has syphilis; the treatment is almost entirely local. As encouragement to those who become discouraged in the treatment of chronic skin diseases, I would state that even the son-in-law of the great Hebra does not cure all his patients, for you see patients here who have been under treatment for 3-6 months, sometimes a year, yet far from being well. In acute eczema in children he is using lycopodium, in adults starch. After the acute stage has passed away he orders emplast. saponis with or without (10 per cent.) of acidum salicylic, which is cut into strips and left on the inflamed surface for 24 hours. This preparation seems to be quite a favorite, for he orders the same in many other forms of skin disease, such as psoriasis, lupus, etc. Parasitic diseases are common, and often the microscope is brought into requisition to show the parasite; for example, this morning in speaking of scabies, he had several patients with the disease at the clinic, and removed from their fingers several of the insects which cause this troublesome disease.

Prof. Kaposi is a man over 40, and below the average height, has a Jewish countenance, sharp eyes, talks fast, sees a great many patients and dismisses them almost too rapidly for the students to thoroughly appreciate each special disease. Professor Neumann has his apartment adjoining Kaposi, and like the latter, has an immense clinic, devoted entirely to diseases of the skin and syphilis (especially the latter). Neumann's lectures are generally well attended, as he is very humorous at times, his poor patients being the victims of his jokes. Last week he showed some patients who had been treated (without mercury as an experiment) for some time after the appearance of the primary sore, but he thought that the secondary symptoms were more severe than they would have been if they had received mercurial treatment somewhat earlier, and he concluded his remarks by saying: "That while the treatment of syphilis without mercury was well enough in theory, he had found it would not work in practice."

In Neumann's wards, as well as in Kaposi's, the male patients are in charge of female attendants, and to one who is not accustomed to seeing this, it is quite a novel sight. Recently in Neumann's ward he opened a large bubo, and his patient who was quite a large and muscular man, showed some indication of fainting, when he was picked up as if he was a child, by one of the female attendants and carried back to his bed some distance away. All patients as a rule in both clinics are exhibited naked before the students, sometimes on a raised chair, at other times they walk around among the students for inspection. This no doubt is a very practical way of studying the disease under consideration, but to me individually, it is simply disgusting to see the poor women exposed as they are to a crowd of students.

There seems to be at the present time a tendency among those, viz.: doctors, professors, assistants, etc., who give private courses here in various branches to increase the price of the same, and make the duration of their courses shorter, so that I think in the future medical men who come to Vienna either to qualify themselves for general or special practice, will find it much more expensive than in the past. In selecting from among these courses, one must use some discrimination, for here as elsewhere, you find incompetent teachers, and one sometimes finds out after he has paid his gulden that he has been "taken in." I have had one such experience since I have been here, and that with a gentleman who is quite well known in our country, through his book on diseases of the nervous system, viz., Rosenthal. He is a man over 40, is small in stature, talks fast with his hands and mouth, *and says nothing*. Such was the verdict in the course recently given by him on "diseases of the nervous system," which was to be six weeks in duration, and was attended by some 20 doctors, most of them being men who had seen some practice, and some of them here especially to study this branch of medicine. All of the Americans ceased attending before the course was half completed. I think those gentlemen in our country who are so fond of quoting him as an authority on his branch, would cease to do so on more intimate acquaintance with the gentleman, I am satisfied that his book is a mere compilation. A great many American students are here at the present time. Harvard College sends more than any other single American college, some of the Western colleges follow close behind in point of numbers. Baltimore has four or five representatives, the majority of them are working hard, and studious in every respect. You can distinguish an American from a German student, not only by address and personal appearance, but there is a push and bustle in an American's manners that is not observed among the Germans. Just at the present time we are having quite a novelty here in shape of four lady doctors from America. Two of them being from Chicago, the others from the North. One of them quite young, and decidedly handsome; they attend Billroth's clinic regularly and seem to take as much interest in operations on the genito-urinary and rectal organs, as on any other portion of the human body. While they are treated very courteously by every one, yet their presence on such occasions does not call forth very favorable comments from the students who are present. W. BRINTON, M. D,

ANALECTS.

Alleged Increase of Insanity in the United States.

We must confess our inability to understand how it comes to pass that the professors of statistical science, in reference particularly to what are known as "vital statistics," do not yet perceive the fallacy of "increments" of integral classes of the population, calculated on the bases of successive censuses. Even if there be a given number for the whole population at one period of census-taking, and another number—say ten per cent. greater—when the next census is taken, it does not necessarily follow that the population has increased ten per cent. in the interval of like duration. It may very well happen that some devastating war or epidemic may have prevented the survival of a certain percentage of those who were alive at the commencement of the earlier interval until the close of it, so that the difference between the numbers polled at the beginning and at the end of the earlier interval may not have been so great as it would otherwise have been, and not so great comparatively as the difference between the census taken at the commencement and the census taken at the conclusion of the latter interval. It seems to be forgotten that mere difference between returns at successive periods throws no statistical light whatever on what has happened in the interval. Comparisons of birth-rate and death-rate are needed to interpret the import of successive census returns, and without such comparisons these returns are not simply worthless, but may be actually misleading. Now, when we come to compare the returns made to the Commissioners in Lunacy at the commencement of each year, we are comparing successive censuses, and no sort of conclusion can be drawn without taking steps to ascertain how any increase which may have occurred is to be explained. Has the number of admissions been greater during this year than formerly? If so, to what extent has this been due to the fact that, more accommodation having been provided, it has been occupied? Again, has there been any proportional decrease in the death-rate? Because, if so, obviously a number of individuals who, according to precedent, would have disappeared from the roll during the year have not disappeared, and now help to swell the total? Further, have any changes in policy or administration, such as a broader interpretation of the meaning of "insanity," naturally leading to the extension of the class thus designated, or greater vigilance on the part of those charged with the duty of searching out and classifying the "insane," occurred? Clearly, these and other factors of the result must be examined and estimated before any trust can be placed in the returns made. Meanwhile these returns are mischief-making; they keep up a vicious circle of activity, producing an increase of asylum accommodation which we believe to be perfectly unnecessary, and which must inevitably lead to an apparent increase in the number of "insane." When, therefore, we hear of a "startling increase" of insanity in the United States, we simply decline to believe in it. General indications of the state of mental health in America do *not* bear out the inference to which statistics point; and, as 'vital statistics' are at present computed in this country and in America, we are convinced that general indications are more trustworthy than figures which may not be facts.—*Lancet.*

Winter Eczema.—Squibb's Formula.

For the relief of winter eczema, a troublesome itching affection, Dr. Squibb's Ephemeris recommends the following : Take of tannic acid, forty grains, of glycerine and alcohol each half a fluid ounce, water to make four ounces. This solution is applied to the itching surfaces by means of a small sponge or rag, morning and evening.—*Detroit Lancet.*

Intestinal Occlusion Due to a Biliary Calculus Impacted in the Rectum.

A very singular case of this kind was reported to the Société Anatomique not long since by M. Babinski. (*Le Progres Medical*, September 15th, 1883.) A man, fifty years old, entered the Hotel Dieu, in the service of M. Vulpian, on February 8th, 1883. No satisfactory history of the patient could be obtained; he was admitted at 10 o'clock P. M., in a state of partial stupor, but his face expressed suffering. His temperature was normal and his pulse small and compressible; his abdomen was distended and painful on pressure; he suffered very much from dyspnœa. On being questioned, he stated that his bowels had not moved for four days, and that during that time he had passed scarcely any urine. The patient died at 4 o'clock next morning—just six hours after he entered the hospital.

On opening the abdomen, the coils of intestine were found to be much distended, and a hard body was found in the upper part of the rectum; at the junction of the upper and middle thirds. On opening the bowel this singular foreign body was found to be imprisoned by the intestinal mucous membrane, which was tumefied but not ulcerated. It was cylindrical in shape, measuring two and one-half centimetres in one direction and one and one-half in the other. It was composed of cholesterine. The whole of the large intestine was filled with fæcal matter, and two other small concretions, also consisting of cholesterine, were found just above the large one. The gall bladder was adherent to the transverse colon, and there was quite a large opening between them, through which the gall stone had found its way into the bowel. The bile duct was a little larger than usual, but presented no unusual appearances and contained no calculi.

There was nothing about the other organs to attract attention.—*Virginia Medical Monthly*.

Knee-Chest Posture for Dislodging Locked Twins.

A new procedure for dislodging locked twins is described, with an illustrative case, by Dr. T. S. Galbraith, of Seymour, Indiana, in the *American Journal of Obstetrics*. Being summoned hastily to a case of difficult delivery, under the charge of a midwife, he found a child delivered except its head, which, with the chin extended, was in the right oblique diameter of the pelvis. The head of another child was also found occupying the cavity of the pelvis, presenting with its occiput to the front, and driven down so firmly as completely to bar the further progress of the labor. With the patient on her back the second head was immovable, but on causing her to assume the knee-chest posture, the attendant found himself able to push it out of the way by introducing his hand, and a few seconds later the first child was delivered still-born; the second was delivered with the forceps, and survived. —*American Practitioner*.

A Formula for Irregular Heart Action.

In the *Boston Med. and Surg. Journal*, Dr. Bowditch highly praises the following:

℞ Pulv. digitalis, gr. x,
Pulv. colchici sem., gr. xx,
Sodii bicarbonatis, gr. xxx.
M. Ft. div. in pil. No. 20.

These are to be taken three or four times daily at first; subsequently to be reduced until only one is taken at bedtime; the treatment to be continued for three to nine months.

He has used it for twenty-five years, and has found it to relieve even the most serious cardiac affections.

Monti recommends that the nipples should be anointed with a (freshly made) solution of gutta-percha in chloroform, just enough of the latter being added to make the solution fluid. As it dries it forms a protecting pellicle, which does not come off even after suckling.

Constant Crying in an Infant from Hunger.

Prof. T. Parvin in Coll. and Cl'n. Record.

This mother brought her child a few days ago to the hospital dispensary, because of its continual crying. Though she is quite young, this is her second child; the first one depended upon her altogether for nourishment during the usual period of nursing, and was a thriving, healthy, cheerful child. But this one, now four months old, she says, has cried night and day since it was born. As a dog hunts in dreams, so this poor child, if it ever dreamed in its sleep, dreamed of crying, of pain and discomfort. It was hard, impossible, indeed, to keep it still during the examination made to ascertain if there was any diseased organ making complaint in its crying. No disease was found. The mother, here let me say, has acted more wisely than many a mother does under similar circumstances, for she has come to find out why her baby cries, while too many others would dose their crying babies with some of the "soothing syrups" or "cordials," which probably accomplish quite as much in the killing as in the curing of the infant population. Having found that the child is not suffering with positive disease, the next question is as to its nourishment. The mother told us she had plenty of milk, quite as much as she had with her first babe, which got on so well. Nevertheless, this babe did not seem as large and as plump as it ought to; and though the quantity of milk was ample, was its quality such as it ought to be? Putting a drop on my finger-nail held obliquely, and letting the milk thus run down the nail, it scarcely left a trace; again, dropping it in a tumbler of water, each drop, as it fell, caused the faintest cloudiness. Finally, one of my clinical assistants, Dr. Grorydon, made an examination with the microscope, and found the number of milk globules was very small. Thus a solution of the problem was reached: the infant was crying from hunger, and from hunger it had been crying these weary months. That this solution was correct is proved by the result of feeding the baby; it is now quiet, happy and improved in appearance, although only a few days have passed since the feeding was begun. The artificial food given this infant was cow's milk diluted with an equal quantity of barley water, and a little loaf sugar added. The practice of diluting cow's milk with water for infant feeding is, I believe, a grievous mistake. That sort of dilution has simply rendered the milk less nutritious, and made it necessary to give a larger quantity of food, and at more frequent intervals, in each way impairing the child's digestive power; but upon this point I will speak to you again. In this case, not water, but barley water was added to the milk. So much depends upon having the barley water properly prepared, let me say a word about this preparation.

Take an ounce of pearl barley, and wash it in cold water; then put it in a vessel containing half a pint of water, and let it be gently heated over the fire, so that the water just simmers a few minutes; now pour off this water, replace it by a pint and a half of water, and boil down to a pint, and you then have barley water.

Rheumatism—Three Types.

The treatment of acute rheumatism has always claimed particular attention from the profession, and will always remain a subject of lively interest. Bartholow says (*Medical Record*) that the chemical theory that it is owing to an acid in the blood is borne out by clinical facts and experiments. But behind this, there is an influence concerned in the production of the excess of acid, which influence is located in the nervous system. He divides the rheumatic cases into three groups: First, spare persons of good bodily vigor and muscular development, with hereditary tendency to the disease. Second, fat persons that use malt liquors and live highly, but who generally have no inherited predisposition to the disease. Third, feeble, anemic, poorly nourished people, who live under malarial influences. For the first he recommends salicylic acid or one of its salts, salicylate of soda, as the proper remedy. For the second group he says the alkaline treatment is the most suitable. He quotes from Dr. Fuller who says: "One ounce and a half of the carbonates should be given in twenty-four hours, and half as much as soon as the urine becomes alkaline." For the third class, he recommends the use of tincture of chloride of iron in full doses, from one-half to one drachm in water, every four to eight hours. He says that under the use of this remedy the pain, fever and swelling subside, the danger of heart trouble is lessened and the whole system strengthened to resist the disease.—*Med. Summary.*

Concentrated Solution of Saline Cathartics.

In the course of an investigation I examined the effect of an administration of a saline cathartic on the concentration of the blood, and I succeeded in demonstrating from experiments on man and the dog that, if the salt be given in the form of a concentrated solution, when the alimentary canal of the animal contains little or no fluid, it produces an immediate and very decided concentration of the blood, owing to the blood becoming deprived of a large amount of its water through the intestinal secretion which the salt excites; if, however, the salt be given dissolved in sufficient water, or if the alimentary canal contain sufficient fluid at the time of the administration of the salt, no such concentration of the blood occurs. In the former case the hematic concentration is very considerable, and is very quickly produced. It reaches the maximum within half an hour after the ingestion of the salt; and is so marked that giving three-quarters of an ounce of sulphate of soda dissolved in three ounces of water to a man, whose alimentary canal must have been practically free from fluid, I found that the number of blood corpuscles in each cubic millimetre of his blood rose from about 5,000,000 to 6,790,000. An almost similar result was obtained with a dog. This excessive state of concentration does not last very long. In from one to one and a half hours after the administration of the salt it begins to decline, and continues to do so until at the end of about four hours the concentration is reduced to the normal. This reduction is effected, not by the absorption of fluid from the intestines, but by the abstraction of the lymph and other fluids from the tissues, and the quantity thus abstracted must be very large. These alterations of the volume of the blood take place apparently without any corresponding change of the blood-pressure. The blood, therefore, would appear to abstract the tissue fluids in virtue solely of its concentrated condition, and, in the nature of its action, to behave somewhat like a sponge. The pressure of the salt upon the blood may also influence the tissue fluids by acting on them endosmotically. Some hours after the administration either of a concentrated or of a dilute saline solution the blood undergoes another concentration, less in degree than the first, but continuing for the greater part of the day. This second concentration is evidently due to the diuretic effect of the absorbed salt. Doubtless, during this period, also, as during the first concentration, the tissue fluids are being drawn upon.

From these remarks it will be readily understood how that a concentrated solution of a saline cathartic ought to prove of considerable service in certain cases of dropsy, where, owing to the great accumulation of transuded serum in vital parts and elsewhere, there is imminent danger to life and an urgent need for an immediate and active removal of a portion of the transuded fluid. In such case the value of saline and other active cathartics has long been appreciated, but I am not aware that use has been made of the more powerful action of a concentrated saline cathartic. It removes the dropsical fluid by two channels; by the intestines and by the kidneys. No other purgative has this double action. It is questionable, also, if any other purgative acts so rapidly in reducing the fluids of the blood. This is of the greatest importance in certain critical cases of dropsy. It is almost perfectly certain that no other purgative excites intestinal secretion so powerfully, and at the same time produces so little irritation of the intestinal mucous membrane and so little disturbance of the body generally. This is an additional recommendation for the employment of the concentrated saline. The diluted salt, the form in which it is always given, has practically, in so far as it affects dropsical fluids, the action only of a diuretic. Based on these considerations, I have made several trials of the concentrated salt in suitable cases of dropsy, and in most of them with very satisfactory result. The conditions necessary for the successful administration of the salt are that the nature of the dropsy should be such as to permit of the full action of the salt. I have found it more useful in general dropsies than in local dropsies and of general dropsies more beneficial in those dependent on a stasis of the circulation, as cardiac dropsy. The cases in which I have employed it are, however, as yet too few to warrant me in making definite generalisations. The other requisite conditions are that the alimentary canal, by the previous abstinence of the patient for some hours previously from food, and especially liquids, should be allowed to become as free from fluid as possible, and that the salt should be administered along with the smallest possible quantity of water. Sulphate of magnesia, on account of being soluble in less than its own weight of water, is one of the most suitable of the saline cathartics for this purpose. Sulphate of soda is, owing to its greater insolubility in water (1 in 4), less suitable. The alkaline tartrates and Rochelle salt do not, however, present this objection, and may therefore be found useful. The phosphate of soda and the sulphate of potash are too insoluble to be of any service.—*Matthew Hay, M. D., in Lancet.*

Albumen in Healthy Urine.

Dr. Millard says that the quantity of albumen found in the urine of healthy persons varies under the following conditions:

1. Albumen is found in the urine of the majority of healthy persons, more or less abundantly and transient in its character. 2. Rest in bed has a clearly marked influence in diminishing the amount of albumen excreted. 3. Bodily fatigue greatly influences the production of physiological and transient albuminuria. 4. Intellectual labor augments with most people the quanity of albumen existing in the urine. 5. Cold bathing exerts considerable influence in increasing physiological albuminuria. 6. Sexual excitement and menstruation manifestly affect albuminuria in the healthy. 7. Albuminuria is as frequent in children as in adults, but the quantity of albumen excreted is less. 8. Digestion, if accompanied by rest, does not exert much influence upon physiological albuminuria.

Three Infectious Diseases in the Same Individual.

Dr. Prior, assistant to the Royal University Polyclinic in Bonn, communicates to the *Deutsche Med. Wochensch*, Aug. 1, a case in which three different infectious diseases occurred in the same individual in the space of one month. Three children were attended on Nov. 18 for well-marked scarlatina, with a temperature of 104° Fahr., copious eruption, and some difficulty of swallowing. Desquamation began on Nov. 21, and proceeded normally, only one child having slight renal symptoms, until, on Dec. 1, the two younger were attacked with rigors, headache, and malaise, and on the following day were covered with a think eruption of varicella. On Dec. 3, in the absence of the mother, a child from the next room, intercourse with which had been carefully avoided on account of measles, was found playing with the child, and showed signs of measles next day. The first patients were now carefully watched, and on Dec. 13 the temperature was found to be raised, with photophobia and slight coryza; on the 15th the eruption of morbilli appeared. Its course was protracted, and caused some anxiety; but, finally, the children recovered. The cases show how the two poisons of scarlatina and varicella may be in the organism at the same time, and how measles may be conveyed by a two hours' intercourse in the prodromal stage, while the crusts of varicella are still present, the measles showing itself as soon as ten days later.—*Med. Gazette*.

Chloral Hydrate as a Vesicant.

Dr. F. D. Ritter, of Gaines, Penn., writes to Dr. T. Gaillard Thomas as follows: "In complying with your request, I write you concerning my experience with chloral hydrate as a vesicant. Some three years ago I accidentally discovered that when powdered chloral, sprinkled on ordinary adhesive plaster and melted by a gentle heat (not more than enough to cause the plaster to adhere to the flesh) is applied while warm to the part where the blister is wanted, within three minutes a gentle heat is felt, increasing in intensity for about three minutes more till it is like a burn, then gradually easing off until at the end of three minutes, the parts feel free from pain.

The secondary effect is soothing; in some instances within half an hour a second burning is felt, though not so intense as at first nor so lasting. If at the end of ten minutes, or as soon as pain has subsided, the plaster be taken off, the surface is found as effectually denuded as by a cantharidal plaster after six hours, though the discharge is not so great. Thus within ten minutes the work of an old fashioned blister is accomplished; and the great advantages of the chloral over the cantharidal are—1st: Its rapidity of action, thus relieving pain and producing the counter-irritation upon an engorged organ before the congestive action has had time to pass into more than the congestive stage. 2: Its ease of application. 3: It need never be taken off to have the blister dressed; but the original plaster may remain until the sore is entirely healed and the plaster loosens and comes off itself. This is in part my experience, and I would have given it to the profession before, but supposed it was well known.—*New England Med. Mon.*

Alcohol in Trichinosis.

A case of trichinosis, in which the only treatment was the administration of alcohol in full doses, is reported by Dr. D. Vincente Ferrer (*Gaceta de los Hospitales*, Valencia). The patient was twenty-three years old, and it was probably the fifth week of the attack when the treatment was commenced. The attack was a severe one, with characteristic pulse, temperature, muscular pains, and rigidity; pulse 124; temperature 103° Fahr. The patient could neither flex the limbs nor stir from the supine position, and was considered by Dr. Ferrer and his colleagues to be in a critical condition. Six ounces of proof spirit (about 56 per cent. of rectified alcohol, R.) were given daily in sugared water in the intervals of feeding. Within twenty-four hours the temperature fell 8°, and the muscular rigidity was distinctly diminished. On the third day of the treatment the dose was increased to nine ounces, and on the fourth to twelve; but this quantity was not borne well, and it was reduced again to nine. On the sixth day the patient was free from pain as he lay in bed, and could move some of the limbs without suffering. The alcohol was continued in the same doses, and from this date convalescence was established. He is stated to have been quite well eighteen days after the alcohol treatment was commenced. Dr. Ferrer considers that the effect was too marked and immediate to be simply a coincidence, but he offers no opinion as to whether the drug affected the trichina, or the muscular fibres, or the reflex irritability of the nerves, or, finally, the areas of inflammatory intermuscular tissue.—*Med. Gazette.*

Influence of Diphtheria upon Pregnancy.

In a communication addressed to the Academy of Medicine of Paris (Med. Rec.), Dr. Oliver concludes that diphtheria may acquire an additional gravity when occurring in pregnant women, because of the liability it has to cause abortion. This accident is due, in the larger number of cases, not to asphyxia nor to an elevation of the temperature of the blood, but to some alteration in this fluid, an alteration which, if it is undefined, is nevertheless incontestable. The possibility of abortion, with its dangers, calls for increased precautionary measures and more strict isolation in the case of pregnant women in the same house or in the same hospital ward with patients suffering with diphtheria.

School Hygiene.

At a meeting of the New York Medico-Legal Society, Dr. A. N. Bell stated that he thought the Board of Education was, perhaps, born in a state of incapacity to estimate the sanitary needs of the schools, and it was impossible for it to overcome this congenital difficulty. An examination some time ago, to test the purity of school-room air, had resulted in the discovery that there was more poisonous carbonic acid gas habitually present in them than in the prisons of the city. The Board of Education had passed a resolution requiring that there should be an average space of seventy cubic feet of air for each pupil, but this had never been carried out, not more than fifty cubic feet being at present the allowance in many of the schools. He believed that out of sixty thousand children, three thousand had died during the last two years, smothered to death. Having called attention to the especially bad condition of one of the school-houses, he stated that the schools in Brooklyn were equally faulty.—*Coll. and Clin. Record.*

Rule for Reducing Dislocations of the Hip Joint.

Having flexed the leg on the thigh, and the thigh on the pelvis, slowly rotate the limb as far as possible, inwards and outwards, according as the toes pointed in or out before beginning the manipulation; then rapidly and forcibly rotate the limb in the opposite direction, and the head of the femur will usually slip into the acetabulum.

For example: In the iliac and the sciatic dislocations, the toes point inwards; therefore, rotate inwards as far as possible, and afterwards rotate outwards. In the pubic and thyroid dislocations the toes point outwards, hence rotate the limb outwards still more, and then inwards.—*Polyclinic.*

Puerperal Eclampsia.

In the Arch. fur Gynäk., Dr. Breus highly recommends his plan of treatment of puerperal convulsions (Med. and, Surg. Reporter), which consists in hot-baths and wrapping in blankets until profuse diaphoresis occurs. He has never seen any evil results, and thinks it desirable to employ this treatment in pregnant women who are the subjects of dropsy or albuminuria, believing that by it the onset of eclampsia may possibly be prevented.—*Weekly Med. Rev.*

An Infant Fifty-Six Years of Age.

M. Sappey communicated to the Academy of Sciences the following fact: When an infant has arrived at its term of development, if any obstacle prevents its expulsion it perishes and becomes a source of great danger to the mother who usually dies. In certain exceptional cases the fœtus acts as a foreign body to which the surrounding tissues become accustomed and a new pregnancy may supervene and follow its normal course. The case of Toulouse, where the child remained in utero, for 26 years; of Sens for 28 years; of Pont-a-Mousson for 30 years, for 31 in that of Joigny; for 47 years in that of Leinzel, in Swabia. To explain these cases two theories have been proposed. The older is that of petrifaction—the infants becoming calcified—observed facts do not support this theory. The second theory is that of progressive desiccation—but the fact I am about to relate sets aside this theory.

The mother became pregnant at the age of 28 years, proceeding until 84 years of age and having been perfectly well all this time she was admitted into the Alms-house of Quimperle and died three weeks after her admission. M. Beaugendre under whose care she had been, performed the post-mortem. On incising the abdominal wall a tumor was found in the right fallopian tube. The tumor was constituted of a cyst with extremely hard walls, its surface unequal and bosselated. The cyst was taken away and its walls divided into two equal parts with a saw. In this envelope, by all its attributes belonging to the mineral kingdom, there was a child, and this child during its long captivity had undergone no alteration The child was in the ordinary position, the limbs flexed upon the trunk and the head upon the thorax. The pupillary membranes completely developed, attested that it was six or seven months of age. The skin, the superficial organs, the viscera situated in the great cavities, all the muscles and soft parts had retained their consistence, their suppleness and their normal colour. The fœtus appeared as if it had just gone to sleep. M. Sappey considers that the fœtus owes its preservation in the cyst to its being protected from the ingress of atmospheric germs, like the bottles of blood and urine presented to the Academy by M. Pasteur, which had continued to keep sweet by the prevention of the admission of atmospheric germs.—GAZ. DES HOPITAUX. —*Western Med. Rep.*

Hot Water Vaginal Injections.

In a recent clinical lecture Dr. Goodell spoke as follows:

A few more words about the injection of hot water. It is not a panacea for all the ailments of the womb. Although it is an excellent remedy in the majority of cases, not only of tenderness, but also of hypertrophy of the womb, you will often be disappointed in it. It diminishes the size of an enlarged womb by its secondary effect upon the capillaries and tissues. If, however, you think that you can reduce a womb that measures three inches and a half to the normal two and a half by the use of hot-water injections, you will be disappointed. It can, perhaps, be reduced to three inches; but to reduce it more would require means which are heroic and unwarrantable under the circumstances, especially when we bear in mind that even these heroic measures may not be successful. You should always say to a patient whose womb is too large: "I cannot make your womb as small as it was originally. You will have some trouble, some backache and some bearing-down pains; but I can make you much more comfortable until the change of life." You may also say: "If I can get you in a condition to become pregnant, there is a probability, although not a certainty, that the womb will grow smaller." Such a case will require, after confinement, remedies that will condense the womb—as ergot, strychnine and quinine. Iron is not the thing. If given after confinement, it is very apt to do mischief. Iron has a tendency to cause a flow of blood to the womb. It will occasionally do great good, but more frequently it does harm. In those cases where a woman is weak and anemic from uterine hemorrhage, a tonic is required, and the best preparations are the vegetable tonics. A good combination is a teaspoonful of Huxham's tincture—the tinctura cinchonæ composita, with ten to fifteen drops of tinctura ignatiæ.—*College and Clinical Record.*

Diagnostic Value of Uterine Hemorrhage after the Menopause.

During the course of a late clinical lecture on malignant disease of the cervix uteri, Dr. T. Gaillard Thomas stated, as an axiom in gynecology, that if a woman who has normally ceased to menstruate begins to have uterine hemorrhage, always suspect carcinoma. Not unfrequently you will see in the medical journals the reports of cases where women who have passed the change of life have begun to menstruate regularly again; but such accounts are altogether deceptive, and, if these cases could be followed out, it would be found with scarcely a single exception, that uterine flow was merely the indication of the presence of malignant disease. In other words, there is absolutely no such thing as a return of the menses when a woman has once reached the normal menopause. Not long since a patient of mine in the Woman's Hospital, who is sixty years of age, began to have a flowing from the uterus, and, as there was no indication of any external disease, I applied the curette to the endometrium and drew out some pulpy masses, which I sent to a well-known microscopist for examination. The report that I got from him was that the growth was not malignant in any respect, but was simply a form of polypus. I am perfectly sure, however, that the microscopist is wrong, and for this reason: in the uterus of a woman of sixty, polypi never develope. The organ at that age is completely atrophied. Sometimes in women who have passed the menopause you will find uterine tumors which have all the appearance of fibroids. They are not by any means fibroids, however, but sarcomata.—*N. Y. Med. Jour.*—*St. Joseph Medical Herald.*

Prolapse of the Transverse Colon.

In the *Polyclinic* (Dec., 1833), Dr. Chas. H. Thomas relates three cases of downward displacement of the transverse colon. A positive diagnosis was not made until after death in any of the cases. The following are the remarks and conclusions deduced from the clinical history of the cases:

No adhesions of the displaced parts were found in any of the cases cited. The intestinal fault was probably not the cause of death in any of them. Taking them together it will be seen that clinical conditions and post-mortem appearances agree in at least one important particular, viz.: the location of the displaced intestines in contact with the anterior abdominal wall and below its normal site.

The normal anatomical relations of the colon have a special significance in the light of these cases, from a diagnostic point of view. The ascending and descending portions of the colon are, normally, to be found in contact with the *posterior* or lumbar wall of the abdominal cavity—behind the small intestines—and are there bound closely down by reflections on the peritoneum. The transverse colon, on the contrary, is normally in contact with the *anterior* abdominal—in front of the small intestines—where it is loosely suspended by the transverse mesocolon; a structure of considerable length.

It therefore appears to be a practical impossibility for the vertical portions of the large intestine to become spontaneously misplaced anteriorly. But of the transverse colon, its displacement downwards—in which changed position its relation of contact with the anterior abdominal wall is retained—these cases show to be a condition of repeated occurrence.

Conclusions.—(1) Displacement of the transverse colon downward within the abdomen may be, to any degree, partial or complete.

(2) Such displacement will present as solid tumor if the bowel be in a state of fæcal impaction, or as a limited area of heightened resonance if the bowel be distended with gas: but in either case the displaced part is to be found *in contact with the anterior abdominal wall.*

(3) The occurrence of an intra-abdominal tumor situated below the normal site of the transverse colon, and having the same general configuration as the colon, such tumor being of a certain consistency, and presenting evidences of being in contact with the anterior abdominal wall; or the occurrence of areas of special tympany with like outlines and similarly located, constitutes a diagnostic sign strongly indicative of downward displacement of the transverse colon.

Tears of Blood.

An article relating to the rare phenomenon of sanguineous lachrymation has been published by M. Damalix (Med. Record). He cites two well-authenticated cases of this curious affection, reported respectively by M. Hasner and by M. Brun. In these cases the eyes filled quickly with the bloody tears, the sanguineous character of which was demonstrated by microscopical examination. This affection is to be carefully distinguished from hemorrhages dependent upon orbital or conjunctival disease, such as polypoid conjunctival vegetations developed in the culs-de-sac of the conjunctiva. Genuine bloody tears are quite independent of any ocular or conjunctival disease and their appearance is irregular. No apparent cause leads to their effusion. In some cases the escape of the tears is unattended by pain. In others the patient experiences pain in the forehead, the eyebrow, and at the root of the nose, or a sensation of pruritus, formication, or heat in the eyelids. These morbid sensations persist only a few instants and disappear with the appearance of the tears; the escape of the tears continues only a few minutes and the quantity of sanguineous lachrymal secretion varies from a few drops to a wineglassfull. This phenomenon is usually intermittent, sometimes regular, but almost always transitory and attended by hemorrhages from various cutaneous or mucous surfaces. Sanguineous lachrymation appears, by preference, in anemic individuals, in those inclined to hematophilia and in hysterical women.—*Weekly Med. Rev.*

The Conversion of Malignant Tumors into Innocent Growths.

Professor V. Nussbaum, in a clinical lecture recently delivered in Munich (*Boston Medical and Surgical Journal,* October 25), expressed the belief that he had discovered a procedure for the positive cure of cancer by restraining the proliferation of the tissue elements of the disease. It appears to him that a total interruption of all peripheral sources of nutrition is the means best adapted to secure this result. He accomplishes this object by the use of the thermo-cautery, with which instrument a deep channel is made quite around the malignant growth, thus cutting off entirely the supply of blood and other nutritive fluids from the surrounding tissues. The small vessels which ascend into the tumor from the parts beneath are sufficient to preserve its vitality, so that gangrene does not occur. He thinks the thermo-cautery far preferable to the ligature, and that it possesses many advantages over the knife. He regards the hot iron and the various chemical caustics worthy of more extensive employment in the domain of malignant growths than they have ever enjoyed. Prof. Nussbaum doubts not that thus circumscribing a cancerous growth, thus cutting off every channel of peripheral nutrition, has a brilliant future, especially in those desperate cases in which death is imminent from hemorrhage. In his experience this method of cutting off the peripheral blood supply has afforded such astonishing results that he recommends this procedure to the attention and practice of all those having occasion to treat a case adapted to its employment.—*Lancet.*

The Cadaveric Poisons.

In concluding an article on ptomaines, or cadaveric alkaloids, Mr. R. N. Wolfenden sums up as follows (Lancet): 1. There are developed in the body, post-mortem, poisons of an alkaloidal character, and which can be obtained also by decomposition of albumen, peptone, casein, muscle, brain, etc. Moreover, they seem to be present in some normal secretions (saliva and urine). 2. These cadaveric alkaloids may be mistaken, post-mortem, for vegetal poison administered with evil intent, but if the body be examined within twenty-four to forty-eight hours after death, any alkaloid there found would be strong presumptive evidence of poison and not ptomaine. After a couple of days it would be a matter of doubt. 3. There is no satisfactory test surely indicating the presence of ptomaine. Physiological characters must be taken in conjunction with chemical tests. 4. Probably the production of ptomaines within the living body may be the pathological cause of many obscure conditions, especially those following on poisoning by bad food, such as stale fish, etc.—*Med. Review.*

FAITH is sometimes personified as a drenched female clinging to a sea-washed rock ; but a better personification would be a bald-headed man buying a bottle of patent hair restorer.

The Medical Chronicle.

A Monthly Journal for the Practitioner.

GEORGE H. ROHÉ, M. D., Editor.

It is requested that all literary and business communications, books for review, exchanges, etc., be addressed to, and all checks, drafts and post-office orders drawn to the order of

DR. GEORGE H. ROHÉ,
95 Park Avenue, - - - - Baltimore, Md.

BALTIMORE, JANUARY, 1884.

EDITORIAL.

The National Board of Health.

We have received the fifth annual report of the National Board of Health, covering the operations of that body for the fiscal year ending June 30th, 1883. The report also gives a summary of the work of the board during the four years of its existence.

The National Board of Health was established by act of Congress approved March 3rd, 1879, and its duties were defined in section 2 of said act to be, " to obtain information upon all matters affecting the public health, to advise the several departments of the government, the executives of the several States, and the commissioners of the District of Columbia, on all questions submitted by them, or whenever in the opinion of the Board such advice may tend to the preservation and improvement of the public health."

On the third of June, 1879, an act entitled, " an act to prevent the introduction of contagious and infectious diseases into the United States," was approved by the president and by section 4 of this act, the National Board was directed to aid "as far as it lawfully may" state and municipal health organizations in the enforcement of their quarantine regulations. A liberal appropriation was made by Congress to carry out the objects of the act, and the Board went actively to work.

The complete success of the Board's work in the same year, in preventing the spread of yellow fever after it had actually broken out in New Orleans and threatened to become epidemic, is matter of history. The efficient aid rendered in that city, and in Memphis in 1879 and 1880, are remembered with gratitude by the *people* of both cities. In New Orleans, however, the officials of the state and municipal health organization, on account of some real or fancied grievance, have been bitterly opposed to the National Board since the summer of 1880, although apparently willing to accept any pecuniary aid at the disposal of the national organization.

In addition to the effective practical work done by the Board in preventing the introduction and spread of epidemic diseases, scientific investigations of the highest importance have been set on foot. Some of these investigations have been completed and are published in the annual reports of the Board for 1879, 1880 and 1881. Others have been suspended on account of the failure of Congress to make the necessary appropriations at the last session. It is hoped that the present House of Representatives, being of the same political faith as that which called the Board into being, will take a broader view of the necessity of scientific research for sanitary purposes than did its predecessor of the opposite party.

The most important of the investigations undertaken at the instance of the board were those of Drs. Wood and Formad on the etiology of diphtheria; of Col. Waring on the flow in sewers, and the ventilation of house drains; Dr. Sternberg on disinfectants and on the suspended matter in the air of places liable to infection; on the adulteration of foods and drugs by Profs. Kedzie, and Diehl, and Dr. Smart; Prof. Remsen's researches into the best method of determining the amount and character of the organic matter in the air and on carbonic oxide in furnace-heated rooms; Prof. Mallet and Dr. Smart's analyses of drinking waters, and a number of others of similar value. Certain wit-snappers of the daily press, and one or two of their imitators in Congress have attempted to discredit the results obtained in these investigations, but sanitarians, not only in this country, but abroad also, have acknowledged their importance.

In its last report the Board asks Congress to restore to it a sufficient appropriation to continue the scientific work it has begun. The sum asked for is small, and we belive that the gross misrepresentation which defeated the objects of the Board in the last Congress w'll fail to influence the present House in a similar manner.

CURRENT LITERATURE.

Practical Clinical Lessons on Syphilis and the Genito-Urinary Diseases. By Fessenden N. Otis, M. D., Clinical Professor of Genito-Urinary Diseases in the College of Physicians and Surgeons, New York; Surgeon to Charity Hospital, etc. New York, Bermingham & Co., 1883. Price, cloth, $4.50.

At various times during the last fifteen years, Professor Otis has made public, through the medical journals, and in monographs, his peculiar views upon the natnre of syphilis, gonorrhœa and its sequelæ, the normal size and shape of the urethra, and the treatment of urethral stricture. In this work he has more fully elaborated his previous contributions to medical literature, and given his opinions a more complete exposition. He believes that syphilitic infection does not take place through the blood, but through the lymph channels, and argues for this view very plausibly.

Prof. Otis believes, with most venereal pathologists of the present day, that the so-called chancroid is a disease " possessing no specific virus, but acquiring its power for destruction and contagion, through the stimulation and vitiation of benign natural processes."

Gonorrhœa is likewise considered to be a non-specific inflammation of the mucous membranes. This view is also held by many modern authorities.

The latter part of the work under review is taken up with a full account of the author's views upon the normal calibre of the urethra, the neuropathic effects of strictures of large calibre, and treatment of urethral stricture by internal "dilating" urethrotomy. These views have been accepted by many American surgeons, and opposition to them is gradually yielding in Europe.

The author's style is clear and practical, his descriptions of the various morbid processes accurate and full, and his therapeutics positive. The work is a good guide to the student and a helpful aid to the practitioner.

The paper, printing and binding are neat and inviting. We have noticed some very aggravating typographical errors, however, for all of which the proof-reader cannot be held responsible. Thus, the name of Biesiadecki appears throughout the book as Beisiadecki, while Cohnheim is presented to us as Conhiem. Surely, a little more care on the author's part would have avoided disturbing errors like these.

Annual Report of the Supervising Surgeon-General of the Marine Hospital Service of the United States, for the fiscal year 1883.

This volume contains, in addition to the general report of Surgeon-General Hamilton, the histories of a number of interesting cases of disease observed by officers of the Marine Hospital service. The appendix consists of a history of the Texas and Florida epidemic of yellow fever in 1882, and a brief report on the sanitary condition of Vera Cruz.

PAMPHLETS.

Lichen Ruber and Lichen Planus. By A. R. Robinson, M. B., L. R. C. P. & S., Prof. of Dermatology in the New York Polyclinic, Prof. of Histology in the Woman's Medical College of the New York Infirmary, etc. ———Deflection of the Nasal Septum and its Treatment. By Jno N. Mackenzie, M. D., Surgeon to Baltimore Eye, Ear and Throat Charity Hospital, Member of the American Laryngological Association, etc. Reprint from Trans. Med. Society of Virginia, 1883.———A New Operation for the Reduction of Chronic Inversion of the Uterus. By B. Bernard Browne, M. D., Prof. of Diseases of Women in the Woman's Medical College of Baltimore ; Fellow of the American Gynecological Society, etc. Reprint from New York Medical Journal, Nov. 24th, 1883.

FLOTSAM.

A SITE has been selected for a Marine Hospital in Baltimore.

MEDICAL Director A. L. Gihon, has been directed to take charge of the Naval Hospital at Washington.

DR. WM. H. COGGESHALL, of Richmond, has become part proprietor and associate editor of the *Virginia Medical Monthly.*

EVERY physician visiting Washington should by all means visit the National Museum of Hygiene. The exhibit will repay careful study.

THE Wiener Medicinische Doctoren Collegium, the largest medical society in the Austrian capital, is discussing the tuberculosis question.

MEDICAL Inspector Adrian Hudson, assistant in the Naval Bureau of Medicine and Surgery, has been ordered to the European squadron.

THE editor of the *Planet* wants to know " whether a cow-boy could get cow-pox?" Can any of our Texas or Nebraska readers enlighten him ?

A NEW and revised edition of Dr. Francis H. Brown's excellent *Medical Register for New England*, will shortly be issued by Cupples, Upham & Co., of Boston.

THE PLANET, one of the liveliest of our exchanges, completed its first volume with the December number. Its appearance has been much improved. We wish it success.

BALANITIS occurring in diabetics may be relieved by any mild astringent lotion, afterward powdering the part with oxide of zinc 25 parts, starch 25 parts and salicylic acid 1 part.

"SEED TIME AND HARVEST" is the title of a neat monthly magazine devoted to the interests of farmers and gardeners. It is published by J. Tillinghast, La Plume, Pa., at fifty cents a year.

PROF. PARVIN says that a strict milk-diet is the best and almost certain remedy for the albuminuria of pregnancy. A recent case thus treated was delivered of twins, no convulsions occurring.

DR. FRANK WOODBURY, who has been one of the editors of the *College and Clinical Record* for several years, has withdrawn from that journal, in order to give more time to his duties as editor of the *Philadelphia Medical Times*.

HAMMOND gives preference to sclerotinic acid in those cases of cerebral and spinal congestion where the use of ergot is indicated. He thinks that it possesses, in a greater degree, the power of contracting unstriped muscular fibre.

DR. W. H. BOBBITT, of Raleigh, N. C., has founded a prize consisting of a gold medal, to be annually conferred upon that member of the graduating class in the College of Physicians and Surgeons, who passes the best examination in gynecology.

DR. WRIGHT claims that the people living upon the Cumberland plateau in Tennessee, are absolutely free from consumption. He has practiced in that region throughout a generation, and recently read a paper before the Tennessee Medical Society, entitled "A people without consumption, and some account of their country."

THE Baltimore Policlinic and Post-Graduate School has organized by the election of the following professors: T. A. Ashby, B. B. Browne, T. B. Brune, J. W. Chambers, T. S. Latimer, H. C. McSherry, J. E. Michael, W. A. Moale, R. B. Morison A. P. Smith, S. Theobald and R. Winslow. A building has been secured on S. Hanover street, and active work will soon be begun.

WE welcome to our table the *Archives of Pediatrics*, a new monthly journal devoted exclusively to the diseases of children. It is edited by Dr. W. P. Watson, of Jersey City, assisted by an able staff of collaborators, both home and foreign, Each number of the *Archives* is to contain 64 pages of reading matter, and no advertisements will be admitted. The subscription price is $3.00 per year.

STRONG efforts are being made by the opponents of Surgeon-General Wales of the Navy, to prevent his reappointment to the position he has filled so acceptably during the past four years. It is to be hoped that the president will not permit the politicians and barnacles in the navy department to influence this appointment. Dr. Wales has introduced so many needed reforms in the administration of the Naval Medical service, that it would be a pity if the good work were spoiled by the nomination of a less efficient officer to the position.

The Medical Chronicle.

BALTIMORE, FEBRUARY, 1884.

ORIGINAL ARTICLES.

ARTICLE I.

The Etiology and Pathology of Croupous Pneumonia.

A paper read before the Medical and Surgical Society of Baltimore, January 9th, 1884.

BY J. W. CHAMBERS, M. D., BALTIMORE.

It is no doubt very profitable to us now and then to take up some well-known disease and discuss it in the light of recent pathology and experience. And this is as true here with croupous pneumonia, as it was some weeks ago with typhoid fever which was so ably and profitably discussed before the New York Academy of Medicine, by Dr. Delafield and others.

Croupous pneumonia is one of those diseases which are as widely spread as mankind itself; on an average, according to Juergensen, three per cent. of all the diseases of the entire globe are due to this cause.

In comparison with internal diseases alone it comprises fully six per cent. of the diseases of England, France and Germany, and this would as well apply to the United States.

Pneumonia ranks equally high among the causes of death. More than six per cent. of the total mortality is due to this disease, and about twelve per cent. of the mortality from internal diseases, and this is not including secondary pneumonias.

Croupous pneumonia seems to have no geographical bounds, and the widest difference in mortality is often shown in places which are geographicaly very near to each other, and possess the same climatic conditions.

The geographical distribution is quite different from that of bronchitis, pleuritis and the other local inflammations of the respiratory tract, and its frequency is affected by the season of the year very differently from pleuritis, bronchitis and catarrhal pneumonia and kindred diseases, as is shown by the table of Juergensen.*

Certain conditions seem to be pretty generally and satisfactorily proven, as for instance, those who lead mostly an out-door active business life suffer far less from pneumonia than those who carry on their occupations within confined apartments. The statistical evidence I think, supports such a view, notwithstanding the contrary opinion held by Flint and others of equally as high standing in the profession.

In England, the average mortality from croupous pneumonia per 1,000 of those living in the rural districts, is .8 while the mortality rate in twenty-five large towns, is two per cent., not including London, which is higher.

In the country population of our own state the mortality is a little less than .8, while in the city of Baltimore, it ranges something over .9 per cent.

It is also shown that soldiers are more frequently attacked with pneumonia while garrisoned, than in the field. This is supported by the reports of the English, French and Russian troops in the Crimean war.

I am aware that it is the custom to enumerate among the exciting causes of pneumonia, such things as may, it is true, cause an inflammation of the lungs, but not by any means a croupous pneumonia.

To this class belong injuries of the chest, such as contusions, gun-shot wounds or those caused by some foreign body in the bronchial tubes, breathing of irritating gases, etc.

*Ziemssen's Cyclopedia.

Statistics seem to show that croupous pneumonia is pre-eminently more frequent in the tropical and semi-tropical climates than in the more northern climates. The reverse is true with bronchitis and other inflammatory diseases of the bronchial tract. Therefore the old idea that there is a relation of cause and effect between cold and croupous pneumonia is no longer tenable, and that the action of chilling or cold, in the causation of croupous pneumonia, at the very most can be nothing more than an exciting factor, as it not unfrequently is in an attack of intermittent fever, which I am sure at this late day, no one would be rash enough to believe to be caused by cold.

If we turn to the records of the board of health of this city, we find that the mortality from croupous pneumonia justifies us in a certain sense to speak of it as an epidemic disease. There is, I admit, a certain continuity during the intermediate periods.

There is no disease with which I am acquainted, whose symptomatology is more varied than croupous pneumonia.

The only invariable element is the change found in the lung, which can be detected only by a physical examination, and by the presence of a surely manifest functional disturbance, the loss of proportion between the respiration and that of the pulse.

A very large proportion of the cases of croupous pneumonia present very few of the symptoms of the typical case which is so graphically described in our text-books. Usually, however, the respiratory affection predominates, but frequently the symptoms extend over the whole body and the patient is simply ill; at one time the attack is violent, the brain seems to be the organ chiefly affected, and death winds up the scene in a few days; at another there is a long prodrome lasting days, perhaps, the only important lesion seems to be with the nutrition and the patient dies slowly but surely o of the vital functio

The duration of ously estimated at days. Most fre comes on the sev and convalesence inaugurated.

There are und abortive pneumoni ease terminates of dent of any form course of one or tw

Croupous pneu begins suddenly wi rigor, or it may de ually, the patient feeling unwell, ver limbs—a general attack is ushered i marked chills or by accession of ranging from 103 (Fahrenheit) with degrees between evening temperatu respiration 40 or 50 right nipple or the to the lung afte however, the pain opposite side; p cough, sometimes even hoarse; ch dust sputa; high c hot skin which late in perspiration; n herpetic eruption a bright hectic s corresponding to coated tongue; cor mental anxiety; and delirium; grea physical depressio the rapidly devel vances, of the typ added to this, the should expect to b solidated lung.

These symptom ed until the sev when they singula subside and the such relief from all toms, notwithstan exhaustion of his physical strength and local condition of his lung as to express himself as well. The principal lesions in those who have died of croupous pneumonia are found in the lungs and pleura. The body is generally well nourished, skin cyanotic and livors numerous. The brain more or less edematous and much congested, also its membranes. The pleura corresponding to the consolidated lung, is always inflamed. The right side of the heart with venæ cavæ distended with blood. The internal organs congested, and, according to Juergensen, the spleen is enlarged to more than one and one-half times its normal size. Catarrh of the pelvis and papillæ is an almost constant lesion of the kidney, occasionally slight enlargement and congestion of Peyer's patches and of the solitary glands of the intestines.

When the chest is opened the lungs generally collapse less than usual and the more affected parts seem raised, due to the consecutive emphysema.

The organ is of dark-red color, specific gravity and absolute weight increased, elasticity is lost, it is less crepitant, and more friable than normal, and pits on pressure. Its cut surface yields a reddish, frothy, tenacious liquid, and very frequently the impressions of the ribs are noticed on the lung.

The primary lesion is spoken of differently by the different pathologists and authors. According to Green, coagulated exudation matter fills the alveoli; according to Cornil and Ranvier, the lymphatics of the surface of the lung are constantly inflamed and filled up with the same matter that fills the alveoli; according to Bristowe, the primary lesion is in the lung substance; according to Niemeyer, in the air cells; according to Fox, in the vesicular structure of the lung; according to Juergensen, in the alveoli and bronchioles; according to Delafield, in the air vesicles and interstitial tissue; according to Flint, in the pulmonary substance, in the air cells and bronchioles, and according to Lynch, begins in the capillaries of the pulmonary system. This last theory or hypothesis, so far as I know, has not as yet been demonstrated.

Now, with regard to the nature of croupous pneumonia, there seem to be two principal theories, first that it is an imflammatory disease simply and only; and second that it is an acute infectious disease or an essential fever depending upon some morbid and specific poison, like typhoid fever or epidemic cerebro-spinal meningitis.

The local inflammation theory does not apply in cases of croupous pneumonia, and does not explain the clinical history of the disease. Artificial croupous pneumonia cannot be produced by experiment upon animals.

Experiments upon the vagus nerve produce catarrhal pneumonia only. There are no cases on record which show that croupous pneumonia has been produced by any of the causes which give rise to other inflammations, though I may state here in the way of parenthesis that Carl Friedlander, and Frobenius and Klebs, claim to have found a special form of microorganism, which, when injected into the lungs of dogs and mice, produces genuine croupous pneumonia; also that Balogh cultivated bacteria from the sputa of pneumonia which, when injected under the skin of rabbits, produced pneumonia wtih kidney affections.

There seems to be a definite relation between pneumonia and latitude as was shown in a paper read by Dr. Sanders before the Academy of Medicine in New York, in 1881.

Bronchitis increases as we ascend from the equator, and pneumonia increases as we approach the tropics. Such is at least true with the United States, as has been shown in a paper read by Flint of New York.

Pneumonia is essentially a disease of the winter and spring months. Those following out-door occupations are less liable to the disease, than those housed in close apartments, and the disease occurs less frequently in the country than in the city.

In regard to the symptoms, a synchronism should exist between the local lesion and the constitutional symptoms if pneumonia is a local inflammation; but the general symptoms of the disease do not bear any relation to the local lesion and the treatment now employed is contrary to all accepted notions as to local diseases. Formerly it was the rule to apply antiphlogistic remedies in the treatment of pneumonia, but this has all been discarded, and the methods now in use do not differ from the treatment commonly adopted for infectious diseases. Local measures are employed, it is true, but they are used solely for the local manifestations just as ice is used in cerebro-spinal meningitis.

The dissent from the local theory of croupous pneumonia is further strengthened by the fact that the disease is uninfluenced by treatment and under favorable circumstances is proven to be self limited, that the attendent fever pursues a cyclical course, and is characterized by an almost pathognomonic temperature curve. On account of these characteristics and other facts that I shall mention, the simple imflammatory basis is now pretty generally abandoned.

How does croupous pneumonia resemble other infectious diseases? An infectious disease is one, according to Virchow, who first introduced the term, in which the harmful influence is not local, but works prejudiciously through the entire organism. Infection does not necessarily imply contagion, but under certain circumstances according to Sanders, Schroter, Bryson, Kuhn and Muller, acute croupous pneumonia may possess a contagious character. Cullen, Sydenham, Tissot, Laennec, Skoda and others of the older authors; Flint, Loomis, Parker and Smith, of more recent authors consider croupous pneumonia to be an infectious disease, while Trousseau and Traube, believe it to be related to idiopathic erysipelas. Traube supported his theory by facts in the clinical history of pneumonia, as the prodromata, pre-inflammatory fever and the independence of the crisis of the inflammation, metastases, etc.

Now what are the characters of an infectious disease?

1st. Infrequency of occurrence and the number attacked; that is, acute infectious diseases do not prevail equally every year, and when they do appear, the number of persons affected varies greatly.

Pneumonia has occured only rarely some years, and it has at times prevailed epidemically in prisons, barracks, etc.

There are reported several well authenticated epidemics of croupous pneumonia.

Again, abortive cases of pneumonia, the occurrence of which being acknowledged indicate it to be of an infectious character.

2nd. Infectious diseases cannot be produced experimentally, except the special poison be inoculated, neither can croupous pneumonia be so produced unless by the same means.

3rd. Acute infectious diseases have prodromata; so often has croupous pneumonia.

4th. Acute infectious diseases pursue a definite classical course; we know of no disease which has a more definite classical course than croupous pneumonia.

5th. In acute infectious diseases there seems to be no relation between the local lesion and the general symptoms; just so with croupous pneumonia.

6th. In acute infectious diseases there are certain tendencies to certain complications in different epidemics; so we likewise have different complications, and the tendency to such in different years, in croupous pneumonia.

7th. Acute infectious diseases have a cyclical course; in no disease is this more marked than in croupous pneumonia.

8th. The rate of mortality varies in each epidemic in acute infectious diseases; so do the mortality tables vary in the different years in croupous pneumonia.

9th. One of the characters of acute infectious diseases is a localization of morbid changes in some organ or organs; this is equally the case with croupous pneumonia.

10th. In acute infectious diseases remedies have no influence upon the natural course of the disease; neither have they in croupous pneumonia.

11th. Patients suffering from an acute infectious disease have a natural tendency to recovery, independent of treatment; so have those who are affected with croupous pneumonia.

12th. I think in conclusion we are justified in stating that croupous pneumonia is a miasmatic, contagious fever, with definite lesions in the lungs, and, according to the experiments of Friedlander and Frobenius, in all probability the specific poison is taken into the body through the lungs.

ARTICLE II.

The Pathology of Pneumonic Inflammations in the Lower Animals.

A Paper read before the Medical and Surgical Society of Baltimore, January 16, 1884.

BY CHAS. FREDERICK PERCIVALL, A. M., M. D., BALTIMORE.

I have found it necessary to introduce in the paper I am about to read, some reference to comparative animal pathology and morbid anatomy, instead of reading to you quotations from books on the diseases under consideration as they occur in the human body, with which you are all acquainted. The existence of pleuropneumonitis contagiosa and bronchitis in horned animals, was lately the subject of differences of opinion between the great veterinary officers of the different great empires of Europe. Dr. Williams, of the new veterinary college of Edinburg, Scotland, carefully studied the post-mortem appearances in both diseases, and has submitted his views to the profession. The opportunity of studying the post-mortem appearances of bronchitis in its earliest stages but seldom occurs, and had it not been for the slaughter of a large number of diseased cattle, the lesions induced by the initial stages of inflammation of the bronchial tubes could not have been so minutely described, and Dr. Williams acknowledges the great assistance he received from Dr. Hamilton, the well-known pathologist to the Royal Infirmary and demonstrator of morbid anatomy in the University of Edinburg, in these investigations.

Prof. Williams says, bronchitis may, according to its seat, be arrayed under four heads, namely: Tracheo-bronchitis, where the lower part of the trachea and larger tubes are the main seats of the inflammation; bronchitis proper, where the medium sized bronchi are made the chief seats of the disease; capillary bronchitis, where the smaller bronchi are chiefly implicated; and catarrhal, lobular or broncho-pneumonitis, where the smallest bronchi and alveolar walls are involved.

The character of the inflammation, whatever part of the respiratory tract may be affected, is what is understood as catarrhal, that is, an inflammation in which, instead of an exudation rich in fibrin, there is a fluid secretion containing a large quantity of mucous and cellular elements. In this particular it differs most essentially from inflammation of the lungs, originating in the parenchyma, and from pleuro-pneumonia, in which the pleural surface as well as the lung structure is involved. The exudate in these is termed croupous or fibrinous. Acute bronchitis consists of congestion of the bronchial tissues associated at first with dryness, narrowing and rigidity, and subsequently moisture, dilatation and relaxation of the tubes. Owing to these changes, the vibrating sounds caused by the passage of air through the bronchi, undergo variations which indicate pretty clearly the dry or moist conditions of the parts, or, as some have it, the dry or moist catarrh. As the symptoms are developed, the cough becomes hoarse, ringing, loud and paroxysmal; the respirations are in some instances greatly accelerated; indeed, out of all proportion to the pulse. For example, the pulse may be seventy or eighty, and the respirations as frequent, or even more so. This indicates bronchitis affecting the smaller tubes and alveolar walls, catarrhal pneumonia, collapse of a more or less extensive area of lung structure, or even occlusion of non-inflamed bronchi and air vesicles by the gravitation into them of the catarrhal fluid. Bronchitis of the larger tubes is naturally less dangerous than the other two, and only proves fatal by inducing the two above named conditions, namely: collapse and occlusion of a more or less extensive breathing surface.

Amongst these animals, it was noticed where the discharge of mucopurulent matter was most profuse, although they seemed to recover from the febrile disturbance and accelerated breathing of the acute stage, that they succumbed in from 14 to 30 days afterward from gangrene of the collapsed lungs, or putrefaction of the fluid incarcerated in the bronchi and air cells. Both of these conditions being expressed by fetor of breath, exhaustive diarrhœa, metastatic inflammation of the articulations, rapid emaciation, gasping respiration, and general septicemia.

With regard to the pathological and morbid anatomy, inflammation of the bronchial tubes, like that affecting other mucous membranes, is attended with changes in their epithelium, the secretion of the glands, and in the surrounding tissues. It is very rare to meet with a fatal case of bronchitis in the human being during its early stages; and, but for the accidental slaughter in Liverpool of the American cattle already referred to, it would have been difficult to have given the details of the morbid anatomy.

Professor Hamilton says: "On careful examination and comparison however, of many cases, we feel assured that the first deviation visible is a relaxation and distention of the abundant plexus of blood vessels ramifying in the inner fibrous coat, immediately beneath the basement membrane; that is to say, of the branches of the bronchial artery. They become engorged with blood, so that on transverse section, they appear like little cavities distended with blood-corpuscles. In a few hours afterward, the basement membrane (which is not apparent in the lower animals as in man,) becomes much more apparent than it usually is, and at the same time more clear and homogeneous, while the surface is thrown in many folds. These changes in the basement membrane are apparently due to its becoming edematous, serous fluid being infiltrated into it from the underlying plexus of distended vessels, and we shall see that as the acute irritation continues, this edematous state of the basement membrane becomes more and more a marked feature. The next change occurs in from 20 to 30 hours after the primary distention of the vessels, and consists in the loosening and desquamation of the columnar epithelium at the foci of greatest congestion. The columnar epithelium is thus shed at a very early stage of the attack, and takes no part whatever in the after changes which ensue. It is never seen again until the other signs of acute inflammation, such as the distention of the vessels and edema of the basement membrane have passed off. Subsequently we shall see that it is gradually reproduced. The cause of this desquamation of the columnar epithelium seems to be the edema of the basement membrane loosening its underlying attachments very much in the same way as the vesicles, which form in an acute inflammatory affection of the skin loosen the attachments of the superficial layer of epidermis. The removal of the protecting covering from the mucous membrane, naturally leaves the latter in an exposed condition, and no doubt the feeling of rawness experienced in acute catarrh of the bronchi, is due to the cold air acting upon an over-stimulated and exposed mucous membrane; and further, it can easily be understood that where this desquamation takes place to an inordinately great extent, the loss of the ciliary action of the columnar cells will seriously interfere with expectoration, and tend to cause the catarrhal products to gravitate downward, towards the smaller bronchi and air vesicles.

"This early shedding of columnar cells and their non-reproduction until after the subsidence of the inflammatory process, is a fact of real importance as it goes a long way to explain the occurrence of those caseous tumors which give rise to tubercle, and are so often confounded with their growth."

The disease may, as already remarked, terminate fatally by the absorption of the putrescent catarrhal products; by gangrene of the collapsed lung, or by the sudden effusion of fluid into the bronchi, constituting what is called suffocative catarrh. If a fatal termination does not ensue, the contents of the alveoli *undergo degeneration*, and are gradually removed by discharge, or by absorption, or by coalescence form caseous masses which may become encapsulated, undergo the calcareous change, and thus become innocuous, or may induce a diathesis leading to the actual development of tubercle in the ox and to symptoms simulating phthisis pulmonalis in the horse. In the last stages of broncho-pneumonitis may also be found secondary abscesses independently of thrombi by the agency of white blood corpuscles and micrococci, which accumulate in the small vessels of the parts affected, and there are facts from the microscopic examination of cases which go to show that death takes place from asphyxia of mechanical origin—embolism of the pulmonary capillaries, caused by the great accumulation of bacteria and micrococci, some of which are dead from want of oxygen, or from putrefaction.

With regard to the last, I shall offer no explanation, as it is even now a question agitating the most distinguished botanists and pathologists of the age. Enough, however, is now known on the subject to render it without doubt that the agency of microscopic organisms in the production of certain diseases rests upon a strong basis of facts.

ARTICLE III.

The Michigan State Board of Health.

[Reported for the MEDICAL CHRONICLE.]

The regular quarterly meeting of the Michigan State Board of Health was held in the office of the Board at Lansing, Michigan, January 8th, 1884, the following members being present: Jno. Avery, M. D., of Greenville, president; J. H. Kellogg, M. D., of Battle Creek; Victor C. Vaughan, M. D., of Ann Arbor; C. V. Tyler, M. D., of Bay City; and Henry B. Baker, M. D., Secretary.

The recommendations to the warden of the State House of Correction, by Dr. Jno. Avery, committee on Buildings, Ventilation, etc., under date of September 7th, 1883, for improving the ventilation of the shops at the State House of Correction, at Ionia, were ordered printed in the next annual report.

The secretary read a resumé of recent work of other boards of health; also a summary of the work of the office of this Board during the last quarter, which showed that a successful sanitary convention had been held at Ionia; that partial arrangements had been made for holding one at Hillsdale; that the proceedings of the Muskegon, Pontiac, and Reed

City conventions had been printed; that special meetings of the Board had been called at the State Reform School to examine plans for a new building; at Detroit to attend American Public Health Association; and at Ionia at the time of the convention; that a leaflet on contagious diseases had been translated into French, Danish, Norwegian, and Swedish, for general distribution among citizens of Michigan who speak those languages; that a very general distribution of circulars on communicable diseases and on the work of health officers had been made to the health officers of cities, villages and townships in Michigan; that similar documents were distributed at Ionia, and at the State Teachers' Association; that circulars, blanks, etc., had been sent to health officers and clerks of all cities, villages and townships in Michigan, for their annual report, including that of the diseases dangerous to the public health; that notice had been sent to health authorities in several parts of the State warning of the shipment of diseased cattle into such localities; that the regular distribution of weekly bulletins of sickness and of meteorology, the yearly distribution of material for meteorological reports, and the quarterly distribution of blanks to observers of diseases, had been made.

The Secretary presented reports from Dr. Hazlewood who as committee of the Board attended the Sanitary Convention at London, Ontario, and the meeting of the Board of Corrections and Charities at East Saginaw. In connection with the first report, Dr. Hazlewood described the water supply of that city (London), and the Secretary, who also attended the convention, described a visit to the Asylum for the Insane near London, Ontario.

By request of the State Board of Corrections and Charities, committees were appointed to examine and report on the sanitary condition of the jails, asylums, etc., in several counties in Michigan.

Drs. Avery and Kellogg were appointed a committee to investigate and report at the next regular meeting on sewerage, ventilation, etc., of the Capitol building.

A committee, consisting of Drs. Baker, Kellogg and Vaughan, were appointed to examine and report on the sanitary condition and needs of the State Reform School and surroundings.

Dr. Kellogg presented and read portions of a very interesting report on the present knowledge respecting diphtheria, which will be published in the next annual report.

Considerable discussion occurred over the examination of text books on physiology and hygiene, with reference to alcohol and other narcotics. Only four books had been presented for examination. The committee reported relative to these books, and asked to be discharged; but the committee was continued, Prof. Vaughan being added to it. It was directed to confer with a similar committee from the State Board of Education, and it is to report again at the next regular meeting of the Board, April 8th. It is hoped that publishers of school books will give early attention to this subject, and that more than one book can be approved at that time.

ARTICLE IV.

Fly Blister on a Young Child, and its Sequela.

By D. W. CATHELL, M. D.

Joseph M., 18 months of age, was suffering from acute bronchitis. For its relief his mother conceived the idea of putting a fly blister on his epigastrium. Accordingly, one 2 by 4 inches in size was applied November 18th, and kept on five hours, after which the blisters were clipped and a free discharge of serum followed.

I was called to see him, November 30th; the bronchitis was nearly gone,

—so was the child—who was pale, with high fever, thready pulse, and great vital depression. The blistered surface, which had become an eroding ulcer, presented a grayish pulpy appearance, and was sloughing in patches here and there. Its edges were everted and surrounded by a margin of angry inflammation. No healthy granulations or efforts at repair were to be found.

Active measures, both internal and external, were at once instituted, but in spite thereof the cellular tissue continued to break down till the abdominal muscles were exposed. The ulcer also kept extending its circumference by erosion till at the time of death, which occurred after great suffering, December 27th. The sore was nearly twice its original size.

A medical confrére related to me some time since, the case of a strumous boy 7 years old, on whose rheumatic shoulder a fly blister one inch in diameter was applied, which relieved the rheumatism but went on eroding skin and destroying cellular tissue till trapezius, deltoid and sterno-cleido-mastoid were all exposed, ending, of course, in death.

I report these cases to illustrate the well-known danger of applying fly blisters to cachectic or very young children, and to suggest that they be banished from the therapeutics of such patients.

ANALECTS.

Observations on Hydrocele.

In infancy one sees acquired hydrocele along the cord or in the tunica-vaginalis sac, or those communicating with the abdomen, "congenital," so called.

Most of them, if left alone, would be cured by nature in the course of time, but the anxiety of parents or the interests of the practitioner demand some interference. As a rule, the simpler this is, the better. I have had them disappear rapidly under the continued application of evaporating lotion, which, as it is inevitably bound on with the clothing, acts not by evaporation, but by stimulation.

In one eight-months baby, badly nourished, and with diarrhœa, a good-sized double hydrocele was rapidly reabsorbed when the child's condition was toned up by change of diet, which checked the diarrhœa.

Long standing infantile hydrocele commonly yields to puncture. The best method is to hold three or four surgical needles side by side between the finger and thumb, and, while making the scrotal sac tense, rapidly repeat the punctual stroke, pricking as many as thirty or forty points. Through the stellate puncture of the surgical needles the fluid quickly escapes into the cellular tissue, and some through the skin, aided by gentle squeezing.

Endeavor to evacuate the sac thus, and the fluid left under the skin is quickly absorbed.

Some cases I have followed a year or two where one acupuncture cured.

Hypodermic aspiration is a simple, and, in time, effective remedy, but, as a rule, has to be often repeated. Two cases of hydrocele of the cord were each cured by one aspiration; one of them contained two ounces, in a child of five years.

The seton is effective, but, unless removed at just the right time, say after thirty-six hours, it will set up a disagreeable suppuration of the sac, necessitating incision.

In the way of medication, I have seen hydrocele in children of six months to two years disappear on the administration of iodide of potash, 2 gr. t. i. d., for two or three weeks, the diminution in fluid beginning soon after treatment was begun.

In the case of one child, whose hydrocele I frequently aspirated, a cure took place only after circumcision for phimosis and preputial adhesions, after which the hydrocele got well spontaneously, and, one year later, the sac was still dry.

In hydroceles of adults I have noticed, with few exceptions, what is not noticed in the text-books, that an induration of the epididymis co-exists either as a hardness of its entire body, or of the globus major or minor alone, showing a very subacute, painless, inflammatory action. This can be noticed only after tapping.

A word regarding encysted hydroceles.

These are developed in the cellular plane investing the epididymis, and probably originate from an obstructed seminal duct. The fluid is invariably as colorless as water (strongly in contrast with the straw-colored fluid of the ordinary variety), or slightly milky from the spermatozoa in suspension, which soon form a sediment on standing. In some cases we find, on microscopical examination, living spermatozoa.

The encysted hydrocele is said to be almost always small—half an ounce to two ounces or so—though Curling says he has seen one as large as twenty ounces.

Among quite a number of this variety I have seen two much larger than that—one of thirty-eight ounces, and another enormous one of forty-eight. The latter was in a man fifty years; had developed during five years; colorless fluid; spermatozoa in action. Waited two months after tapping, till it had filled to fifteen ounces, when, after tapping, I injected half an ounce of tincture of iodine. One year later no trace of fluid or thickened sac remained. It was cured. In the patient of sixty-three years old, with a thirty-eight ounce hydrocele of this form, of seven years' standing, there was one of three ounces on the other testicle also. Spermatozoa were abundant in the fluid. One drachm of tincture of iodine was thrown into each sac after tapping, and a little inflammatory fluid returned in a month or so, as is usual, but was reabsorbed, and, one year later, both sacs were dry.

Thus, as I have found in smaller encysted hydroceles too, Curling's statement, that this form is not cured by iodine, is disproved. I think, in fact, that its cure is almost certain.

This variety I have found exclusively in old gentlemen from fifty to seventy years. In one patient of seventy it began fourteen years before, immediately after his wife's death, when he became continent. It grew to fifteen ounces; fluid colorless, spermatozoa abundant.

A number of smaller encysted hydroceles have remained as perfect cures by the iodine injection.

Dark fluid hydroceles are apt to contain either blood or cholesterin, and I have thought the former sometimes degenerated into the latter, as illustrated by a twenty-five-ounce cyst in a patient of seventy years, giving a sediment of blood and spermatozoa and sperm cells when tapped in October, 1879, but when next seen and tapped, in June, 1883, yielding fluid containing cholesterin crystals in abundance. Suppuration of the sac followed simple tapping, and a small slough occurred at the puncture point.

I have seen two cases of thickened sac, with cholesterin crystals, in the fluid, suppurate freely after tapping, and believe the irritation of the crystals escaping in the course of the puncture set up irritant action. This accident, however, does not always follow evacuation of such fluid, as shown in a ten-ounce hydrocele carried eight years by an old gentleman, the fluid of which deposited one fifth of its bulk of crystals. No suppuration followed tapping.

CURATIVE TREATMENT. — First. By internal administration of iodide of potassium in selected cases, cure may be brought about after tapping, where there is well-marked induration of the epididymis. The power of this drug to produce absorption of plastic exudation or chronic induration is well recognized, even where (as is most often the case) there is no syphilis suspected. Of course, if this disease does exist, potash *must* be used. I have record of a case of double hydrocele, ten ounces on each side, where the testicles were both somewhat enlarged and hard. The man proved syphilitic, and but one tapping, followed by medicine, cured him.

Second. Injection with iodine will, if rightly used, be a competent curative method in most cases. I have resorted to it about forty times, and note the following points :

There is almost always some little shock after injection. The pulse commonly falls from 80 to 60 or 50 beats for a few minutes. Some pallor is usually shown, and a good deal of pain experienced, following the course of the vas deferens.

I have once seen very profound shock. The patient was sixty-six years old, and had an old hydrocele of ten ounces, which I evacuated, and had injected but half a drachm of iodine when the patient showed prostration, pallor, and collapse; became pulseless, and was restored only after half an hour of stimulation by whiskey, ammonia, and hot bottles.

I should prefer not to use the iodine injection in a patient with weak heart.

Occasionally, for some unaccountable reason, a case is utterly rebellious to this method of cure, as in a man of twenty-one years whose hydrocele had been injected with iodine, three times in seven years, by Dr. Fowler, of Altany, and Dr. Otis, of New York, and no impression was made on it. To test the matter, I did it with thoroughness the fourth time, and also failed to cure it.

After iodine injection one expects first an accumulation of some inflammatory fluid, rapid for a week or so, then slow, and finally a reabsorption, leaving the sac dry.

Third. Injection with pure carbolic acid, as demonstrated by Levis, of Philadelphia, has taken rank as probably the best method of radical cure of hydrocele,

I had resorted to it in about a dozen cases, and find that its two decided advantages are, that it gets up a grade of *plastic inflammation* different from and better than that by iodine, and that it is almost always painless and gives *no shock*. The pulse never varies after the injection. I have had but one man complain of pain, and he for three minutes said his "testicle felt as if it was in a frying-pan." After operation the patient usually keeps at his work. There is less reaccumulation of fluid, and more often a plastic lymph that can be felt in the sac.

One drachm of deliquesced crystals should be thrown through the cannula, distributed in the sac, and left.

The scrotum should be well greased, to prevent the caustic action of the acid on the skin if a drop or two of it escapes from the cannula.

I once injected three drachms into a large sac and had acute suppuration follow, requiring incision, which, of course, cured the hydrocele effectually. I used too much. One drachm will always suffice. Carbolic acid poisoning never follows this injection.

Finally, I regret to report one death following the simple operation of tapping without injection.

An old and feeble book-agent of temperate habits of life was tapped by me three times in 1879 for a hydrocele of twelve ounces. No reaction followed but in the next year, after a simple tapping, there ensued acute inflammation of the sac, and phlegmonous cellulitis of the scrotum, with fatal exhaustion, due to his enfeebled condition.

It was the only serious result of over one hundred and fifty cases, representing, perhaps, five hundred tappings. —*Dr. Abbe in N. Y. Med. Jour.*

Let Nature Remove the Placenta.

In Deutch. Med. Woch., September 26, 1883, Dr. Dohrn thus sums up his experience :

1. In one thousand lying-in women, in whom the expulsion of the

placenta was left to nature, the results were far better than in one thousand others in whom Credé's method of expulsion was used.

2. The one thousand lying-in women in whom the placenta was spontaneously expelled, had considerably less hemorrhage and fever after delivery. In those cases treated by Credé's method, portions of the membranes were frequently retained, and there were more fatal cases than in the others.

3. The disadvantages which are conditional to the method of Credé, are especially seen in the cases in which the placenta is expressed during the first five minutes. After a longer time the expression was more complete, but never as safe as by the spontaneous method.—*The Medical Age.*—*Texas Courier-Record.*

On the Radical Cure of Exomphalos.

A hernial protrusion at or near the umbilicus is an exceedingly troublesome condition in the adult. In children, it can be cured by the careful use of a well fitting truss in the great majority of cases; indeed, I have never seen an umbilical hernia in an adult which dated from childhood. It must be by far more common in women than in men, for I cannot find amongst my surgical friends, who see men as patients, that it is common in males; whilst those of us who deal with the abdominal viscera of women, see it very often. It occurs chiefly in very fat women, or in those whose abdominal walls have been greatly stretched by many labors, or by large tumors, and we all know that it is peculiarly liable to strangulation. It is never cured in the adult by the use of a truss; in fact, in my experience, it generally gets worse in spite of every or any kind of truss, and the employment of such means of retention is always irksome and sometimes quite impossible.

I have not made anything like an exhaustive research into the literature of the radical cure of umbilical hernia, but what search I have made has been singularly barren of results. In most of the text-books it is not even mentioned; and, even in the special books, very little is said about it. I have found record of a few cases, as in Professor John Wood's book, where stitching operations have been done subcutaneously, but they have been mostly in children, and no definite statements are made as to the subsequent results.

The peculiarities of exomphalos, that the omentum is inevitably present in the sac, that it is almost always adherent to the inner surface of the sac, and generally irreducible, have stood very much, indeed completely, in the way of the means of the subcutaneous operations; and the extreme difficulty of being sure that all the intestine is returned before the wires are tightened, forms a serious danger in their performance. Still another difficulty exists—one much less known—that it is almost exceptional to find a single hernia aperture; they are generally multiple.

Concerning the adhesion of omentum to the sac, Mr. Wood says that it would not constitute a serious objection to the operation, since the presence of an omental plug would contribute to the closure of the aperture, and strangulation of this structure by the ligature might be avoided in its application. A very extensive acquaintance with the omentum leads me to differ entirely from these two statements, and to conclude that the retention in the ring of a piece of omentum would be a complete bar to any permanence of its closure. Mr. Wood further says that the presence of much permanent distension of the abdominal cavity by fat or other causes, would preclude any attempt at a radical cure by operation, and this, of course, removes the great bulk of sufferers from any hope of relief. A final objection to all subcutaneous operations is, that the utmost that is gained by them is the union of opposing surfaces of peritoneum, such a union as is not at all likely to resist a stretching force for any length of time. I have seen only one such operation done, very many years ago. It was perfectly successful for a few months, but after that, the patient slowly relapsed into her former state.

The operation I am now about to describe I was led to first by being obliged, occasionally, to operate in cases of strangulated exomphalos. In such cases, I have never done what is recommended as the extraperitoneal operation, as I am sure it cannot be so safe as the operation by opening the sac; and it leaves the patient, after her recovery, with a larger hernia than she had before it. In such cases, as far as I can find (for in my earlier practice, and before my present method of record was in fashion, such abdominal sections were not thought worthy of specific record), eleven in number, I have opened the sac, freed all adhesions, removed redundant and irreducible omentum, pared the edges of the ring, and stitched them together. Every one of the eleven recovered; and I cannot discover that I have had a death in such a case—certainly it would be an incident not likely to be forgotten. I know three of these patients now, and the cure of the protrusion is permanent, after eleven, eight and five years, respectively. What has come to the others, I do not know

But since the time when I began to discard the superstitions of the peritoneum, between five and six years ago—that is, after the clamp was given up in ovariotomy, for all true progress in abdominal surgery dates from that—I have turned my attention to the radical cure of exomphalos, as one of the legitimate advances of my department. I have deliberately opened a number of hernial sacs, at or near the umbilicus; have reduced the intestine; cut off adherent omentum; pared the edges of the ring or rings; stitched them together by a continuous silk thread (which I leave permanently there); and have thus secured complete occlusion of the sac. The cases are included in the various series of abdominal sections I have published, and several have been performed since my last series was published. As might be expected, such an operation has had no mortality—I should be immensely surprised if I lost a case—and the results, so far, are all quite permanent. All the patients have been fat, some very fat, and the last one was pregnant.

This short paper I purpose to be a mere preliminary note of my practice on this subject: and, therefore, I have given no details. I shall take the matter up at length in a coming annual series of cases.

Let me conclude by saying, that I have an impression that the radical cure of hernia of other kinds than umbilical, will, by-and-by, be undertaken by abdominal section. I am not sure but that it will be extended to operations for strangulated hernia. A few weeks ago, I removed an ovarian tumor from a woman with a femoral hernia, in which intestine was adherent. It was a very easy matter to undo the adhesions, and, by means of a handled needle and a silk thread, to obliterate the ring in a manner which, I am sure, no operation from the outside could have effected. So much can be done through a two-inch incision, that, if I should be ever called upon again (as I very rarely am) to operate on a strangulated femoral hernia, I believe I shall proceed by abdominal section, and complete the radical cure of the protrusion at the same time that I relieve the obstruction.—Lawson Tait in *Brit. Med. Journal.*

The Use of the Bromide Salts for Abdominal Neuroses.

There is so strong a bond of therapeutic association between the bromides and the neurotic troubles of the head and chest that we are apt to forget how useful the same drugs may be for sundry disturbances of the digestive organs; and yet all the physical analogies of the subject would lend support to this doctrine. No one claims for the potassic and sodic bromides that they can clear away heterologous exudation, and mend damaged textures. But those of us who are still old-fashioned enough to believe in "functional derangements," or dynamic force temporarily perverted, can easily understand that there are certain aberrations of the cerebro-spinal system, which, being of the same kind wherever they are situated, may be expected to yield to the same medicines.

For an elderly widow lady, tormented rather often with "emotional diarrhœa," I prescribed a few years ago some ordinary astringent remedies, with minute doses of opium, to be taken according to her needs. But for another malady, sleeplessness, I gave occasionally moderate quantities of bromide of potassium. She discovered, however, that the latter remedy did her diarrhœa more good than anything else, and that, whenever it was taken at bed time, the next day passed without any alvine looseness.

Fourteen years ago Dr. Waring Curran recommended potassic bromide for the vomiting of pregnancy; but its real value could not be determined, as other things were combined with it (*Medical Press and Circular*, July 14, 1869). But I have given the medicine in the pure form, and simply dissolved in water, and never without marked, though perhaps temporary, success.

The distant echoes of cholera justify us in recalling some important observations by the late Dr. James Begbie, who spoke of bromide of potassium as able to strip that dread disease of some of its terrors (*Edinburgh Medical Journal*, December, 1866). He gave it in the earlier stage of the collapse, and in quantities of twenty or thirty grains, at hourly, or even half-hourly, intervals; and he records the cessation of vomiting, the arrest of cramp, and the speedy return of warmth and color to the previously cold and livid surface. He tells us that the medicine was tried fairly, both in the Leith and Edinburgh Cholera Hospitals, and that its use in both institutions did not disappoint expectations. It is good to feel fortified against the most painful and mortal of all abdominal neuroses.

Lastly, I may glance at the use of the bromides in the treatment of saccharine diabetes. Here again Dr. Begbie started a line of therapeutic inquiry which has been successfully worked by other practitioners; and at this moment I have under my care a lady between fifty and sixty years of age, whose special diabetic symptoms are clearly kept much in abeyance by a large dose of bromide of ammonium every night. Would this illustrate what has been called the "alterative and absorbent effects" of the bromides on the liver?—*British Medical Journal*.

Painless Treatment of Condylomata.

Nussbaum recommends the treatment of small condylomatous patches on the penis by daily washings with salt solution, followed by the sprinkling over them of calomel powder. Chemical change takes place and corrosive sublimate is produced, the condylomata disappear, and no pain is felt. Solution of corrosive sublimate in collodion, which acts more quickly, gives rise to much pain, and requires the patient to rest in bed. The proposed method is not new, but has fallen into unmerited disuse.—*Practitioner*.

A Clinical Study of the Action and Uses of Caffeine and Convallaria Majalis as Cardiac Tonics.

In the *Therapeutic Gazette*, August 15th, 1883, Dr. Beverly Robinson, of New York, thus concludes a paper on this subject:

Summary of cases seems to show:
1.—In caffeine and convallaria we have two efficient heart tonics.

2.—Diuretic action of caffeine is more marked than that of convallaria.

3.—Convallaria is well borne by the stomach of most patients suffering with chronic cardiac disorders.

4.—When not well supported, rejection of medicine by the stomach is probably due to the uræmic condition already commencing.

5.—As cardiac tonics, it is difficult, as yet, to assign a decided superiority to either of these drugs, they both giving increased cardiac power.

6.—Cumulative effects do not occur from their continued use during a period of ten days or more.

7.—Their power of restoring the rhythm to the cardiac pulsations, and increasing the bulk of urine, is not equal to that of the infusion of digitalis.

8.—In this latter drug we have still the most efficient heart tonic and regulator which has been discovered.

9.—Digitalis is a more powerful diuretic than caffeine.

The Influence of Syphilis upon the Progress of Cancer.

The reciprocal influences of diatheses are not well known yet, from want of attention being drawn in that direction. That of syphilis upon cancer can, in certain cases, be given with precision, of which the following cases are examples: A woman, whose antecedents are unknown, was taken with a cancerous tumor of the breast about a year ago. The progress was at first very slow, but she contracted syphilis eight months since, which is now in the full period of secondary accidents. On investigation how the syphilis had acted on the cancer the conviction is reached that it has considerably augmented its progress and its generalizations. Indeed the entire left breast and the axillary ganglia have undergone a cancerous degeneration. The subclavian ganglia form a considerable mass and reach up to the mastoid apophysis. Considering that the duration of the cancer is of one year only, and that it attained its present development in the last few months, that the invasion of the subclavian ganglia is only exceptional, and then it is considered a formal contra-indication of all operative interference, the conclusion is inevitable that syphilis was the origin of this abnormal process. This case presents another unusual fact. When cancer is largely developed and the ganglia are affected, pain is always very great, but in this case the patient does not suffer any pain at all.—*St. Louis Med. and Surg. Journal.*

The Co-existence of Chancre and Chancroid.

The question as to whether this is possible, receives some affirmative confirmation from a case reported in the *Med. News*, October 20, 1883, by Dr. John Ferguson, of Toronto. The patient, a medical student, in whose word Dr. F. seems to have implicit confidence, had connection on the same evening with two women. Three days afterwards he had a chancroid; five weeks subsequently he had a chancre, followed by constitutional syphilis, though in the meantime he had not had connection with any woman. It was ascertained that one of the women was suffering from chancroids, and a man who had connection with the other woman at about the same time, subsequently had constitutional syphilis.—*Med. and Surg. Rep.*

Pathology of Old Age.

A contribution to the pathology of old age is the subject of an article by Sommerbrodt from his experience in the Pensioners' Hospital at Berlin from 1873 to 1877 (Boston Med. and Surg. Jour.). Twenty-five autopsies were made on men over 70 years of age. Acute disease, as has been generally noticed, occurs but rarely, and when present is generally connected with the organs of respiration. The heart was affected in but few cases, while in every case evidences of endarteritis were to be seen. Chronic inflammatory changes were frequent in the meninges, while hemorrhage into the substance of the brain was rare. Gall stones, which in extreme old age never caused colic, were found in eight cases. Malignant disease (cancer of the postate) presented itself but once. The course of such troubles is probably run in previous decades. Pleural adhesions were often met with, but exudation into the pleural cavity very seldom. In about one half the cases tubercles, that is, cheesy centers, were scattered throughout the lungs, and this was notably oftener the case in persons who were quartered together in barracks than those who had a separate dwelling. This fact, the author thinks, points to the contagiousness of the disease. In general its course was run almost without symptoms; especially was it to be remarked that hæmoptysis was absent in the majority of cases.—*Weekly Medical Review.*

Successful Abdominal Surgery.

Dr. Robert Battey, of Rome, Ga., reports to the *Virg. Medical Monthly* eighteen consecutive cases of ovariotomy and performed by him, all successfully. He employed a modified antiseptic treatment. He insists on having the patient under his immediate charge subsequent to the operation, and concludes as follows: "The friends of a patient are by no means the best nurses for an ovariotomy case. Whilst in England I was assured that no operator who had any character to lose would venture to stake it upon an operation to be done under such disadvantages. They all require their cases to come to them, and put them into the hands of their trained nurses."
—*Pacific Med. and Surg. Journal.*

Prevention of Sea-Sickness.

Dr. Henry Bennet, in the *British Medical Journal*, recommends the following plan for the prevention of sea-sickness: A good, easily-digested meal should be taken four hours before embarking. Just long enough before embarking to secure its absorption, a cup of strong black coffee should be taken. The stomach should be entirely empty; a full stomach rather promotes sea-sickness. The influence of the coffee on the nervous system last about eight or ten hours, during which time the body may get accustomed to motion of the ship. It is better to take no food nor drink till hunger or thirst shows itself. For thirst soda or Apollinaris water, with brandy or champagne, clear, may be sipped. To allay hunger, *cafe au lait*, with or without bread, may be taken, and that aggrieving, a little curry may be tried as advised by Dr. Randall. On long journeys, after the coffee, one should lie in his berth. In the continued sickness of long voyages, great and often permanent relief may be obtained by rectal injection at night of fifteen or twenty drops of laudanum in an ounce and a half of warm water, which, if not retained, may be repeated in an hour and a half. —*American Practitioner.*

Corrosive Sublimate in Gonorrhœa.

Dr. Joseph McChestney, of Deming, New Mexico, contributes to the *Therapeutic Gazette*, for December, a report of a series of seven cases of gonorrhœa treated with injections of corrosive sublimate, one grain to six ounces of water, once every four hours after the subsidence of the acute stage. He is confident that this solution will cure gonorrhœa within ten days. In several cases this injection was resorted to after a long and unsuccessful course with the ordinary remedies; the result was uniform success.

"My poor man," said the doctor, "you are dangerously ill. Is there any word you want to send to your friends?" "Am I really so ill?" asked the sufferer. "Alas, I can offer you no hope." "Very well, then," said the sick man; "just telephone for another doctor."

The Medical Chronicle.

A Monthly Journal for the Practitioner.

GEORGE H. ROHÉ, M. D. Editor.

☞ It is requested that all literary and business communications, books for review, exchanges, etc., be addressed to, and all checks, drafts and post-office orders drawn to the order of
Dr. GEORGE H. ROHÉ,
95 Park Avenue, - - - - Baltimore, Md.

BALTIMORE, FEBRUARY, 1884.

EDITORIAL.

The Annual Message of Mayor Latrobe.

In the annual message of the mayor of Baltimore, transmitted to the City Council on January 28th, occur several matters of especial importance to physicians.

The cost of the health department for the year 1883 was $183,284.33. This large expenditure was partly due to the small-pox epidemic of last year. The entire number of cases of small-pox reported during the epidemic was 4,930, of which 1,184 died, a small fraction over 24 per cent. The death-rate for the year in an estimated population of 408,520, was 22.93 per thousand.

The completion of the new quarantine hospital at Hawkins' Point is briefly referred to, and it is recommended that steps be taken to permit the occupation of the new station by the 1st of May. The present station should continue to be used by the city as a city pest hospital.

Upon the necessity of a proper system of sewerage, His Honor speaks with definiteness and characteristic business sense. He says:

"I recommend an application to the Legislature for an enabling act authorizing the issue of bonds to an amount not exceeding $5,000,000, bearing not more than 4 per cent. interest, the proceeds of the sale of which shall be applied to the construction of a general system of sewers for this city. Should this power be granted, and the people endorse the recommendations, I then suggest the appointment by the Mayor and City Council of a commission similar to the Water Board, with power to appoint a suitable engineer, *the said board to decide upon a proper system and proceed to have it constructed.*"

The recommendation to place the entire matter in the hands of a commission, strikes us as a wise and important one. In this city this plan has always worked satisfactorily in the past, and in such a commission when properly constituted, the interests of the taxpayers are much more likely to be safe than in the hands of a single salaried officer. The "one-man power" has never been very popular here, and even when temporarily introduced, has failed to gain the support of the people.

A Cowardly Attack.

Dr. P. H. Millard, of Stillwater, Minnesota, has recently been the victim of an infamous attack upon his professional character by a trio of homœopaths of that city. A patient of Dr. Millard, suffering from puerperal mania, died eight hours after receiving a hypodermatic injection of Magendie's solution of morphia. The dose administered was less than eight minims. The husband of the patient requested a homœopath of Stillwater to make an autopsy, which was done with the aid of two other practitioners of the same faith. After a lengthly examination, these three worthies signed the following statement:

"We the undersigned recognizing that Emelia Ludwig was very sick, and that the condition of the generative organs, such as to cause some apprehension, still the condition of the patient as revealed by the postmortem, was not in our opinion sufficiently grave to cause death in the time and manner of the above named person. Considering the collapsed state of the lungs, the conjestion of the Pons Varolii and base of brain, the coma suddenly appearing; the absence of pyæmic or septicæmic symptoms, the condition of the patient the evening previous, we feel compelled to believe that her demise was precipitated by the administration of of some narcotic of which opium probably formed a base.

Signed, WM. L. CRADDOCK, M. D.
W. H. CAINE, M. D.
ALEX. DONALD, M. D."

Immediately upon becoming aware of this extraordinary statement, Dr. Millard demanded a coroner's investigation, and a new post-mortem was ordered, which was made by Dr. C. A. Wheaton, of St. Paul, assisted by Drs. Stone and Quinn. The followers of Hahnemann who had made the first autopsy, and several of the physicians of Stillwater were present. After the inquest the jury promptly and fully exonerated Dr. Millard.

The real animus underlying the attack upon Dr. Millard's character is probably the fact that this gentleman is chairman of the state board of medical examiners of Minnesota, and in executing the duties devolving upon him in this position, he has stirred up the bile of the quacks and irregulars in the state, who took advantage of what seemed to them a good opportunity for revenge. Happily the attempt failed, and Dr. Millard is to be congratulated upon this prompt and complete exposure of the unworthy motives and dishonorable practices of his enemies.

CURRENT LITERATURE.

Proceedings and addresses at a Sanitary Convention held at Pontiac, Mich., January 31 and February 1, 1883, and at a similar convention held at Muskegon, Mich., August 23 and 24, 1883. Published by the Michigan State Board of Health, Henry B. Baker, M. D., Secretary. Lansing, 1883.

These two pamphlets of 161 and 65 pages respectively, contain thirty-three addresses and papers read at popular sanitary conventions held under the auspices of the Michigan State Board of Health, in the two cities above named. The plan of holding sanitary conventions is one first introduced, we believe, by the Michigan Health Board, and it has recently been followed by the State Boards of Kentucky and of Maryland. It seems to be a practical way of familiarizing the public with the results of sanitary work. In the volumes here noticed may be found terse, entertaining and instructive papers upon adulteration of food; toy pistols and their dangers; the dangers in dirt; limitation and prevention of typhoid fever; relations of the soil-water to health; popular errors about medicine; sewerage and drainage; water supply; communicable diseases, and others of like importance to the public. The proceedings of the conventions are fully noticed in the local press, and the papers are afterwards printed by the State Board of Health, and freely distributed to the citizens of the State. We can only reiterate the opinion heretofore expressed in our columns, that the Michigan State Board does more effective, practical sanitary work than any other similar organization in the country.

PAMPHLETS.

Plastic Surgery of the Face. By L. McLane Tiffany, M. D., Prof. of Surgery, University of Maryland. Reprint from Transactions Medical Society of Virginia, 1883.——Morbid Somnolence. By Rudolph Matas, M. D. Reprint from N. O. Medical and Surgical Journal.——Sewerage of Cities. By C. W. Chancellor, M. D. Reprint from Transactions of the Sanitary Convention of Maryland, 1883.——The Recent Advances of Sanitary Science; being the annual address before the American Academy of Medicine. By H. O. Marcy, A. M., M. D., President of the Academy. ——An essay on Medical Legislation.

By Harry Hakes, M. D., Wilkes-Barre, Pa. Read at the annual meeting of the Luzerne County Medical Society.

FLOTSAM.

THE New York Post-graduate School has removed to new and more commodious quarters.

THE circulation of the *British Medical Journal* is eleven thousand six hundred and fifty copies, weekly.

AMONG the delicacies of the Paris markets are artificial oysters. We confess to a preference for the natural bivalves.

A case of epithelioma of the conjunctiva extending to the optic nerve is reported by Griffith in the *Ophthalmic Review*.

THE *Index Medicus* will be continued, a sufficient number of subscribers at $10.00 per year having been obtained to justify its continuance.

THE Baltimore Medical Association celebrated its anniversary, on the 14th of January. Dr. E. G. Waters was elected President for the ensuing year.

THE publication of the *Annals of Anatomy and Surgery* was suspended with the December number. The editors hope to resume its issue next year.

THIRTY cases of resection of the stomach have been reported in Germany. In 26 there was cancer; of these, 7 recovered. In 4 there was gastric ulcer, and of these, three recovered.

WE have added to our list of exchanges, the *Texas Courier-Record of Medicine*, edited by Drs. F. E. Daniel and W. B. Brooks. It is published at Fort Worth, Texas, at $2.00 per year.

A "collective investigation" into the causation of croupous pneumonia is to be set on foot under the auspices of the New York county Medical Society.

WE have received a number of pamphlets on "Opium Addiction," by Dr. J. B. Mattison, of Brooklyn, N. Y. The author will send copies of his writings on this subject to any one applying for the same.

IN a recent number of the *Popular Science Monthly* the statement is made that consumption is more prevalent among animals in a wild state than when in captivity. We don't believe the statement is true.

DR. DEMBO claims to have discovered the ganglia concerned in the production of cancer of the uterus. He says they are situated in the anterior wall of the vagina, and are independent of the spinal cord.

THE excellent paper on Canning Houses and the Public Health, which was read before the State Sanitary Convention by Dr. W. Stump Forwood, has been reprinted entire, in the Havre de Grace *Republican*.

A man who abstains from alcohol, as shown by insurance tables, at 20 years of age has a chance of living 44.2 years; at 30, 36.5 years; at 40, 28.8 years. An intemperate man's chance at 20 is 15.5 years, at 30, 13.8; at 40, 11.6 years.

WE print, in this number of THE CHRONICLE, two papers recently read before the Medical and Surgical Society of this city, upon Pneumonia. In the next number several other papers upon the treatment of this disease, will be given.

E. S. ULMAN, a member of the graduating class at the College of Physicians and Surgeons, died on the 21st of January of Pneumonia, Mr. Ulman was a popular member of the class and his loss is deeply felt. Appropriate resolutions were passed by his classmates.

DR. ELISHA HARRIS, secretary of the New York State Board of Health, died January 31st, of peritonitis. Dr. Harris was well known as an active sanitarian. He had been sanitary superintendent of New York city and president of the American Public Health Association.

PROF. Da Costa, from his own experience is so sure that cold baths, when possible, and otherwise, cold sponging, is the only remedy, and so effective a one, in the high temperature complication of acute rheumatism, that where it will not be used he will, hereafter, withdraw from the case.

THE Cartwright lectures for the current year were delivered in New York, on the 2nd, 4th and 6th of this month by Prof. Burt G. Wilder, of Cornell University. The subject was "Methods of Studying, the Brain." The full text of the lectures will be published in the *New York Medical Journal.*

THE Annual Meeting and banquet of the Medical and Surgical Society of Baltimore was held January 23d. Dr. Chas. Frederick Percivall was elected president, Drs. J. W. C. Cuddy and B. F. Leonard, Vice Presidents; Dr. C. B. Ziegler, Recording Secretary, Dr. Wm. N. Hill, corresponding Secretary and Dr. Wm. H. Norris, treasurer.

DR. J. K. BAUDUY, Prof. of Nervous and Mental Diseases, Missouri Medical College, says: After a thorough and continued trial of bromidia at St. Vincent's Asylum, I can cheerfully certify to its great therapeutic value and purity. Its effects are much more rapid and efficient than the ordinary chloral mixtures. We could not for some time be induced to try the remedy, entertaining some prejudice against all such preparations. But experience in its use requires us, as a matter of justice, most emphatically to indorse the preparation and give it most extended and impartial trial.

M. MARTINEAU, who claimed to have successfully inoculated a monkey with syphilis a little over a year ago, has recently reported the further history of the inoculated monkey. The initial lesion was succeeded by skin lesions characteristic of the syphilis, and after an interval of ten months after the inoculation by a syphilitic ulcer of the palate.

PROF. Bartholow says iodide of ethyl is a very valuable antispasmodic, singularly and immediately beneficial in spasmodic asthma, also lessening the liability to subsequent attacks, In capillary bronchitis it is conspicuously beneficial, as also in catarrhal pneumonia. In chronic bronchitis it is a most valuable agent, from its local action. It will probably take the place of iodine vapor for respiratory diseases. The dose is gtt v-xx three or four times a day, by inhalation, generally from a handkerchief.

ONE of the preposterous bills now before Congress is that introduced by Senator Call appropriating a million dollars for endowing a university of Medicine at Washington, and a hundred thousand more for grounds and building. A noticeable feature of this project is to place "allopathic, homeopathic, and eclectic" physicians on a common footing in the Faculty. If the fool killer gets around to our national Capital this winter, we would suggest that he begin his work on the Senator from Florida.

A NEW quarterly journal, entitled the *International Review of Medical and Surgical Technics,* has just appeared. It is edited by Drs. Jos. H. and Chas. Everett Warren, and W. E. Smith, and published by the International Medical Exchange, Boston. Its special feature will be to publish accounts of new instruments and methods of treatment. It is also the official organ of the American Association of the Red Cross. The first number contains 130 pages, and is handsomely printed on heavy tinted paper. The subscription price is $2.00.

The Medical Chronicle.

BALTIMORE, MARCH, 1884.

ORIGINAL ARTICLES.

ARTICLE I.

Amputation at the Hip-Joint.—Arrest of Hemorrhage by a New Method.

By C. A. WHEATON, M. D., St. Paul,
Professor of Surgery, Minnesota College Hospital.
(Read at a Meeting of the Ramsay Co. Med. Society.)

MR. PRESIDENT:

This boy, whom I present for your inspection to-night, came under my professional supervision about a year and a half ago. At that time he was suffering from a periostitis of the left femur in the neighborhood of the knee-joint. I did not see him until the disease was well advanced, when it was too late to look for benefit from abortive treatment. Large poultices were applied and in a few days free incisions were followed by the evacuation of large quantities of pus. In February last, after several months of suffering and suppuration, although his condition forbade an extensive operation, I urged upon his parents the necessity of interference, inasmuch as the probe encountered necrosed bone in several situations. Small sequestra were being discharged spontaneously, and the thigh was becoming riddled with sinuses. The limb from knee to hip was very much enlarged, and unless an arrest of the extensive waste could be effected I did not think he could survive long. Accordingly, in February 1883, the boy was put under ether, the sinuses laid open, and as much as possible of the diseased bone removed. It was found that the femoral shaft had not been more fortunate than the soft parts which enclosed it; it too was seamed, furrowed and perforated, and so extensively diseased as to preclude the possibility of removal of all the necrosed tissues. Little good was done by the operation beyond securing direct drainage. The tortuous sinuses were converted into straight tracks, and many of the old openings closed in a few weeks after. Under the influence of ferruginous tonics, a nutritious diet, and fresh air, he improved sufficiently to warrant my proposing a radical operation in June last. Dr. Hand kindly saw the case with me at that time and urged immediate operation; this, however, was not permitted until the latter part of last September, when he was turned over to me bodily with the suggestive admonition: "Now, doctor, don't butcher him, and do save the limb if possible."

The foregoing is a brief history of the case from the time of my introduction to it, to September last, when the limb was removed at the hip-joint.

In reviewing the literature of hip-joint amputation, we find, for controlling the circulation to the part to be removed, Dupuytren's abdominal tourniquet as modified by the elder Pancoast, the mechanism most commonly employed for this purpose. Through the kindness of Dr. Wm. Davis, of this city, my attention was called to a new method employed by Mr. Jordan Lloyd, and described in the *London Lancet* of May 26, 1883. I take the liberty of quoting a description of Mr. Lloyd's method, which answered the purpose admirably:

"The limb is first elevated and stripped of blood. A strip of black India rubber bandage about two yards long is then doubled and passed between the thighs, its centre lying between the tuber ischii of the side to be operated on and the anus. A common calico thigh roller must next be laid lengthways over the external iliac artery. The ends of the rubber are now to be firmly and steadily drawn in a direction upward and outward, one in front and one behind, to a point above the centre of the iliac crest of the same side. They must be pulled tight enough to check pulsation in the femoral artery. The front part of the band passing across the compress occludes the external iliac and runs parallel to and above Poupart's ligament. The back half of the band runs across the great sacro-sciatic notch, and, by compressing the vessels passing through it, prevents bleeding from the branches of the internal iliac artery. The ends of the bandage thus tightened must be held by the hand of an assistant placed just above the centre of the iliac crest, the back of the hand being against the surface of the patient's body. It is a good plan to pass the elastic over a slip of wood held in the palm of the hand, so as to diminish the pain attending the prolonged pressure of the rubber bandage. In this way an elastic tourniquet is made to encircle one of the innominate bones, checking the whole blood-supply to the lower extremity. The elastic bandage may be secured above the iliac crest in the usual manner with tapes, and may be prevented from slipping downward by being held with a common roller tied securely over the opposite shoulder. Experience has shown, however, that no mechanical means answer so well as the hand of a trusty assistant. When the band is once properly adjusted the assistant has only to take care that it does not slip away from the compress or over the tuber ischii. The former is prevented by securing pad and tourniquet together with a stout safety pin, and the latter by keeping the securing hand well above the iliac crest, or even more safely by looping a tape beneath the elastic near the tuber ischii, passing it behind under the sacrum and having it held in that position. The solid rubber tourniquet may be used instead of this bandage. I prefer, however, the bandage. The soft parts are less damaged by reason of its greater breadth, and it is less likely to roll off the compress placed over the external iliac.

"The ligature, being altogether above the limb, is out of the way of the surgeon in any operation at or about the hip-joint. The great trochanter is fully exposed, the hip being free upward as far as the iliac crest, and inward to the perineum.

"The bandage has the following advantages over Davy's lever: (1.) The simplicity and certainty of its application; no previous experience being necessary to compress the vessels, there is no possibilty of going wrong. (2) The security with which the vessels are controlled, regardless of the movements of the patient or manipulations of the operator. (3.) The freedom from danger of injury to the rectum or abdominal contents. (Davy related a case at a recent meeting of the London Clinical Society in which he himself had wounded the rectum with his lever, the patient dying on the following day of peritonitis.) (4.) Its applicability to cases in which the rectal lever could not be employed, as in strictures of the bowel, intra-pelvic growths, and arterial abnormalities. (5.) It requires no special apparatus."*

To the successful application of this method to the case in question, I am indebted to Dr. Hodges, who applied and maintained in its position this simple contrivance so accurately that but a very small quantity of blood was lost. Taking into consideration the possible injury of some of the abdominal contents, the difficulty of making efficient pressure in fat subjects, or the failure to compress the aorta against the body of the 4th lumbar vertebra in subjects where there is an anomalous deviation of the artery to the right or left of the mesial line,

*Boston Medical and Surgical Journal, Sept. 13, 1888.

would seem to be sufficient argument against the abdominal tourniquet. The fatality attending the use of Davy's lever as attested by the report just read will certainly militate much against the general application of this device. The method of Brandeis, who ties his patient to the operating table, and controls the aortic circulation by means of a stick and roller bandage interposed between the ligature and the anterior abdominal parietes; the more primitive method of controlling the circulation by digital pressure of the external iliac against the pelvic bone, or the preliminary operation of ligating the femoral artery and vein in the ileo-femoral triangle, all require additional time, and may give much additional trouble, and should not be employed when so simple and efficient a method as this of Mr. Lloyd's is at our command.*

I have brought this boy before you for the purpose of showing the shape and character of the stump which has resulted from a form of amputation described by Esmarch as the circular and modified by Dieffenbach by a vertical incision extending from above the summit of the great trochanter to the circular incision. This vertical incision allows ample room for the easy and rapid disarticulation of the head of the femur. This method was adopted in this case, as anchylosis was thought to exist, and we thought enucleation could be more readily effected than by the ordinary transfixion operation.

The patient, as you see, has almost entirely recovered, and has left the hospital for his home. He is stronger than he has been for nearly two years, and has every reason to be satisfied with the result of the operation.

The specimen shows how extensively the femur was diseased. The entire bone is roughened and spiculated. On the posterior surface just above the condyles is a large opening, whence a sequestrum was removed.

ARTICLE II.

Symptomatology of Catarrhal Pneumonia.

BY E. M. REID, M. D.,

President of the Medical and Surgical Society of Baltimore.

Read before the Society, January 10th, 1881.

A few years since, Mr. President and gentlemen, I was summoned in great haste to see a lady about twenty-five years of age, who was then thought to be dying. When I reached the bedside, I beheld a picture of such suffering and despair that it will take more than ordinary influences to erase it from my memory. With glistening eyes and gasping efforts, she—whilst sitting, supported by her attendants—endeavored to impart to me the following history of her case:

That she had recently been exposed to the contagion of measles, and now had a troublesome cough with an eruption on her face and body, which she thought was the disease. On this she concluded that she had taken cold, causing her distressing symptoms. A glance at her face showed the eruption to be dark and her lips cyanotic. The circulation was hurried, though the pulse was not tense nor full in volume; her temperature was high and respirations quickened. She seemed anxious for rest, but could not obtain it in consequence of the dyspnœa. Her moaning and sighing gave additional evidence of her condition.

This case, gentlemen, carried with it, many of the prominent symptoms that are to be found in a rapidly advanced catarrhal pneumonia. That there were other symptoms simulating a capillary bronchitis, such as superficial respiration with playing of the nostrils, retraction of the lower ribs with pain at each inspiration, that manifested themselves before the case came under my observation, I have

---

*I have since used Mr. Lloyd's method in a second case of amputation at the hip-joint, with equally happy results.

no doubt, and if the *vis medicatrix natura* and treatment combined had not come to the rescue, the probabilities are that it would have terminated as acute catarrhal pneumonia frequently does, by lessening of the cough, decrease of the restlessness, the on-coming of apathy, and, in the language of Juergensen, developing a picture of carbonic acid intoxication, with cerebral symptoms not unlike those of tubercular meningitis, the scene closing in coma or suddenly with convulsions. Now I have presented in as concise a manner as I possibly could, the symptoms that commonly appear in a typical case of acute catarrhal pneumonia, which may occur incidently in measles.

I further call your attention to the fact that about the same class of symptoms serve to represent an acute catarrhal pneumonia, whether it be found as a complication of a contagious malady or springs from those inflammatory processes that prevail in a severe bronchitis. It is also my bounden duty to mention another form which frequently results from the bronchitis of whooping cough or a general diffuse catarrh running a subacute course. Whilst it differs but little from the acute in its essential attributes, it nevertheless has become distinct, and maintains its individuality by its slowness of growth and residence in a feebler pathological soil than the acute form. I mean that slow form described by Ziemssen, and later supported and elucidated by no less an authority than Juergensen. Its very name sub-acute, indicates its true characteristics. It begins slowly and generally ends slowly.

The patient may make a good recovery, but in the majority of cases the process of repair is very imperfect. The fever is moderate and the breathing is not as difficult as it is in the acute form. When it is secondary to whooping cough, or an extensive bronchitis, their accompanying cough subsides on its development. Its progress is followed by a depression of the vital forces; cyanosis and extreme emaciation foretell the coming of serious lesions, and if there be no intercurrent excitation to light up an acute attack, which sometimes happens in the career of a chronic pneumonia, those cases where the fatality is fixed, are gradually overcome by the more profound symptoms of carbonic acid poisoning which ultimately leads to coma and death.

ARTICLE III.

Treatment of Catarrhal Pneumonia.

BY J. W, C. CUDDY, M. D.

Read before the Medical and Surgical Society of Baltimore, January 16th, 1884.

MR. PRESIDENT AND GENTLEMEN:

In giving a brief description of my method of the treatment of catarrhal pneumonia, while I can present nothing new, I hope to be able to give what is scientifically correct. I shall, to the best of my ability, confine myself exclusively to the department allotted to me, although it will be difficult in telling how a medicine acts, to steer clear of symptomatology and pathology. But as these are in the hands of such able members of our society, I will use my utmost endeavor to say just as little as possible on those subjects. I cannot forbear, however, to express myself very positively on the nomenclature of this disease, although I know that I am differing from a large majority of writers.

I am decidedly opposed to the name catarrhal pneumonia, believing that it does not in the least convey a true meaning of the disease as now understood. In my opinion, there is but *one* pneumonia, and that the one which is now invariably known by the name of croupous pneumonia. What is so elaborately described by our writers as catarrhal pneumonia, is nothing more nor less than a true bronchitis; its inflammatory action extending down into the fine bronchioles, calling forth the adjective capillary.

Therefore, in my opinion, the proper term should be capillary bronchitis, and in my practice I always so designate it. If, as often happens, the lung tissue becomes involved along with the bronchioles, then a separate disease is manifested, and true pneumonia is set up, the two together being well and truly designated by the compound word broncho-pneumonia. So much by way of introduction.

The very first indication to be met in this disease is hyperemia, an increased circulation and elevated temperature. To overcome this hyperemia should be our first object, and for this purpose we have some remedies that seldom fail us. First and foremost among my choice of remedies is that grandest of arterial sedatives, veratrum viride. This medicine given promptly and in sufficient quantity, will, in my opinion, readily unload engorged vessels, thereby removing pressure from sore and inflamed mucous linings, and will thus abort many cases of this terrible malady, and spare the sufferer days and weeks of pain and disease. To be sure, not every case will demand or stand this treatment. It is only the sthenic cases that call forth this line of medication, but they are the very ones that we wish to abort, for these are the cases that if not checked early, so rapidly develope and often run to a speedy and fatal termination.

In this variety of the disease under discussion and in its primary stage, the inflamed mucous surfaces are constantly throwing out a secretion which greatly prevents the entrance of a proper amount of air into the lung. To keep down the formation of this viscid matter is an important element in the successful treatment of capillary bronchitis. It is believed that the two most effectual agents for this purpose are ammonia and potash. While it is probably true, as many assert, that ammonia acts the more readily of the two just mentioned agents, it is certainly, by its stimulating properties, in many cases much less desirable than the other mentioned remedy. I therefore usually prefer the potash, and of its preparations the bicarbonate is by far the most preferable. These two medicinal agents then are the ones required in the initial stage of the disease. A favorite prescription of mine is as follows, the dose given being what is required for an adult:

℞ Potas. bicarb.   ℈j,
   Tinc. verat. vir.   M xxiv,
   Liq. ammon. acetat.   ℥ iv.

M. Sig. tablespoonful every three hours.

This vehicle for the administration of the potash and the veratrum is generally agreeable to the patient, and although possessing but slight medicinal power, yet it probably does aid to some extent in preventing the formation of muco-purulent matter. Another important remedy in this hyperemic stage is quinine; especially is it valuable when the temperature is very high, and day by day undergoes but little change. Pretty free doses are demanded, and not less than from 5 to 10 grains should be given 3 or 4 times daily. If quinine is used early in the disease, I believe it very materially aids in fortifying the system against a long and continued attack, and prevents the disease from assuming a low form in the advanced stage.

When the disease is not aborted, and assumes those more unfavorable phases which our histologists and symptomatologists have so clearly laid before you, the three best remedies at our command are ammonia, quinine, and alcohol. Either the muriate or carbonate of ammonia is extremely useful, and should be given in 5 grain doses every 2 hours. The continued use of quinine is useful in any and every stage of this affection. Alcohol, in the form of whiskey or brandy, should be given in all cases where there is a lowering of the vital forces, and in combination with milk, makes an excellent stimulant and nutrient. Local applications, such as sinapisms, poultices and stupes, are often useful in allaying the pain and dyspnœa consequent upon this disease, but I do not believe that blistering has the same advantage here as it has in croupous pneumonia.

A very important part of our treatment is that which is required to allay the persisted coughing which is not only troublesome and annoying, but extremely dangerous. A continuous cough greatly prevents the introduction of fresh air into the bronchioles, and the absence of this needed air is one and probably the main cause of atelectasis or collapse. To prevent this, various cough syrups and mixtures are almost universally used, although many suppose that they are but little if any service. I think that they are really advantageous, and that their good results are manifest to any careful observer. One of the best prescriptions of this kind is the following:

℞ Morphiæ acetat. . gr. iij,
    Tinc. sanguinaria· . ℨ ij,
    Vin. antimonii . .
    Vin. ipecac . aa ℨ iij,
    Syr. prun. virg. . ℨ iij.

M. Sig. teaspoonful every 2 or 3 hours.

These, then, in my opinion, constitute all the main requirements in the management of this disease, the treatment of which you have requested me to discuss. Sedatives, antipyretics and stimulants, such as I have mentioned, will, if persistently used, abort and cure most of our cases, so much so that the results will certainly be more satisfactory than that which occurs to most of our writers, who lay it down as a rule that 50 per cent. of these cases prove fatal.

And now, gentlemen, this brief and hurriedly prepared paper is before you either for your commendation or disapproval. If commended, I will be gratified, and will be encouraged to persevere in a line of treatment which seems to me correct and generally satisfactory; if disapproved, I will listen with interest to your criticisms, and will endeavor to profit thereby.

FOREIGN CORRESPONDENCE.

Clinical Teaching. Profs. Von Bamberger and Nothnagel.—Some Obstetrical Statistics from the Vienna General Hospital.—How to Live in Vienna.

VIENNA, JANUARY 21, 1884.

The students who attend the medical department of the University of Vienna, pursue a course of study which we recognize in our country as the graded course; that is, the first two years are spent in studying anatomy, physiology, chemistry, materia medica, etc., and the students only enter on the practical study of diseases at the beginning of their third year at the university. From this time to the completion of their studies, a considerable portion of their time is spent in attending the clinics and lectures on "Internal Medicine." In the University of Vienna, besides a host of "Ausserordentlich" professors and private docents, there are two regular professors, Prof. Heinrich v. Bamberger and Prof. Herman Nothnagel; the former succeeding the famous Prof. Skoda, who died here in Vienna less than three years ago. Prof. Nothnagel is quite a new man here, being called to fill the chair of Practice of Medicine in the University about eighteen months ago. Previous to this, he was a professor in the University of Jena, and is well-known to the medical world by his contributions to medical literature. Both of these gentlemen are approaching middle life. Prof. Bamberger, in appearance, reminds one of a typical Englishman, and while speaking, takes his chair; Prof. Nothnagel, on the contrary, never sits while he is talking to the class; he is constantly moving around the bed on which the patient is lying whose case he is describing. In appearance, he denotes what he really is—a cultivated German physician and an intelligent gentleman.

The clinics are held five times a week, from 8 to 10 o'clock in the morning. As Prof. Nothnagel is by far the best lecturer, his lecture-room is crowded so that one coming a few minutes late can hardly find standing room, and you find, here as is unfortunately the case in most of the lecture-rooms, a total disregard for the health and comfort of the students, as ventilation is something not thought of, or if considered, is not observed. So after one remains here two hours among four hundred average German students, you can almost imagine yourself in a miniature black hole of Calcutta, and you go out in the fresh air at the expiration of the clinic with a feeling of great relief. The teaching is purely of a clinical character; a patient on his bed is brought into the lecture-room, the professor will call one of the students to him, and together they will question and examine the patient. The examination includes not only a physical examination, of all the organs of the body, but a chemical and microscopical examination of the urine, and sometimes of the feces. After the diagnosis is made, the professor will spend the balance of his time in speaking of the pathology, the clinical history, the accepted method of treatment, the prognosis, etc. of the disease under consideration. To show the variety of disease presented, I would state that during the past five days there have been before the class, patients with echinococcus of the liver, diabetes mellitus, diabetes insipidus, peritonitis, dilatation of the stomach, caused by a cancer of the pylorus.

Profs. Bamberger and Nothnagel have each two assistants; all of these gentlemen give private courses, the duration of each being about six weeks. The number of men in each class is limited to six. These courses are very much in demand, especially by Americans, and it is only by giving your card and waiting two or three months, that one is able to participate in the benefits to be derived from these really excellent and practical courses. The method of instruction is as follows: With a companion, you are left in charge of a patient in one of the wards, and you are expected to make a correct diagnosis of the case, besides marking out accurately by percussion the location of the heart, lungs, liver and spleen, and in some cases a microscopical and chemical examination of the urine. At the end of a certain time (generally over one hour), you and your companion have completed your examination, and have agreed to agree or disagree in the diagnosis of the case before you; you then send for the assistant, who will question you what you have found in the lungs, heart, urine, what is your diagnosis, re-examine the patient with you, and if you are not correct in the diagnosis, show you your mistake; then he will spend some ten or fifteen minutes with you in speaking of the pathology, treatment, and prognosis of the disease from which the patient before you is suffering.

After four months of almost daily visits of this kind through the wards which are devoted to patients with medical diseases, I am very much impressed with their thoroughness and accuracy in making the diagnosis of disease, but not with their methods of treatment; and a medical man in private practice could hardly afford to treat his patients in the *do nothing* manner that is in vogue here. Most all of the acute diseases as pleuritis, pneumonitis, bronchitis, endocarditis, peritonitis, metritis, etc., run their course without any special treatment with the exception of cold applications made over the organ which is affected; this cold application is changed from time to time, and is either ice in a bladder, or a towel dipped in ice water. With this and proper food, a great many cases receive no other form of treatment during the entire duration of the disease. In other cases the symptoms receive more attention; if the patient is suffering much pain, opium in decided doses is given. When the the fever is high, quinine is the remedy used; it is given in fifteen grain doses at a time, and generally not more than two doses in twenty-four hours, although in some cases, three doses of fifteen grains each are given at short intervals.

Prof. Braun of the first obstetrical clinic, read his report before the class this week, of the results and the work done in his department during the last three months, from which I send you some extracts:

The number of women confined, 800; forceps applied, 15 times; turning, 11 times; craniotomy, 3; decapitation, 0; premature births produced on account of contracted pelvis, 3, (one child living); retained placenta, 8, although it was only necessary in one of these cases to introduce the hand for the purpose of removal; prolapse of the umbilical cord, 8, in five of these cases the children were born dead; episiotomy performed, 13 times, twice on both sides. Of the 15 forceps cases, two of the children were born dead, and in 11 of these cases the perineum was ruptured, two into the rectum; 37 of the women had some form of puerperal illness, viz: eclampsia, metritis, endometritis, phlegmasia dolens, etc. Five of the number died, viz: two from eclampsia; one from rupture of the uterus (dying undelivered); two dying from peritonitis and septic absorption. In one of those dying from septic absorption, a small piece of retained placenta was found at the autopsy, which had been overlooked by those who had charge of the case at delivery. You may be able to judge from this very brief synopsis of quite a long report of the conservative character of the Vienna School of obstetrics, when you know that the forceps are used in less than two per cent. of the cases which are delivered here.

As more American medical men are coming here now than ever before, it may be interesting to some of your readers to know how students live here, and the cost of the same. The majority of the students hire a room which can be obtained in close proximity to the "Krankenhaus," from 12 gulden ($4.80) to 40 gulden ($16.00) a month, according to the style in which the student wishes to live. This includes all attention, or as the Germans term it, "bedingung." Then he takes his Vienna breakfast of coffee, bread and eggs, at a café, and his other meals at the restaurants. Other students, and I think the lesser number, take board at a "pension," the same as our boarding houses in Baltimore. I think the former method of living rather more expensive than the latter, but in some respects it is more agreeable, unless one is fortunate enough to obtain board with a German family that will cook with some regard for the American stomach.

A man can live here comfortably and attend the regular lectures on $500.00 a year, but if he indulges in the private courses (which are the most beneficial to a medical man seeking to improve himself), takes a recreation trip of a month in the summer, if he lives well, and from time to time attends the magnificent operas which are presented here in a manner not surpassed in the world, it will cost him fully $1200.00 a year.

WILMER BRINTON.

From the far East.—Medical education in Turkey.—"Go East, Young Man, Go East!"

BEYROUT, Syria, Jan. 5, 1884.

Beyrout is, you may say, the seaport of Damascus, 60 miles distant, though there is no port here. It is situated just on the banks of the Mediterranean, and the new part of the city is on a very rocky cape which juts out in an easterly direction. The population is variously estimated at 80,000-100,000 inhabitants, the majority of whom belong to the Christian sects. It is just like all eastern cities

—stone houses, flat roofs, narrow and dirty streets, without sidewalks, and all of the houses surrounded by stone walls. I speak of it as being dirty, but it is the best of all the eastern cities that I have seen, being far ahead of Smyrna and Constantinople in cleanliness. The houses are a little more European in appearance than the latter places—there being quite a number of red-tiled houses. A number of Europeans are in business of different kinds here, and we have an American population of 40-50 souls. To the rear of the city is a very fertile plain, in which is one of the largest olive orchards in the world. Also we have here nearly all of the tropical fruits, and only a few days ago while riding out I saw ripe, on the trees, oranges, lemons, citrons, bananas, dates, etc. The figs and grapes are now out of season, having been gone only a few weeks. The climate is now delightful, it being scarcely cold enough for fire, but in the summer it is said to be very oppressive, and all who can, go from the city to the mountains. The Lebanon mountains are just east of us, at a distance of 15-20 miles, and the tops of most of these are now covered with snow. They are very rugged, being composed of one mass of limestone, with here and there a few strata of sandstone. In the plain to the rear of the city we find some quarries of excellent sandstone for building purposes, and out of this are built all of the houses, the blocks of stone being brought here on donkey and mule back.

But now we will look at the medical aspect of the country for a short while. As far as I can ascertain, there are only four medical colleges in all of the Turkish dominion. The one at Constantinople and the one at Cairo are prominent institutions, and the men they turn out are, I believe, intended chiefly for the military service. The one here at Beyrout is incorporated in New York State, and recognized by the Turkish authorities to this extent—that the graduates have to go to Constantinople and stand a second examination, and pay about $35.00 for a second diploma. The examination, if it is like the one I had to stand there, is a perfect farce, the money being all they want. The fourth one is at Aintab, and is not recognized by the government in any way. Were I to compare the merits of the different colleges, 'twould, to say the least of it, be immodest; but I can say that I know of no place, even in "the states," where the students have a better opportunity for clinical work than they do at the "Syrian Protestant College." The Johanniter Hospital, under the order of the knights of St. John, is always filled with interesting cases—it has from 50-60 beds, and the out-door clinic is well attended. The classes of eye, skin, and glandular diseases are seen here in all shapes and at all stages. Vesical calculi are frequent, and not a month passes but what one or two cases are operated on—crushing and cutting are resorted to as the case may call for. Deformities of the extremities are very frequent and give very satisfactory results in the plaster bandage. Burns and scalds call for quite a number of plastic operations. Most of the amputations are for accidents attending blasting, and these are quite common. Caries and necrosis are also frequently met with, and in some of the cases amputation has to be resorted to. Tumors are quite common, but not many of those I have seen as yet, have been of a malignant type. All capital operations here give a much smaller mortality than in Europe or America, but I am not prepared to give the exact statistics. The cause of this low mortality may be due, in part, to the climate, to the total absence of alcoholism in this country, and to the fine hospital accommodations and careful nursing, but to some extent it must be due to the operator, Dr. Geo. E. Post, son of Dr. A. C. Post, of New York. And now to your medical students, I'd say to all those who want to rise in

the profession as specialists, or as general practitioners, go East! The East is the place for a man who wants work in the medical line, and who really wants to find where he can do the greatest amount of good. There you can have any amount of work and in any line that you like, except ovariotomy. Civilized communities seem to particularly claim this specialty.
T. W. KAY.

ANALECTS.

Tuberculosis One Hundred Years Ago.

A remarkable chapter in the history of the infectiousness of tuberculosis is given by Dr. J. Uffelmann, in the Berlin Klin. Woch. In 1782 the Medical Councillors of the Central Sanitary Bureau of Naples, said that tuberculosis was an especially dangerous disease. In accordance with this opinion the Sanitary Bureau issued an order for the protection of the people against the spread of this disease. The substance of this order is given by the Boston Med. Journal thus: "1. Every practising physician is ordered to give immediate notice to the bureau of the appearance of consumption in any patient under his care. For the first failure to report he is liable to a fine of three hundred ducats. For a second, he is to be exiled ten years from his native country. 2. Poor patients who may be afflicted with this disease are to be brought to a hospital designated for this purpose without delay or ceremony. 3. The directors of hospitals are to keep the clothes and bed linen belonging to the departments containing phthisical patients entirely separate from those intended for use in other departments of the hospital. 4. The superintendent of each hospital shall keep an inventory of all articles of clothing belonging to patients affected with tuberculosis and on the death of such patients shall personally compare the inventory and the effects of the patients to ascertain that every article is accounted for. Any violation of this regulation is punishable by imprisonment or the galleys. 5. All articles not supposed to have been infected are to be at once thoroughly cleansed; those articles supposed to be infected are to be immediately burned or rendered harmless in some other satisfactory way. 6. The directors are to thoroughly disinfect any rooms or wards occupied by patients with tuberculosis, by white-washing and painting the floors, ceilings, and walls. The doors and windows are to be removed and burned, and replaced by new. 7. Newly erected buildings are not to be occupied as dwellings within one year from the date of their completion. 8. Heavy penalties are attached to the sale of any article of wearing apparel from the effects of a phthisical patient, and the penalty affects the purchaser as well as the seller."

Thus it appears that consumption was placed upon a plane with the plague. It will be apparent to all that the most disastrous consequences were suffered by all classes of society. The breaking out of tuberculosis in a family was looked upon as the greatest of misfortunes. At last no amount of money would afford a place of shelter for phthisical patients. The friends of the patients were looked upon as the carriers of contagion and avoided. Thus whole families fell a prey to misery and want. The most exorbitant prices were exacted for the dwellings of the sick. Houses in which a person had died of tuberculosis could not be sold at any price. Many even among the rich were beggared. In Portugal similar laws were enacted. The law continued to be executed in Naples till the beginning of the present century. Since then there has been a gradual letting down until for more than a generation practically the same laws have existed as in other nations. It does not seem probable that even the establishment of the doctrines of Koch would be followed by barbarous practices like those we have quoted. Still it would have a great disturbing influence upon many classes of people.

Divulsion of the Internal os for Dysmenorrhœal Headache.

Dr. George F. French of Minneapolis, reports the following case in the *Northwestern Lancet*:

Mrs. Z., age thirty-nine, began menstruating when but twelve and a half years old.

A year later she fell from a horse and menstruation ceased, re-appearing but once in a year. Retroversion was discovered at the age of twenty-two, at which time Dr. H. R. Storer dilated the os internum for suppression of menstruation, with slight relief.

At twenty-six Mrs. Z. was married. Two years later she suffered a miscarriage, from which time date menstrual headaches of most violent character, lasting from three to seven days, and continuing periodically for ten years. Opiates and chloroform afforded no relief, potassium bromide and chloral aggravated the symptoms; ergotine sometimes mitigated the distress.

Six years ago these headaches became intense beyond description—the patient becoming at times almost maniacal in spite of the free use of opiates and the administration of chloroform.

In 1876, Prof. T. G. Thomas made a successful operation for vaginismus, and the same year one for coccygodynia, caused by a fall. In 1877, Dr. Buck, of Oakland, Cal., instituted systematic dilation, with sponge tents, by which means the headaches could be invariably averted. When dilatation was omitted, the headaches appeared and menstruation was scanty. These dysmenorrhœal sufferings were never referred to the pelvis, but always to the head.

The patient came under my care in September, 1881.

In watching the case, sometimes dilating the os, and occasionally omitting to do so, I saw that there existed a causative connexion between the headaches and the undilated os internum.

Fully convinced of this, I determined upon divulsion, and on June 14th, 1883, forcibly ruptured the internal os with a Thomas' dilator, the patient being profoundly etherized. The resistance encountered was somewhat formidable; when the ring gave way after prolonged and exhausting effort, the rupture was audible.

Patient remained in bed for a fortnight. No effort was made to prevent recontraction. No rise of temperature or other constitutional disturbance followed the operation, since which the patient has never had a headache or any form of dismenorrhœa, and her general health is much improved.

Trichiniasis in Illinois.

In the last quarterly report of the Illinois State Board of Health, Dr. John H. Rauch, the secretary, writes as follows:

Three outbreaks of trichiniasis—one of them resulting in three deaths—have occurred, the first during the early part of November, in a family near Gardner, Grundy county; the second and third during December, in Woodburn, Macoupin county, and in Bloomington, respectively. The Gardner and Bloomington cases resulted from eating uncooked pork and sausage, and the Woodburn cases from raw smoked sausage. Specimens of the meat from Gardner and Woodburn were sent to the Secretary for examination, the character of the disease being only suspected, until the microscope showed, in one case, about 2,000, and the other, about 8,000 trichinæ to the cubic inch.

Dr. A. T. Darrah reports the Bloomington outbreak quite fully, and Drs. Taxis and Reid, of Gardner and Woodburn respectively, have promised detailed reports of their cases. The matter, however, possesses little sanitary importance, except that it is well to put on record every authentic instance of the occurrence of trichiniasis and to determine its cause. Since 1866 I have noted every such instance in this State, and all of the deaths resulting, which now number sixteen; and without exception they have been caused by eating uncooked or imperfectly cooked pork in some form. I see no reason to modify the opinion expressed in 1881, in reply to an inquiry addressed to me by a committee of the Chicago Board of Trade and the State Department at Washington, to wit: That, as a sanitarian, I regard the danger to human life from trichinæ as practically amounting to nothing, it being so easily prevented by thorough cooking.

The investigations which have been made during the past four years both in this country and abroad, show American pork to be freer from trichinous infection than that of other countries. The hog in every country is subject to the parasite; even the wild swine in European forests have been found infected, and an outbreak of trichiniasis in 1881, at the village of Khiam, near the sources of the Jordan in Palestine, was caused by the flesh of a wild boar slain in the woods near the village.

Prof. Virchow is recently reported to have condemned the outcry against American pork, as utterly illogical, unnecessary and unjustifiable by sanitary reasons, and adds that "no case of trichinæ in American hog meat has been proved to exist in Germany for ten years." Neither in Switzerland nor England has it been found necessary to interfere with the importation of American hog products; and yet in these countries their reputation is higher than ever before. It is only where the custom of eating raw pork obtains that severe or extensive outbreaks of trichiniasis occur. Such an outbreak was that at Emersleben, in Saxony, last fall. MM. Brouardel and Grancher, who made an investigation, found that it was not due to American pork at all, but that the trichinous hog, which was the origin of the disease, was born and reared in a stable at Emersleben, the offspring of an English boar and a native sow. Killed on the 12th of September, 1883, a slice of the carcase was eaten raw on the 13th by two men who were taken ill on the 16th, and died a month later.'

Meanwhile, the rest of the meat, mixed with other, was minced up and sold between the 13th and 19th of September. Except by five persons, who cooked it a little, this minced meat was eaten perfectly raw, and within a short time there were two hundred and fifty persons sick, of whom forty-two died; and one hundred and twenty-six more cases, with eleven deaths, occurred in neighboring villages among persons who ate sausage made by the same butcher. Trichinæ were found in abundance by MM. Brouardel and Grancher in the bodies of two of the victims. This is the most extensive outbreak that I know of; but as previously remarked, the question is one of economic and commercial importance, and in only a very limited sense has it any sanitary interest. Proper cooking will render the most badly infected piece of trichinous meat absolutely innocuous. Exposure to a temperature of 150-160 degrees, F., is fatal to the trichinæ.

Hints on the Treatment of Constipation.

Our pharmacopœias, officinal, non-officinal, and popular, are richer in purgatives than in remedies of any other class. I must not digress into a comparison of the relative value of our cathartic drugs, although the subject is a very tempting one. The practitioners of rational medicine have accumulated a vast store of precise and valuable information concerning the actions of purgative medicines, and this important branch of therapeutics is still growing. Each of us has his favorite cathartics; if we have tried their action well, we should not lightly change them. For cases of habitual constipation which do not yield without drugs, my favorite remedy is socotrine aloes. I have little faith in belladonna, and none in nux vomica.

Aloes is especially useful in the fecal sluggishness of sedentary persons. Properly given, the drug may be taken daily for years, without either losing its aperient efficiency, or producing any but the best results. I give one, two or three grains of socotrine aloes in a pill, combined with a quarter of a grain of sulphate of iron, and one grain of extract of hyoscyamus, at bedtime every night. I find out, in each case, the exact quantity of aloes required to produce one full alvine evacuation after the morning meal. In this combination, the quantity of aloes will need readjustment from time to time, usually in the direction of reduction. I shall mention only one other drug for the class of cases I am now considering, namely, the American cascara sagrada. From my former experience of so-called new drugs, I have learned to employ such preparations with much caution, and to recommend them with more. But I now venture to state that I have used cascara sagrada in two or three cases of severe habitual constipation with marked success. I have given from fifteen to thirty minims of the American liquor, thrice daily, adapting the dose by the result, and endeavoring to secure one, or at most two dejections, in each twenty-four hours.—*Brit. Med. Journal.*

Syphilitic Neuralgia.

Prof. Seeligmueller read a paper on the subject of syphilitic neuralgia at the Fifty-sixth Versammlung Deutscher Naturforscher which recently met in Freiburg (Med. News). Neuralgiæ, he said, which are certainly related, etiologically, to constitutional syphilis are nothing like so uncommon as would be supposed on reference to the literature of the subject. He does not refer, of course, to the cases of neuralgia following syphilitic periostitis, or to the osseous pains, but only to such cases in which the pains occur along the tracks of nerves. Such cases have been observed by Fournier in the course of the supra-orbital and sciatic nerves. Seeligmueller has also observed them in the course of other nerves, as the intercostals, the brachial plexus, and the great occipital. Lately he has observed, it seems, a very typical localization of syphilitic neuralgia in the head, and certainly along nerve tracts, which were formerly supposed to be cases of isolated neuralgic affections in unusual places. In these cases the pains were spontaneous, as though pressure had been made along a track two or three fingers wide, and which extended on both sides from the ear upward to the top of the head. He has further seen cases in which the pains were confined to a limited zone and to the course of sensitive nerves, as the auriculo-temporal and small occipital. There was no middle-ear disease in any of the cases. The time at which the neuralgic affection comes on after syphilitic infection varies from two to fifteen years. The treatment is, of course, antisyphilitic.— *Weekly Medical Review.*

Cancer of Rectum Relieved by Scraping.

If we can afford relief in this terrible disease by so comparatively simple a process as scraping, we should hail the fact with delight. Dr. J. Crawford Renton reports a case in the *Glasgow Medical Journal*, September, 1883, where it was resorted to, and now, for a period of thirteen months, the patient has continued to experience great relief. The bleeding was easily controlled by finely-powdered matico. It would be well in suitable cases, such as this one, where the growths are villous in character, to try scraping before resorting to the much more serious operation of excision of the diseased part.—*Med. Surg. Rep.*

Bacteria; their Mutability.

Dr. Carpenter, at the British Medical Association, said that he believes that the same germs may, under altered circumstances, produce different diseases. A severe attack of any particular disease may so affect the system that a disease arises which cannot be recognized as related to that from which it proceeded. Under favorable conditions an ordinary intermittent fever may develop into a virulent form, which is highly contagious. Even the innocent hay bacillus may undergo such an alteration in its type as to become the germ of severe disease.—*Lancet.*

[Not one of the things which Dr. Carpenter says may occur has ever been demonstrated to occur. *Ed.*]

Diagnosis of Diabetes.

A correspondent writes to the *Gazette des Hopitaux* on a simple means of recognizing this disease. Every time a patient in consulting him passed the tongue several times between the lips in the course of conversation, he concluded at once that his patient was diabetic. Out of thirty-four cases not once did he observe an exception to the rule. The reason why is easily understood—dryness of the mouth—a fact well known to all.

Determination of Sex.

Dr. Andrew Wilson (*Brit. Med. Jour.*) advocates the theory that post-menstrual impregnation is followed by the birth of a female child, and that pre-menstrual fertilization results in the formation of a male child. He says: "I have the firmest faith in my theory—a faith substantiated by facts I have been able to ascertain from human histories—that the difference in sex is due simply to the greatest or least power of development exhibited by the ovum, according as it is pre-menstrually or post-menstrually fertilized."—[Credat Judæus Apella!]

Cascara Sagrada in Internal Hemorrhoids.

Dr. John Elfers, of Sugar Branch, Indiana, speaks very highly in the *Therapeutic Gazette*, for January, 1884, of his use of cascara sagrada in internal hemorrhoids. Among the many cathartics which he has employed in this condition, this one is *par excellence*, the best, while its protracted use, by relieving the cause to which the hemorrhoids are largely traceable, contributes to a permanent cure. He strongly recommends the use of this drug in those cases where, either from reluctance on the part of the physician or objection on the part of the patient, operative interference is not resorted to.

The Ether Spray an Immediate Cure for Neuralgia.

Dr. McColgan extols the value of the ether or rhigolene spray for the instantaneous relief, principally, of facial neuralgia. He first had occasion to observe its good effects upon his own person, he having suffered greatly from facial neuralgia. Since curing himself, he had occasion to test its efficiency in about twenty cases. The result was invariably a most gratifying success. In many instances a permanent cure was established. He attempts to explain its action by supposing a complete change to take place in the nutrition of the affected nerve in consequence of the intense cold acting as a revulsive.—*St. L. Med. Journ.*

Vaccination in India.

Several years ago the British Government passed Acts of compulsory vaccination for Great Britian and India. Recent reports from India present the most gratifying results as to the carrying out of the law. Its enforcement has not been attended with the difficulty which was anticipated. The people in most cases yield to simple persuasion, and in a few instances where they prove refractory the issue of a summons is almost always effectual. Opposition fostered by caste prejudices is in some places still offered, but as a rule the masses now accept vaccination with readiness, and in some parts it is even sought after and paid for. In the district embracing Bengal, Madras, Bombay and some other sections, the number of persons vaccinated in 1883 was over 4,400,000, and the ratio of successful results reached the unusual percentage of 98.39.—*M. and S. Jour.*

Vesication in Diphtheria.

Dr. W. F. Bartlett, of Buffalo, N.Y., communicates to the *Therapeutic Gazette* for December, the results of his experience in the use of cantharidal blisters in diphtheria. His plan is to apply the blister immediately on the appearance of the exudate in the throat. The theory is that the materies morbi is eliminated through the blistered surface, while the counter-irritation thus caused relieves also the engorged pharyngeal surfaces. He regards the exudate in the throat as merely an announcement of the presence of the poison in the blood, and that from the nature of the epithelium or impinging of inspired air primarily upon those surfaces, the partial elimination of the morbid element is accomplished.

[Dr. E. M. Reid, of this city, has urged this method in the treatment of diphtheria for some years, and has reported in the local medical societies numerous cases in which patients apparently in *articulo mortis* have recovered after the application of a blister to the chest.—Ed.]

A Reason why Phosphorus should not be given to Red-haired People.

Dr. Jas. S. Tracy writes as follows to the *Medical Record*:

Once in a while in one's practice something happens so different from bad roads, poor pay, and sleepless nights, as to cause for a time the every-day experiences to be forgotten. A case in point would seem to present a new contra-indication to the administration of phosphorus, at least it is new in this part of the country. A lady patient whom nature had adorned with a color of hair which considerably out-auburned auburn, needed, it was thought, phosphorus, and was accordingly given some pills containing that medicine. After taking them faithfully for some time, she noticed, either in the excreta or some place else, the phosphorescence, and rightly divining that the pills were causing the phenomenon, returned, and expressing a desire to discontinue the treatment, gave as a reason for so doing that she was afraid the medicine would get into her hair and ignite

The Treatment of Saccharine Diabetes by Bromide of Potassium.

On the 28th of August last, M. Dujardin-Beaumetz presented to the Académie de Médicine a review of an article having this title, by M. Felizet. The subject itself is not a new one, but M. Felizet's paper and the discussion to which it gave rise are of interest.

The treatment of diabetes mellitus by bromide of potassium is in keeping, according to Felizet, with theoretical considerations and the results of experiment and clinical observation. He refers briefly to the three views which have been entertained with respect to the pathology of the disease, namely, the "alimentary" theory, the "hepatic theory" and the "nervous theory." Bromide of potassium suggests itself to those who adopt this latter view of its pathology.

It is unnecessary to refer to the experiment of the author of the paper in cases of artificially produced glycosuria. He reported, however, twenty-nine (29) cases of diabetes or more in which the sugar disappeared from the urine after the use of the potassium bromide, and he mentions that

MM. Hérard and Dreyfus-Brisac have obtained good results in many cases.

In M. Felizet's case, however, bodily exercise, alkalies, and in some cases quinine and arsenic were resorted to in addition to the bromide, so that it cannot be determined with any certainty how much of the good effect obtained in these cases was due to the latter drug. He states, moreover, that it is only in cases of moderate severity that benefit followed its use; in severe cases, no good resulted, whether the agent was given alone or was associated with other means of cure. He acknowledges, furthermore, that considerable nervous depression may result from the use of the bromide, and that in order to avoid this action exercise should be insisted upon. He suggests that some of the other bromides might give as good results, and might be free from injurious properties of the potash salt. In conclusion, he states his belief that the bromide of potassium is an agent of some value in diabetes mellitus, but that it is necessary to use it with prudence.

M. Dujardin-Beaumetz agreed with this statement, but added that the agent was often too depressing and debilitating to be used even in cases in which it would seem to be indicated otherwise.

M. Bouchardat was fully in accord with M. D. Beaumetz with respect to the depressing action of the salt in diabetes, and he stated that it was impossible to say how much good was done by it in the cases reported by M. Felizet.

M. Hardy had used the remedy in three cases apparently with some benefit, though in one case its use had to be suspended. He reminded the members of the Academy that bromide of potassium, when given in large doses, and for some time, gave rise to an eruption of acne, and he said that this eruption increased very considerably a tendency to boils, which is always present in cases of diabetes.

M. Ricord said that he had given the bromide to seven or eight diabetics, in doses of two, or three, or even four grammes, and had never seen any depression or debility therefrom; on the contrary, he had obtained excellent results.— *Va. Med. Monthly.*

In the *Medical Bulletin* for February, Dr. M. Landesberg reports very favorable results from the use of Duquesnel's aconitia in facial neuralgia The dose at first is $\frac{1}{320}$ grain to be cautiously and gradually increased to $\frac{1}{80}$ grain, repeated three times a day. The effect of the remedy must be carefully watched.

At a recent meeting of the Philadelphia County Medical Society, Dr. Carl Seiler called attention to the value of tincture of benzoin in the treatment of chapped hands and frosted feet. He has used it in a number of cases with much success. It is applied by simply painting it on the skin. The stocking may be prevented from sticking to the feet by rubbing some oil over the benzoin.

In Edinburg, Scotland, physicians are required by law to report all cases of infectious disease, for which, however, a fee equivalent to about 62 cents for each notification is paid. During the last six months nearly five thousand dollars were paid to physicians by the health department for such notifications.

Dr. Richard McSherry, Professor of Principles and Practice of Medicine, University of Maryland, Baltimore, Md., says: " I have used the preparation known as BROMIDIA, prepared by Messrs. Battle & Co., of St. Louis, in my practice, and have found it a very satisfactory agent in cases for which it is deemed most appropriate."

The Medical Chronicle.

A Monthly Journal for the Practitioner.

GEORGE H. ROHÉ, M. D., Editor.

☞ It is requested that all literary and business communications, books for review, exchanges, etc., be addressed to, and all checks, drafts and post-office orders drawn to the order of
Dr. GEORGE H. ROHÉ,
95 Park Avenue, - - - - Baltimore, Md.

BALTIMORE, MARCH, 1884.

EDITORIAL.

The Report of the State Board of Health.

We have received from the Secretary, Dr. C. W. Chancellor, the fifth biennial report of the State Board of Health of Maryland. The volume contains, besides the general report of the secretary, in which we have looked in vain for a financial statement, of a number of tables of vital statistics of no value in their present form and relations, of an appendix of 15 pages consisting of rules for the prevention of the spread of contagious diseases, and of the papers read, and discussions at the sanitary convention held in Baltimore on Nov. 27 and 28, 1883. This portion of the report, which is by far the most interesting and instructive, consists of addresses by Dr. Richard McSherry, the president of the convention, and Mayor Latrobe, and of the following invited papers: The Necessity for Local Boards of Health, by Mr. Henry C. Hallowell; the Sanitary Requirements of Baltimore Co., by Dr. Jackson Piper; Canning Houses, and their Relation to the Public Health, by Dr. W. Stump Forwood; Malaria or Bad Air, by Dr. W. Chew Van Bibber; What shall be done with the Sewage? by Dr. A. N. Bell, of New York, Editor of the *Sanitarian;* Dry Earth as a Disinfectant, by Dr. St. Geo. Teackle; the late Small Pox Epidemic, by Dr. E. J. Henkle; Etiology of Baltimore Catarrh, by Dr. John Morris; Vital Statistics, by Dr. Jas. F. McShane; Necesity for a Law Regulating the Practice of Medicine, by Dr. James A. Steuart; Quarantine, by Dr. Walter Wyman, U. S. M. H. Service; the Conflict of State Power and Individual Rights in Sanitary Matters, by Dr. Richard Gundry, (See MEDICAL CHRONICLE for December); Sewerage Systems, by Mr. Chas. H. Latrobe, C. E., Liernur's System of Sewerage for Baltimore, by Col. Geo. E. Waring, Jr., of Washington, and City Sewerage—a Reply to Col. Waring; by Dr. C. W. Chancellor.

These papers all deserve careful reading by the profession and the public for whom they are especially intended. They evince an interest in matters of sanitary importance which only needs cultivation to bring forth good fruit. It is hoped that the success of the first convention will stimulate the board to hold others, for it is especially by this means that a knowledge of the importance of sanitary works can be brought home to the public.

While this volume shows that our state board has not been entirely idle, it leaves much yet to be desired, and we trust that we may be able to place the next biennial report of the board upon our shelves by the side of those of Massachusetts, Michigan, Connecticut, New York and West Virginia, without feeling like offering an apology for its many short-comings.

The Annual Report of the City Health Department.

In our opinion florid language has no proper place in a scientific or statistical publication, and we have endeavored to keep it out of the pages of the CHRONICLE, but we cannot resist the temptation to abstract from Dr. Benson's report the following specimens from his "well of English undefyled." "While grim pestilence" he says, "has invaded our country covering our sister cities, as well as our own, with its blighting wings, and though we were the last to be polluted, yet, by indomitable energy and faith in the right, we have come out first, bright as the noonday's sun. Science has triumphed and ignorance has been rebuked." "The conflict was heroic and decisive." This triumph of science over ignorance; or, in other words, the extermination of small-pox by the enforcement of vaccination seems to have given our vigorous ex-health commissioner but little respite for, as he says, " much to our discomfiture, in the latter part of July yellow fever was exhaling its death-laden breath at the mouth of the Chesapeake Bay." This is quite an exquisitely constructed phrase and we are glad to have the opportunity to give it a more extensive circulation through the CHRONICLE, than it would otherwise obtain.

In September last, the health commissioner divided the city into two sanitary districts, and requested the assistant health commissioner to make "a topographical survey and medical sanitary inspection of all the streets, alleys, lanes, and courts, as well as of all the factories, of every kind, in that portion of the city east of the falls," while the same work for the city west of the falls was assigned to an official entitled "Medical Sanitary Inspector and Acting Supervisor of Vaccination."

The assistant health commissioner seems to have ignored the request of his chief, for he submitted no report, while the report of the "Medical Sanitary Inspector, etc.," is given in full, and especial attention is directed to it by the commissioner, who states that it "shows the inspection to have been systematically and thoroughly made," and that its perusal will give "a faint idea of what has been done, and what can be done in the future." This is another of those felicitous expressions to which we have already called attention above, for after carefully reading the report of the "Medical Sanitary Inspector, etc.," we must confess that we really have only a *very faint* idea that any work of the kind indicated was done at all. On the other hand we have an abundance of suggestions and opinions among which is one to the effect that the "Medical Sanitary Inspector, etc.," thinks it "quite fair to claim" that the reduction in the death-rate and the unusual exemption of the city from zymotic diseases "is largely due to the vigilance of our Health Commissioner."

Dr. Benson makes two suggestions to which we cannot agree, however unwilling we may be to differ with him. In order to limit the spread of diphtheria he wants parents to examine the throats of their children every morning, "and, on the appearance of the least redness about the tonsils or palate, take a quill, or an oat straw, and blow upon the inflamed membrane a small quantity of either powdered chlorate of potash, sulphate of iron, sulphite of soda or carbolate of soda, or with a camel's hair brush paint the parts with tincture of iron." We certainly hope that this suggestion will *not* be generally adopted by parents. The other recommendation with which we disagree is that the customary outdoor "recess" of school-children should be discontinued, and "some childish plays or games, under the supervision of the teachers in the school room" substituted therefor. Such a change would be a very disastrous one to the health of the children. There is probably no need to apprehend that it will be adopted.

There are a number of very excellent recommendations in Dr. Benson's report, which the City Council and the public should carefully consider. Such are those relating to sewerage, street-cleaning and sprinkling, removal of garbage and fecal matter, and various others. The mortality tables are also more complete than we have been accustomed to see them in the publications of our health department, but as "vital statistics" they still leave much to be desired.

The Baltimore Polyclinic.

We call attention to the announcement of the Baltimore Polyclinic and Post-Graduate Medical School, which appears in our advertising pages. The building occupied by the school is located at 112 Hanover Street, and is admirably adapted for its uses. The Faculty is composed of gentlemen of ability and energy, and will doubtless make the school a success. Baltimore is throughout the year one of the pleasantest cities in the country to live in, and we have no doubt that many of the practitioners who annually visit one of the large cities for the purpose of "brushing up," or studying a specialty, will hereafter give the Monumental City the preference. We are sure that none of those who do so will have cause to regret their decision.

CURRENT LITERATURE.

A Manual of Medical Jurisprudence with special reference to Diseases and Injuries of the Nervous System. By Allan McLane Hamilton, M. D., one of the consulting physicians to the Insane Asylums of New York City, etc., with illustrations. New York and London. Bermingham & Co., 1883. Pp. 386.

Dr. Hamilton has produced a very useful guide for physicians liable to be called into court as expert witnesses in cases of litigation in which the mental responsibility of one of the parties is in question. The work treats of insanity, hysteroid conditions, epilepsy, alcoholism, suicide, and cranial and spinal injuries in their medico-legal relations. The definitions of the various conditions are generally clear and exact, the advice to physicians acting as witnesses is judicious, and the questions discussed are illustrated by many interesting and instructive cases cited from the literature and the author's wide experience.

The paper, printing and binding are excellent.

Thirtieth Registration Report upon the Births, Marriages and Deaths in the State of Rhode Island, for the year 1882. Prepared by Charles H. Fisher, M. D., Registrar of Vital Statistics and Secretary of the State Board of Health.

This report contains an elaborate analysis of the vital statistics of the State of Rhode Island for 1882. From it we learn that the death-rate was 18.3 per thousand, and the birth-rate 24.7 per thousand. Divorces have increased to a considerable extent. The registrar states that during the three years from 1869 to 1871, inclusive, the proportion of divorces to marriages was 1 to 13.5; from 1872 to 1876, inclusive, it was 1 to 13.1; from 1877 to 1881, inclusive, it was 1 to 11, and for 1882, it was 1 divorce to every 9.7 marriages. This indicates an increase of nearly 4 per cent. in 1882 over the average for 13 years. The number of divorces granted was 271, out of a total population (census 1880) of 276,531.

Excessive Venery, Masturbation and Continence. By Joseph W. Howe, M. D., author of "Emergencies," "The Breath," "Winter Homes for Invalids," late professor of Clinical Surgery in Bellevue Hospital Medical College, etc. New York and London. Bermingham & Co., 1884. Pp. 299.

In this neat and handsomely printed volume, Prof. Howe gives the results of a large and varied personal experience and extensive reading upon the disorders of the sexual organs and their effects upon the general health. The work is concise and practical, and yet sufficiently full to make it a valuable work of reference. The chapters on treatment are especially complete, the cases being classified, and the appropriate treatment for each class accurately indicated.

In all the essentials of good book-making—paper, printing and binding—the volume reflects great credit upon the publishers.

PAMPHLETS.

The Reciprocal Attitude of the Medical Profession and the Community. By Alexander Hutchins, A. M., M. D. Brooklyn, N. Y.——First Annual Report of the New York Skin and Cancer Hospital.——Address of the Flushing Committee of the New Orleans Auxiliary Sanitary Association to the Mayor and City Council of New Orleans.——Annual Report of the Board of Managers of the Maryland Hospital for the Insane. ——Study of a Case of Multiple Sarcomata of the Skin. By Jas. Nevins Hyd , A. M., M. D., Professor of Skin and Venereal Diseases, Rush Medical College, Chicago, Ill. Reprint from Edinburg Medical Journal, Jan. 1884.——Annual Announcement of Cooper Medical College, San Francisco, Cal. Session 1884.

FLOTSAM.

The Baltimore *Polyclinic* spells its name with a *y* after all. Y ?

Over ten million gallons of sewage are daily discharged by the new sewerage system of Boston.

One of our brightest exchanges, *The Proceedings of the Medical Society of Kings County*, New York, has suspended publication.

All the European powers have accepted the proposal of Italy to have a conference at Rome for the construction of an international Sanitary Code.

The *Æsculapian* and the *Analectic* are two new exchanges coming to us from New York. They are both well filled with interesting matter and well edited.

The collections on Hospital Saturday and Sunday, in New York, amounted to $42,803.69 this year, an **excess** of over $12,000 over last year's fund.

And now santonine is recommended in the treatment of gleet. The dose is 5 grains triturated with an equal quantity of sugar of milk, and to be taken twice a day.

A Philadelphia medical weekly has an editorial headed "Our self-sufficient egotism." We are glad our contemporary is beginning to see itself as others see it.

A Professor in the Westminster Hospital College, London, is said to condense the etiology of phthisis in the following Baconian epigram :
Some are born to phthisis,
Some acquire phthisis, and some have Phthisis thrust upon them.

The National Board of Health and the Marine Hospital Service have had several interesting matinées before the Public Health Committee of the House of Representatives. The washing of dirty linen in public is not a very creditable proceeding on the part of either organization or its representatives.

In his first Cartwright Lecture, Dr. Burt G. Wilder says that owing to the marked flexure of the brain of the embryo, "the mesocele becomes cephalic in position, the procele and diacele ventral, while the metacele and epicele remain dorsal." A new dictionary of anatomical terms is imperatively demanded !

The Mayor has appointed Dr. Jas. A. Steuart Health Commissioner of this city, and has re-appointed Dr. Jas. F. McShane, assistant Health Commissioner, and Dr. Sidney O. Heiskell, Resident Physician at the Quarantine Hospital. These are all excellent appointments, and give general satisfaction.

J. H. Chambers & Co., the enterprising western publishers, will begin the issue of a new journal devoted to ophthalmology, in April. Its name will be *The American Journal of Ophthalmology;* its subscription price $2.50 a year, and its editor, Dr. Adolf Alt, one of the most prominent ophthalmologists in the country.

The Medical Chronicle.

BALTIMORE, APRIL, 1884.

ORIGINAL ARTICLES.

ARTICLE I.

NON-PARASITIC SYCOSIS.

BY GEORGE H. ROHÉ, M. D.

Professor of Hygiene and Clinical Dermatology, College of Physicians and Surgeons, Baltimore; Member of the American Dermatological Association, etc.

[Read before the Med. and Surg. Society of Baltimore.]

The characteristic features of non-parasitic sycosis are inflammatory papules, pustules and tubercles, each perforated by a hair, and occupying especially the region of the beard, although the eyebrows, scalp, axillæ and pubes may also be seats of the affection.

The following is the usual history of a case of sycosis: A number of painful reddish papules or pustules appear in the beard or moustache, the single lesions being each perforated by a hair. The skin around the papules or pustules is usually reddened, and somewhat swollen and infiltrated. In some cases, however, the characteristic lesions remain perfectly isolated, no extension laterally of the inflammation taking place. The pustules are usually small, flat, or slightly elevated, with scanty contents which they show little disposition to discharge unless punctured or broken by pressure or friction. There is often burning and exquisite tenderness to the touch; rarely severe itching. In cases of long standing, the pus has dried into crusts and scabs, under which the surface is frequently excoriated. At times there are broad, elevated, papillary masses,—fungoid excrescences—bearing some resemblance to mucous patches. In other cases there are boils and deep abcesses. As the disease progresses, the hair follicles are destroyed, the hairs, at first still firm in their follicles, fall out, and a flat shiny, reddened, or venated scar results, which often strongly resembles the cicatrix remaining after the involution of lupus. Recovery from the disease rarely takes place without appropriate treatment.

The etiology of the disease is not established. Wertheim believes the primary irritation to be due to a disproportion in size between the hair-shaft and the hair follicle. Hebra and Kaposi attribute it to the after-growth of a new hair at the bottom of the follicle before the mature hair has been shed. The disease is sometimes caused by the extension into the hair-follicles of a more superficial dermatitis, such as eczema. At other times it is evidently due to the constant contact with the skin, of an acrid discharge, for example, a catarrhal discharge from the nose, which is frequently accompanied by sycosis of the upper lip and the parts of the nostril studded with the fine hairs called vibrissæ. When the inflammation is once lighted up it is kept up by the movements to which the hairs are constantly subjected as well pointed out by Dr. Hyde: "Each free hair operates like a lever upon the inflamed ring of tissue beneath, and this whenever by the touch of the hand, by the action of brushing, by currents of air, or by any agency whatever, a movement is imparted to it. Every such movement must tease to a variable degree the surface beneath already irritated, and when estimate is made of the hundreds of such movements to which each hair is subjected during a period of twenty-four hours, the relative importance of this apparently insignificant factor may be appreciated." The form of sycosis under consideration is not contagious; is not caused by a parasite, and cannot be conveyed from one individual to another through the utensils or manipulations of the barber. It is not caused by shaving, as the most severe and persistent cases occur in persons who do not shave. It is not very rare, the lighter forms constituting, perhaps, 4-5 *per cent.* of all forms of skin disease seen in this part of the country. It is most frequently seen in individuals between 25 and 40 years of age.

The pathology of sycosis has been shown by Robinson to be primarily a peri-folliculitis, progressively attacking the follicle itself. There is reason to believe, however, that the inflammation may sometimes begin in the follicle and extend secondarily to the peri-follicular tissues.

The diagnosis of non-parasitic sycosis is comparatively easy if the salient features of the disease are borne in mind. Each papule or pustule is perforated by a hair, and the disease is essentially an inflammatory affection of the hair-follicle and the immediately surrounding structures. In fact, sycosis bears a nearer resemblance to acne than to any other skin disease, and in most dermatological text-books, it is described in immediate connexion with the latter disease. In acne, the sebaceous glands and structures immediately adjacent are the seat of the morbid process, while in sycosis the hair follicles and surrounding tissues are the parts affected.

From eczema of the bearded portions of the face, sycosis is differentiated by the absence of the characteristic features of the former disease. In sycosis there is unusually no itching or discharge of sticky serum, which symptoms especially mark an attack of eczema. In eczema there is likewise more infiltration of the skin, and the inflammation extends beyond the borders of the beard and may even involve the entire face; in sycosis, the inflammation is limited to the parts covered by thick hairs. It should be remembered, however, that a long-standing eczema of the beard may result in, or rather be complicated by sycosis. Even the deep abscesses, furuncles and fungous sores may sometimes be seen in cases of very intense chronic eczema in strumous individuals.

From parasitic sycosis the differentiation will be aided by a history of the case. The latter disease usually begins as a ringworm—tinea circinata—and the fungus which is the cause of the disease can usually be found without much difficulty in the scales and affected hairs, with the aid of a good microscope. In this form of the disease the hairs also fall out much earlier than in the non-parasitic variety. The hairs are also dry, lustreless, broken off, and split at the broken end. When the inflammation extends deeper in the parasitic form, there are usually numerous deep and very painful abscesses which give a knobbed appearance to the lower jaw. On opening these abscesses, a mucous or muco-purulent fluid is discharged.

The pustular or tubercular syphilide should offer no difficulty in differentiating it from non-parasitic sycosis. I have, however, seen two cases where the two diseases were present in the same individual, and caused considerable hesitation in arriving at a conclusion. In these cases I found the sycosis especially obstinate; both had a catarrhal discharge from the nose which kept up the irritation of the upper lip, where the disease was principally located. In one of the cases the eyebrows were also affected by the sycosis. In syphilis, the generalisation of the eruption, and the tendency to destructive ulceration of the lesions when long continued, will enable the diagnosis to be made with little difficulty.

The prognosis of sycosis is favorable. It demands, however, more personal attention from the physician in its treatment than almost any other skin disease. A neglect of certain precautions—to be presently pointed out—on the part of either physician or patient, will result in almost certain failure to cure the disease, and consequent disappointment to the patient and discredit to the doctor.

The important points to be insisted upon in the treatment of non-parasitic sycosis are four: Shaving of the affected part, puncturing all abcesses and pustules, the proper application of appropriate ointments, and epilation. I consider it of such importance that the diseased spot should be shaved daily, or every other day, that I decline to begin the treatment of a case unless this advice is followed. There is always strenuous objection on the part of the patient, who urges various reasons for not carrying out this procedure. It will be found, however, upon trial, that shaving—if the barber is expert and the edge of the razor keen—is not nearly so painful as the patient anticipates, and the rapid improvement which follows soon removes all objection to the practice. When there is considerable crusting and scabbing, the accumulated crusts are first softened by the use of sweet oil, lard, simple ointment or a poultice, and then shaving commenced. In order to facilitate the removal of the crusts the beard can be first shorn with scissors. After the face has been shaven, all pustules, tubercles, papules, boils and abscesses should be opened with a fine, sharp bistoury, and the discharge of their contents and of the blood which flows pretty freely, encouraged by douches of hot water. This is best done by dipping a large, soft sponge in very hot water and applying it to the diseased surface, continuing this for five or ten minutes. When the bleeding has ceased some soothing ointment should be applied on cloths and bound to the parts.

Hebra's ointment, or the ointments of ammoniated mercury, calomel, ($ \mathfrak{z} $ ss- $ \mathfrak{z} $ j to $ \mathfrak{z} $ j), yellow oxide of mercury, (gr. x-xx to $ \mathfrak{z} $ j) or oxide of zinc will be found to answer the purpose.

The irritation soon subsides, and on daily repetition of this procedure, the face shows marked improvement in a few days. When abscesses and pustules cease to form, I generally direct the 5 per cent. oleate of mercury ointment, and know no other application which gives such satisfactory results. The diffused redness that remains can be made to disappear more rapidly, by an occasional superficial scarification, and the application twice or three times a week of a solution of carbolic acid in alcohol, (1 pt. to 4). The shaving must be continued for at least a year after the final disappearance of the eruption, for upon allowing the beard to grow again the disease is exceedingly liable to return.

In many cases of this disease it will be advisable,—and will hasten the cure—to pull out the hairs from the inflamed follicles. It will be found that this procedure, if consistently carried out, shortens the duration of the disease very materially. It is, however, not so necessary in the non-parasitic as in the parasitic form, and it is very painful to the patient and trying to the practitioner.

In those cases where fungus vegetations occur, they may be destroyed by means of caustics or removed by the curette. It is only in very rare cases, however that such severe measures are required. In most of the cases coming under the notice of the physician in this country, the simple means briefly described above, will suffice for the cure.

In sycosis no internal remedies are requisite, unless there should be disturbance of function of some internal organs, the digestive apparatus for example, when the appropriate remedies demanded by the case should be given.

Dr. John G. Archer, a native of Maryland, died in Pointe Coupee, La., on March 17. He was a brother of Hon. Stevenson Archer, of Harford County.

ARTICLE II.

A Case of Acquired Amenorrhœa with Complete Uterine Atresia; Atrophy of the Uterus; Probable Atrophy of the Ovaries, and absence of Molimen.

BY B. F. LEONARD, M. D., BALTIMORE.

In March, 1881, I was consulted by Mrs. J., a white married woman, for the relief of palpitation of the heart, associated with general debility and some emaciation. Physical examination demonstrated that her heart and lungs were sound, but there was present an anemic murmer, of which I did not inform her. Upon inquiring into the case, the following history was given me:

She grew up a healthy and robust girl, but she menstruated late—but once—at her 17th year. Before her second period was due she married, and it did not make its appearance. In due course of time she was delivered, by forceps, of a boy. The placenta was retained for twenty-four hours, when it was removed while she was under chloroform. Her lying-in was long and tedious; she had pains, foul smelling discharges, and fever; but in about two months she recovered her usual good health. She nursed her boy until she consulted me, nearly three years and nine months later, under the impression that prolonged lactation would prevent pregnancy. I pointed out to her the injury she was doing to health, and she weaned her child. But her functional heart trouble was obstinate, and she remained under observation some time. After waiting a due period and menstruation being still absent, she consented to an examination, when I found the uterus was smaller than normal, in a condition of hyperinvolution; and that the external os uteri was occluded, its locality being simply marked by a little pit about one-third of an inch deep.

I have seen her recently, and I find the same condition present.

She has menstruated but once during her life; and since the birth of her child, has had no show, vicarious or otherwise, and above all, she has had absolutely no menstrual symptoms. She is now robust, but she laments the absence of her "health." She will, however, allow no attempt to restore the patency of the uterine canal, for fear of another pregnancy. This change in her sexual condition does not affect her appearance, for she has a fine bust, her voice is feminine, and her venereal appetite and enjoyments are normal.

I have no intention of discussing theories of menstruation, although this case affords a tempting opportunity. Accepting the view of Pflüger as stated by Schroeder, (Ziemssen's Encyclopedia, Vol. X,) that the growth of the Graafian follicles causes an irritation of the ovarian nerves, which, after a certain intensity is reached, produces, by reflex effect, an arterial congestion of the genitals, this hyperæmia resulting in ovulation and menstruation; we must assume in this case, that as a result of inflammatory puerperal conditions, there followed, first, an atrophy of the ovaries with consequent destruction of the Graafian follicles; and secondly, atrophy or hyperinvolution of the uterus with complete occlusion of the uterine canal. The absence of all menstrual symptoms confirms the first proposition; and the second one must be true, else there would be secretion into the body of the womb, with consequent distention and greater or less increase in the size of the uterus. Exactly the opposite condition is present, the womb is below the normal size.

As far as I know, this case is unique. After quite an extensive research, I have been unable to find a similar one. Quite a number of cases of congenital uterine atresia have been reported. The editor of this journal has kindly furnished me with notes of two such cases: one was reported by Duplay (Arch. Gen. de Med. 1834, tome 4, p. 8, 418); and by

Alberts (Berlin Klin. Wochenschr. 1865, p. 213). But these were cases of congenital atresia, supposed to be due to endometritis commencing during fetal life, and though curious, are not to the point.
314 E. Baltimore St.

[Monteros reports a case of Jobert's (cited in Schwarz, *Complicationen der Blasenscheidenfistel*) in which, on post-mortem examination, the uterine cavity was found obliterated. There was vesico-vaginal fistula, destruction of vaginal portion of the cervix. The supra-vaginal portion of the cervical canal was pervious, but the uterine cavity was entirely obliterated. (Kroner, *Arch. f. Gynæk.* xix, 1.) refers to the case.—ED. CHRONICLE.]

ARTICLE III.

TWO CASES OF EXTIRPATION OF THE OVARIES.

Operations performed at the New York Woman's Hospital.
BY Prof T. GAILLARD THOMAS;
ASSISTED BY H. D. NICHOLL, M. D.
[Reported by A. SANFORD, M. D.]

CASE 1st.—Miss Sarah W., aged 32. Menstruation irregular, duration 7 days, scanty, very painful, especially before the flow, and a constant sufferer from pain in the back and legs, and headaches.

Diagnosis: Anteflexion, prolapsed ovaries.

Treatment: An incision was made in the median line down to the peritoneum; this was found and carefully opened with scissors, the hand thrust in and quickly returned with the ovaries, and ligatures of carbolized silk were tightly applied. The ovaries were then removed, the cavity carefully sponged out and the wound closed by interrupted wire sutures, embracing the peritoneum. The operation was completed in 13 minutes.

Remarks by Prof. Thomas: Unless the ligatures are tightly drawn, hemorrhage will follow and prove fatal. When searching for the peritoneum (which in this case was found with difficulty), one of the chief dangers of the operation is in wounding the intestine. This is a terrible calamity, and should be carefully avoided. The ovaries were found apoplectic, or much enlarged by blood cysts.

CASE 2d.—Mrs. Kattarina A., aged 37—married 15 years, no children, no miscarriages, menstruation regular, amount normal, pain before and during flow, constant pain in the abdomen, back and head. Tumor 2 years growth, commencing in left side of abdomen causing vesical irritation and pressure on rectum.

Diagnosis: Multiple uterine fibroids.

Treatment: Removal of ovaries. This was done as before, the Prof. explaining that a single thread of the silk ligature was carried through with the needle, and in making the knot, two turns should be made in the first stitch to prevent slipping. The carbolized silk would be absorbed and give no trouble. When the fibroid came in view, Dr. Thomas remarked that the removal of these uterine tumors was a very serious affair and wholly unnecessary, as they would soon atrophy after cessation of menstruation following removal of the ovaries. The operation lasted 11 minutes.

Dr. Thomas is the well-known Prof. of Gynecology in the College of Physicians and Surgeons, N. Y., and admission to his Hospital operations is by sections of class in rotation, about 10 being present at one time. He does not make any point as to *time* spent in this operation. Each laparotomy patient is assigned a cottage, isolated, and containing one room each, for patient and nurse, and previous to the operation, these rooms are thoroughly scoured with disinfectant solutions, and the patient is also briskly rubbed all over with bichloride sol. 1 to 1000. The operator and assistants also vigorously use the same solution upon the arms and hands. No other disinfectants are used during the operations. One of these patients had been taking 90 grs. of sulph. morphia per week. Eighty per cent. of laparotomy cases recovered at the N. Y. Woman's Hospital in the year 1883.

ARTICLE IV.

A Hairpin in the Bladder.

BY J. H. SCARFF, M. D., BALTIMORE.

Was called at 7 A. M., November 12th, to see Clara B., aet 11, who, I was informed, was suffering great pain in the region of the genital organs. Her friends with whom she was stopping in the city, in the absence of her parents, had become much alarmed at this sudden onset of pain, and in interrogating her as to the probable cause, ascertained that she had pushed a hair-pin into the vagina.

After hearing this history, I placed the girl upon a table and made an examination of the external genitalia, having no instruments with me to explore the vagina or bladder, which were found extremely sensitive. The clitoris was much enlarged, and showed every evidence that masturbation had been practiced for a considerable time. It being impossible to examine the vagina or bladder without producing excessive pain, I concluded to defer the examination until a later hour, when, with the aid of chloroform and instruments, it could be properly done.

At 12 M. the same day, I promised to return and make a thorough examination under the influence of an anesthetic. Assisted by my friend, Dr. Jones, who gave the chloroform, I examined the vagina, and found nothing indicating a foreign body. I then passed a uterine probe through the urethra into the bladder, (the urethra was very much dilated and patulous,) and lying diagonally across the fundus of the bladder was the hair-pin. After several attempts, I finally succeeded in withdrawing it with a pair of uterine dressing forceps.

I afterwards ascertained that the girl had been taught this method of titillating her genital organs by a female servant, and that she had indulged in the practice for over a year. As I have not been able to find any record of a similar foreign body being found in the female bladder, I have ventured to think the case of sufficient interest to place upon record.

[In one of our exchanges, we notice a reference to a somewhat similar case. The statement is made that a "prominent surgeon once had a female patient in whose bladder was a calculus concreted around a hair-pin, and he remarked that the patient's misfortune was probably due to an attempt to pin up her water-fall."
—ED. CHRONICLE.]

CORRESPONDENCE.

The Contagiousness of Croupous Pneumonia.

SALISBURY, N. C., March 5, 1884.

To the Editor of the "Medical Chronicle."

SIR:

I read with much pleasure the paper in the February number of your journal on "pneumonia," by my friend, Dr. Chambers. I was more than interested, and anxiously looked for his conclusions. The reason why I was curious to know what his summary would be is this: I have had much to do recently with the above named disease; have treated twenty-nine cases in the last eighty or ninety days. My recent experience with this disease warrants me in corroborating his statement that "croupous pneumonia is a miasmatic, contagious fever." In my experience, it has been as contagious as measles or scarlatina; when the epidemic first made its appearance, it attacked a child in a family of five, father, mother, and three children. Soon after the first was attacked, another of the children took it, then the father, then the other child, and lastly the mother,—all had pneumonia. A friend came and nursed them; he went home sick and died of pneumonia. His wife and brother waited on him, and both had severe attacks of pneumonia. Thus the disease continues to spread from house to house; old and young, male and female, robust and debilitated suffering alike.

Dr. Chambers states that the disease is confined more to cities than to the country. This may be true in many instances, but in this epidemic the reverse is true. The disease seems to be confined to malarial districts following the banks of the Yadkin and of creeks and ponds where malarial fevers are the terror of September and October. In these districts I have dispensed to patients, on an average for six weeks, an ounce of quinine a day.

Some of these attacks of pneumonia are ushered in with a distinct chill, others are developed more gradually. Most cases are unilateral, though in three cases both lungs were involved; some are lobular, while others nvolve a whole lobe, and in a few cases the whole lung seemed to be involved. In some, the disease is acute, and convalescence rapid; in others, t lapses into a chronic condition. The brain in many cases has given me much anxiety; indeed, the pain in the head at times is so intense that the patient, though perfectly rational, complains of nothing else. In some instances a diagnosis was retarded for days on account of all the symptoms of disease being referred to the cranium and spine; in some I really suspected meningitis or encephalitis, but in thirty-six or forty-eight hours the head symptoms would subside, and a diagnosis of the true malady was easily made.

Dr. C. says, "we know of no disease which has a more definite classical course than croupous pneumonia." Now, I do not wish to be understood as saying that these twenty-nine cases were all *croupous* pneumonia, yet, they were pneumonia, and many of them *croupous*, and you have noticed the vast difference in the symptoms present in different cases.

As is apparent, the treatment in this epidemic can not be a routine of drugs. In some cases the treatment is almost nil, yet in others the most heroic measures have to be resorted to. The mortality has been very small up to this time. I shall be glad to read Dr. C's plan of treatment in the next number of the CHRONICLE.

Respectfully,
C. N. POOLE, M. D.

The Report of the Maryland State Board of Health.

To the Editor of the "Medical Chronicle."

MY DEAR SIR:

I am truly glad to observe that you have *independence* enough to express your judgment and criticisms on the report of the State Board of Health. The reports of said Board from the 1st to the 5th inclusive, are before me. You call attention to several points that have also attracted my attention; first, the "absence of any financial statement." An examination of the reports will show that not one of the reports except those of 1875 and '78, show any reference, whatever, to the expenditures of the Board; a most significant omission. The report shows that nothing worth the paper on which it is printed, appears from the *members of the Board or its secretary*.

The only papers of any value, whatever, are contributed by physicians having no connection whatever, with the Board in an official capacity, and are voluntary contributions. Then, too, if the whole five reports published, be carefully considered, it will be plain to any competent judge of their contents, that not all of the papers contained, put together and boiled down to solid extract, would take the *second* prize before any prize committee, whilst the State paid not less than $20,000 for the trashy contents which these reports contain. I do not wonder that you say most truthfully that "we trust that we may be able to place the next biennial report of the board upon our shelves by the side of those of Massachusetts, Michigan, Connecticut, New York and West Virginia, without feeling like offering an apology for its many shortcomings."

In conclusion, I would add that not one of the reports of the State Board of Health would command 25 cents a volume in the judgment of any intelligent physician, whilst each biennial report cost the State not less than $2,500. Yours, truly,

J. S. CONRAD.

ST. DENIS, MD., March, 16, 1884.

ANALECTS.

The Management of Chorea.

In the management of chorea it is essential to make a prompt and thorough cure of the first attack, if possible, for while benignant nature often supplies an efficient therapy for this disease, she more often fails, and violent cases may die or pass on to choreic insanity, and the less violent in the beginning, may, without medical interference, become paralytic or a chronic habit, and if recovery does eventually take place, a latent diathetic condition of the voluntary nerve centres may become a part of the patient's constitution, to reappear whenever subsequent neuratrophic conditions exist in the patient. In the management of this affection, therefore, no plan could be more prejudicial to the real welfare of the patient, present or future, than the so-called expectant plan, a most pernicious plan when carried out in many other diseases as well as in chorea, and only justifiable when we are in doubt as to the proper therapeutic measures to be employed. He who has become familiar with the possibilities of chorea from observation of a large number of cases, will never counsel expectancy, or be satisfied with letting the disease wear itself out, if he can do better by more efficient treatment.

An essential therapeutic procedure in a large majority of cases promotive of a tendency to recovery, is the removal of the child from home and the unsanitary surroundings (speaking in a neurological sense), under which the morbid condition has been engendered.

The change from usual environment should be agreeably diverting to the patient and calculated to call into exercise the volitional powers, while being of such a sanitary character as to be promotive of exalted nutrition, invigorating sleep, mental tranquilization and hemic enrichment. Pure air, free sunlight, and an agreeable temperature should be sought in making the change.

Despite the theories that have been advanced of the dependence of chorea upon rheumatism, based upon its frequent association with antecedent rheumatic fever and co-existent cardiac bruit, it will be found to often follow after a scarlatina, aggravated measles, whooping-cough or other cause of depressed vitality if of sufficient intensity to implicate the stamina of the cerebro-spinal axis in such as possess inherent neuropathic tendencies. It is often associated with hysteria and epilepsy. For all the cases put forth by Mr. Hughlings Jackson and Dr. Kirkes, to show that the origin of the trouble is rheumatic, other cases can be offered to show the non existence of previous rheumatism, though rheumatism is markedly if not primarily a disease of the nervous system, as a careful examination of all the facts will show (which it would be out of place here to present), and it should not therefore be strange to find rheumatism as one of the links in the chain of nervous phenomena, and that chorea is not unfrequently the neuratrophic substratum just as the lesion of the trophic nervous system which underlies rheumatism may give rise, and does sometimes, to the phenomena of chorea.

The essential neuropathic condition of chorea is a neuratrophia and consequent instability of the cerebro-spinal motor area, seldom grave enough to be considered organic, strictly speaking, though in a sense or degree we must concede that all disease is organic, and the post-mortem changes that have been found in the corpora strata, cortex and elsewhere in the brain, such as erosions, hemorrhages, etc. in the fatal cases, are sufficient to satisfy us that in many cases the lesion is grossly structural, though hyperemia and irritation of the motor area of the cortex and subjacent portions of the brain and cord are often primarily at fault and this is obviously due to atonic vaso-motor conditions. Beginning in the motor area of the brain and cord, chorea may in its progress, and often does, invade the psychical sensory regions, giving rise to imbecile and insane states and anesthesia.

To treat chorea successfully, therefore, we should suppress, as far as we can, involuntary movement from the very beginning, by giving the child the necessary moral encouragement and strengthening its will power by new demands upon its attention and volition as well as by medication. The sympathetic treatment that fosters hysteria is equally objectionable in chorea. The child wants encouragement that it may not yield any more of its control than it is obliged to, in order that it may not become discouraged and give up entirely to the erratic movements. The will should be made to pass, even though so imperfectly, over the channels of motor nerve conduction so that the "insanity of the muscles" may not become complete, pending our efforts at physiological reconstruction.

The medical treatment should be descending cerebro-spinal galvanism and arsenic to restore trophic nerve power and tranquilize the psycho-motor area, chloral hydrate and sodium bromide in moderation, especially at night, to secure complete cerebro-spinal rest and the neurotic and hematic tonics, iron, the hypophosphites, zinc, cod-liver oil and strychnia; the latter very sparingly. A milk diet is preferable to all other simple substances, but the patient should be fed on a generous variety of food.

After the involuntary tumult of the muscles has subsided, the physician should still look after the patient until a reassuring vigor of constitution is established, and such advice should be given as will tend to promote continued growth in new strength and give the best assurance against the return of this singular and sometimes formidable expression of nerve irritability.

If we watch our patients closely we shall find some of them troubled with symptoms of laryngeal nerve irritation and spasms. When the spasm is not great enough to attract our attention in the day time, we may often learn of its existence from statements made by the patient or nurse in regard to the child's having a troublesome night cough.

I do not know why the cough should appear at night and be absent all day. I have seen it regularly recur at bed-time and continue through the night to the great disturbance of the patient's rest.—*Dr. C. H. Hughes in Weekly Med. Review.*

Punctured Wounds of the Skull.

In a recent discussion on this subject, before the Academy of Medicine of Cincinnati, Dr. P. S. Conner in introducing the subject for discussion, said he was well aware that it might be looked upon by many as rather trite, and yet the gravity of the sometimes apparently slight injuries renders it of great importance. The treatment of simple punctured wounds of the cranium is still a matter of discussion, from the fact that it is frequently difficult to decide whether the injury received is one of the skull alone, or whether the structures underneath the brain and its coverings are also involved. If the injury be of a definite character, the question arises whether we are justified in interfering actively in order to prevent the development of dangerous complications, or whether it is more prudent to wait until further symptoms arise. As regards active interference, we have the advocates of the extreme use of the trephine from Ambrose Paré to Pott, and the expounders of the doctrine, as Stromeyer, that the trephine ought not to be used in any case. Stromeyer claims that, although the injury inflicted may be of the utmost gravity, the trephining of the skull will but increase the dangerous symptoms.

The speaker alluded not to the general fractures of the skull, but to the punctured form. No one would fail to recognize an injury where the skull is driven in, but in a punctured wound the gravity is often overlooked; and yet, without any apparently severe injury externally, such an injury may perhaps prove most dangerous.

The skull may be punctured by the blade of a knife, a bullet, a piece of glass, a sharp instrument, as a pick, and various other substances. The depth of penetration may be out of all proportion to the extent laterally, and the symptoms may be masked for hours or days. The injury is probably greater to the internal than the external table of the skull, or a diploic injury may be followed by inflammation of the veins or pyemia, but usually the internal table is broken off and the meninges or the encephalic vessels pierced. Hemorrhage and inflammation may thus result, and sometimes the brain substance itself may be injured, the penetration extending perhaps even to the opening of the lateral ventricles. With all these serious consequences, a diagnosis is frequently not made.

The speaker remembered one instance where death resulted in forty-eight hours, and the wound in the skull had been overlooked altogether. Knowing the liability of suppuration of wounds of the external and internal tables of the skull, we can understand the necessity for drainage so that a steady outflow is necessary for the safety of the individual. Death is often attributed to a punctured fracture of the skull, and it is therefore desirable to call attention to the danger of injuries about the head, even if they are simple scalp wounds, to decide whether the trephine should be used or not.

The speaker could not see where the danger lies *per se* in the use of the trephine; it is not followed by a great mortality, and the latest examinations made by Walshman, of London, show that there is but little danger. The trephine simply converts a wound with a ragged edge into a smooth one, and the removal of a button of bone frequently prevents inflammation of the meninges, or a localized inflammation of the cerebral mass, or an abscess. A wound of the skull may cause death without a warning, setting in either with convulsions or coma. In order to show how slight an injury may take the life of an individual, the speaker presented a specimen obtained twelve years ago, where a man was cut in a fight on the head, the injury being, however, scarcely perceptible, and yet death occurred in twenty-four hours. At the post-mortem examination, a small scalp wound was found, underneath which there was an extravasation of blood; on reflecting the scalp it was discovered that the skull had been pierced with a small pocket knife, severing a branch of the middle meningeal artery, the cut extending to the depth of half an inch.

This man might have been struck a hundred times about the head in other situations, and yet he might have escaped much injury. The injury was not recognized during life; if it had been recognized the trephine might have saved this man's life, as the hemorrhage could readily have been stopped with a little white wax. Another man was struck on the head with an ice-pick. Paralysis of the right upper extremity, but not of the face, resulted, and two weeks afterward, when Dr. Connor first saw him, a hardness was to be felt at the seat of the injury, as if the pick had been broken off. The doctor at once removed a button of bone with the trephine and came upon the abscess cavity, which he evacuated, but the man died in two or three days. The cavity was not very large; it was situated at the superior portion of the first frontal convolution. The symptoms following the injury in this situation ought not to have been produced according to our present understanding of localization of the brain. If the crown of the trephine had been applied in this case immediately after the injury, it would have permitted an outflow of fluids, and prevented these serious symptoms.

The next specimen, obtained from Dr. E. W. Walker, was one of singular interest. A boy being provoked at a man, picked up a piece of a broken pane of window glass and threw it at the latter, striking him on the head. The man went to bed, but was found dead the next morning. An examination showed a piece of the glass sticking fast in the skull. Had this piece been removed immediately there might have been a chance of life. Death resulted from extravasation of blood. Sub-cranial extravasation of blood is not necessarily fatal; the speaker had himself saved a patient's life by trephining and removing the clot.

A practical lesson to be drawn from these illustrations is that a careful examination ought to be made of every head where a punctured fracture is suspected, and if such be found it is the wisest course to apply the trephine. There is no more danger in removing a button of bone from the head than from the tibia. The special danger of these injuries lies in lesions underneath the skull. It is not necessary to carry out all the extreme precaution for antisepsis, yet with this method the results have been still better than by any other method. The speaker had seen quite a number of cases where death would have resulted if the treatment had not been active.

The speaker had occasion, in preparing an article on this subject some time ago, to look up the authorities, and he was struck with the many instances of recovery from a gunshot wound in the brain on record. There is this difference between a gunshot and a pick wound, that the ball in its course is apt to leave a sufficiently large opening behind it for drainage. The speaker was rather skeptical that when a ball strikes a piece of bone, there is no injury except that made by the surgeon in the operation. If he were thus injured he would rather have the pieces removed than left in the brain. We are not now so far from a decision when to use the trephine as a good while ago. The mere cutting of bone does but little damage, and when a conical crown is used, the dura mater can be sufficiently protected. There is not so much danger from injury to the dura mater as from leptomeningitis later; and this is prevented by the removal of the irritating bodies and the securance of free drainage. To show how much injury the brain will tolerate, the speaker mentioned the case of a convict who tried to injure himself by driving pieces of wire into his head, and yet without doing any damage. Certainly these are rare cases, but they show that we need have no exaggerated fear of injuring the dura mater, when the constant injury caused by the presence of bone is so much more dangerous.—*Cincinnati Lancet and Clinic.*

Prevention and Cure of Seasickness.

Dr. Bennet communicates his own personal experience in preventing seasickness, from which he had been a great sufferer in his early life whenever he was compelled to take a journey by sea. He discovered by accident that two cups of *cafe noir*, taken, with sugar only, an hour or more before embarking, entirely prevented the expected attack of seasickness on the occasion of a very stormy voyage. Subsequent investigation on himself and others has led him to the conclusion that coffee, if taken according to specified directions, will entirely prevent seasickness on short voyages.

By following this plan he has himself enjoyed immunity from seasickness for twenty-five years. Moreover, scores of his friends and patients have found the plan equally effective. It is as follows: The coffee used must be of good quality. A medicinal infusion of about an ounce and a half, made by boiling for ten minutes in four ounces of water, will furnish a dose of about the requisite quantity and strength.

It is to be taken about one hour before the voyage is begun, if sugar alone is added; if milk also is used, it must be taken about two hours and a half before leaving. The object is to ensure its entire absorption, and to leave the stomach empty when the start is made. Furthermore, the coffee should be taken on an empty stomach. However to prevent exhaustion, a nutritious but easily digested meal should be taken long enough beforehand to be well out of the way when the time arrives for taking the coffee. A full stomach at the beginning of a voyage, if there be any predisposition to seasickness, tends rather to cause than to prevent an onset. And the failure of remedial agents taken by the stomach is due to the inability of that organ to absorb them after the malady has begun.

On longer voyages it is well to take the coffee as above described, and then to lie down. The action of the coffee will last for eight or ten hours, and during this time the system may become accustomed to the motion of the vessel.

No food, liquid or solid, should be taken until there is a feeling of hunger or thirst. For the latter, a mineral water, soda or Apollinaris, with or without champagne or brandy, may be sipped.

For hunger, *cafe au lait*, alone or with a little bread, may be taken, or other articles of food that have been recommended may be tried, for instance, curry.

According to the experience of a naval surgeon, the best means of controlling confirmed seasickness is the constant drinking of lukewarm water. This is placed in quantity within reach of the sufferer, who is to drink half a tumbler when the sickness comes on. It is immediately thrown up, but easily, and by and by calm comes.— *N. Y. Med. Times.*

Carbonic Oxide in the Air.

On the subject of carbonic oxide in the air of heated rooms, Dr. Max Gruber last year read a paper before the Bavarian Academy of Sciences, which, in a more extended form, has just been published in the *Archiv fur Hygiene*. Gruber finds that the method for detecting carbonic oxide which was proposed by Fodor is the most delicate of all, and capable of detecting as small an amount as one volume of carbonic oxide in 20,000 volumes of air, that is 0.05 in a thousand. From experiments conducted on animals and on himself he draws the following conclusions:

1. That there is a certain degree of dilution at and beyond which carbonic oxide produces no injurious effects upon the system, and this, probably, lies between 0.02 and 0.05 per cent. by volume.

2. That even the long-continued breathing of an atmosphere which contains carbonic oxide in such a state of dilution produces no accumulation of this gas in the body.

3. That carbonic oxide can be detected by Fodor's method when diluted far beyond the limit of injurious effect.

4. That even with the aid of this delicate method no carbonic oxide could be discovered in rooms which

were heated by red-hot iron stoves and furnaces, and he further concludes that the use of iron stoves and furnaces does not involve the dangers to health which have been very generally supposed to exist.—*New York Medical Times.*

Oral Pathology.

A red line on the gums, with fetor and metallic taste, indicates ptyalism; a blue line, lead poisoning; great sponginess, with sloughing and great fetor, scurvy; a red line about the teeth and along the gums, periostitis; purple gums and purulent discharge, necrosis; gums hot, red, swollen, very tense, phlegmon; gums inflamed and soft, with fluctuation, alveolar abscess; swollen gums, fetid discharge, mucous patches, shallow ulcers under the tongue, eroded palate, eruption of mouth, skin and scalp, gums everted, fetid matter from necks of teeth, syphilis; a white-coated tongue, denotes febrile disturbance; a brown, moist tongue, indigestion; a brown dry tongue, depression, blood-poisoning, typhoid fever; a red, moist tongue, feebleness, exhaustion; a red, dry tongue, inflammatory fever; a red, glazed tongue, general fever, loss of digestion; a tremulous, moist and flabby tongue, feebleness, nervousness; a glazed tongue, with blue appearance, tertiary syphilis.—*Independent Practitioner.*

Coca.

Dr. H. D. Hicks, of Boston, writes as follows (*N. Y. Med. Jour.*) regarding the value of coca:

I have used it both personally and in my practice, and find it of great service in the following conditions:

To prevent and relieve fatigue.

In those cases of backache accompanied by high-colored urine with excessive amounts of urates and uric acid.

In short breathing dependent upon weakness of the muscles of respiration.

Palpitation of the heart, without valvular lesion, due to dilation or to weakness of the heart muscle.

It renews the vigor of the intellect, and relieves mental exhaustion, rendering the flow of thought more easy and the reasoning power more vigorous.

It dissipates "the blues," leaving the mind calm. By its use the depression following an indulgence in alcoholic liquors is relieved, and it invigorates the exhausted sexual function due to excessive venery.

It destroys the craving for alcohol, and, in small doses, is useful in sick headache and headache resulting from over exertion. Its habitual use as part of the daily diet conduces to mental clearness and activity, freedom from fatigue, and sound sleep.

Fœtus in Fœtu.

Dr. Lubimoff, Kasan, Russia (*Vratch Vedomsiti*), has recently reported an interesting case of this kind. He found on a little girl born at term, and living, a perineal tumor, of which the right half was hard and the left half soft. On autopsy there were found two cysts in the left half. The right half contained different portions of a fœtus—a well developed foot with six toes, a rudimentary arm, and a stomach. Between the two tumors were found small dermoid cysts, containing epithelial cells, striated muscular fibre, bits of cartilage, and bones containing marrow in the interior.

Treatment of After-Pains.

At a recent meeting of the New York Clinical Society (*N. Y. Medical Journal*), Dr. L. E. Holt reported a case in which he had used the fluid ext. of gelsemium for the relief of after-pains. The patient could not bear opium, and all the usual local applications had given no relief. He then gave the gelsemium in fractional drop doses, frequently repeated, which relieved the patient promptly. —*The Medical Summary.*

Bromidia and Morphia in Delirium Tremens.

Dr. J. F. Goldman, Huntsville, Ala., writes:

Case 1.—Mr. W. R. W., aged thirty-five, a healthy, strong man, had been drinking hard for a number of days, resulting in delirium tremens. I put him on a sol. morph. and tr. valerian, one ounce each, tr. verat vir. (Norwood's) one drachm; teaspoonful every hour till sleep. I then went to bed, and to sleep, confidently expecting my patient would do likewise. But in this I was doomed to disappointment. Messenger came early in the morning with the information that my patient had been wild all night and slept none. I then prescribed bromidia two ounces; sulph. morph. two grains; teaspoonful every hour till sleep. The result was most happy. My patient fell into a sound sleep of some twelve hours duration, from which he awakened, and went at once to his place of business, a well man.

Case 2.—J. S., aged forty, strong, muscular and vigorous. Found him treading the border lands of horrors, with every symptom of delirium tremens. I put him at once on the bromidia and morph. treatment, with the same result as in case 1—sound sleep and perfect recovery. Since treating the above cases, I have relied implicitly on the bromidia and morphia, and have never been disappointed.

Panaritium.

Panaritium is the unfortunate designation of an acute inflammation of the finger that may attack as well the first as the second or third phalanx, and that has its seat in the subcutaneous cellular tissue, whence the name *panaritium subcutaneum*, or in the sheath of the tendon (*panaritium tendinosum,*) or, lastly, in the bone (*panaritium osteale*). The disease may arise in consequence of crushing, or wounds, or most frequently from infection; it usually begins with pain, from the degree of severity of which a conclusion may be drawn as to the seat of the inflammation, for in those inflammations that have their origin in the bone, the pains are so intense that the sufferers, as a rule, are disturbed in their rest. The swelling in the case of *panaritium osteale* is so light that it bears no proportion to the agony endured. Such intense pain is produced by the retention of the pus beneath the periosteum. When it raises this up and escapes into the cellular tissues, the pain gradually diminishes. From the commencement of the affection until spontaneous rupture externally takes place, usually from twelve to fourteen days elapse; early incision is therefore a great relief to the patient. Incisions can be made even when the pain is most intense, the patient being narcosed, but the incision must, of course, reach down to the bone. The ostitis of the third phalanx generally ends in either total or partial necrosis of the bone. Three or four weeks elapse before the bone is separated from its surroundings— from the tendons, the articular ligaments, or, in the case of partial necrosis, from the still living bone. During this period new bone is already developed by the raised up periosteum, and even if the sequestrum capsule is not completely tubular, in course of time the development of the new bone may still be considerable. If an incision has been made, examination with the probe must be resorted to from time to time—about once a week—to ascertain how much of the surface of the bone is free, and if found to be fairly freed from its surroundings, it should be seized with a strong pair of forceps and quickly removed. The wound will now close, but at the same time the formation of new bone will be limited, and in consequence of contraction, to a certain extent only a rudimentary phalanx may be developed.

The finger will, of course, be somewhat deformed; it generally becomes slightly clubbed. The incision is usually made by the side of a tendon; the tendon may already be necrosed, but it is not always so, and consequently it would not be proper to aid the occurrence of necrosis by incision. Spontaneous bursting most frequently takes place around the tip of the finger ; there are cases, however, in which it takes place under the nail, or at the root of the nail. In such cases the pain is always intense as the nail is only raised up gradually, and the process of elevation is extremely painful. In cases in which the matrix is affected in the process of perforation, the nail becomes necrosed. As far as the nail looks red, it has life in it, just like hair that remains in the cutis ; when matter is collected under the nail it no longer looks red and translucent, but becomes dull, milky colored, and later on it becomes greyish black, a sign that the nail is already dead. Death of the matrix, however, is not always associated with death of the nail; this may occur, but the death of the nail-bed is not a neccessary result of the process; the nail-bed may remain, and the nail may be formed anew. One thing remains ; the inflamed nail-bed never retains so smooth a form as before; it becomes uneven, knotty, and in consequence the nail is never developed with such beautiful smoothness ; it remains uneven, and of a dull milky color. In the course of years this condition may improve a little, but it never becomes good. Various attempts have been made to restrict this uneven growth of the nail by even compression, or by scraping, but the results are only transient, as the cause of the irregular growth is not removed ; the matrix still remains uneven and lumpy. When the pus is originally formed in the subcutaneous cellular tissues, an opening soon appears in the skin, where, first, a vesicle forms, from the cuticle becoming raised up from the rete malpighii. The panaritium subcutaneum has already found its way through by the fifth day, and by the twelfth the wound is generally healed. There are also cases of panaritium in which no pus is formed, but in which complete spontaneous gangrene of the tissues takes place. How is this gangrene to be explained ? In inflammation, gangrene may arise through two causes: 1. The inflammatory process may from the first be so intense that the structure immediately dies ; 2 Clotting of the blood may take place and gangrene, in consequence of the arrest of the circulation. This last possibility we cannot except in the case of panaritium, for how could such a disturbance of circulation as leads to gangrene take place so suddenly ? I have already mentioned to you that the circulation in the fingers is so active that a finger may be completely cut off, except a thin bridge of the skin and the separated part may grow on again, the circulation being carried on through the bridge of skin only.

I think gangrene would take place here from the first cause. The acute inflammation is a chemical process in the tissues which is associated with dilation of the vessels with consequent exudation of serum, with increase of number of cells in the connective and fatty tissues, and with extravasation of white blood corpuscles, which come to light as pus. The most essential part of the affair, however, is the chemical process which changes, in a manner not yet understood, the intercellular substance and the vascular tissues. There are naturally different degrees, and these degrees are manifested in such a way that the inflammatory change and the disturbance of nutrition are small in one case, whilst in another they are extreme—indeed, the peculiar disturbance of nutrition may be so intense that the vitality of the tissues ceases. This cessation of vitality is principally of importance as regards the vascular tissues, for when once the walls of a vessel are dead--as held by Bruecke--clotting of the blood readily takes place. At a temperature of 1 C. (33.9 F.) no freezing takes place, and the blood, as far as it alone is concerned, may still circulate, but at this temperature the tissues of the vessels die, and clotting then takes place in consequence of their death. The like is the case in various other processes—the first in order is the death of the tissues, and the stoppage of the circulation is secondary. When gangrene takes place through the action of liquid caustic alkalies, we must look upon this in the same way as being the result of the destruction of the tissues. The conditions are similar in the case of certain animal poisons, particularly the poison of serpents, for we cannot suppose that such a disturbance of circulation is set up that gangrene follows by the mechanical injury from the teeth; it is probable that the poison itself acts chemically in such a way that it kills the tissue, and that, as a consequence of the death of these, stagnation of the blood supervenes.—*Trans. from Billroth in Med. Press and Circular.*

Fresh Paint.

The current belief among householders that the smell of fresh lead paint is noxious is founded on pretty general experience, but is opposed by the belief, equally current among chemists, that lead compounds are not volatile. A fact recently brought to our notice seems to support the domestic theory. The basis of the useful and popular luminous paint is known to be sulphide of calcium. Now, this compound, when unprotected by varnish, glass, or some other impervious substance, is slowly acted on by the acids of the air and sulphuretted hydrogen is evolved, which blackens lead paint. This is well known, and can easily be avoided by proper protection of the paint. But the curious thing is that unprotected luminous paint is found to be perceptibly blackened by the fumes from fresh lead paint. There seems to be only one possible explanation of this—namely, that a surface freshly covered with lead paint does actually emit some volatile compound of lead. We believe that many physicians could confirm this view from their own observations in regard to painted houses.—*Lancet.*

Non-Vesicating Croton Oil.

An important discovery seems to have been made by Mr. Harold Senier, of the London Chemical Society, to judge from an abstract given in a recent number of the *Lancet* of a paper read by him at a meeting of the Pharmaceutical Society. It amounts to nothing less than that croton-oil may be separated into two different oils by the action of alcohol, one of which is irritating but not purgative, and the other purgative but not irritating. When alcohol of the specific gravity of 0.794 to 0.800 is added to the croton oil in proportion of seven or more volumes to six, the oil separates into two parts—one of them (the vesicating oil) dissolves in the alcohol, and remains soluble in alcohol in all proportions; the other, (the purgative oil) separates, and is then found to have become insoluble in any proportion of alcohol. This insoluble oil is said to be a safe and pleasant purgative, free from any undesirable action, in doses of one-tenth to one-half a minim, in the form of pills made with magnesium carbonate and extract of henbane as excipients. —*N. Y. Medical Journal.*

According to the *British Medical Journal*, the female medical students of St. Petersburg have been compelled to reside in a large boarding establishment provided by the authorities, instead of being free, as heretofore, to live where they pleased. They are required to be at home before 9 o'clock every evening, and are charged ten roubles per month for board and lodging. Princess Shakafskoy is the present resident superintendent. This change was made through fear of Nihilistic plots.

The Medical Chronicle.

A Monthly Journal for the Practitioner.

GEORGE H. ROHÉ, M. D., Editor.

☞ It is requested that all literary and business communications, books for review, exchanges, etc., be addressed to, and all checks, drafts and post-office orders drawn to the order of
DR. GEORGE H. ROHÉ,
Cor. Greene & Mulberry Sts., - Balto., Md.

BALTIMORE, APRIL, 1884.

EDITORIAL.

The Twelfth Annual Commencement of the Baltimore College of Physicians and Surgeons,

On March 4th, the twelfth annual commencement of the College of Physicians and Surgeons of Baltimore, was held in the Academy of Music, in the presence of a large and brilliant audience. Hundreds of bright eyes showered affectionate glances upon the newly-created *doctores medicinæ* as they came forward to receive the coveted diploma from the hands of Prof. Lynch. After prayer by the Rev. Mr. Lefevre, the Dean, Prof. Opie, gave a brief history of the origin and rapid progress of the school, and pointed out the causes of its unexampled prosperity. The Graduating Class numbered 127, and were from all parts of the country, as shown by the following list:

Allen, J. R.	Va.
Anderson, J. E.	N. J.
Atkinson, Clarence L. C.	W. Va.
Banner, L. L.	Va.
Barton, Robt. White,	Tenn.
Bates, Woodville,	Mo.
Battle, J. T. J.	N. C.
Berry, J. W.	W. Va.
Best, B. W.	N. C.
Briggs, David K.	S. C.
Brooks, G. C.	N. C.
Brown, William E.	S. C.
Burner, D. F.	Va.
Bush, J. C. F.	N. Y.
Byers G. W.	Pa.
Carpenter, E. G.	Ohio.
Chambers, John Jay,	Ohio.
Chapman, W. C.	Ky.
Chesney, J. W.	W. Va.
Clayton, Charles E.	N. C.
Coffman, W. H.	Va.
Cooper, A. T.	N. C.
Cooper, F.	N. C.
Cornell, M. C.	Pa.
Cox, J. W.	Mo.
Daily, Griffin T.	W. Vu.
Daniels, J. B.	W. Va.
Derby, G. A.	N. Y.
Doughton, George,	N. C.
Dunne, A. J.	Mass.
Edmiston, M. Jr.	W. Va.
Edwards, William,	N. C.
Erwin, T. G.	N. C.
Eubank, C. D.	Va.
Fowlkes, W. M.	N. C.
Follmer, J. Brooks,	Pa.
Fisher, D. S.	W. Vu.
Fitzgerald, E. M.	Ct.
Flippin, J. M.	N. C.
Fleming, J. Frank,	Pa.
Futrell, M. F.	N. C.
Garvey, J. B.	Pa.
Gearheart, E. A.	Pa.
Gentry, J. M.	Pa.
Glass, J. H.	Ky.
Graham, W. R.	N. C.
Green, J. E.	Ga.
Green, Albert W.	N. Y.
Hall, C. C.	Pa.
Hall, Robert E. L.	Mo.
Harrell, W. J.	N. C.
Heilman, A. E.	Pa.
Hersman, C. C.	W. Va.
Hiers, C. M.	S. C.
Holroyd, Wm. H.	W. Va.
Hood, E. V.	Ga.
Hopkins, C. F.	Pa.
Horne, A. F.	Va.
Horton, E. H.	N. C.
Houck, A. F.	N. C.
Howard, C. I.	Pa.
Jameson, C. H.	La.
Jamison, J. A.	W. Va.
Jarrett, J. H. S.	Md.
Johnson, S. H.	N. J.
Jones, D. H.	Md.
Kellam, B. C.	Va.
Kelly, Carl M.	Pa.
Kidd, J. W.	W. Va.
Krebs, J. S.	Pa.
Laing, H. M.	Pa.
Lane, R. Y.	Ga.
Line, L. M.	Md.
Little, W. E. E.	Canada.
Loughridge, John T.	Ohio.
Love, William Preston,	W. Va.
March, E. J.	Ohio.
Martin, Isaac J. Jr., G. C.	Md.
Mathews, C. O.	Texas.
Manley, J. A.	Pa.
McCleary, W. W.	Pa.
McGovern, M.	Pa.
Morehead, P. W.	Va.
Murray, Hosea Powers.	N. C.
Nash, Charles P.	W Va.
Neblett, Norman H., G. C.	Va.
Ninde, F. F.	Va.
Noel, E. E.	W. Va.
Nordman, F. R.	Md.
Oates, T. F.	Ark.
Palmer, J. G.	Ga.
Payzant, J. A.	Nova Scotia.
Perry, Mark P.	N. C.
Pickle, J. W.	Ark.
Pritchard, W. B.	N. C.
Pruner, W. H.	Md.
Quinn, Wallace C.	Pa.
Riddlemoser, W. T.	Md.
Riegel, W. A. L.	Pa.
Robinson, Jabez P.	S. C.
Robinson, J. S.	N. Y.
Robinson, T. E.	Md.
Rodreick, S. S.	W. Va.
Rogers, H. M.	Va.
Sampsell, D. M.	Pa.
Showalter, J. B.	Pa.
Simon, Frank,	Wis.
Slicer, J. B.	Md.
Schlicher, E. J.	Pa.

Smith, Robert J., G. C.	Mich.
Smith, T. J.	R. I.
Sooy, R. M.	N. J.
Spalding, James W.	Texas.
Sproesser, Alfred F.	Pa.
Stiger, J. D.	N. J.
Taylor, W. R.	Ohio.
Tulloss, Wm. R.	Va.
Twigg, Ashford.	Md.
Wachter, C. L.	Md.
Wade, J. T.	Mo.
Walsh, Fred. W.	New Brunswick.
Walter, A. P.	Pa.
Watson, S. P.	S. C.
Webb, M. W.	Ohio.
Wedgworth, W. M.	Miss.
Wyatt, Z. W.	W. Va.
Yeager, C. F.	Texas.

GRADED COURSE.

T. H Brayshaw, 2d year.
N. T Carswell, 1st year.
J. S. Daniels, 1st year.
Gilbert Hess, 2d year.
C. La Forge, 1st year.
C. R. Marshall, 2d year.
W. McNaul, 2d year.
W. V. Philbrick, 2d year.
J. G. Sullivan, 1st year.
W. H. Van Geisen, 1st year.
Chas. H. Vees, 1st year.
J. J. Wilson, 1st year.

The Cathell Medal was presented by Prof. Cathell to E. V. Hood, of Georgia, and the College Prizes were delivered by Prof. Arnold as follows: The Brown Memorial Medal to David K. Briggs, of S. C.; the Howard Memorial Medal to Robert J. Smith, of Michigan; the College Distinctions to Alfred F. Sproesser, of Pa.; J. Frank Fleming, of Pa.; J. T. Wade, of Mo.; C. L. Wachter, of Md; Wallace C. Quinn, of Pa.; S. S. Rodreick, of W. Va.; and J. D. Steiger, of N. J. The Bobbitt Prize, a handsome gold medal, was awarded to E. V. Hood, of Ga., for excellence in gynecology.

The valedictory address, by Rev. Prof. Edsall Ferrier, of Easton, Pa., was an eloquent and masterly effort, and was listened to with rapt attention by the large audience. We hope soon to print the address in full in the CHRONICLE.

The spring session began on March 17, and will continue until July 1st. The exercises will be limited to clinical lectures and practical work in the chemical and biological laboratories.

The Alumni Association of the College met March 3. Dr. William Rickert of the class of '79, was elected President, Dr. E. V. Hood ('84), Vice-president, Dr. J. H. Branham ('79), Secretary, and Prof. Opie, Treasurer. The committee on prize essays reported that less than three essays had been submitted, hence no award could be made. A resolution was adopted, removing the restriction requiring at least three essays to be submitted, and offering for the next year two prizes, a first prize of *one hundred dollars* for the best essay, and a second prize of *fifty dollars* for the next best.

The association now numbers over one thousand members. In order to keep up a proper *esprit de corps*, it is desirable that a notification of all civil and professional honors and distinctions received by the members should be sent to the secretary, who will place the same on record and report them to the association at the next annual meeting.

The Medical Service at Bay View Charity Hospital, and the Medical Colleges of Baltimore.

For many years the immense amount of clinical material in the Bay View Almshouse, the great charity hospital of Baltimore, has been running to waste, so far as its utilisation for purposes of teaching was concerned. The medical schools of this city have made frequent and earnest, but heretofore unavailing, efforts to obtain the privilege of furnishing the medical attention to the sick, and give clinical instructions to their students in the institution.

It was represented to the Trustees that, aside from the desirability of furnishing to medical students the advantage of studying, under competent teachers, the varied forms of disease to be found in a hospital of this character, such a change would be of very great advantage to the sick themselves, and for very obvious reasons. Previous boards have held tenaciously to the political power, which the appointment annually of two visiting physicians conferred, and no arguments based upon the benefit to the patients had any weight. Political influences were too strong to be resisted, and hence all previous efforts in the direction of improving the medical service in the institution in question failed.

It is not intended in this article to question, in any way, the qualifications of any of the medical gentlemen who have held the position of visiting physician to Bay View, but merely to point out the defects involved in the system. Under this system there were no responsible resident physicians appointed, and the visiting physicians could not give the time and attention demanded, during a brief daily visit of one, two or three hours. Besides, the science of medicine at the present day is so vast a body of knowledge, that no two individuals, however well fitted by natural ability, or acquirements, can compass the whole of it, and consequently many patients, especially those afflicted with the rarer diseases, must suffer, unless the aid of specialists be called in to make a diagnosis or suggest a line of treatment.

Although these considerations had little weight with previous Boards of Trustees, as stated above, they were sufficient to convince the present Board, appointed last February by his Honor, Mayor Latrobe, and consisting of Messrs. Joseph Friedenwald, Black, Hartman, Kemp and Blake. This Board has recently taken action which completely changes the system of medical service for the poor in this city. Arrangements have been consummated in consequence of which the Faculties of the COLLEGE OF PHYSICIANS AND SURGEONS, and of the University of Maryland will hereafter assume the duty of providing medical attendance to the almshouse. Two resident physicians will be appointed annually, at a salary of $500 per year, with board and lodging. These resident physicians are nominated by the Faculties, subject, of course, to confirmation by the Board of Trustees. One member of each of the above named Faculties shall visit the hospital daily and give the necessary attention to the sick.

In addition, the Board of Trustees has granted to the above faculties the privilege of giving clinical instruction in the institution, and for this purpose, suitable lecture-rooms will be fitted up through the liberality of the Trustees, as soon as the necessary room can be obtained, which will be in about three months, when a large addition to the hospital, to accommodate the large number of insane inmates is completed.

The Faculty of the College of Physicians and Surgeons has elected Dr. W. Page McIntosh, (class of '82) as one of the physicians. His appointment dates from April 1. Dr. McIntosh has been for the past two years resident physician at the Maryland Lying-in Hospital, and is well-qualified for the responsible position to which he has been appointed. Dr. Hiram Woods, who has previously served with much credit at Bay View, has been nominated by the University of Maryland. The term of service of the visiting physicians will begin on the 1st of May.

Thus has the medical service for the poor of this city been "taken out of politics" in a practical manner by the action of an enlightened Board of Trustees, which has instituted a great reform against extraordinary pressure from the politicians, who were unwilling to see the patronage slip out of their grasp. The gentlemen comprising the Board deserve the gratitude of the medical profession and the public for their action. It is to be hoped that the reform will prove of permanent benefit to the institution.

The large amount of clinical material thus rendered available for purposes of instruction will prove of immense benefit to students coming to this city for a medical education, and places the facilities of the two schools mentioned above nearly all similar institutions in this country.

Dr. Quinan's Medical Annals of Baltimore.*

Everybody who has any knowledge of medical men in Baltimore, is well acquainted with the fact that what Dr. Quinan doesn't know about the history and literature of medicine, everywhere and at all times, isn't worth inquiring about. He has on a number of occasions corrected the inaccuracies of writers who have either falsified history by incorrect dates, or who have committed the graver fault of misquoting one of his beloved ancients. He has on all appropriate occasions, insisted upon a proper recognition of the advanced position which the profession of Maryland has always held, and has done much to place enduringly upon record, their services to the state, to science, and to humanity.

The work whose title is given in the foot-note, and which has just issued from the press, under the auspices of the Medical and Chirurgical Faculty of Maryland, is a monument of patient toil and unwearied industry. It will be to the future historian of medicine in the United States, what official documents are to the writer of secular history; not history, but the materials out of which history is constructed. That errors should creep into a work of this character is unavoidable, but the few that have come to our notice, are mostly attributable to the proof-reader. To most persons the amount of labor represented in these memorials of the medical profession in this city, must appear almost incredible. With Dr. Quinan this has been a true labor of love for many years, and only those who were

---

* Medical Annals of Baltimore from 1608 to 1880, including events, men and literature, to which is added a subject index and record of public services. By John R. Quinan, M. D., member Medical and Chirurgical Faculty of Maryland.

often brought in contact with him during his search after facts in the history of this or that corypheus of medicine, who has "joined the choir invisible," and left but scanty records behind, can appreciate the toil involved. The medical profession of this city and state owes the author a debt of gratitude that can be only partly discharged by a hearty acknowledgment of the value of his work.

We should like to quote examples of the thoroughness with which Dr. Quinan's self-appointed task has been fulfilled, but our space is limited, and we will only add a citation which he has himself written over the biographical notice of one of those whose memory he here enshrines, and which applies to himself with singular exactness:

"Incredibili industria, diligentia singulari."

CURRENT LITERATURE.

The Hip and its Diseases. By V. P. Gibney, A. M., M. D., etc. New York and London, Bermingham & Co., 1884.

The first chapter is introductory to the subject. The second, descriptive of the anatomy of the hip, is full, accurate, and, like the whole book, written in good style; the only drawback being the very poor wood-cuts which deface all the pages on which they occur. One of the best features is the full and vivid clinical pictures with which the book abounds; and one of the most commendable is the cases in which errors of diagnosis or treatment were made. These add much to the value of the work, and speak well for the honesty of the author. Many clinicians seem to have the faculty of forgetting such occurrences.

Much space is given to differential diagnosis, and the distinctive features of the various diseases are clearly brought out. The excellent classification adds much to the clearness of the treatise, and to the ease with which the book is understood.

Less space is given to treatment than would be expected in a work of the kind. Rest, blisters and poultices being the agents generally used. The last half of the book is devoted to chronic articular ostitis. The writer believes that the bone is the primary seat of this disease in most cases, although it may be secondary to other affections about the joint, and that struma, congenital or acquired, is the principal etiological factor; injuries being of secondary importance, they being the exciting causes in some cases.

The treatment of this disease is fully treated of in several chapters, all the different surgical procedures being fully considered. The book is a credit to American authorship, and should be read by every one who wishes to understand this subject with all the recent advances.   J. H. B.

FLOTSAM.

FLINT believes in the bacillar origin of tuberculosis. Virchow is still one of the doubters.

ON March 27 the medical department of the University of Louisiana, celebrated its semi-centennial.

THE Annual Meeting of the Association of American Medical Editors will be held in Washington. May the 5th, at 8 P. M., in Medical Hall, S. E. corner of Sixth and F Streets.

The Annual Address will be delivered by President LEARTUS CONNOR, M. D., on "*The American Medical Journal of the Future, as Indicated by the History of American Medical Journals in the Past.*"

Dr. N. S. Davis will open the discussion on "*How far can Legislation Aid in Elevating the Standard of Medical Education in this Country?*"

THE *Atlanta Medical and Surgical Journal* has changed editors, publishers, paper, type, cover and character of contents. It is much improved in every respect. We wish it a long and successful career henceforth.

THE veterinary experts who investigated the outbreak of disease among the cattle in Kansas, have come to the conclusion that the malady was due to ergotised rye among the hay.

DR. JULIUS WISE has succeded Dr. D. C. Gamble as the St. Louis Editor of the *Weekly Med. Review*. Dr. Wise is favorably known to the editorial fraternity as former editor of the *Mississippi Valley Medical Monthly*. We welcome him back into the ranks.

VIDAL regards capsicum as the best remedy in piles. He prescribes three or four three-grain pills daily, half at breakfast time and half at supper time. Under its influence congestion and all the painful symptoms which accompany it disappear rapidly.

DR. LUNSFORD P. YANDELL, senior editor of the *Louisville Medical News*, and professor of principles and practice of medicine in the University of Louisville, died at his home on March 12, of angina pectoris. Dr. Yandell belonged to a family whose name is well known in medical literature.

BETWEEN 1874 and 1881, 445 cases of trichinosis have been reported in the German Army. Fifteen of the cases ended fatally. In the United States Army during the same period, not a single case has been reported. This is certainly a point in favor of the American hog.

DR. THOS. H. HUGHES, class of 1879, College of Physicians and Surgeons, died at his home, in Rappahannock Co., Va., January 29, 1884, of consumption. Dr. Hughes was only 28 years of age, but he had already won an enviable position in the community where he practiced.

TWO doctors were disputing by the bedside of a patient. "I tell you the liver is diseased," said one. "Nonsense; nothing of the kind. It is the spleen." "Very well; we shall see at the post-mortem who is right." Great sensation on the part of the patient, whom in the heat of the argument they had quite forgotten.—*New Orleans Times-Democrat*.

We have a suspicion that we have seen this story before; it has a rather ancient flavor. We don't believe the *T.-D.* intended to palm it off on us as original.

A well-written short story of some medical interest appeared in *Swinton's Story Teller* for February 20. It is a sympathetic history of a case of leprosy occurring on the bayou Lafourche in Louisiana, where not a few cases of this dreaded disease are known to exist. The salient points in the clinical history of leprosy are well brought out, without the offensive realism that so often accompanies the novelist's study of pathology. The author of the story is Mr. John Dimitry, a descendant of a well known Louisiana creole family.

ON the evening of March 13th, Dr. Wilmer Brinton, who is so well known to our readers as the writer of the interesting letters in the CHRONICLE, from Vienna and other European medical centres, celebrated his return home by an elegant supper to a few personal and professional friends, at the St. James Hotel. Those present, in addition to the genial host, were Drs. Chambers, Scarff, Leonard, Hartman, and Robinson, Messrs. D. L. Brinton, John T. Stone, and the editor of the CHRONICLE. Methods of medical education abroad were discussed over the lubricous oyster, the savory terrapin, and various other good things which yet linger nameless in the memory, and many witty sayings passed across the table "between the sherry and champagne."

The Medical Chronicle.

BALTIMORE, MAY, 1884.

ORIGINAL ARTICLES.

ARTICLE I.

Report of an Operation by Galvano-Cautery on Internal Hemorrhoids; Cure.*

By B. F. LEONARD M. D., Baltimore.

Many surgeons, at home and abroad, speak of the galvano-cautery with great respect, and but little familiarity. It has been used by Byrne and others, with marked success in uterine surgery, but so far as I know, mine is the first operation of the kind in this city, and possibly in this country, by the galvano-cautery.

I saw in December last, through the kindness of my friend, Dr. C. F. Percivall, a case of both internal and external hemorrhoids, with a history dating from 1869. It was only in the last few years that the patient's suffering became intense, due mainly to complicating fissures. Under the treatment of a specialist, these fissures were rendered almost painless, though cure was not possible as long as the cause remained. The patient was compelled to use an enema daily for years, and the distress after defecation persisted for hours. He was told by several surgeons that the only relief was the knife; this he declined, and suffered on. Finally, hearing Dr. P. speak of the galvano-cautery he determined to submit to an operation.

On inspection, several small external piles were seen, and on straining, there protruded from the anus an indurated internal hemorrhoid, about as large as a walnut. On one side of this, and attached to it, was seen a venous pile, both having a common cord-like semi-sessile pedicle, reaching nearly two inches above the sphincter, in which could be seen an artery and a vein, the former running to the indurated and the latter to the venous pile. On pressure, this latter could be entirely emptied, leaving a collapsed sac.

I operated on the internal piles on December 22, last, with the able assistance of Dr. Percivall. The sphincter was first dilated, and the clamp was applied as usual, but the attachment of the pedicle was so long, that the clamp had to be applied the second time. The patient refused to be chloroformed, but he inhaled a few whiffs, himself holding the cone. The operation took about twenty minutes, and was comparatively painless, but of course the stretching of the sphincter was painful, as well as the necessary contact afterward with the contused tissues. About a week later a second operation was done on the external piles with the galvano-ecraseur.

The cautery used was the Seiler battery (see cuts), made by Mr. Otto Flemming (furnished by Mr. Willms). It worked to a charm, being absolutely under the control of the operator, and requiring no assistant. I have used it a number of times since, with the greatest satisfaction. In this particular operation, I found the best way to use it was by keeping the knife in contact with the tissues to be cut, and applying the white heat intermittently by means of the circuit-closer. By working slowly enough, and cauterizing the parts thoroughly, there is no resulting hemorrhage—there was absolutely none in this case.

A concise description of this excellent battery may not be uninteresting. The cell is quite large ($6\frac{1}{2} \times 6\frac{1}{2} \times 7\frac{1}{2}$ in.);

---

* An abstract of this paper was delivered at a meeting April 12, 1884, of the Medical Society of the Woman's Medical College, Baltimore.

the elements consist of 5 pairs of zinc and carbon plates. This cell fits in a box resting on a platform which is elevated at any height by means of a treadle in front, thereby immersing the elements to any desired extent, thus regulating the amount of force. A rack holds the treadle at any desired point. When not in use the cell and platform are lowered, and the latter acts as a drip-cup. The conducting cords fit into a "universal hard rubber handle" to which various instruments (knives, ecraseur, etc.) are attached. In the handle is a "current closer,"—a knob, by pressing which the current may be made or broken at pleasure, thus placing the battery under the control of the finger. The battery is run by a fluid of complicated formula, and which polarizes but little.

A few days since, I received the following letter from the patient:

BALTIMORE, April 10, '84.

* * It gives me pleasure to say the results of the operations performed upon me with the galvano-cautery have been in every way satisfactory. The operations themselves were comparatively painless. I was confined to my room but three days, more from precaution than from any inconvenience. Since the first week, I have not experienced even soreness in the parts, and I now consider myself as good as new. * * *

Yours, very truly, ———

In view of the efficiency of the battery, the ease and comparative painlessness of the operation, the freedom from hemorrhage, and the quick recovery, I believe the galvano-cautery has a wide and useful field before it in the surgery of rectal diseases.

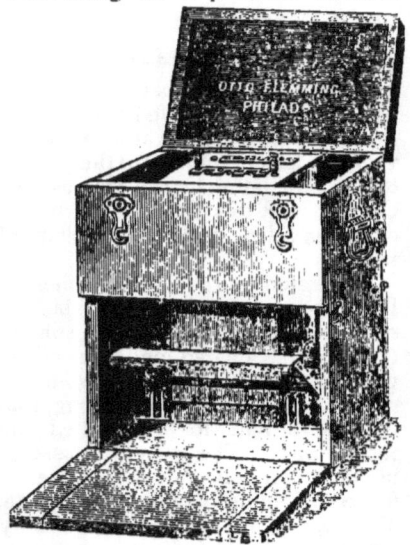

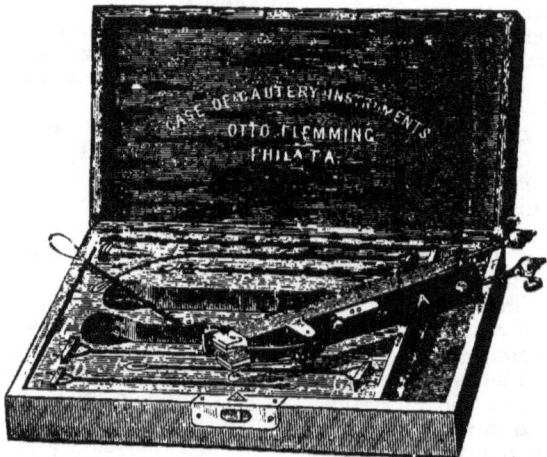

ARTICLE II.

FETAL AUSCULTATION.

BY J. H. BRANHAM, M. D.

Assistant Demonstrator and Lecturer on Regional Anatomy, College of Physicians and Surgeons, Baltimore.

In 1818, Meyer, of Geneva, first discovered that the sounds of the fetal heart could be heard through the walls of the mother's abdomen. Notwithstanding the importance of this discovery, it received very little notice until three years after, when Kergaradec of Paris, called attention to it, and stated that he had verified its truth. Then it became widely known and appreciated. The sound is by most observers likened to the tick of a watch heard through a pillow. To me, this resemblance is slight, while the adult heart, when the ear is placed over a remote part of the thorax, gives almost the same sound.

At what time can the sound of the fetal heart be heard? Depaul claims to have heard it eleven weeks and four days after possible conception; other observers have detected it in the fourteenth week. I have had very few opportunities of examination in the first weeks of pregnancy, and have never heard it before the last of the fourth month. It can always be heard after the middle of pregnancy, when there is a living child, if careful and repeated auscultations are made. The sound is dicrotic, and the point of greatest intensity is midway between the left anterior superior process of the ilium and the umbilicus in a large majority of cases. This is because the sound is transmitted through the posterior wall of the thorax, and is heard where the back of the child is applied to the uterus. In right anterior positions, it is most distinct at the corresponding point on the right side. In posterior positions, the sound is discovered with difficulty, and is situated far back. In face and breech presentations, it is situated at or above the line of the umbilicus. It can generally be heard over but a small area and when the amnionic fluid is scanty and the sound is more diffused, the point of greatest intensity can easily be found.

From the foregoing, it will be seen that the fetal pulsation is of great importance in ascertaining the position of the child in utero. It cannot be relied on alone, but should always be taken into consideration. Every accoucheur, when engaged to attend a case, should carefully examine the patient during the latter part of the gestation. By means of careful auscultation and palpation, he can ascertain the position of the child. If this be abnormal, it can be corrected by external, or by combined external and internal manipulation. He can also detect multiple pregnancy, and whether or not the child is dead.

This is by far the most reliable sign of pregnancy. Jerking of the abdominal muscles may so closely resemble the movements of the child, that accurate and experienced observers have been led into error, but, to the careful examiner, nothing can be mistaken for the fetal heart.

It is often necessary to decide if the child in utero is living or dead, and here again, we have to depend principally upon auscultation. If the sounds have once been heard, and afterward cease, there can be no doubt that life is extinct. I have diagnosticated the death of the fetus by this means in two cases; in both my opinion was confirmed.

In 1859, Frankenhausen, of Jena, made the remarkable statement that he had foretold the sex of fifty children by the rapidity of the heart-sound, without a single mistake. He stated that the average rate for male children was 124, and for female, 144 per minute.

This question has since been discussed by many observers with various results. A large number have confirmed, partly, his theory, while others state that there is no relation between the sex and heart-rate.

Dr. Naylor, (Edinburg *Med. Jour.*, 1876), calls attention to the effect of digestion on the fetal heart rate. He states that two (2) hours after a full meal, the heart beat is increased from four to thirty-two per minute. Dr. Cummings, in an elaborate paper, concludes that the heart rate varies with the size of the fetus; but that in two children of the same size, the male pulse is slower.

Dr. Wilson, (*American Practitioner*, 1873 and 1875) reports 232 cases, and from them arranges the following table: If the rate is from 110 to 125, almost certainly male; from 125 to 130, probably male; 130 to 134, doubtful, with probabilities in favor of male; 134 to 138, doubtful, with probabilities in favor of female; 138 to 143, probably female; 143 to 170, almost certainly female.

I have examined a large number of cases with the view of determining the sex, position and condition of the fetus. I will first give a small number of cases in which the probable sex of the child was recorded before its birth, and then will see what conclusions we can draw from the foregoing data.

The cases are twenty-three in number, from patients examined by myself or Dr. McIntosh, late resident physician at the Maternité Hospital of this city. There are 13 males with an average pulse of 130, average weight, 7½ lbs.; and 10 females, average pulse, 143, and weight, 8 lbs. Of the males, nine were correctly diagnosticated, and two were recorded as doubtful; 136½ and 135½, weight, 7 lbs. and 8 lbs. and 14 oz.; and two incorrectly, 160 and 145, weight, 9 lbs. and 4 oz., and 9 lbs. Of the females, seven were correctly predicted, and three were doubtful. The pulse in these being 131½, 131, 137, and the weight, 7 lbs., 7 lbs. 10 oz., and 10 lbs. and 8 oz.

Does the maternal pulse influence the fetal? When the mother's is in a normal condition, I think not. Having examined a number of patients to decide this point, I was unable to detect the slightest relation between the two. When there is any physical or chemical cause which acts at the same time on mother and fetus, of course, both are increased (as in fever, etc.) There can be no doubt that the rate of the fetal pulse often changes to a great degree, and very rapidly. This is the case especially just after active movements. I think that we are justified in concluding that the sex of the fetus can be ascertained with considerable accuracy, if frequent examinations are made when the mother is quiet, and not after a meal, and if the pulse is counted for at least a minute at a time. By this we eliminate the error which might arise from counting during transient increase.

In conclusion, let me urge that every physician on being called to a case of confinement, ascertain at once, the position and condition of the fetal pulse, so that if any emergency arise, he can have a sure guide as to whether the child is suffering, is dead, or is doing well.

ARTICLE III.

HEMORRHAGIC MALARIAL FEVER.

By JOHN S. LYNCH, M.D.

Professor of Principles and Practice of Medicine, and Clinical Professor of Chest and Throat, College of Physicians and Surgeons, Baltimore.

[The following valuable paper was read by the distinguished author, before the Medical and Surgical Society of Baltimore, and published in the *Physician and Surgeon*, of February, 1876. It is now republished with changes and additions, in response to many requests from our readers. ED. CHRONICLE.]

Mr. President and Gentlemen:

The disease selected for discussion to-night, is known throughout the Southern States by various names: but the State Medical Association of Alabama having in 1870 suggested the name of Hemorrhagic Malarial Fever; it was subsequently adopted by the Royal College of London, and has since been generally accepted by the profession.

Though of rare occurrence previous to 1867; in which year it assumed the proportions of a formidable epidemic throughout the Southern or

Gulf tier of States, it is undoubtedly not a new disease. Sporadic cases of it have been seen from time to time by nearly all physicians practising in the more intensely malarious regions of the South; and my valued friend, Dr. E. D. McDaniel, of Camden, Ala., in an able contribution to the Transactions of the Alabama State Medical Association for the year 1874, quotes numerous authors who have described the disease as witnessed by them in Brazil, Mexico, Italy, the Spanish Peninsula, and some of the West India Islands. These observations run back through a period of over one hundred years. Notwithstanding these facts, I find some difficulty in preparing myself for this discussion, as the complaint is not yet included in any of our systematic works on medicine and what literature there is on the subject is scattered through various Southern medical journals and the transactions of Southern State Medical Associations, or works now out of print. There is also a great scarcity of post-mortems by capable and reliable observers, and especially is there a total absence of microscopic examinations of the kidneys and liver, so that we are ignorant of what may be the nature of those finer anatomical lesions of these organs which lead to the hemorrhage. In the description I am about to give, therefore, I shall rely principally upon my own observations, which were unfortunately quite numerous through the years 1867-72 in the southern part of the State of Alabama.

ETIOLOGY.

The disease is unquestionably malarious in its origin, since it never occurs except where this poison abounds, and rarely, if ever, except in those who have been the victims of frequent attacks of intermittent fever, or the subjects of malarial cachexia. I explain the fact of its sudden development into an epidemic or endemic disease in the Southern States, by the complete disorganization of our system of labor; in consequence of which, the low-lying plantations were left undrained by the neglect of ditches, and fences decayed, and were overgrown with vines, weeds, etc., thus giving rise to a more abundant, or more deadly, crop of malaria. It is quite probable, too, that moral or psychical causes had some influence. Worn out in waging the most gigantic war in modern history against vastly superior odds, greatly disappointed and depressed at its (to them) most unfortunate termination; deprived of their property and reduced from a state of opulence to abject poverty, their physical systems were doubtless ill-prepared to bear up against even ordinary morbific influences—to extraordinary ones they succumbed at once. This theory assumes greater probability in view of the fact that the negro race seems hardly ever to be the subjects of this fever; though the ordinary forms of malarial fever were more frequent among them than during their enslaved condition.

SYMPTOMS AND COURSE.

As a rule, the disease is developed during an attack of ordinary intermittent or remittent fever, and generally in those who have already suffered from repeated attacks. I have seen no exception to this; but a very few instances are recorded in which it developed during the first attack. Suddenly then, during such an attack, the patient has a chill more pronounced, or of longer duration than usual, and upon emptying the bladder, he or she is horrified to find that the urine is intensely red and partaking more or less of the character of pure blood. This bloody urine is sometimes passed in enormous quantities, the patient not unfrequently filling a large chamber full of it in one or two hours. At the same time the skin has begun to turn yellow, and this icterus deepens to a dark bronze color, which varies from day to day, and sometimes from hour to hour. This jaundice rarely assumes the bright lemon color which we witness in true icterus from resorption and evidently has a different pathogeny. Nausea and other evidences of gastric derangement, if not present during the chill, now come on, and continue during the entire course of the disease. Everything—even ice water—is vomited. The patient becomes restless and anxious, tossing from side to side, and the respiration is hurried and sighing. The fever is of unusual intensity—the thermometer running up to 105 to 110; but even in the continued form there are quite frequent slight variations almost from hour to hour. In the highest grade of this fever all the above symptoms continue; it may be with slight variations or remission, but never with any intermissions until the end, which is usually *death*.

But every case does not of course end in this way. Between the extreme case I have described and the mildest forms, there are many grades. Thus the fever, hematuria and nausea may be continued, remittent, or intermittent, and sometimes all these symptoms end in a single paroxysm, and the patient rapidly recovers. If the fever is intermittent, then the nausea and hematuria, and even the jaundice, may disappear during the intermission, to return again during the next paroxysm; and this feature has a most important bearing upon the prognosis, as death or recovery bears a distinct or unvarying relation to the continued or intermittent character of the fever and symptoms.

To speak more particularly of the clinical features: The bowels are generally constipated, and respond very slowly to cathartic medicines. The skin is usually dry, and even in the intermittent variety the paroxysm does not terminate with the profuse perspiration which characterizes ordinary intermittents. The vomited matters consist generally of thin mucus, more or less colored with some shade of green from admixture of bile. In the milder cases profuse bilious vomiting occurs; in the severe ones the fluids have the deep bluish-green color of sulphate of copper. This last I have almost come to consider as a fatal symptom. Notwithstanding the high temperature, the brain seems to be little affected. Delirium is rare, and the patients generally retain complete consciousness up to the last moment.

The jaundice which is so prominent and invariable a symptom, is evidently not due to resorption of bile; for, as just remarked, in some cases the profuse bilious vomiting proves that the biliary ducts are intact, and that the hepatic cells are in a state of super-activity. This jaundice then is hematogenous, and caused by a solution of the red blood corpuscles, whose coloring matter set free, stains all the tissues, and in some cases plugs up the capillaries. Whether this death and subsequent solution of the red corpuscles is due to the directly poisonous action of malaria, or is caused by the fact that these cells have been slowly diminishing during previous attacks of intermittent fever, and is analogous to that hematogenous jaundice which appears in extreme anemia from loss of blood, I am unable to say. Probably both of these causes combine to produce the result.

The hemorrhage from the kidneys, (I have never witnessed hemorrhage from any other source), is perplexing and more difficult to explain. Is this hemorrhage or apparent hemorrhage due to the corpuscular necrosis alluded to above, and are the kidneys merely discharging their excretory function in removing these dead corpuscles from the circulation; or does the enormous amount of pigment set free in the blood act as an irritant upon the kidneys, producing intense congestion of these organs with rupture of the Malpighian tufts, and hemorrhage into the tubuli uriniferi, just as cantharides or turpentine and other medicines do? The entire absence of any reliable microscopic investigation (so far as I am aware) into the condition of the kidneys renders the discussion of this question purely speculative.

Most of those who have written upon this subject seem to take it for granted that the hemorrhage is due entirely to congestion, and adduce the fact of the hemorrhage itself as conclusive proof of it. I confess that for a long time I was of the same opinion; but I had entirely overlooked the fact that beside the hematuria there is not the slightest evidence that the kidneys are in any way disordered. We know that as a rule a fluxional or obstructive congestion of the kidneys capable of producing extensive rupture of the capillaries is usually attended with very serious symptoms; among which *the most constant is suppression, more or less complete, of the urinary secretion*, with severe pain in the lower dorsal and lumbar regions, followed by dropsy and symptoms of uremic intoxication. Now, in the disease under consideration, while there is undoubtedly a large amount of blood, or at least of red blood corpuscles discharged, there is a still larger quantity of urine voided also; in fact, instead of suppression, there is a hypersecretion. Nor do the patients complain any more of pain in the back in this than they do in other forms of malarial fever; while the clearness of intellect which is maintained to the very last is in marked contrast to the convulsions and coma which characterize uremic poisoning. The intermittent character of the hemorrhage, too, and the sudden and complete changes which occur in the urine, render the theory of congestion highly improbable. It quite often happens that after passing large quantities of bloody urine at the last micturition, the very next will consist of an equally large quantity of normal urine, whose color does not cause a suspicion of the presence of a single drop of blood. Now, in ordinary congestive hematuria we know that the blood does not disappear suddenly, but gradually; and the urine generally shows traces of it for several days, and the amount of blood corpuscles present is in inverse ratio to the amount of urine. It seems to me, therefore, that it is improbable that the hemorrhage is due to congestion of the kidneys alone; but on the contrary, that it is principally if not exclusively due to those changes in the blood itself already alluded to.

It is true it may be asked, can red blood corpuscles pass through the walls of the capillaries of the Malpigian bodies without a previous rupture of those walls? I firmly believe that they can; and they always *will* do so *when deprived of vitality*, and with that vitality, of those electro-chemical properties which distinguish them as *living corpuscles*. Deprive the red globule of its vitality, and consequent affinity for, and power of absorbing oxygen, and it is reduced to the same condition as the white corpuscle and obeys the same laws; and one of these laws is, that when subjected to lateral pressure in the capillaries, they escape through the minute fenestra in the capillary walls.

I believe, therefore, that both the jaundice and hematuria are due to the same cause, and that is, that the red blood corpuscles, poisoned by the malarial influence or other causes not understood, are some of them dissolved, liberating their coloring matter, while the most of them escape undissolved through the capillary walls. This escape will always be more rapid in the kidneys than elsewhere, in consequence of the greater lateral pressure always existing here, on account of the absence of the usual disparity in size between the artery and accompanying veins. And, by the way, it is a singular fact that no anatomist, so far as I know, has pointed out this beautiful arrangement to secure the separation of water from the blood in the kidneys. Everywhere else an artery either has *two* venae comites of equal size with itself, or numerous other channels are provided for a free return of blood; while here there is only *one* vein, of equal or less size than the artery. By this arrangement a sufficient pressure is always preserved in the kidney to secure the filtering away of the blood serum through the Malpighian tufts, the serum of course carrying with it the urea and other salts it may hold in solution.

The intense catarrhal affection of the stomach, with its attendant nausea and vomiting, is a phenomenon generally witnessed in all the graver forms of malarial disease, and as Frerichs has pointed out, is doubtless caused by plugging of the hepatic capillaries by pigment granules, and in the disease under consideration, probably by the debris of the dead corpuscles also. I need not, therefore, enter into any extended discussion of this symptom, at least so far as its pathogeny is concerned, but content myself with the remark that it is one of the most important symptoms of the disease in a clinical point of view, because it baffles all our efforts to introduce either food or medicine by the natural channel. Indeed, in the severer cases, so intense is this catarrh of the stomach, and so complete is the destruction of the epithelium, that for many days after the fever, hematuria and jaundice have disappeared, the organ remains utterly incapable of digestion or absorption, and as inert as a leather bag; so that not a few of the cases die from inanition and the extreme anemia from loss of blood, long after danger from the other symptoms has ceased.

PROGNOSIS.

From what has preceded it will be readily understood that the most important prognostic sign is the type of the fever, that is, as to whether the latter is continued, remittent, or intermittent, the several forms being the more dangerous in the order named. The quantity of blood lost is important also, but this symptom as a rule will always depend upon the type of the fever; and the hemorrhage invariably follows the type of the latter as to its continuance, remission, or intermission. The intensity of the accompanying gastric disturbance is also important, for, as before remarked, the continuance of this symptom may endanger life, even after the malaria has been neutralized and the fever and hemorrhage arrested.

Upon the whole the prognosis is grave in all cases, since, while a few cases of the continued type recover, many of the intermittent type die; and the lowest percentage of mortality claimed by any *reliable observer* is from fifteen to twenty per cent., and this was based upon a very limited number of observations. My own experience would lead me to believe that the general mortality is much higher than this; while in some years and in some particular localities it has reached the enormous rate of seventy-five per cent.

TREATMENT.

Strange as it may appear, upon this subject the student meets with the utmost confusion and contradiction in the views and reports of those who have written upon the subject. While some insist upon the efficacy of large doses of quinia; others rely upon purgatives, others upon diaphoretics, and others still upon astringents and hemostatics. Some consider arrest of the hemorrhage the leading indication, others arrest of the paroxysms, and others the gastric disturbance. The truth probably is that none of these plans of treatment exclusively are of any value. Any one who has had the courage, or who has been compelled by circumstances to treat periodic fevers on the expectant plan alone, knows that the tendency in these, as in most other fevers, is towards recovery. The continued type of fever has a strong tendency to become remittent, the remittent to become intermittent, and the quotidian intermittent to be become tertian, the tertian a quartan, and finally to cease altogether. One thing is certain to my mind, and that is, that those who ignore or forget the condition of the stomach in this disease will always be puzzled by the uncertain and apparently contradictory results of their treatment. I have been much surprised to see that so able an observer as Dr. E. D. McDaniel, in the paper already alluded to, places the arrest of hemorrhage as the leading indication, and arrest of the paroxysms as only secondary, entirely ignoring the fact that the hemorrhage always follows the type of the fever, and is continued, remittent, or intermittent, exactly as the accompanying fever presents these characteristics. He and some others maintain that quinia (exhibited by the stomach) always increases the hemorrhage. It is quite probable that it does so, but only because that medicine, being a local irritant, intensifies the gastric catarrh, but never reaches the circulation, and consequently never exerts its anti-periodic or anti-pyretic effect when so administered. In my opinion, the leading and most important indication in all cases is to arrest the paroxysms; the second, to allay the gastric irritation; while the hemorrhage may be left to take care of itself; for if the pathological views I have heretofore expressed are true, the elimination of the dead red blood corpuscles from the circulation is not only salutary, but absolutely essential to the safety of the organism.

The first indication can only be met by quinia, since this is the only medicine we are acquainted with that can be absolutely relied on for this purpose. But we must exhibit the quinine in such a way that it will certainly and promptly enter the circulation. It is worse than useless to introduce it into the stomach; for that organ with its mucous membrane congested, inflamed, and denuded of its epithelium, has no more digestive or absorptive power than a gum-elastic bag, and the quinia will only intensify this condition. The rectum is not much better off; for in consequence of the plugging of the hepatic capillaries by pigment, the entire mesenteric system of veins is overloaded with blood, and they are rather inclined to part with the fluid they contain than to take up other fluids by absorption. On one occasion, before I had reached these conclusions, I gave from thirty to forty grains of quinia every day for an entire week without arresting the paroxysms of a hemorrhagic intermittent. They were at once promptly and permanently cured by the exhibition of eighteen grains hypodermatically. And this is the mode which should always be resorted to for the administration of the medicine. Twenty to thirty grains of quinia thus given arrest the fever with absolute certainty, and the hemorrhage ceases with the fever. Quinia can be thus administered with absolute safety, provided proper precautions are taken to insure a perfect solution of the drug, and the proper points are selected for the injection. I have given upwards of two hundred and fifty injections of quinine, and have seen cellulitis follow in only one instance, and that was a case of scarlet fever which was mistaken for a fever of malarious origin.

The second indication, viz: to relieve the gastric catarrh, is best met by the direct action upon the mucous membrane of calomel and bi-carb. of sodium, and ice slowly swallowed, and the indirect action of cathartics, which, by exciting free serous transudations from the intestinal mucous membrane, relieves, to some extent, at least, the engorgement of the portal system.

For the first purpose, half a grain or a grain of calomel and five grains of bi carb. of sodium may be given every half hour or hour. These doses, if retained, will soon purge, and thus fulfill the second indication also. If they do not, however, I have found nothing so effectual as from six to eight drops of croton oil in six or eight ounces of mucilage or thin gruel, given as an enema; to be repeated every two hours until the desired effect is produced. The paroxysms having been arrested by the quinia, and the portal congestion relieved by the means above indicated, the hematuria always ceases at once, and the patient may be left alone to enter upon a prompt convalescence, provided the loss of blood has not been so excessive as to paralyze the nervous system, and especially the trophic nerves, which regulate and control the gastric, hepatic, and pancreatic secretions. Fluid food in small quantities, and especially milk, should be tried at short intervals to ascertain whether the stomach has regained its digestive and absorptive power. As soon as this is ascertained, iron in some form and cod liver oil should be given for the purpose both of rapidly renewing the lost red corpuscles, and increasing the oxygenophorous powers of those remaining. Quinia should also be given just as soon as it can be safely exhibited, to prevent relapse.

If the stomach is slow in regaining its digestive power, and death becomes imminent from combined anemia and asthenia, nutritious and stimulant enemata of eggs, milk and brandy should be given at proper intervals; and if these are rejected or fail to give the proper support, then as a last resort transfusion should be resorted to, and repeated until the integrity of the digestive system is restored.

ARTICLE IV.

Michigan State Board of Health.

[Reported for the MEDICAL CHRONICLE.]

The annual meeting of the State Board of Health was held at its office in Lansing, April 8, 1884.

The members present were President Avery, Drs. Lyster, Hazelwood, Vaughan, Tyler, and Secretary Baker.

Reports of the sanitary condition of the Wayne County Poor House and Asylum; and of the Barry County Jail, were made by the Committees who examined these institutions; and these reports were ordered printed.

Dr. Vaughan read a paper prepared by Dr. C. P. Pengra, which gave results of investigations relative to the purification of water by freezing. As a result of a series of elaborate experiments conducted in the University laboratory, Dr. Pengra found that contrary to the general impression freezing does not render water pure. Ordinarily he found less infusoria and bacteria in ice than in the water from which it was frozen, but the ice contained them in numbers sufficient to preclude its use. In harvesting ice the greatest care should be taken to get it from a pure source. This valuable paper will be published in the report of the Board.

The Secretary presented a summary compiled from lists of medical practitioners, registered under the new law. The number of counties in the state is 80; from 76 of which reports have been received. The number of registrations returned is 3,285, but in some cases physicians are registered in two or more counties. The number reported to have graduated is 2,351; those who had attended some college but not graduated, 208; those who had attended no college, 726. The number, belonging to all schools, reported as having graduated is 72 per cent. of the whole number; the non-graduated collegiates are 6 per cent., and the non-collegiates are 22 per cent. of the whole number. The "graduates" are from all classes of medical colleges, hospitals, medical societies, etc. The number of different "schools" of medicine reported in these sworn statements is about 75, including "Cureopathic," "Indian," etc. In at least one instance, it is reported that the sworn statement had to be signed by a "mark," the practitioner being unable to write even his own name. The number registered as belonging to the four most prominent schools of medicine are as follows: Regular, 1,533; Homeopathic, 490; Allopathic,

398; Electic, 366. The proportion of graduates to practitioners is: Regular, 87 per cent.; Homeopathic, 74 per cent.; Allopathic, 82 per cent.; Eclectic, 48 per cent. (Of all schools, as above stated, the per cent. is 72.)

It was decided to print the names and addresses of the health officers in Michigan as soon as full returns are received. The number in the state is nearly 1,400. A new edition of the document on the prevention and restriction of scarlet fever was ordered, the last edition of 30,000 copies being nearly exhausted. It was also decided to publish facts relative to several outbreaks of trichiniasis in Michigan.

The following resolutions were unanimously adopted:

Resolved, That the Michigan State Board of Health respectfully and earnestly memorializes Congress to pass the bill, introduced into the House of Representatives, Jan. 8, 1884, by the Hon. Casey Young, or of some similar bill, providing for the prevention of the introduction of infectious diseases into the United States, and for procuring information relating to climatic and other conditions affecting the public health.

Resolved, That we consider the National Board of Health the best existing, and the proper agency to carry on the work mentioned in the preceding resolution

The Board discussed the merits of several text-books on physiology and hygiene with special reference to the effects of alcohol on the human system, and approved for use in the schools: Martin's "Human Body," briefer course, second edition, containing special chapter on alcohol and other narcotics; and Dr. Eli F. Brown's "Alcohol; Its effects on Body and Mind."

The amount of office work during the quarter has been large, and has included: The perfecting of arrangements for holding a Sanitary Convention at Hillsdale; preparation of the proceedings of the Ionia Sanitary Convention for the printer; the making of a compilation of the public-health laws of Michigan; proof-reading on 96 pages of the Annual Report; issuing blanks for the return of the new health officers in each city, village and township in Michigan; issuing the regular weekly bulletin of meteorology, and of sickness in Michigan; the correspondence of the office (postals are not usually copied), covering 750 pages of letter-copying book, of which over 150 pages have direct reference to the prevention and restriction of communicable diseases in Michigan; and the regular computations of data relating to meteorology and sickness.

CORRESPONDENCE.

STEUBENVILLE, Ohio, April 4th, 1884.

Editor "Medical Chronicle."

SIR:—As physician to Gould's Tunnel, Pan-Handle Railway, from July 1st, 1883 to April 1st, 1884, seventy-eight cases of scalp wounds came under my care, all caused by falling rock from the roof of the tunnel.

All the wounds were from one to eight inches in length, all penetrating to the skull. Of these cases, forty were in colored, and thirty-eight in white men. The average distance through which the rock fell was eighteen feet. The weight of each piece I endeavored to keep, but failed. All the wounds were sutured with silk, as they were clean cuts, the edge of the scaly rock causing the injury. The maximum temperature in any of these cases was 103° in one case. This one assumed alarming symptoms, which responded to the liberal administration of calomel.

In but one other case did the temperature reach 102°, and this for only a few hours. In seventy-six cases, in some of which the wounds were quite large and ugly, the temperature at no time rose above 100°.

All the injuries were dressed with pulv. acidum boracicum, freely sprinkled over wound, and padding it well and firmly with cotton, and letting it alone for five days before removing sutures, many of the men working full time. But one case did not heal by first intention, and he went on a drunk; this case finally healed by granulation.

Pneumonia existed among the men this winter to a considerable extent; four cases are worthy of mention: subjects, colored; first winter north, large and full habit; I felt in duty bound to follow Prof. Arnold's advice, "to bleed when in your judgment you see fit." Two of these I bled till they fainted; they recovered. The other two are in heaven, I trust.

I shall always feel that I did not do my whole duty, but there is one consoling thought: the sight of so much blood was "a holy terror" to the others and their friends, who threatened to mob me if I "spilt" more.

I feel quite sure that I had a lateral dislocation of the ankle, without any fracture of tibia or fibula, but as I'm not a Gross or Agnew, I dare not record it.

JNO. D. MULHANE.

ANALECTS.

Diabetes.

The good, hard and fast rules of the examination table are being found less and less infallible as the practitioner travels on his medical path in actual practice. When sugar was found in the urine of a patient wasting away, the hypothesis was erected that the presence of sugar in the urine was significant that the person would soon belong to the past. And it cannot be denied that the teaching of the schools is to the effect that glycosuria means diabetes, and diabetes is a malady which in no long time ends in death. Aretæus gives a clear description of the malady, and thought that the disease was a colliquation of the flesh and limbs into urine. It was not till the time of Willis that the presence of sugar in the urine was fully recognized. Later authorities have decided that diabetes is "a disease in which a saccharine state of the urine is the characteristic symptom." Diabetes, then; is not a wasting disease in which the body is gradually starved to death by the sugar escaping by the kidneys; but the presence of sugar in the urine tells of the oncome of a wasting disease. If the last is seriously meant, then very often glycosuria lies like Ananias and Sapphira.

The other day, meeting an eminent physician and falling into chat with him while inspecting Barnum's "Toung Taloung," the so-called "white" elephant, the conversation ran on the pitfalls of practice arising for some of our cherished theories. During this turn of talk, the question was put, "How do you determine in a case of glycosuria, whether the patient has diabetes or not?"

He looked at me with a steady, inquiring gaze, and slowly replied, "I look at him." Now, it struck me this was just about the best and most sensible remark upon the subject that could well be made. Diabetes is a disease which prints its mark on the organism in such a way that when its symptoms are detailed and the urine is examined and found to contain sugar, the conclusion is not far to seek.

At chest-hospitals, it is almost a rule to strip all the patients and examine the chest as a first preliminary, without premising one or two leading questions to the patient—in other words, assuming that because a patient comes to a chest-hospital, therefore there is present some mischief in the chest. So, when there are "Renal Hospitals," a day not so distant as to be over the horizon, it will probably become a rule to make an examination of the urine as the first step. And when this is done, how many patients will be found to have saccharine urine? A good many more than are actually diabetic. When some apex-consolidation is found, how do we decide upon whether it is old or new? We look at the patient and ask a few questions —at least that is my way of approaching the difficulty—after the stethoscope has had its word (which is often an inarticulate sound); and, depend upon it, in maladies affecting the whole system, as phthisis and diabetes undoubtedly do, it is a good and sound plan "to look at the patient."

The trained eye is our main guide as to the general condition of the patient and his health or ill health. When a corpulent, florid-complexioned man, well-fed and vigorous, passes sugar in his urine, only a tyro could conjecture that he was the victim of the classical diabetes—a formidable wasting disease. Between the matter of examining the sputum for bacilli in a case of lung-consolidation, to determine the precise histological condition of the neoplasm, and looking hard at a man who has perceptible quantities of sugar in his urine, lies a mighty tract of knowledge. But still it is only what a medical man must command if he has either to win the confidence of his patient or hold his own in the present battle for existence.

When a patient looks haggard or worn, complains of muscular lassitude, feels his work growing too much for him, and troubled with thirst (and sugar-thirst is indefinitely less quenchable than salt thirst) then the presence of sugar in the urine becomes of the highest significance ; and, though this perhaps will be regarded as rank heresy, relaxation from labor, a diminution of the tax upon the nervous system, is more important than the shallow line of avoiding everything that can be converted into grape-sugar. It may be well to give the liver physiological rest as to its glycogenic function, until it has come round; but that is not the whole of the pathology of diabetes ; while the proposal of a French professor to treat diabetes by feeding the patient on the flesh of carnivorous animals, was about the height of shallowness and folly.—*J. Milner Fothergill in Phila. Med. Times.*

Treatment of Hay Fever and Allied Disorders.

In a very valuable paper on this subject in the *American Journal of the Medical Sciences* for January, 1884, Dr. Harrison Allen claims that the means of effecting the cure of this hitherto considered incurable disease is simply to overcome the tendency to obstruction in the nasal chambers.

The symptoms of hay fever are always associated with some degree of obstruction of one or both nasal chambers. A cause of this obstruction is dilatation of the bloodvessels. There is no doubt that the local phenomena are in most instances the same, and that the multiform related symptoms, such as injection of the eye, headache, malaise, asthma, etc., are due to reflex vasomotor disturbances. But many patients report for treatment who exhibit swelling in the nasal mucous membrane, occlusion of the respiratory passages, and mucoid or semi-purulent discharge, without any of the related reflex phenomena. Yet a third and intermediate group exhibit perhaps a tendency to turgescence of the mucous membrane, together with one or more of the more common constitutional symptoms of typical hay-fever. Indeed, there is nothing peculiar to the disease just named save its sharply defined periodicity, particularly in that phase of it where the periods of recurrence happen to coincide with the time of fruitage of certain plants, or the gathering of certain crops. In a small group of cases, where, in addition, other signs and symptoms become prominent which would invalidate the above proposition, Dr. Allen is inclined to attribute them to mental impression—in some of the varied phases of hysterical or neurotic excitement.

Or, the case may be stated in different language, as follows: In an imperfectly defined group of cases of nasal catarrh, a sensation of sudden obstruction of one or both nasal chambers is a conspicuous symptom. This sensation is accompanied by a constant change in the chambers themselves, viz: engorgement of the membranes over the turbinated bones, producing pressure against the septum and occlusion of the respiratory passages of the nose. The sensations are recurrent, but vary greatly as to the time of the day or the season of their return. With some patients they are nocturnal, and are associated with the recumbent position; with others they occur after meals only; with some they occur in the summer season; with others yet again, in the winter. The sensations may be confined to either chamber or be present in both. In aggravated cases they are associated with numerous reflex symptoms, among which may be mentioned lachrymation and hyperesthesia of the conjunctiva, headache and asthma. Patients having a disposition to obstruction during the summer and autumn report themselves as suffering from "hay-fever;" while those having alternating attacks in the right and left chambers report with "nasal catarrh."

The cases so far studied exhibit one feature in common, viz: that the inferior turbinated bones lie well above the plane of the floor of the nasal vestibule. In many persons, not the subjects of "hay-fever" and allied disorders, the lower free portion, including, of course, the inferior border of the bone, lies below the plane of the floor of the nasal vestibule; and in ordinary inspection the inferior meatus is out of sight.

It will thus be seen that the mucous membrane, which is known to be the most erectile, is also the most exposed to irritation from extraneous substances, and to changes in the temperature of the surrounding air.

The conclusions to be drawn from the study of the six cases reported by Dr. Allen, may be summarized briefly as follows:

(1). That the treatment of all conditions of obstruction in the nasal chambers, no matter from what cause arising, can be successfully carried out by destroying the causes of obstruction. If the cause be an overgrowth of bone-tissue, it must be filed, sawed or drilled away. If it be caused by a deviated cartilaginous portion of the septum, such portion must be re-set in a new place. If, as is often the case, it is due to periodic turgescence of the mucous membrane or the resulting secondary hypertrophies, such growths must be destroyed, either by the galvano-cautery, by the snare, or by caustic acids.

(2). That the treatment of hay-fever and allied periodically recurring nasal affections in no way differs from the treatment of other nasal diseases accompanied by obstruction, and that the treatment may be conducted during an attack as well as in the intervals between any two attacks.—*Esculapian.*

Neuralgia of the Second Branch of the Trigeminus.

Dr. F. Lange presented a patient, about forty years of age, a tailor, who suffered from neuralgia of the second branch of the trigeminus, on the right side, which had resisted for a long time the usual external and internal remedies and applications, until finally the patient submitted to an operation, which was performed in March, 1882, after the method of Lueke, modified by Braun and Lossen, consisting in an osteoplastic resection of the zygomatic arch and bone, finding the nerve in the depth of the spheno-maxillary fossa, at its exit from the skull, and besides, a separation of the nerve at its exit from the infra-orbital foramen, and extracting the anterior piece from the base of the skull at this point. He was also able to destroy the spheno-palatine ganglion, and so far the result has been permanent. Anesthesia followed the operation immediately, and was complete also on the corresponding side of the palate. The patient at present had a certain kind of formication, which he described as like the crawling of worms, but had no real pain. The operation was performed by making a horizontal incision along the upper edge of the zygomatic arch extending to the external angle of the orbit, and then a perpendicular one downward over the base of the zygoma, and with a fine saw separating the zygoma, from its attachment to the superior maxilla, directing the saw so that the blade was more parallel to the sagittal plane, in order to prevent subsequent disfigurement from depression of the separated bone. Then by bone scissors the arch was cut across half an inch in front of the meatus auditorius externus. This triangular flap of skin and bone was pulled downward, and then the spheno-maxillary fossa laid open, the temporal muscle drawn backward, and the nerve found, after some adipose tissue had been pulled aside or removed. In the patient presented, the operation had not offered any peculiar difficulty, but Dr. Lange presumed that it was probably on account of his lack of fat, and could readily conceive that sometimes in stout, fleshy persons the operation might be very tedious. He was able to see the internal maxillary artery, but there had been no disagreeable interruption on account of hemorrhage. The wound healed entirely by the first intention, and as an accident the rubber drainage tube was healed in. After a time the tube was cut out. The result, so far as disfigurement went, was rather gratifying, and also with respect to the recurrence of the disease. Dr. Lange did not think that any other operation afforded the possibility of excising the nerve to so great an extent and with so little danger and disfigurement as the one described. For some time the patient had slight difficulty in opening his mouth in consequence of inflammatory contraction of the temporal muscle; but at present he had no difficulty which prevented him from taking his food, though the movements of the jaw were not normal yet. The little wound by which the nerve was exposed at its exit from the infra-orbital canal had hardly left a visible scar.—*New York Med. Jour.*

Diagnosis of Disease of the Stomach.

Prof. Leube (*Deut. Archiv. f. klin. Med.*, p. I, vol. xxxiii), recommends as a diagnostic measure, that a soft india-rubber tube should be passed into the stomach and its contents examined at various periods of digestion. A meal consisting of soup, a large beef-steak, and a piece of white bread, is completely digested by a healthy stomach in seven hours, so that if it was washed out at the end of this time the fluid comes back clear, or mixed only with a few flakes of mucus. Leube recommends that this should be done at the commencement of the treatment in every case of gastric disease, with the exception of those where the disease is likely to terminate of itself in a few days, or where there is a tendency to bleeding, as in gastric ulcer or pernicious anemia. He regulates the treatment by the result he obtains. If the fluid returns clear it is evident that the stomach digests in the normal time, and if dyspeptic symptoms are present it is probably gastralgia, or nervous dyspepsia, perhaps even ulcerated. In order to ascertain the power of the stomach to secrete gastric juice he washes it out with warm water until the water returns neutral, then pours in fifty centimetres of thirty per cent. soda solution, and leaves it twelve minutes in the stomach. He then introduces 500 centimetres of lukewarm water, and tests the fluid which returns. If the stomach is normal the gastric juice should neutralize the soda, and if the fluid return strongly alkaline the secretion of gastric juice is deficient. The healthy stomach is also stimulated by thermal irritation, and Prof. Leube uses this method by injecting 100 centimetres of ice-water into the empty stomach, and washing it out with 300 centimetres more water after ten minutes. Generally, though not always, the water thus obtained from a healthy stomach contains both acid and pepsine. In chronic dyspepsia the water remains neutral, and has no digestive action. In cases of purely nervous dyspepsia the result is the same as in healthy stomachs. A very remarkable result was observed in a case of uremia, in which, notwithstanding great disturbance of digestion, the functions of the stomach were readily and perfectly performed, and not only was the meal completely digested in the normal time, but the secretion of gastric juice was exceedingly rapid. It is therefore probable that the gastric disorder in uremic conditions is due chiefly to nervous disturbance. In cases of severe dyspepsia not of a nervous nature the digestion of a meal is almost always delayed, and the fluid removed after the injection of soda or ice-water is almost without exception free from acid and pepsine. The author directs attention to a peculiar form of dyspepsia due to malaria, and which is cured quickly and permanently by quinine. In one case the disease was treated for months with all kinds of diet and mineral waters in vain, until a tertian type became evident in the dyspepsia, and quinine quickly cured it. In another case, a patient who had suffered from ague had loss of appetite and sickness in the morning. In the evening it was better, and the patient could take the most indigestible food without difficulty. Seven and a-half grain doses of quinine cured all these symptoms in four or five days.—*The Practitioner—Lancet and Clinic.*

Subscribe to the MEDICAL CHRONICLE.

A Method of Rendering the Skin Insensible.

M. Jules Guerin read a note at the Academie des Sciences on a method of rendering the skin insensible in those operations which do not admit of chloroform by inhalation, and cited a case in which he had employed it to advantage. A lady, aged sixty, consulted him three months ago for a tumor in the right breast, of eight years' standing, which on examination proved to be a scirrhus. The general health was bad, bronchial and cardiac troubles were manifest, and the kidneys were not in a very satisfactory condition. However, the operation was urgent. Chloroform having been considered dangerous, M. Guerin applied around the tumor a circular layer of Vienna paste, limited by a double band of diachylon. At the end of twenty minutes the caustic was removed, leaving in its trace a black ribbon-like line. The knife was then applied, and the tumor removed without the patient feeling the slightest pain, and she did not seem to be aware of the operation. The results were all that could be desired.—*Med. Press and Circular.*

Perspiration in Albuminuria.

Dr. Jansen finds that nephritic patients constantly lose large quantities of watery vapor from the skin, but no regularity can be observed in the quantity. Edematous parts of the body lose more water than non-edematous parts. Less water is lost by perspiration in acute nephritis, and possibly also, in nephritis with contracted kidney. The proportion differs in different individuals suffering from nephritis with enlarged kidneys; they sometimes lose more, and sometimes less, than healthy patients. No regularity could be found in the excretion of carbonic acid by the skin in nephritic patients.—*Esculapian.*

PROF. WILLARD PARKER, the prominent surgeon of New York, is dead.

The Medical Chronicle.

A Monthly Journal for the Practitioner.

GEORGE H. ROHÉ, M. D., Editor.

☞ It is requested that all literary and business communications, books for review, exchanges, etc., be addressed to, and all checks, drafts and post office orders drawn to the order of
Dr. GEORGE H. ROHÉ,
Cor. Greene & Mulberry Sts., - Balto., Md.

BALTIMORE, MAY, 1884.

EDITORIAL.

The Meeting of the Medical and Chirurgical Faculty of Maryland.

The eighty-sixth annual convention of the Medical and Chirurgical Faculty of Maryland was held in Hopkins Hall, Johns Hopkins University, on April 22 to 25 inclusive. Under the direction of the courteous president, Prof. Richard McSherry, the business of the Convention was despatched with commendable promptness. For the first time within the recollection of the writer, the Faculty adjourned on time, with all its work completed.

The president in his annual address made a number of most valuable suggestions and recommendations. A portion of the address, referring to the relations of the profession to certain sanitary needs of the community, was referred to a special committee, consisting of Drs. George H. Rohé, John Morris and James A. Steuart, which will bring certain of the matters discussed by the president, specifically before the Faculty for its action, at the next annual meeting.

The annual oration was delivered by Prof. William Pepper, Provost of the University of Pennsylvania, who gave an interesting discourse on some Practical Views on Dietetics in Disease. Prof. Pepper's address was replete with wholesome advice, and was well received.

The reports of the various sections were excellent summaries of recent progress, and, in a number of instances, contained evidence of good original work.

The number of volunteer papers presented was larger than usual. A good feature of most of the work done, was its markedly practical character. It is no small praise, and yet is entirely deserved, to say that the current volume of the transactions will represent better work as a whole, than any previous volume issued by the Faculty.

The Library Committee reported a continued increase in the value of the library, both intrinsically and in the greater advantages furnished to the members of the Faculty by its large and constantly increasing collection of books and current medical periodicals. The care with which the library has been fostered during the last eight years, has unquestionably contributed much toward developing the literary tendency which is so decidedly manifest among the younger generation of Baltimore physicians.

The work of the convention was fitly closed by the election of Dr. Thomas S. Latimer as President, Drs. John R. Quinan and I. E. Atkinson as Vice-Presidents, Drs. G. Lane Taneyhill, Robert T. Wilson, T. Barton Brune and Richard H. Thomas as Secretaries, and Dr. W. F. A. Kemp as Treasurer.

The American Medical Association.

The approaching meeting of the American Medical Association in Washington, will doubtless be attended by many of the members of the profession from this city. As nearly all of those attending from this city will go and return daily, it becomes worth while to secure a reduction of fare from the railroads. We take great pleasure in informing our readers that the railroads running between this city and Washington, will sell round-trip tickets to delegates and permanent members of the association, on presentation of their credentials, for $1.65.

CURRENT LITERATURE.

Report of the State Board of Health of West Virginia, for the years ending December 31st, 1881, 1882 and 1883.

The report of Dr. James E. Reeves, the energetic secretary of the West Virginia State Board of Health, makes a neat and well-printed volume of 308 pages. The contents are: the text of the law establishing the board, the minutes of the meetings of the board, explanations of the manner in which the law regulating the practice of medicine is enforced, lists of practitioners qualified to practise in the state, various papers relating to local boards of health, and a number of special articles, all valuable as exponents of the most recent sanitary knowledge. The titles of the various papers are as follows: Small-pox in Mercer and Wyoming Counties, by Hon. Isaiah Bee, M. D.; Epidemic and Contagious Diseases, by G. McDonald, M. D.; Nailer's Consumption, etc., by J. L. Dickey, M. D.; How to Nurse the Sick, by Geo. B. Moffett, M. D.; The Relations of the Soil to Health, by George H. Rohé, M. D.; Prevention of Malarial Diseases, by Chas. Smart, M. D.; Our Eyes and Our Industries, by B. Joy Jeffries, M. D.; Ventilation, by Justin M. Hull, M. D.; Treatment of the Drowned, by Hon. A. R. Barbee, M. D.; Prevention of Hereditary Constitutional Diseases, by B. W. Richardson, M. D.; Excessive Use of Tobacco, by James Evans, M. D.; Legislation on Insanity, by Geo. L. Harrison, L. L. D.; The Eminent Domain of Sanitary Science, by James E. Reeves, M. D.; The Texas Cattle Fever, by D. E. Salmon, D. V. M.; Foot and Mouth Disease, by L. D. Wilson, M. D.; Foot-rot in Sheep, by C. B. Robinson, V. S.; Pink Eye and Horse Scarlet Fever, by John C. Peters, M. D., and Treatment of Horse Scarlet Fever, by C. B. Robinson, V. S.

An *itemized* financial statement closes the report, from which it appears that the total expenses of the board for the three years, including the salary of the secretary, were $3,241.51. From this is to be deducted $1,745.00, received for fees and special taxes collected from itinerant physicians, thus reducing the total cost to the state to exactly $498.83¾ per year. Evidently Dr. Reeves is a business man, as well as a good sanitarian.

The contrast between the amount and quality of the work done by the West Virginia Board, and that of the Maryland Board, especially when the cost to the state is considered, is very unfavorable to the latter. As the Maryland Board still owes the public a financial exhibit for the last two years, we defer further comment at present.

Diseases of Children. A hand-book for practitioners and students. By Armand Semple, B. A., M. B., Cantab; M. R. C. P., London. Physician Northeastern Hospital for Children; Physician to the Royal Society of Musicians; author of "The Voice Musically and Medically Considered," "Aids to Medicine," etc. G. P. Putnam's Sons, New York, 1884.

As a condensed manual, the above work is unusually clear, concise and complete. The author's object seems to have been the practical application of medical knowledge to diagnosis, prophylaxis, and therapeutical indications. There is little space consumed with obsolete opinions and doctrines. Discussions relating to mooted pathological questions are avoided.

As regards scope, the book is peculiarly complete, embracing all diseases and their facies, as met with in children, and a scrupulous care has been exercised in descriptions of the characteristic conditions of ill health and distinctive features of infantile ailments. It fairly represents the existing state of the science of medicine with respect to the subjects treated of, and will no doubt be found to reflect the views of those who exemplify, in their practice, the present stage of the progress of medical art. The book is well printed on clean, white paper, and neatly bound.   G. T.

Shakespeare as a Physician. Comprising every word which in any way relates to medicine, surgery, or obstetrics, found in the complete works of that writer, with criticisms and comparisons of the same, with the medical thoughts of to-day. By J. Portman Chesney, M. D., Ex-Secretary Medical Society of the State of Missouri, etc. St. Louis, J. H. Chambers & Co., 1884.

The author of this work thinks that "the conception of presenting Shakespeare's medical knowledge in a complete and connected form" is original with himself. However this may be—and our knowledge of Shakespeare bibliography is not sufficiently full to question the accuracy of the statement—so much of the book as is compiled from the writings of the immortal bard is full of interest, as everything from that source must be.

The medical allusions in Shakespeare are many, and indicate a profound knowledge, both popular and scientific of the subject, current in his day. The pedantic comments of the author of this volume, however, often appear to be added merely for the sake of "padding." But in spite of this, the book is one which the physician will find it of advantage to own and to study in connexion with a good edition of the poet's works.

Conversations between Drs. Warren and Putnam on the Subject of Medical Ethics. With an account of the medical empiricisms of Europe and America. By Frank Hastings Hamilton, M. D. New York and London, Bermingham & Co., 1884.

The "conversations" between the mythical Dr. Warren and Dr. Putnam attracted considerable attention when they appeared in the columns of the now defunct *Medical Gazette.* To most of the profession outside of the state of New York, they present little interest, however, as in no other state is there a contest on the code question. The present form in which these dialogues are printed will serve a useful purpose by keeping them together; and Dr. Hamilton's happy style makes a very hackneyed subject interesting.

PAMPHLETS.

Second Annual Report of the Baltimore Eye, Ear and Throat Charity Hospital.——Fifth Annual Report of the Board of Health of Memphis.———Sixth Annual Report of the Presbyterian Eye, Ear and Throat Charity Hospital.——Case of Impetigo Herpetiformis; Recovery. From the *Medical News.*——Two Cases of Paget's Disease of the Nipple. From the *American Journal Med. Sciences.* ——A Case of Sarcomatous "Inflammatory Fungoid Neoplasm." From the *Medical News.*——On the Value of a Lotion of Sulphide of Zinc in the Treatment of Superficial Lupus Erythematosus. From the *Medical News.*——A Case of Ainhum. From the *American Journal Med. Sciences.* ——The above five reprints are from the pen of Dr. Louis A. Duhring, the distinguished Professor of Dermatology in the University of Pa. The last two have been given, in abstract, in the supplement to the November number of the CHRONICLE. ——A New Operation for the Reduction of Chronic Inversion of the Uterus. By B. Bernard Browne, M. D. From the *N. Y. Med. Journal.* ——Dental Jurisprudence. By Richard Grady, D. D. S. From the

American Journal of Dental Science, January, 1884, pp. 21.——Health Counsels for Working People; School and Health Circular, No. 2. Published by the State Board of Health of New Jersey.——Aneurism of the Femoral Artery. A Knife-wound of the Intestines. By W. O. Roberts, M. D. From the *American Pract'r.* National Board of Health.——Remarks and Arguments before the Committee on Public Health of the House of Representatives, by Members of the National Board of Health in refutation of charges made against the Board, by the Supervising Surgeon-General of the Marine Hospital Service.——Three pamphlets, Washington, Gibson Bros., 1884.——Iodoform in Dental Surgery. By C. F. W. Bodecker, D. D. S., M. D. S. Reprinted from the *Independent Practioner.*——The U. S. Marine Hospital Service and Quarantine. Reprinted from the *Sanitarian.*

FLOTSAM.

THE U. S. Ship Portsmouth arrived at Newport, R. I., with yellow fever on board.

SALICYLATE of sodium is said to cause menorrhagia. There is negative evidence that it will not produce abortion.

DR. C. C. HERSMAN, (class of '84, C. P. S.) has been appointed assistant Physician to the West Virginia Insane Asylum, at Weston, W. Va.

DR. WILLIAM H WELCH, of New York, has been elected professor of pathology in the Johns Hopkins University.

IN the *N. Y. Med. Jour.* for March 15th, Dr. F. Lange describes a new method of treating large bone cavities in the lower end of the femur in adults. The paper will well repay perusal.

IN the *Medical News* for April 26, Dr. Thomas M. Markoe reports two cases of sarcoma of the synovial sheaths, the first on record.

THE annual meeting of the West Virginia State Medical Society will be held at Clarksburg, May 21. A large attendance and an interesting meeting are anticipated.

THE latest development of abdominal surgery is the removal of uterus, tubes and ovaries for dysmenorrhœa. Dr. R. S. Sutton, of Pittsburg, advocates, and has done the operation. As our German friends would say: this is like using 24 pounders to kill sparrows.

AN ovariotomy was done on a girl aged fifteen years, by Prof. A. J. Stone, of St. Paul, on March 15. The entire tumor weighed over $81\frac{1}{2}$ pounds. What remained of the patient after removal of the tumor was estimated at between 50 and 60 pounds. Four weeks after the operation the patient was out of bed and moving about.

THE State Board of Health of Louisiana has been re-organized. The governor has appointed Dr. Joseph Holt president of the board. Among the other new appointments are Col. W. M. Smallwood and Drs. L. F. Salomon and T. R. Oliphant. The medical gentlemen named are active and progressive, while Col. Smallwood is one of the best informed business men of the crescent city.

THE editor of the CHRONICLE hopes to see many of his friends at the meeting of the West Virginia State Medical Society, at Clarksburg, on May 21. He will be accompanied by Dr. J. W. Chambers, who is not unknown to many of the West Virginia doctors. Dr. Chambers and the editor have been appointed delegates to this society from the Medical and Chirurgical Faculty of Maryland, and expect to read papers at the meeting.

The Medical Chronicle.

BALTIMORE, JUNE, 1884.

ORIGINAL ARTICLES.

ARTICLE I.
INDIGESTION IN YOUNG CHILDREN.

By J. HARVEY HILL, M. D., BALTIMORE.

It is not my purpose to enter elaborately into the treatment of this subject and to fill out all the details of description, but to catch up the salient points as we pass along, hoping thereby to elicit from others, an expression of opinion and experience which will lend interest to the discussion.

The function of digestion during the period of infancy—at least of the early part of it—differs so greatly from that of adult life, when the organs have attained their full development, that the treatment of the diseases of that time calls for special consideration. The absence of teeth and the functions of salivation and mastication, the undeveloped sacculated form of the stomach of later life, the peculiar susceptibility of the nervous system to external and internal influences, the special food arranged by nature for the infantile period exhibited in all forms of higher animal life, the frequency of the ingestion of food, the perishable and changeable character of suitable food—and those changes to such conditions as are absolutely hurtful—the growing prevalance of artificial nourishment, and the ignorance of those who attend upon the wants of young children artificially fed; for in nursing children, the ordinary mother's wit and the instincts of the child are quite sufficient to secure its physical welfare but when the course of nature is departed from a much higher intelligence and judgment is required for the proper management of the child. All these considerations, and many more which might be offered, go to establish the importance of a careful study of the conditions belonging to infant digestion and its disorders, important, not only for the immediate welfare of the patient, but even more so for its future.

By a continued existence of these disorders, cachectic conditions are established, deformed and crippled states brought about, and evils set into being, which may be handed down to posterity. Many an infantile dyspepsia is a childhood anemia, and an adult phthisis or necrosis, mental weakness, early senility, or for aught we know, bad morals.

Certainly no class of disorders come so frequently under our care, as those of the alimentary function; and scarcely any disease amongst children can be intelligently treated without taking into account the question of digestion, and this more especially in young children artificially nourished. With children at the breast of a healthy mother, I always feel relieved of a considerable portion of the responsibility of the treatment. Alimentation is apt to be the best possible. I shall not offer statistics to show the frequency of digestive disorders, but appeal alone to the experience of each one here to-night to prove that indigestions immediate and remote stand preeminent in the list of affections we have to treat of children. Therefore in no branch of our professional work ought we to have our opinions more clearly defined, our judgments more evenly balanced, and our methods of instruction to our clients more concise and unmistakable. General direction on the presumption of an intelligent comprehension of what is needed will too often fail and too frequently show us how little intelligence sensible people have in the matter of children's food.

It is scarcely possible for us to discuss the subject of indigestion without entering more or less upon the consideration of nutrition. In the treatment of all the diseases belonging to this class, the very first element to regard is *diet;* and I trust you will not think me digressing when my remarks tend toward that portion of the subject.

Of the general causes leading to the development of disease in digestion, there stands first, artificial nutriment, "bottle raising." There is a growing tendency amongst women to excuse themselves of the cares of nursing and avail them of the more convenient bottle. Again the inability to furnish milk is becoming more frequent; I find it no uncommon thing for mothers to lose their milk in the second or third month, or earlier, and possibly sometimes the willingness thereto, is the parent of the loss. Poor milk, partially changed, therefore unpalatable, not to mention its hurtful qualities, leading children to dislike and refuse it, the too early resort to the ordinary diet of adults or in the more careful the starch foods only. This is a frequent error, and I think, too readily sanctioned by physicians. When consulted upon this point, I invariably reply "milk is the staple for the first year," exclusive of everything else for the first half, unless especially directed because the baby is sick, and for the second half, only a little starch food under special directions.

The numerous advertised artificial foods and their claims to partial or complete use in indigestion, are calculated to lead us away from this principle. They are thrust upon us by the different enterprising firms who prepare them, and if we believe the small half that is said of them, we will abandon our old fogy ways of believing in milk, and go to Mr. A's package of food, worth fifty cents a pound, to cure all the ills of the infantile stomach. Commercial interests do not add to the statements they make of their preparations, the full measure of reliability.

In the references to these foods and their excellences by my patients and others, I am often reminded of the results of treatment by a certain article when it is the one of a number entering into the prescription used, and to this one particular favorite article all the benefits received are ascribed. One mother tells me to recommend Mellin's food to all my patients, for it made her baby the robust, thrifty child that it is, when she mixed a teaspoonful to a pint of the best milk which could be obtained. Another ascribes all praise to Imperial Granum, and shows me the beautiful lithograph of five babies it has fed into being, when she, too, uses one part of the food to one hundred of fresh milk, and so on through the list.

Another important factor of these troubles is the inherent susceptibility of childhood to external impressions. Children recuperate more quickly, likewise respond more readily to disease-producing influences. Cachectic conditions likewise lend susceptibility to indigestions, scrofula, syphilis, anemia, etc. City life with its confinement in superheated rooms without the privileges of open-air recreation, partially fermented or stale food, which is largely inseparable from dwelling at a distance from the place of production.

Inherited Peculiarities.—Our American life is largely a dyspeptic one, and the children reap their portion. Dyspeptic parents as well impress these weaknesses, as their physical resemblance, upon their children. Insufficient clothing—and clothing too warmly—often are causative, together with unwatchfulness or over-anxiety of attendants; again the disposition to overfeed. In these days we will perhaps partake too much of the mania to feed—to feed up those whom we are called to treat. It is often the very source of the trouble we would escape. Many a dyspeptic child is simply an overfed child. I remember a child who came under my care, puny, sick, vomiting, whom the over zealous mother had been filling up with a pint of rich cream every day. A timely interference alone saved its life. Ill conditions of the nurse, growing out of dyspepsia, cachexia, pregnancy or menstruation, sometimes violent emotions, etc., these points should all engage our attention in seeking the causes of the nursing child's dyspepsia. These are some of the general causes. I shall now refer to some of the special conditions:

Infantile Colic.—Everybody knows what a colicky baby is. This trouble often manifests itself with the first food—sometimes before food has been taken at all. There could hardly be an indigestion before food has been taken, and yet flatulency may exist from the retained contents of the bowels. I can but think an important cause of this early trouble and frequently extending onward for several weeks, is the use of the abdominal bandage; and for its use, I am not able to find one substantial reason. What indication in nature is there to bind up the abdomen of a babe with a flannel bandage? Surely not to keep it warm, for that is better done by loose fitting garments. Not to support the walls; for the child is or ought to be finished in utero. Not to prevent protrusion of the contents at the umbilicus; else why not adjust inguinal trusses also for hernia will sometimes occur there. Not to enable us to care better for the cord; for that is better wrapped in a little absorbent cotton, and allowed to hang loosely upon the abdomen. What then does the bandage do for the infant? This, if well and carefully applied, it does *no harm;* but as the abdomen is a changing portion of the body, now flat and soft, now hard and full by food, crying or gas, the bandage may be comfortably loose one half hour, and the next be so loose as to slip about, or so tight as to give absolute distress. Nurses do not always have good judgment, and in their anxiety to do a thing well, draw the bandage so tightly as to compress the abdomen, interfere with peristalsis of the bowels, and thus confine the gases and give cause to colic.

If undigested food passes or the natural contents of the bowels are retained, fermentation will develope gases which give rise to pain. A very slight pressure upon the abdomen of a young child may suffice to make a virtual obstruction, and imprison gases, which, without, would pass easily away or never be developed. The abominal bandage of the child is worse than the abdominal bandage of the mother. I cannot account for the general prevalence of colic in nursed babies more reasonably. In my experience, it is the exceptional child who escapes flatulency.

It is certainly not in the nature of things that this first digestion must be painful. I have never yet counseled the leaving off the bandage in any but such children as were prematurely born, and it is a fact, that these, when nursed, have been singularly free from colic. After careful search, I am compelled to believe there is not one good reason why I should continue the use of what may do so much harm, and on the contrary, find many good reasons why I should abandon it. I am aware that some authorities have advised the discontinuance of this old time practice, but the general and continued sanction of the profession is my justification for referring to the matter at some length; I trust you will pardon the digression.

While colic is only a symptom of indigestion, yet in many cases of very young children it is so prominent that I have chosen to deal with it rather as a condition of disease—for if the flatulency is relieved by being brought up or passed downward, there will be no other evidence of disease. Meddlesome nurses are frequently responsible for the misery of their patients, aside from the malpractice of the bandage, by dosing and feeding between the birth and the milk flow. Nothing but the most positive orders will prevent this stuffing usually.

The food of the mother is often responsible, but this we are accustomed to look for, and nurses themselves are quick to recognize the effects of acid fruits, etc., but there are cases where the utmost care and healthfulness of maternal diet is maintained, but by reason of her confined habits and reduced strength, a condition of acidity of her digestion may exist; not enough to attract her attention, and yet sufficient to give her milk irritant properties. In several instances my attention has been directed to this cause by the child being taken with flatulency in the early part of the night and extending on for a longer or shorter time, until complete relief is gained, resting quietly during the day, only to begin the same trouble with the next night; thus proving to my mind that it was the milk elaborated from the more liberal dinner meal which was the source of irritation, the meal most apt to be attended by evidences of indigestion with us all. Such cases I have seen greatly benefitted by copious draughts of lime water, or other suitable treatment of the mother's stomach. In one case I particularly remember to have seen relief as if by magic, the very first night after lime water had been taken by the mother after dinner, and this was emphasized by several attempts of the mother to discontinue the lime water, to whom it was very distasteful, by the immediate return of the violent colic in the otherwise perfectly healthy baby.

The so-called troubles of teething are, as a rule, some form of dyspepsia, due entirely to other causes. A physiological process should not be saddled with ailments found frequently, and during several months of child life. Why should all the reflexes imaginable be ascribed to the teeth? General convulsions, strabismus, diarrhœa, cough, laryngismus, stridulus, skin eruptions, *et id omne genus*. I do not deny that there may be a pathological condition due to the eruption of the teeth, but too much stress is put upon this function as a factor of disease. The period is a time of indulgence by parents, of undeveloped judgment of the child as to appetite and gratification of diet, change and weaning, and enteric susceptibility; and it would be more correct to say the *time* of dentition is one of disease liability, but to dentition itself, there attaches very little that is pathological. I cannot bring myself to think that a reflex cough or other trouble is due to a tooth yet deeply imbedded in the gum, and causes not the slightest evidence of local inflammation or pain. Upon very few occasions have I found it necessary or desirable to cut the gums.

I venture the opinion that a careful search into the nature of the food and digestion of the teething child and its nurse, will generally reveal sufficient reason for its ailment, without resorting to so natural a process to account for it.

Teething in animal life is never heard of as a source of disease. The books generally give considerable space to the troubles of teething, but I still maintain that when so many other more direct causes for disorder constantly exist in the digestive machinery, it is hardly needful to look to so occult a process, unless the signs of disease are manifested by inflamed gums. Where strumous, syphilitic, or other cachectic conditions exist, let them rather be held responsible than the teeth. So long as we mislead ourselves with the idea that the teeth may be responsible for every disorder we cannot readily account for otherwise, we are doing truth a great violence. So long as mortality reports differ so widely as to the ill results of dentition from almost nothing up to a very large proportion of deaths under 2 years, we can be assured there is some lack of observation somewhere. I repeat, if careful search of alimentation is made, the cause will most frequently be found.

A condition of dyspepsia manifested by apthæ or the parasitic thrush fungus, occurs frequently in early childhood—oftener in artificially fed children; at first a functional disorder, but at length perhaps ending in a gastrio-enteritis. I desire to mention this as a digestive disorder rather than a local disease of the mouth, and an appreciation of this fact will often lend aid to the effectual treatment.

Vomiting may be the first evidence of irritability of the stomach, followed by weakening and failure of growth One needs to distinguish between vomiting and simple eructation or regurgitation. In the former state there will be evidence of gastric irritation by the mucus thrown off, or by the dejections. Food, however, may be retained and the stomach show little evidence of disorder, yet there will be violent colic pains, green watery or mucous diarrhœa, containing lumps of caseine or jelly—a true dyspeptic diarrhœa.

Inquiry into the food or the manner of feeding will generally reveal the cause, but not always, for in some cases there seems to be an inherent want of tone in the digestion in the child, even the nursed child. Food taken into the stomach undigested, passes on to ferment, and irritate the bowels into catarrhal state. There is then acidity or extreme offensiveness of the stools and breath, or gases passed by rectum. Emaciation will now progress rapidly, unless a check is given to the disease. In such conditions, apthous patches are apt to appear, and the disease will often be pronounced a case of thrush, when it is a true dyspepsia. Constipation is likewise at times an expression of indigestion, the caseine being separated and accumulated into masses, acts by a mechanical obstruction, exciting flatulency and pain. This condition may be due to excessive acidity of the stomach, insufficiency of the digestive ferments or excess of caseous matter in the food administered, or simple overfeeding. Children frequently ingest too much milk, more likely so with the bottle than when naturally fed.

Eruptions of the skin, usually eczematous, are frequently the outcome of intestinal irritation, and require as a first consideration to be treated as dyspeptic ailments.

Marasmus, or atrophy, is often but a symptom of faulty assimilation of fatty food, or that together with the albuminous. The energy of the vital process during the early years, is such when wasting begin, there must be some gross outrage being done the economy. Until organic disease of the liver or mesenteric glands or other organ is clearly manifested, it is well for us to search carefully for functional failure of the digestive organs.

In a case recently under my care a nursing child of two months, the mother being a prime specimen of woman, and having nursed other children well, and exhibiting no evidences of failure, either in quality or quantity of milk supply, the child was emaciated to the last degree, and rapidly weakening by a diarrhœa of mucous and green curdy passages, abdominal pain and loss of rest; but being unable to check the diarrhœa or relieve the pain, I was almost ready to grope out into the darkness by changing food, when I determined to try pepsin persistently alone. This gave in a short time perfect relief, the child gained flesh rapidly, and is now fat and well. This success in treatment proved to my mind a clean case of functional dyspepsia. The father is a confirmed dyspeptic. Had the case occurred a few months later, I doubt not "*dentition*" would have fallen heir to the diagnosis.

Tendencies toward indigestion are transmitted, and some children suffer because they belong to a dyspeptic race. I have known idiosyncrasies of taste and appetite to be manifested before intelligence could possibly discern.

Cholera infantum is often a genuine acute dyspepsia at first, and if it could be recognized and treated as such sufficiently early, could be arrested. A child during a period of great heat, will for days manifest great restlessness at night, turning over in bed, sweating profusely, have intense thirst, offensive stools, perhaps constipation, offensive breath, and yet when awake, appears well, except perhaps a little unusual fretfulness of temper. The stomach is doing its work badly; the great thirst causes milk food to be taken in extra quantities; the intestines are overloaded with solid residue, and that condition of gastro-intestinal irritation is brought about which will culminate in a genuine cholera attack, no doubt an effort of nature to relieve the oppressed bowels of irritant contents and to deplete the congested mucus surfaces.

If in this early and really dyspeptic state the patient could be seen and the trouble brewing fully apprehended, no doubt a wise treatment would be successful. The entire withdrawal of food, and the free use of water and ice for such time as seemed necessary, would probably abort many an overwhelming attack of cholera infantum.

The intense thirst in this dyspeptic stage is something familiar to us all, and I cannot too strongly urge its gratification with *water and ice*. Menstruation and pregnancy of the nurse may be a cause of dyspepsia in the child; seldom the former. Intense emotions in the nurse may also have similar functional disturbances in the child as a result. In the treatment of this class of disorders, the subject of dietetics takes so prominent a place, that I find it impossible to avoid entirely the field of a former paper I had the honor to read before this body.

The tendency of our times in and out of the profession in all disorders is toward overfeeding. We concern ourselves too soon lest our patients weaken. Certainly to an overworked stomach the first indication is rest, as nearly absolute rest as possible. In the large proportion of children's troubles, we find this condition of overtaxation to exist. We are not apt to make a mistake when we attempt to restrain the anxiety of mothers to feed and stuff their sick children. Fortunately for us and the patient, nature interposes a repugnance to food, which is not easily overcome in the modern baby, except it be when thirst demands liquid, and fluid food only is allowed, and the child is thus forced to drink it.

That a nursed child is infinitely better off than a bottled one is hardly necessary to mention here, except it were for the frequent opposition that experience receives amongst the laity. That milk—generally cow's milk—is the one most suitable and available food for the first year where nature's supply is denied, seems also superfluous to mention, yet these facts need to be reiterated again and again in the successful management of children. That during the latter part of the first year and the second, only soft or easily softened starch preparations may enter the dietary; and albuminous articles at the latter part of the second year, are also well-known, but they are fundamental truths in infant dietetics.

To get good milk is not so difficult as formerly, as bottled milk is now brought to the market, and if honestly prepared at the dairy where produced, is likely to have undergone the least change possible, and yet it has little advantage over that of a first-class dairy. The "one-cow idea" is not important, except to be condemned when the cow is kept near the city, and most likely in an ill ventilated stable and fed upon slops. With good milk, sufficient dilution is important. Too often, food is too concentrated, and oftener when condensed milk is used.

It is far easier for the child to dispose of too much water than too much caseine. The almost nuvarying acidity of city milk requires us constantly to guard this point, and I am in the habit of recommending the regular use of lime water as an antacid and dilutent, and in liberal quantity. It has an attenuating influence upon the coagulum of the caseine. There is no question but this feature to divide and soften the caseine of coagulum of cow's milk is well attained by the use of some starch food, always to be cooked, and better, one of the reliable prepared foods, my choice from experience being Mellin's.

Another most excellent method when the caseine passes off in lumps undigested, is to coagulate the milk by use of rennet, and strain off the coagulum, after which a little cream may be added. This form of food the most delicate stomach will often digest, and is applicable to the adult as well. All milk should be boiled, unless the source is well known to be from a cow, sufficiently far away from the calving to be free from the irritant colostrum in the milk.

To peptonize milk, makes a most desirable preparation for the weakened stomach. Messrs. Fairchild Brothers & Foster deserve commendation for placing in the hands of the profession their peptonizing powders, a most easy method, with full directions for their use, consisting of 5 grs. of their ext. of pancreas, and 10 grs. bi. carb. soda, in separate papers. I have found this process to be a great aid to digestion in sick children. We do well at times to fall back upon these easily digestible foods, when children older may have passed to the use of meats, and food to be masticated.

The use of glucose syrup or sugars for adding the needed sweetness to children's food is far better than the use of cane sugars; one remove further from the condition to be absorbed, or better still, to use a reliable malt extract, of which I think none is better than Trommer's. This, especially if the entire wheat flour is used, or any of the unchanged starch foods.

The medicinal treatment proper of children's dyspepsias must, of necessity, occupy a secondary place in the large proportion of cases to dietetic management. He who depends upon drugs much, will lose his patients.

The classes of remedies chiefly in demand are: digestives, laxatives, emollients or soothing agents, antacids, anti-ferments or antiseptics. Of the agents which I enumerate as digestives, pepsin stands prominent. The question has often been put to me by myself and others as to the really positive good from the use of pepsin. Too frequently I have had to evade the point by saying I had used it upon general principles, and I hoped and believed that no evil had come from it. More recently I have been confining myself to the use of the pure pepsin, usually Beale's or Fairchild Brothers & Foster's scale pepsin, and I can testify to the positively good results obtained. In the case of a child before alluded to, I gave Fairchild Brothers & Foster's scale pepsin in ¾ grain doses after each nursing or just before, if the child might be expected to sleep, and I had the satisfaction to see a decided and continuous improvement from the first use, noticeable in the less pain, and better digested appearance of the stools at once.

A genuine pancreatic extract no doubt has a useful place if administered, but more so, I think, if it is allowed to have its effect upon the food before administration. Extract of malt is highly useful when starch foods are administered. It is usually well taken too, and that is something. Of laxatives, the one prominent and least objectionable in a large proportion of cases is calomel, in minute doses. Others there are which I frequently use, but I cannot refrain from this passing tribute to our old time tried friend. Of the soothing or quieting agents, I mostly rely upon ext. hyocyamus, sub. nitrate of bismuth in liberal doses. Of the antacids, the chief are lime water, bi-carb. soda, prepared chalk, and magnesia.

In certain conditions attended by diarrhœa and putrefactive changes in the intestinal tract, I have found decided benefit from another class of remedies, antiseptic in their character, given for this effect alone.

Dr. Alex. Hutchins, of Brooklyn, first called my attention to them, acknowledging the Guy's Hospital reports as the source of the suggestion to him. I refer to the salicylates of sodium and calcium. He used them extemporaneously, prepared by adding the acid to sodium bi-carbonate or to prepared chalk for serous diarrhœas. I have found them highly beneficial for adult dyspepsia with sulphurous fermentation.

ARTICLE II.
INFANT MORTALITY.

BY WM. N. HILL, M. D., Baltimore.
Read before the Med. and Surg. Society of Baltimore.

A constant agitation of a known evil is the only possible way to its final eradication. People are accustomed to lying supinely on their backs and taking everything as a dispensation of Providence, when the real state of the case would show the cause to be their own selfishness.

The crying shame of civilization is infant mortality, and this "massacre of the innocents" which annually takes place over the entire civilized world can be directly attributed in the vast majority of instances to man's inhumanity to man. To a city physician this is specially striking. He is called on the eve of a hot summer day to see an infant. If he is honest and not a self deceiver, he goes with fear and trepidation in his heart as to the final result of the case. He knows that in all probability the system of the patient has been exhausted by the intense heat, the physiological tissue change going on in a normal body has been interrupted, the blood is surcharged with effete particles owing to non-oxygenation, organic lesions of the brain, lungs, or bowels, are liable to supervene at any moment, his efforts to relieve prove futile, death ends the scene, and another victim is taken from the "surplus population." Religion tells us another soul has gone to eternity; and science, that the small quantity of force centered in a child's body has been returned to the infinite quantity scattered throughout the universe.

So constantly does this result follow, that the physician satisfies his conscience by refuge to the prevailing system of philosophy that the death he has just witnessed is a physical necessity, and, according to a supposed law of nature, requiring a certain percentage of humanity to die annually to make room in the world for the rest. This inhuman doctrine has permeated the whole system of society; its effect, on those who would mitigate this great evil, being to paralyze their efforts to a great extent. The public is not fully aroused to the necessity of any action, and everybody who attempts to give a few lungfuls of air (supposed to be the one necessity of existence not yet taken from human beings by the greed of their fellows) to a dying infant, is looked upon with suspicion by many, who, if they were sufficiently educated in the matter, would be devoted adherents to any plan of relief.

Many municipalities have prepared lungs for their towns, but their usefulness has been impaired by various causes; long distances from points of dense population; the consequent inability of the poor to reach them, and last but not least, the custom of beautifying (falsely so called) the landscape by laying out roads and walks. The roads are used by those rich enough to possess teams, and the hard, gravelly walks are given to the poor.

Disraeli refers pointedly to this matter, when he says, "gravel walks were not found in the garden of Eden." The most conspicuous legend always to be found on entering a park is, "keep off the grass," and an appeal on behalf of the little ones should be made to public sentiment against this misappropriation of the public domain for the benefit of a class, and the children should be allowed to roam where they list, without the fear of a mangled corpse on the one hand, or the park police on the other. The most laughable object in a park is a concrete pavement. The beauties of this pavement for pedestrian exercise can only be appreciated after a ten-mile walk over the same. The sensations felt by a mother who has carried a nursing child around one of these breathing spots for several hours have to be experienced to be appreciated, and the milk secreted for the nourishment of the child, is it not reasonable to suppose that it has been affected by the pain from her well corned feet? Walking over grass or a path made by the feet of pedestrians without gravel, concrete, or other improved pavement is so much easier that the fact cannot well be called in question.

The magnitude of infant mortality needs constantly to be borne in mind. In Massachusetts, where possibly, the chance of life is fairly up to the average, during the 15 years ending 1870, there were 514,233 children born, and 71,536, or 13.91 per cent. of these died in 1st year, and 131,784, or 25.52 per cent. before they had reached their 5th year, The percentage falls in the newer states where the lands and air have not yet been monopolized by private individuals to such an extent as in Massachusetts, and it rises to a higher rate in the countries of the old world, where our present social system has reached its highest development. There is no doubt that many infants are born without sufficient vital force to keep the machinery of life going, and the cause lies in the inability of the mother to procure a sufficient quantity of light, air, and the proper kind of food. Adulteration of the food of mother or infant, arising from the greed of manufacturers, is a refined cruelty, perpetrated on innocents, that would revolt the heart of a savage, if he were capable of understanding its consequences—but this subject is too vast to be more than referred to in a paper of this kind.

Three illegitimate children die to one legitimate. Our local health authorities are regulated by a law which prohibits the collection of statistics of births and deaths of illegitimates. This is the proper thing to do in a State that offers a premium of $4.50 per capita to each prostitute, by charging a licence of that amount on lawful wedlock. An illegitimate has not entered the world in the regular manner, has no business here, and does the best thing for himself and society by getting out of it as soon as possible. His existence is a nuisance to all concerned, and an epitaph for him and many of his legitimate brothers might read:

"Now that I am so soon done for,
I wonder what I was begun for."

Children need fresh air for respiration, but should be protected from the cold. The mortality increases in Russia where these conditions are not obtained, and decrease in Sweden where they are. The comparison between Russia and Sweden is remarkable. In Russia where a human being is only a unit, the per cent. is 53, and in Sweden where he has much more right to call himself a man, the figure is 39, that is of those under 5 years. The insane notion of hardening a child by exposure to cold without sufficient clothing can only be defended on the Spartan principle of killing the weak for the benefit of the State.

The influence of locality on mortality rate is shown in Scotland to be, islands 15, mainland 18, cities 30. There is no doubt the islands would show a lower figure if it was not for the extortion that is practiced on many of the inhabitants, resulting in their having but insufficient food and clothing. Society cannot capture the Atlantic's breeze, nor capture all its waters. The progress of humanity has diminished the mortality in the last three centuries. This gratifying fact should make us hope for still greater benefits to be derived from the close study of the subject now going on.

The old fogy notion, that a child should be seen and not heard, is fast dying out. The wants and wishes of children are much more studied than they formerly were, but the death wail of millions who have gone to join the silent majority, calls on each of us to remove such preventable causes of death as yet remain.

Much has been written of the joys of paternity and maternity, but neither parent is very joyful when awakened at midnight by the cry of their child in agony; their first resource in many instances is some patent nostrum containing a large quantity of opium. They find it apparently successful, and use it again and again. The ultimate evils of this plan of treatment are too well known to discuss.

A child's best chance of life lies in its mother's or nurse's intelligence, and it is our duty, as practitioners, to constantly lecture our patients on the rules governing the hygiene of maternity. Our influence is paramount, and, in most cases, our audience receives our words with attention, mothers generally being more alive to the interests of their children than to their own.

Now let us consider for a moment what diseases are preventable; in its ultimate analysis the question may be answered that there is no disease that is not preventable except old age, which is the natural ending of human life, and not properly speaking, a disease at all. By a proper study of the science of stirpiculture by physicians, much good might be done to humanity, and infant mortality among other things diminished. It is an astonishing fact that we should exercise so much care in the breeding of our horses, pigs and cattle, and that the vast majority of human beings should beget children without any thought of what kind they are going to get. The race is susceptible of great improvement in this regard, and physicians with their influence may accomplish much good. Sentimental nonsense should not be allowed to interfere with a consummation so devoutly to be wished for. The death of a child after birth is so obviously dependent in most instances, on preventable causes, that it is not necessary to refer to them in this body.

ARTICLE III.

A TRIP TO WEST VIRGINIA.

At the last meeting of the Medical and Chirurgical Faculty of Maryland, Dr. J. W. Chambers and the writer were appointed delegates to the Medical Society of the State of West Virginia, whose annual session was to be held in Clarksburg on May 21 and 22. Accordingly on the day before the former date, we packed our gripsacks and started on our journey across the mountains, reaching Clarksburg, a pleasant little city, at 8 o'clock on the following morning. Comfortable quarters were secured to us at the Walker House, through the intercession of Dr. D. Porter Morgan, the chairman of the local committee of arrangements.

The meeting of the society was called to order in the City Hall at 3:30 P. M. of the 21st, and the members and delegates cordially welcomed in brief speeches by Dr. Morgan and the Mayor of the city, Gen. Northcott. A number of new members, among whom we noticed several old C. P. & S. students were elected.

After hearing reports from the committee on publication, treasurer and secretary, the report of the committee on climatology and epidemics, Dr. R.

W. Hall, chairman, was read by the secretary. The report stated that diseases of the respiratory organs were most frequent throughout the state; that diphtheria prevailed to a considerable extent, advices having been received of its prevalence in at least two-thirds of the state. The reports indicated, however, that the disease was less malignant than formerly. Attention was called to the fact that some physicians reported many cases of diphtheria with a remarkably low death-rate, while others in the same section reported but a few cases with a high rate of mortality. The committee explain the difference by the custom of some physicians calling many cases of simple pharyngitis, or follicular tonsillitis, diphtheria. They also comment upon the tendency of physicians to ignore the teachings of clinical observation, and to place too much dependence upon the conclusions of microscopical experts.

Malarial, scarlet, typhoid and typho-malarial fever did not prevail to any very great extent in any part of the state.

The report being presented for discussion, Dr. Reeves stated that diphtheria was unquestionably a specific disease, transmissible by contagion; that the uncertainty of the diagnosis, which was made so evident by the conflicting reports of physicians practicing in the same localities, made it important to bear the fact of its contagiousness in mind, in order that proper measures should be taken to limit its spread. Referring to another portion of the report, Dr. Reeves said that he believed that typhoid fever was also frequently communicated by contagion. For several years past he has treated typhoid after a new method which has given him more satisfactory results than the antipyretic plan formerly pursued. He now rarely gives quinine to his typhoid fever patients, unless the tongue is broad, moist and indented upon its sides by the teeth. When, however, the tongue is dry, red and pointed, he regards quinine as little less than a veritable poison to the patient's nervous system. In the latter condition he uses ergot. He gives half a drachm of fluid extract of ergot with an equal quantity of tincture of cinnamon, every three hours. Has continued this for 2–3 weeks with the best results. When the temperature is high, he reduces it by applying cold to the wrists. He has used this method for a number of years with entire satisfaction. Cloths kept constantly wet with ice water are applied to the wrists, and rapidly bring down the temperature. Recently he has varied the method slightly. He uses a coil of rubber tubing, which is placed around the patient's wrists, and a current of cold water passed constantly through the coil from the reservoir of a fountain syringe. The end of the coil is prolonged and conducts the water into a pail or other receptacle under the bed. The ergot appears to reduce the liability to intestinal hemorrhage, and also seems to have some effect in keeping down the temperature.

Dr. Sharp referred to the fact that mild cases of what are sometimes called follicular tonsillitis are occasionally followed by paralysis and other sequelæ of diphtheria, and that cases of severe and undoubted diphtheria follow contagion from such equivocal cases. His own experience has frequently furnished him with illustrative cases. He has never seen cases to convince him of the contagiousness of typhoid fever.

Dr. Carpenter related the history of an outbreak of diphtheria in his own family. Not a single one out of eleven escaped. The first person in the house attacked, was a nurse. No one in his family had been exposed to the diphtheritic contagion, and he attributed the outbreak to the effluvia from a damp cellar in which considerable vegetable decomposition was going on. An interesting fact was that the prophylactic use of quinia, tincture of chloride of iron, and chlorate of potassium seemed to reduce the severity of the attack, although not preventing it in any of the cases.

Referring to typhoid fever, Dr. Carpenter said he did not consider the disease contagious, but spread by the use of polluted water,

Dr. Schriver thinks typhoid fever is not contagious. Has seen second attacks in same individual. Gives nitro-muriatic acid in the dry tongue condition of typhoid fever.

Dr. Miller believes diphtheria is contagious. Uses salicylic acid internally. Locally, he applies Monsel's solution, which dissolves the membrane almost immediately.

Dr. Chambers, of Baltimore, said that diphtheria is doubtless often caused by defective drainage and other insanitary conditions; that it is often acquired in schools, either by contagion, or in consequence of the bad hygienic conditions to which the children are often exposed there, although at their own homes the sanitary surroundings may be perfect. He believes that typhoid fever is contagious, although less so than many others of the class of infectious diseases. The disease should be treated on general principles; the patient, not the disease should be treated. His experience had led him to the conclusion that quinine is very pernicious in its effects in many cases of typhoid. The temperature can be better controlled by cold water. Is glad to learn the convenient method of application mentioned by Dr. Reeves.

Dr. Hoff, a delegate from the Ohio State Medical Society, startled the members by declaring his unbelief in the contagiousness of diphtheria. He had seen multitudes of cases in which contagion could be positively excluded. He has, furthermore, never seen any evidence in favor of its contagion. He usually gives patients with diphtheria an emetic, and uses ice, creosote, and inhalations of slaked lime locally. Internally, gives tincture of iron and whiskey. In typhoid fever, he believes that mercury should never be given. He has always lost his patients with this disease if mercury was administered. He has great faith in the power of alcohol in typhoid fever, however. Allows the patient whiskey *ad libitum*.

Dr. Rohé, of Baltimore, cited the cases of Frick, Foulis, and other surgeons, who contracted diphtheria from patients upon whom they performed tracheotomy for laryngeal diphtheria, as incontestable evidence of the contagiousness of the disease. There were differences in individual susceptibility, as well as variations of susceptibility in the same individual at different times. The same conditions had been frequently observed in other infectious diseases. He related his own case among others to show this. Does not believe that sewer gas or bad sanitary environment is ever causative of diphtheria, but is convinced that individuals living under bad hygienic conditions are much more susceptible to the contagious principle of this disease, than when their hygienic surroundings are good. He has seen severe cases of diphtheria following exposure to mild and simple cases of follicular tonsillitis, and has likewise seen laryngeal paralysis following what appeared to be very mild cases of the disease. In this respect, his experience agreed with that of Dr. Sharp. Inasmuch as the diagnosis cannot always be made with certainty, he thinks the patient and those brought in contact with him should be given the benefit of the doubt, and in suspected cases, the most appropriate treatment for diphtheria should be given. He also called attention to the constitutional symptoms, which are not accounted for by the local inflammatory condition alone.

As regards the treatment of diphtheria, he would urge the necessity of great watchfulness on the part of the physician over the nurse, or person charged with the administration of medicine, in order that this may not be neglected. He had frequently seen patients get worse under treatment, and after close questioning had found that the patient was receiving much less medicine than had been directed. After correcting the negligence of the nurse, the patient would almost invariably improve. He always gives a solution of quinine and tincture of iron, in syrup, repeating the dose at hourly intervals. When the case is severe, or obstinate, gives in addition solution of benzoate of sodium. This treatment he had learned from Prof. Erich, of Baltimore, who had been unusually successful in the treatment of this disease. He believes local treatment by swabbing with carbolic acid and other medicines, or inhalations of vapor of water, either simple, or medicated, to be of very little advantage. In diphtheria of the larynx, he urged tracheotomy as a life-saving measure if the membrane threatened suffocation. His colleague, Dr. Chambers, had saved over 25 per cent. of his cases of tracheotomy for diphtheritic laryngitis.

Regarding the etiology of typhoid fever, Dr. Rohé thinks not sufficient attention has been given to the evidence in favor of Pettenkofer's ground water theory, as set forth in a paper by Dr. Rohé in the recently published report of the West Virginia State Board of Health. He believes a careful study of the problem from this point of view will yield valuable results.

The committee on New Remedies reported through its chairman, Dr. R. McC. Baird. The recent literature upon convallaria majalis, jequirity, kairin, and paraldelyde, was referred to and the judgment of the reporter upon these remedies given.

Dr. Fleming Howell reported a very interesting case of esophagotomy for the removal of a silver fifty-cent piece. The coin lodged in the esophagus just below the cricoid cartilage. Various methods were tried but without success. Esophagotomy was done by Dr. Howell assisted by Dr. Morgan, and the coin easily removed. The incision in the esophagus was closed with fine silk sutures, the latter cut short and the external wound closed. The case recovered without a bad symptom, and the wound healed by the nineteenth day. Dr. Howell then gave statistics of the operation from various sources. Gross (Surgery, 6th edition) reported 39 cases, of which 33 recovered and 6 died. The case now reported added one to the list of recoveries. In concluding his well-written paper Dr. Howell stated his belief to be that the immediate operation of esophagotomy was indicated by the following conditions:

First. When a foreign body becomes lodged in the cervical portion of esophagus and has resisted a fair and careful effort for its extraction.

Second. When a foreign body has become lodged in the esophagus at any point within a finger's length below the upper end of the sternum and it has resisted a careful and thorough effort for its extraction.

Third. When a foreign body has become lodged in the esophagus at a point beyond a finger's length, below the end of the sternum, and its character is known or can be pretty definitely ascertained to be such that it would not be likely safely to pass outward or become loosened by ulceration and pass downward into the stomach, and it has resisted the most thorough and careful efforts for its dislodgment.

Dr. Rohé, fraternal delegate from the Medical and Chirurgical Faculty of Maryland, read a paper on the Treatment of the Later Syphilitic Lesions of the Skin and Subcutaneous Tissue, of which the following is a brief abstract:

The writer expressed the opinion that the view of Hutchinson, that the so-called tertiary manifestations of syphilis are merely sequelæ and not symptoms of the syphilis. could not be accepted without more definite evidence in its favor than had yet been furnished. The tubercular syphiloderm and the subcutaneous gumma are regarded as anatomically identical. The author of the paper said the prognosis of syphilis is generally favorable. He regards it as curable and deprecates the hopeless prognosis given by so many authorities. In the treatment of tertiary syphilitic lesions, potassium iodide holds the first place. It should be given in free doses,—twenty grains 4 to 6 times daily are sometimes necessary to produce the effect desired. Mercury is of much less value in this than in the secondary period, but should not be entirely omitted. Tonics are of importance in all stages of the disease, to counteract the spoliative effect of the disease upon the red corpuscles. Good food, fresh air, cleanliness and moderate exercise should be insisted upon. Cod-liver oil and iron, in the form of tincture of the chloride, or of pills of the proto carbonate, made by W. R. Warner & Co., under the name *Pil. chalybeate*, are often indicated. Locally, the application of mercurial plaster to the lesion, before ulceration, assists in promoting rapid absorption. After ulceration the syphilitic infiltration should be scraped out with a curette, and iodoform applied.

Dr. Sharp read an elaborate paper on Listerism in Obstetrics—shall we adopt it? He reviewed the recent theories of the nature of puerperal fever, and gave the practice of leading German, French, English and American authorities during the puerperal period. He carefully considered the evidence in favor of Listerism in obstetrics and concluded that cleanliness and common sense are the best preventatives of septic infection during the puerperal period. He laid down the following propositions:

"Proper care during labor, proper rest and diet after. We may draw the following conclusions: The attendant should see that his hands and instruments be kept scrupulously clean, for which purpose plenty of soap and water and nail brush are sufficient, except when he has been handling objects from which it would be expected that infection should arise; then the use of germicides becomes necessary.

"That the first stage of labor should not be interfered with by the too early rupture of the membranes—before the os uteri be fully dilatable; the second stage of labor not unduly protracted, but shortened by the judicious use of the forceps; the third stage properly managed by securing complete contraction by massage and ergot; thus having the genital canal free from all material liable to decomposition, and then rest from harrowing after-pains by the use of morphia. During the lying-in, there should be complete rest, so as to secure perfect uterine involution and the healing of the slighter lacerations and contusions which may have occurred. Natural drainage of the vagina and uterus can be secured by letting the patient use a chamber either on the bed or on the floor, when necessary, as advocated by Dr. Goodell.

"In cases where more extensive lacerations of the cervix or perineum occur, proper operative procedures should be taken. The nurses and attendants should be taught the necessity of rest of mind and body, proper diet and the necessity of pure air and perfect cleanliness of the patient, her bed, clothing and suroundings."

Dr. Chambers, fraternal delegate from the Medical and Chirurgical Faculty of Maryland, then delivered a lecture illustrated by diagrams, and specimens, on Cerebral Localization.

The lecturer first gave an outline of the recent discoveries in the physiology of the brain. He rapidly sketched the results of the researches of Hitzig and Fritsch, Ferrier, Vulpian, Goltz, and others, illustrating his remarks by reference to a number of diagrams and to a specimen of the normal brain of a monkey. After calling attention to the accuracy with which the centres of motion in the cortical substance of the brain of the lower animals had been localized by the experimenters mentioned, he referred to the clinical and pathological observations of Charcot, Ferrier, Benedikt, and others, who in great measure corroborated the results of experiment on the lower animals by cases of lesions of the brain in the human subject.

He related cases of his own, and exhibited the specimens in which an accurate diagnosis of the seat of the lesion had been made before death. In conclusion, Dr. Chambers stated his belief that the time was fast approaching, when the nature and locality of lesions of the brain could be as accurately diagnosticated, as are now the pathological alterations in the lungs and heart.

Dr. Chambers was tendered a vote of thanks at the conclusion of his interesting discourse.

On motion of Dr. Fleming Howell a resolution was adopted directing the appointment of a committee to memorialize the legislature at its next session to provide proper compensation to physicians when summoned into court to give expert evidence.

Dr. Geo. Baird, of Wheeling, was elected president, and Dr. S. L. Jepson, of Wheeling, was re-elected secretary for the ensuing year. The next meeting will be held at Weston.

The attendance of members, the papers read, and the discussions thereon, were exceedingly creditable to the profession of the State, and show that the physicians of West Virginia are fully alive to the progress being made in the art and science of medicine.

On the evening of the 21st, a musical entertainment was given to the society by the pupils and teachers of Broaddus Female College, under direction of Rev. E. J. Willis, the principal of the institution. The concert was largely attended, and the various performers were liberally applauded.

After the meeting adjourned, we paid a visit to the West Virginia Insane Asylum, located at Weston, 25 miles distant from Clarksburg. We reached Weston on the cars of an accommodating narrow-gauge railroad, which runs through a very rich and picturesque farming and stock-raising country. By the courtesy of Dr. A. H. Kunst, president of the road, we were invited to ride on the engine. As the temperature outside was about 85°, and that in the engine cab seemed to be about 150°, we enjoyed it for a little while, but we desire to be excused in future. We shall prefer the smoking car hereafter.

On reaching Weston we were warmly greeted by Dr. W. J. Bland, the superintendent of the Asylum, and his medical staff, Drs. T. G. Edmiston, J. L. Lewis and C. C. Hersman, these latter being all graduates of C. P. & S. The following day we were conducted through the building by Mr. Clifton, a member of the board of trustees, and Dr. Bland's assistants. We found the institution excellently managed throughout. Although improvements in the sewerage and ventilation could be suggested, the general condition of the building in these respects is much above that ordinarily found in institutions of this character. At the time of our visit there were 676 patients in the hospital. These represented all classes of mental disease.

The writer and his colleague will long remember the generous hospitality of their old and new West Virginia friends, and look forward with pleasant anticipations to equally pleasant meetings in times to come. R.

A CASE of death from chloroform is reported by Dr. Luther Sexton in the *New Orleans Medical and Surgical Journal* for May. The patient was about to undergo an operation for necrosis of the tibia. The autopsy showed interstitial nephritis.

CORRESPONDENCE.

Editor of the "Medical Chronicle."
DEAR SIR:
  Will you kindly grant me the use of your correspondence column to request from any physician, who may have observed squamous, or other pathological conditions of the skin, following the internal administration of borax (whether for epilepsy or not), very brief notes of the cases for publication?
  Treatises upon the diseases of the skin do not appear to recognize such conditions; which have yet been observed in England by Gowers, and also by other writers upon mental and nervous diseases, as well as in Boston in this country.
  Very respectfully,
  EDWARD WIGGLESWORTH, M. D.
79 Boylston St., Boston, Mass.

ANALECTS.

Sore Throat in Children.

Henry Ashby, M. D., M. R. C. P., (*Practitioner*, *London*, Dec.,) mentions four principal varieties:
  1. Simple tonsillitis. 2. Scarlatinal tonsillitis. 3. Pseudo-diphtheritic. 4. Diphtheria.
  Weakly and scrofulous children are especially subject to the first. It is oftener seen as a complication of alimentary disorders, as those of liver and stomach, than of the respiratory tract, as bronchitis and laryngitis. It frequently precedes rheumatic attacks. It may be the result of the scarlatinal poison. In proof of this he cites an interesting series of eight cases occurring in a hospital ward within a few days. Several nurses also took the disease. The first patient attacked, it was found, had been exposed to the genuine scarlatina a few days before. None of the cases had an eruption. One, a patient in previously bad condition, died. No insanitary conditions prevailed.

  In view of the difficulty—at times the impossibility—of diagnosticating scarlet fever from simple tonsillitis, the writer recommends the isolation of all children with febrile sore throat as long as faucial congestion remains. The points in favor of scarlatina are: The presence of vomiting and diarrhœa in the stage of invasion; a pulse of 130-160; not necessarily a high temperature; marked injection of the uvular pillars of the fauces and tonsils. Later, the enlargement of the cervical lymphatics, with tenderness; the implication of the nasal mucous membrane, and a yellow exudation over the tonsils and uvula make the diagnosis of scarlatina tolerably certain.
  Under pseudo-diphtheria the writer includes a class of cases which are said to bear the same relation to diphtheria that epidemic tonsillitis bears to scarlatina. It prevails where diphtheria does, is attributed to sewer gas and other poison. They differ from it in that the cervical glands are rarely involved, the membrane is less tough, the nasal mucous membrane unaffected, the urine does not contain albumen, the usual sequelæ of diphtheria are absent. The prognosis is always good. The duration is rarely over a week.
  The sore throat of diphtheria is differentiated from anginose scarlatina, by the fact that in the latter we rarely have true membrane. A yellowish exudation may cover the tonsils, perforations and even sloughing of the palate may occur, and there may be much external cellulitis, but the leathery, whitish, adherent exudation of diphtheria is absent. The amount of albumen in the urine of scarlet fever is usually slight; in diphtheria it is often fifty per cent.—*Archives of Pediatrics.*

  DR. J. ROBERT WARD, president of the Maryland State Board of Health, died at Govanstown, April 29, aged 76 years.

Symptoms of Iodoform Poisoning.

The following on the various manifestations of iodoform poisoning is from the Independent Practitioner:

M. Schede (Centrbl. f. Chirurgie, No. 3, 1882), who is known to have observed the greatest number of cases of poisoning by iodoform, describes six different forms of the same. The most common phenomena are: a considerable elevation of the temperature, up to one hundred and four degrees Fahrenheit, with noticeable disturbances of the general health of the patient, manifesting itself soon after the iodoform has been applied. The symptoms of another form, as described by M. Schede, are: great mental depression, headache, loss of appetite, and the taste of iodoform in everything taken into the mouth; the pulse is accelerated and small, but after the removal of the iodoform these symptoms soon disappear. A third variety is mentioned in which was observed a great frequency of the pulse (from 150 to 180 per minute,) with relative little disturbance of the patient's general health. But in the fourth form he observed in connexion with frequent pulse a corresponding rise in the temperature. This form, says M. Schede, might be mistaken for septicemia, although in iodoform poisoning the wound is perfectly aseptic, the tongue red and moist, and sensorium clear. A fifth form is mentioned, but as this occurred after extensive surgical operations, its etiology is doubtful. The symptoms of the sixth variety are: disturbances of the functions of the brain, appearing either as phenomena of acute meningitis or actual brain disease. The symptoms of acute meningitis were met with mainly in young patients; they present themselves as an accelerated pulse, vomiting, depression of the sensorium, sometimes to a degree of complete coma, and contractions of certain groups of muscles. Schede regards it unsafe to fill the cavities of large fresh wounds with iodoform, as it adheres to the tissues in such manner that, if alarming symptoms should present themselves, its removal may be found difficult.—*Weekly Medical Review.*

Veratria in Muscular Tremor.

After small doses of veratria each muscle when stimulated reacts more vigorously, and the contraction lasts longer than in the normal condition. The increased duration of the single contraction is shown not only by the greater length of the myographic curve, but also by the fact that while thirty stimuli per second are needed to set a normal frog's muscle into tetanus some ten suffice to tetanise the veratrised muscle. The tremors of alcoholism, of central nerve-degeneration, of fever, etc., are due, according to Dr. Feris, to a condition of muscular contraction in which the impulses are not sufficiently rapid to give rise to tetanus. This may be owing to defective innervation as well as to muscular degeneration. Dr. Feris has used veratria in such tremors, giving it in pills of half a milligramme each (one-one hundred and twentieth grain), of which four were taken daily at intervals of an hour. Of thirteen patients so treated ten were suffering from alcoholism, two from disseminated sclerosis, one from sequelæ of typhoid. In all the tremors disappeared entirely in five to fifteen days. Improvement appears after the first day, as is shown by making the patients write before and (one hour) after each pill. The treatment should be kept up for ten days at least, or relapse may occur. The cases have continued well for two months at least after the veratria was stopped.—*The Practitioner.*

THE Baltimore Polyclinic is now established in roomy and comfortable quarters at 112 Hanover St. There are about twenty students in the different departments. Clinical material is abundant. During April, 1381 visits of patients were registered.

The Medical Chronicle.

A Monthly Journal for the Practitioner.

GEORGE H. ROHÉ, M. D., Editor.

☞ It is requested that all literary and business communications, books for review, exchanges, etc., be addressed to, and all checks, drafts and post-office orders drawn to the order of
Dr. GEORGE H. ROHÉ,
Cor. Greene & Mulberry Sts., - Balto., Md.

BALTIMORE, JUNE, 1884.

EDITORIAL.

The American Medical Association.

The thirty-fifth annual meeting of the American Medical Association, was held in the city of Washington, May 6 to 9 inclusive.

Prof. Austin Flint, Sr., of New York, presided. In his annual address the president described the movements which led to the formation of the association, and discussed the relations of the body to the profession at large, the elevation of the standard of medical education and the code of ethics. Dr. Flint also suggested that the International Medical Congress should be invited by the Association, to hold its meeting in 1887, in the United States. This suggestion was adopted and a committee appointed to carry it into effect.

The Sections on *Practical Medicine, Surgery, Obstetrics and Gynecology,* and *Diseases of Children,* each did a large amount of excellent work. Many of the papers read were above the average in quality and the discussions instructive and interesting. In the remaining sections, however, the scientific and practical value of the papers was hardly up to what ought to be the "minimum requirements." This was especially true of the section on State Medicine, where a few prosy papers were read and an immense deal of time frittered away over insignificant matters.

The address of Dr. Shoemaker, the chairman of the section on Practice of Medicine, gave a clear and succinct review of the progress made in medicine during the past year.

The address in Obstetrics, Dr. T. A. Reamy, Chairman, consisted in an analysis of 231 cases of operation for laceration of the cervix uteri. Not a single one of the patients died from the effects of the operation.

The address in Surgery by the chairman, Dr. C. T. Parkes, was devoted to an experimental study of gun-shot wounds of the abdomen. Dr. Parkes concludes that opening the abdomen in the middle line, cleaning out the cavity, and resection of the intestines if necessary, give better results than the expectant plan of treatment.

Dr. D. J. Roberts, the chairman of the section on State Medicine, discussed in his address the relations of state supervision over medical education and medical practice. He was opposed to the principle of giving to state boards of health the power to regulate the practice of medicine. He also advocated the establishment of a department of Health, whose head should be a cabinet officer. His various suggestions were apparently not received with favor by the association.

The discussion on tuberculosis in the section on practice of medicine attracted most attention. It is somewhat significant to note that the only two members who were at all known in connexion with previous work in experimental pathology, Drs. Formad and Sternberg took the ground that all of Koch's conclusions should not be accepted without reserve.

Some discussion arose over the report of the Trustees of the *Journal*, and a strong minority report was made by Dr. Packard, in which the management of the *Journal* was sharply criticised. By a nearly three-fourths majority, the minority report was laid on the table. The vote, however, showed that a large minority of the association is dissatisfied with the *Journal*, as at present conducted,

The usual number of resolutions. good, bad and indifferent were introduced and passed. Many of the members have come to the conclusion that there is entirely too much "resoluting" in this and other organizations of similar character. It is suggested that a Committee on Resolutions be hereafter appointed, to which all resolutions shall be referred for comment or revision before being acted upon by the association. This would save the association from many a *faux pas*.

The following officers were elected for the current year :

President, Dr. H. F. Campbell, of Ga.

Vice Presidents, Drs. Jno. S. Lynch of Md.; S. D. Mercer of Nebr.; J. W. Parsons of New Hampshire and H. C. Ghent of Texas.

Treasurer, Dr. R. J. Dunglison of Pa.

Librarian, Dr. C. H. A. Kleinschmidt of Dist. Columbia.

Chairman Committee Arrangements, Dr. S. Logan of New Orleans.

Assistant Secretary, Dr. W. H. Watkins of New Orleans.

The Association adjourned to meet in New Orleans on the last Tuesday in April, 1885.

CURRENT LITERATURE.

Eczema and its Management. A practical treatise based on the study of three thousand cases of the disease. By L. Duncan Bulkley, A. M., M. D., physician to the New York Skin and Cancer Hospital, etc. Second edition. New York, G. P. Putnam's Sons, 1884, $3.00, pp. 344.

The appearance of a second edition of the above work is an indication that the author's labors are appreciated by his professional brethren. Dr. Bulkley's experience in the treatment of diseases of the skin has been very extensive, and hence a work giving the results of that experience cannot but be valuable. Inasmuch as fully one-third of all skin diseases coming under the notice of the practitioner in this country, are classed under the head "eczema," it becomes important that our knowledge of that disease, its various manifestations, its causes, and its successful management should be clearly defined. We say without hesitation that this object has been accomplished by Dr. Bulkley. While we disagree with him on some minor points connected with the pathology of eczema, we can unreservedly recommend the book as a safe guide to the practitioner. The hints on the management of eczema are full and clear, and if borne in mind by the physician, will render the treatment of most cases easy and satisfactory.

The paper, type, printing and binding of the volume are a delight to the eye, and creditable alike to the good taste and liberality of the publishers.

Addresses and Exercises at the One Hundredth Anniversary of the Foundation of the Medical Schools of the Harvard University, October 17, 1883.

This beautiful specimen of typography from the "University Press" of John Wilson & Son, contains the addresses of Dr. Oliver Wendell Holmes, President Eliot, Dr. Francis Minot, Mr. Harry Lee, and Prof. H. W. Williams. It is a worthy memorial of the first centenary of the Harvard Medical School.

FLOTSAM.

THE Maryland State Pharmaceutical Association held its second annual meeting in this city on May 13 and 14. The meeting was a very interesting one, and was well attended.

THE New York State Board of Health is about to undertake a "collective investigation" upon a very important subject. It is intended to collect facts bearing upon the question, when a patient convalescent from an infectious disease ceases to be capable of conveying the infection.

THE following treatment has been successfully used by Dr. Brooks, of Paducah, Ky., in tapeworm: ℞—Chloroform fl. extract of male fern āā. ʒj, emulsion of castor oil (50 per cent.) f℥jjj. M. S.—Take at once after a 24 hours' fast. Dr. B. says this remedy "anesthetizes or suspends vitality, and any active purge during anesthesia of the tenia is all that is required to expel it."

FROM a statistical table prepared by Col. Geo. E. Waring, secretary National Board of Health, we learn that during the last fourteen years 115,406 cases of yellow fever occurred in the United States. The total mortality from this disease during that period was 21,797, a death-rate of 18.8 per cent. These figures ought to appeal to Congress to place in the hands of a proper organization the power to prevent such a waste of life in the future.

PROF. SAMUEL D. GROSS, M. D., L.L.D., D. C. L., died at his home in Philadelphia, on May 6. Prof. Gross' fame as a surgeon was world-wide, and his numerous contributions to surgical literature rank among the first. His last great and crowning work, the System of Surgery, has passed through six editions, the last being issued in 1882. The immense amount of labor he performed during the course of his long and useful life was rendered possible by a strict economy of the odds and ends of time which most men waste. His life is in all respects a model for the young physician. It may most truly be said of him,

He wasted not the treasure of his time.

THE timely articles of Drs. J. Harvey Hill and Wm. N. Hill have crowded out much other matter prepared for this number.

GOVERNOR MCLANE has appointed Dr. Richard McSherry president of the Maryland State Board of Health. A better selection could not have been made.

DR. GEO. M. STERNBERG, U. S. A., has been ordered to the Johns Hopkins' University to continue his researches in bacterial pathology.

BY a recent fire in London, the entire second edition of Dr. Morell Mackenzie's work on Diseases of the Throat and Nose, was destroyed. The author fortunately has in his possession the proof-sheets, but some delay will occur before the work can be reprinted.

NEW editions of Dr. Murchison's Clinical Lectures on Diseases of the Liver, Jaundice, and Abdominal Dropsy, and Treatise on the Continued Fevers of Great Britain, are in the press of Wm. Wood & Co., New York. The former work will be revised by Dr. Lauder Brunton, and the latter by Dr. W. Cayley of the Middlesex Hospital.

THE Secretary of the Treasury has issued a circular notifying the officers of the Marine Hospital service, that the importation of rags from Egypt will not be allowed unless they have been subjected to disinfection by one of the following processes:

1. Boiling in water for two hours under a pressure of 50 pounds per square inch.
2. Boiling in water for four hours without pressure.
3. Subjection to the action of confined sulpurous-acid gas for six hours, burning 1½–2 pounds of roll brimstone in each 1000 cubic feet of space, with the rags well scattered upon racks.

The Medical Chronicle.

BALTIMORE, JULY, 1884.

ORIGINAL ARTICLES.

ARTICLE I.

THREE CASES OF SPINDLE-CELLED SARCOMA.

BY O. J. COSKERY, M. D.,

Professor of Surgery, College of Physicians and Surgeons, Baltimore.

CASE I.—Fred. B., aged 47, a German, baker, early in March, 1883, discovered a movable tumor under the skin, situated one and a half inches to the inner side of, and about the same distance above the left nipple. The tumor was then smaller than a medium sized hazel-nut. It grew continuously until on June 20th, 1883, or only three months after it was first noticed, it had reached the size of the fetal head, and was nodulated. On the above date he entered the City Hospital, where, some days afterward, the lump with a portion of the integument was removed. The patient left hospital on July 15th, 1883, the wound having nearly cicatrised. On December 11th, 1883, he again entered the hospital with a distinctly nodulated mass of nearly the same size as at the time of the former operation; the centre of the mass from above downward being a little nearer the clavicle than before. It was again extirpated with a portion of the skin and pectoral muscle, both of which seemed to be involved, although the greater portion was easily shelled out with the fingers. It was found to consist of a number of roundish masses, from the size of a small hazel-nut to that of an unhulled black walnut.

These pieces were friable, some very much so, and were greyish in color. The naked eye appearances, both in shape and color, closely resembled what was found at the time of the first operation. Patient left hospital again January 18th, 1884, with a large surface still granulating. Soon thereafter he noticed that the growth was returning at several points and when he again came to the hospital on April 28th, 1884, the following was noted: The wound made at the time of the second operation had never healed over a space of nearly one and a half inches square. This space was now occupied by a new growth. In front of and extending nearly an inch above the outer end of the left clavicle, was a rounded mass which seemed somewhat movable. Just to the inner side of this was another lobule, also seemingly movable, and of nearly the same size as the first one mentioned. To the outer side of the track of the second incision, and reaching towards the axilla, another and larger mass. To the inner side of the incision, a lump seemingly firmly attached to the walls of the chest.

In consideration of the extent of the growth during each interval from March to June, 1883, and from January to April, 1884, notwithstanding very careful removal on each occasion; of the man's anemic condition, and of the doubtful extent of invasion of deeper parts (which depth could not be positively made out by palpation), I advised the patient strongly not to have any operation done. His expressed fear of death from increasing growth, the absence of any pulmonary complications, and the personal solicitations of the patient overcame my scruples.

Under chloroform on April 30th, the operation for the removal of all the masses was attempted. Although only slight hemorrhage had followed the second operation, remembering that it had been rather profuse at the first, I decided to use the knife as little as possible. An incision over the inner and upper tumor, only large enough to admit two fingers was made, and one of the masses fished out. This was found to be much larger than expected, and to have dipped down behind the clavicle, fully to below its lower border.

The incision required for the removal of this portion, passed through a large branch of the external jugular vein. This was quickly tied. Another incision over the outer mass was made and the lump hooked out with the fingers. The hemorrhage was so profuse that it was found necessary to lay open the skin so as to make one incision of the two, that a better view might be gotten of the bleeding points. These were found to be entirely too numerous to attempt ligation of each. A sponge was accordingly thrust deeply in above the clavicle, and the portion of the cicatrix with all the masses to the inner side quickly scooped away. There still remained the mass on the outer side.

The fingers passed around this portion, followed it as far as the axillary vessels, which could be felt pulsating, and still did not grasp the whole. This probably was the cause of the intense neuralgia the patient had suffered from since the second operation (and which should have been mentioned before), down the arm and forearm.

Because of the unknown depth of this piece, the profuseness of the hemorrhage everywhere, (and which I had already decided in my mind could only be arrested by packing,) knowing the difficulties of packing the axilla, and as the patient's respiration had been decidedly ugly once or twice under the chloroform, I decided to abandon the operation at this point, leaving the largest of all the pieces *in situ*. Sponges were pushed into the pockets under the skin, pads of lint over them, and the whole tightly bandaged.

There were some variations of temperature and pulse, not as much as might be expected under the circumstances, nor particularly noteworthy; and forty hours after the operation, the bandages were cut across. Eight sponges were at once removed together with the lint, but the deeper ones were left. A wash of forty per cent. carbolic acid was ordered to be poured freely upon the wound and remaining sponges. On the fourth day two deep sponges were torn away, giving a good deal of pain, and some brisk granulation hemorrhage.

On May 5th the remaining four sponges were removed. The surface of the extensive wound was healthily granulating, oozing slight. The temperature and pulse have neither been high since the operation. In the wound were two easily recognized masses of new growth that have made their appearance since the operation.

May 12th, the patient was up and about the ward.

Since this note numerous lumps of new tissue have made their appearance in the scar and neighborhood, and the large mass, formerly in the axilla, and left at the time of last operation, has been brought forward by the cicatrization going on.

The following is the report of microscopic appearance of tumor removed at last extirpation, by Dr. N. G. Keirle. "This, the third tumor growth, is of the same species and variety as the two preceding, with this distinctive feature: the spindle-cells are loosely intertwined, not compactly felted as at first, which text ural condition favors metastasis. There is nothing further noteworthy in this, the well known medium sized, spindle-cell sarcoma."

CASE 2.—Mrs. M. L., aged 44 yrs., mother of six children, first noticed, twenty years ago, a tumor the size of a hazel-nut in the right breast, a good inch above the nipple. She did not remember having received any blow upon the part about this time. The tumor was painless, rounded and movable. About one year ago she noticed that it was increasing in size, and in March, 1884, it commenced to grow very rapidly. On April 28th, 1884, when I first saw her, there was a freely movable, nodulated tumor, occupying the position of the right mammary gland, and involving it, about the size of a cocoanut. This was painless both before and after handling.

The superficial veins in the immediate neighborhood of the breast were dilated and tortuous. The tumor was removed by the usual elliptical incision. In turning out the mass a cyst burst, from which probably an ounce of greenish-yellow, glairy fluid escaped.

The patient did uninterruptedly well, the incision healing by first intention. The first dressing, of dry lint, was not removed until the fourth day, and all the discharge that took place came from around the two ligatures required at the time of operating. The sutures were removed at odd times from the seventh to the twelfth day, and the ligatures on this latter date.

May 15th, patient discharged and went home, to New Jersey, wound nearly cicatrised.

June 1st, patient reported in writing that she was entirely well.

Report of microscopical structure of specimen by Dr. N. G. Keirle. "The mammary tumor is a spindle cell sarcoma, which cells so dilate and distort the gland and tubules as to cause the latter to simulate cysts, but the recognition of aciniform structure prevents such error. The vessels are numerous, of large calibre, and simple spindle-cell walls. In the nomenclature of Rindfleisch it is a 'sarcoma pericanaliculosi diffusum'."

CASE 3.—Mrs. F. L. C., aged 50, ceased menstruating two years ago. About two years and a half ago a tumor made its appearance on the outer side of the left thigh about one inch above the outer border of the patella. This grew slowly until in April of this year, when having struck it, pain was increased and swelling came on. When first seen by me in May, 1884, the lump was about the size of a large orange, distinctly nodulated, and while evidently adherent to the skin at one or two points, was freely movable over the deeper structures.

On May 14th, 1884, under chloroform, an incision about two and a half inches in length was made over the most prominent portion of the growth, two fingers of the left hand introduced, and the mass scooped out with difficulty. In some places the knife had to be used, at one point a portion of the skin was removed. One skin vessel required ligation. In pulling out the mass a small cyst, containing about a teaspoonful of yellow watery fluid, burst. The wound was stitched together with three sutures and dry lint put on, over which a bandage from the toes up. On the fourth day after, some slight bloody oozing having occurred through the lint, the dressing was removed. The wound was in good condition, no redness of edges. The ligature came away with the dressing, and there was some slight oozing. A greased rag with a pad over each flap was then applied and the part rebandaged.

May 21st, flaps in good position, but discharge slightly offensive. Sutures still left in. No ugly symptoms except that for a few hours last night the patient had some pain.

June 1st, wound nearly closed, no nodules.

June 14th, 1884, wound entirely healed.

Dr. Keirle, to whom the specimen was handed for microscopical examination, reported it to be a "spindle-celled sarcoma."

PROF. JOHN S. LYNCH, of the College of Physicians and Surgeons, has been elected first vice-president of the American Medical Association. A well-deserved compliment.

ARTICLE II.

BILIARY CALCULI.

BY WM. H. NORRIS, M. D.

Surgeon in charge of the Baltimore Eastern Dispensary, and late Surgeon U. S. Army.

[Read before the Med. and Surg. Society of Balto.]

This name is given to concretions which form in the gall-bladder, the hepatic and biliary ducts.

They differ in number, size and position. There may be only one, or there may be thousands.

They may be of the minutest size, or large enough to fill the whole cavity of the gall-bladder.

They are found in the gall-bladder, tubuli biliferi, and biliary ducts, and occasionally in the bowels.

Concretions of very great size have been found in the bowels, and it has been a question, whether they were formed in the bowels, or passed from the gall-bladder through the gall ducts into the duodenum.

Dr. Wood states that he has seen them so large as to fill the bowel and moulded exactly to its shape, and to have obstructed the bowels. They were entirely too large to be passed through the gall-ducts, and must have grown by accretion, or must have formed in the bowels.

Sometimes when they cannot pass through the ducts, they produce inflammation, and ulceration, and thus make their way into the bowels.

Gall-stones are usually of a yellowish, brownish, or of a brownish yellow color, and of a soft consistence.

They are of various shapes, generally of irregular form, and rounded angles.

Their composition is various, but consists most frequently of cholesterin and coloring matter of the bile; sometimes, however, they are found to consist entirely of phosphate or carbonate of lime.

They are probably formed by the depositions from the bile around a solid nucleus; which may be insoluble matter precipitated from the bile, coagulated blood, fibrinous, or albuminous exudations, or concreted mucus.

Whatever impedes the flow of bile favors their production.

It is possible that a deficiency of alkali in the bile may have some effect in producing them.

Dr. Powell states (contrary to what is generally believed) that gall-stones are rarely, if ever, found in tropical or hot climates, and this he attributes to the fact of the bile being more liquid in hot countries.

These concretions often remain in the gall-bladder a long time without occasioning any inconvenience, and are only discovered after death. They may lie in the ducts without producing any trouble, or of ever being suspected of being there during life.

It is only in the act of expulsion, or when so large as to occasion distension, or obstruction, that they become a source of trouble.

One of their ordinary effects is severe pain, caused by putting the coats of the gall ducts upon the stretch, and thus causing it to contract spasmodically.

In such cases the pain is sometimes exceedingly violent, as much so perhaps as any to which the human subject is liable.

The paroxysms usually come on suddenly in the right epigastrium, or toward the right side, just over the origin of the common duct, and thence shooting to the back.

The pain almost always comes on in paroxysms. Yet we may have a dull, aching pain in the interval. We generally have a pale skin, small and feeble pulse, nausea and vomiting, great anxiety and restlessness, and great prostration.

The paroxysms may continue for a few hours, or for many days. The stone at length passes into the duodenum and passes away with the stools, and we have instantaneous relief.

Another morbid effect of gall-stone is inflammation. This may arise from irritation of their presence, or direct pressure, or distending force, or from bilious accumulations which they occasion.

The inflammation sometimes ends in suppuration or ulceration, and through adhesions of the connective tissues find their way into the cavities, or externally to the surface.

Another effect is obstruction. A duct may be distended by one of these concretions so as to produce spasm, inflammation and ulceration, without a complete stoppage of the flow of bile, which may find its way alongside of the calculus. But more frequently we find complete occlusion of the ducts by these concretions, and in such cases the accumulation behind the obstruction is enormous.

The precise seat of obstruction depends upon the position of the stone. If this be in the hepatic duct, the distention will be in the tubuli biliferi, and the liver may become so large as to yield a sense of fluctuation when examined externally. If the cystic duct be obstructed, the gall-bladder will only be distended. If the common duct, both the gall-bladder and all the biliary ducts behind the point of obstruction.

The absence of bile in the alimentary canal, derangement of digestion, general jaundice, are all the symptoms of this affection.

If the obstructions should not be removed, inflammation, ulceration and perforation will result; with the escape of bile into the peritoneum, bowels, or externally through the skin, with generally a fatal result.

Treatment.—In the treatment for biliary calculi, the first indication is to obviate their effects.

The second, to cause their expulsion or solution, and to prevent their formation.

The effect that most urgently calls for interference is the spasmodic pain. For this, various remedies have been brought prominently to the attention of the profession. The older practitioners recommended general and local blood letting, emetics, opiates in some form or other, warm baths, hot fomentations, tobacco enema, etc. Dr. Durand, of Dijon, at one time had considerable repute in Europe for curing this disease by the use of a mixture composed of 2 parts of sulphuric ether and 3 parts of oil of turpentine, in drachm doses every 30 minutes. This was supposed to have the power to dissolve the calculi, but it is more likely to have had its effect in relieving the spasms by its antispasmodic action.

But, Mr. President and gentlemen of the Society, happy for the practitioners of the present day, we have at our command other and more potent remedies. And of first importance among these is chloroform.

In cases of violent and severe agony attending the passage of a gall-stone, the inhalation of a few drachms of chloroform will often act like a charm in affording instantaneous relief from pain and spasms. It is probable that it produces a relaxation of the spasms of the ducts, and muscular or nerve fibers of the diaphragm, duodenum and abdominal muscles, all of which are thrown into convulsions by the passage of a calculus. Hypodermic injections of morphia often act like a charm in relieving pain and overcoming the spasms. Jaborandi and pilocarpine may be used with good results.

The second indication, that is, to cause their expulsion or solution, and to prevent their formation. Chloroform, alkaline medicines, and hydrated succinate of peroxide of iron may be used, generally with success, in connection with proper dietetics.

Another morbid effect of these concretions, is distention of the gall-bladder. This may result from various causes, the most frequent, however, are such as produce obstruction in the common duct, as gall-stone. In these cases bile is the distending fluid, and the accumulation may be enormous, as much as 12 lbs. or more. We may also have paralysis from over-distention. In all of these cases the chief danger is rupture or perforation of the coats of the gall-bladder, and the escape of the bile or pus into the abdominal cavity—although it may find an outlet by an ulcerated opening into the bowels, or to the surface through the skin.

The treatment to be used in such cases should be directed to the removal of the obstruction, and overcoming the spasm if possible, and to meet these indications, chloroform and sulphate of morphia are of first importance. If, however, we should fail in this, we should resort to the aspirator, and if necessary, to free incision into the abscess.

It was at one time deemed questionable, on the part of the surgeon, whether we would be justified in opening the gall-bladder, inasmuch as all such operations had generally proven fatal.

But, in the light of more advanced surgery of the past decade, we find that many cases recover after such operations.

The British and continental surgeons advocate such a mode of practice, and particularly so with English surgeons in the East Indies.

ANALECTS.

The Causation of Nervous Diseases.

While the symptoms and lesions of the so-called "system diseases" of the spinal cord have been carefully studied, but little light has been thrown upon their etiology. Why an inflammatory process, acute or chronic, should extend longitudinally through the organ for several inches, but fail to involve cells or fibres lying in close proximity to it on all sides, has received no explanation. In 1881, Adamkiewicz discovered that the various capillary vessels lying in and supplying with nutriment the various tracts in the cord, and the various segments of its gray matter, were connected with different branches of the spinal arteries, so that a disease of one branch would effect but one tract, and not all parts of the cord indefinitely. His attempt to bring this fact into a causal relation with the system disease was, however, unsuccessful; for it only carried the question a step farther back, and failed to explain why certain arteries, to the exclusion of others were affected in certain diseases. Professor Strumpell, of Leipzig, in an inaugural address on taking the chair of Practice of Medicine at the Policlinic, quite recently, has made a valuable contribution to this subject. His opinion is worthy of careful attention, as he is not only a well-known scientific worker and a man of very wide experience, but also the author of a work on Practice which is superseding that of Niemeyer throughout Germany. Admitting that anatomical structure furnishes no explanation for the existence of system diseases, Strumpell seeks their cause in physiological, embryological, or toxicological facts.

Any voluntary effort calls into play certain definite centres and tracts which are distinct from all others, not on account of their structure, but because together they form a physiological unit. All physiological action is accompanied by chemical change in the parts which act. If that action is excessive the chemical changes may pass the line of safety and go on to pathological changes. Such changes will be limited, however, to the parts which form the physiological unit; or, in other words will affect one system alone. There are numerous examples of diseases thus caused by overaction of a part. Writers' cramp and other occupation neuroses are examples of overstrain producing temporary inability without known lesions. Strumpell would also assign to this cause progressive muscular atrophy, bulbar paralysis, and amyotrophic lateral sclerosis, all of which are known to follow severe exertion, and to present definite pathological changes limited to the *motor system* in the gray matter or white tracts.

The researches of Flechsig have demonstrated that various tracts in the cord develop at various periods in the embryo, and that each system has its own time of obtaining its medullary sheath. This fact Strumpell brings into connection with two forms of system disease, both of which appear early in life, and both of which may be ascribed to a failure in the normal process of development; viz., the hereditary form of locomotor ataxia described first by Friedreich, and the congenital pseudo-hypertrophic paralysis recently investigated by Erb.

External agents manifesting a power of specific action upon certain parts of the nervous system form the third great cause of system diseases. These agents may be inorganic or organic. It is well known that strychnine excites the reflex centres, atropine the secretory centres, morphine the sensory tracts, conium the mo or nerve terminations, etc. A selecttve action of poison is therefore provein to exist. Strumpell cites lead and mercury as inorganic agents possessing a specific action upon the motor system of the spinal cord, and assigns lead palsy and mercurial tremor a place among the group of system diseases. But organic agents also show a selective action upon the nervous system. An epidemic of erSot poisoning occurred in Marburg not long ago. Those who were affected presented symptoms which resembled almost exactly the symptoms of locomotor ataxia, and the post-mortem examination demonstrated sclerosis limited to the posterior columns of the cord in all cases. In Northern Italy the peasants mix lathyrus beans with corn when food is scarce. The result is a peculiar form of poisoning, in which all the symptoms of spastic paraplegia develop and a lesion of the lateral columns of the cord is found. These facts seem to Strumpell to prove that organic agents, germs, may cause nervous disease of a systemic character. Following this line, he seeks to show that the connection between syphilis and locomotor ataxia may be due to a selective action of the syphilitic germ upon the posterior columns of the spinal cord. But if this is doubtful, there are numerous nervous diseases whose course and termination demonstrate a germ origin. Cerebro-spinal meningitis is infectious ; hydrophobia is contagious ; tetanus is best explained by the entrance of some external organic agent into a wound ; trigeminal neuralgia is most frequently malarial in its origin, and is only affected by anti-malarial remedies. Further, there is a form of nervous disease, commencing with a chill and acute febrile symptoms, running an acute course for some days, with general constitutional symptoms, enlargement of the spleen, occasional albuminuria, etc. ; in a word, presenting for a time all the features common to diseases which are known to be of germ origin. This form of disease is infantile spinal paralysis and its ally, acute infantile encephalitis. In these Strumpell finds examples of a germ disease in which a selective action of the germ upon certain motor-trophic cells is as evident as the selective action of lead upon other motor-trophic cells.

It is evident that under these three divisions, physiological overwork, embryological malformation, and toxicological agents, inorganic and organic, Strumpell has succeeded in classifying all the primary system diseases of the cord.

As an original and suggestive effort to explain a hitherto unknown subject his address will command attention. It is possible that his hypotheses will need to be modified as facts collect about them. It is possible that other causes, as well as those which he mentions, may exist. But there are many points of interest in his presentation of the matter, and not the least is the fact that by it neurologists are to be open to the attacks of the whole army of bacteria.—*Med. Record.*

The Dietetic Treatment of Diabetes Mellitus.

At the meeting of the American Medical Association, Dr. Austin Flint, Jr. read a paper on the above subject. He said that it occasionally happens that the presence of sugar is detected in persons who seem to be in thoroughly good health, though this is very rare. From an extensive experience in examining for life insurance, he would estimate that it occurs in one person out of every three hundred and seventy-seven persons. In most cases attention is called to the trouble by the symptoms. There are thirst, polyuria, dryness of the feces and of the skin, weariness on exertion, etc. Pruritus of the vulva is an extremely common occurrence, and when not explicable otherwise, should always lead to an examination of the urine.

The usual symptoms, however, are not always all present by any means. As to the detection of sugar in the urine, which is, of course, *the sign* of the disease, he said that the great desideratum has been a test that would be simple and easy and yet accurate. Fehling's test when accurately used is certain, but it is apt to become inoperative when the solution is kept for a long time. He considered that two liquids which had been prepared by Squibb, of New York, answered every requirement. Without taking the time to describe them fully, he gave the method by which they should be used. Mix equal parts of the two fluids and pour the mixture into a test-tube to the depth of an inch. Bring it to a boil; then add an equal part of urine and bring the mixture thus made to a boil. Then allow it to cool. These steps are most important to be observed. If on cooling there is no distinct opaque yellowish or reddish precipitate, there is no sugar. The promptness and amount of precipitate indicate approximately the amount of sugar. For the more accurate determination of this, the differential density method of Roberts is good. The specific gravity of urine has no definite relation to the amount of sugar. Owing to the proportion of urea, diabetic urine may have a specific gravity as low as 1011. Normal quantity and specific gravity of urine do not *exclude* the existence of diabetes.

The author then touched upon the symptoms, etc., of the disease, and to some extent upon the glycogenic function of the liver. In this connection, he said that he thought his own experiments had harmonized with those of Bernard and Pavy. He believed that sugar was formed in the liver, but was very rapidly washed out of the organ by the blood current. The discovery of Bernard, however, had not thrown the light upon the etiology of diabetes that had been hoped at first. Besides the sugar from the liver, we have the sugar resulting from digestion. In diabetes much of this is discharged through the kidneys. The failure of the body to consume the hydrocarbons results in a loss of heat. The temperature is below normal. He spoke of a patient of his whose temperature is $96.5°$ F. How far can diabetes mellitus be treated? Cantani says, "Diabetes has become a disease *easily and certainly curable*, if treatment be not begun too late." Dr. Flint did not think this statement extravagant when we consider the results of the dietetic treatment, provided it be submitted to. A cure is the result or, at least, a removal of the symptoms, except an occasional slight glycosuria. Our main reliance is upon diet, which must be one that *absolutely excludes starch and sugar*. This is difficult to enforce. There is often a craving for starchy food, especially bread. There are numerous so-called antidiabetic breads, which are said to contain no starch. Dr. Flint has had many of them analyzed. They are all frauds, sometimes containing more starch than ordinary bread. If the patient will not submit to the diet, he may be allowed a piece of the crust of a roll with plenty of butter twice a day, under protest. The craving for starchy food and for sugar diminishes. It is difficult to make a diet-table of foods that do not contain these ingredients, but it can be done, especially if the patient be in well-to-do circumstances, and he may live even luxuriously. Even in mild cases this rigid regimen must be kept up for at least two months. Then a gradual return to usual diet may be allowed, the urine being examined every five days, and the strict diet at once enforced if any sugar be found. As regards general treatment, the action of the skin must be excited, general untiring exercise, a mild course of training, massage, Turkish or Russian baths, may all be tried in cases in which they are not contraindicated. The patient must not drink much. The anti-diabetic diet will lessen the thirst. The sucking of cracked ice is good. Alcoholic drinks are injurious and should be avoided, especially champagne and spirits are to be interdicted. If something of the kind must be taken, claret in small quantities is the best. The patient cannot bear sustained effort, and all causes of mental anxiety must be avoided. As a rule, the insomnia does not require narcotics. When boils appear, sulphide of calcium is of great benefit, though it does not affect the disease itself much. The lowered temperature of the body makes great care necessary to avoid taking cold.

The medicine which he recommended chiefly, was Clement's solution of the arsenite of bromine, in three-drop doses three times a day in a wine-glassful of water (two drops represent one-twenty-fourth of a grain of the salt). The system can tolerate this drug for months. But no drug will be of use without diet. Patients should be informed that they are suffering from a serious disease and must follow directions. There is always danger of a relapse.—*Medical News*.

Gallic Acid in Hemorrhage from Urinary Organs.

Of all the remedies usually recommended for this condition, Dr. Lionel S. Beale (*Lancet*, March 15), prefers gallic acid, which he says seldom disagrees in any way. Some patients complain of its taste, but it is generally well borne by the stomach. It does not cause constipation, and even when the crystals are swallowed in a state of suspersion in water or mucilage no inconvenience results, and the stomach is not disturbed by their presence. The glycerine of gallic acid is, however, the most pleasant form in which to prescribe the remedy. This contains one part of gallic acid in four. Forty minims will contain ten grains, and may be given in distilled water, peppermint, orange, or other water. But it is most essential that the patient should persist in taking the doses regularly for several days. Gallic acid is absorbed by the blood and passes away unchanged in the urine, and it is probable that it acts directly on the parts from which the bleeding is taking place; and therefore a certain strength of solution is necessary to get the good effects, and this can only be obtained by its persistent introduction into the stomach, and so into the blood at short intervals of time. He has given gallic acid in ten-grain doses every three hours without intermission for three weeks, no objection having been made on the patient's part. Whether much larger doses would be absorbed he doubts; but he is not aware to what extent the remedy may be pushed, nor does he know in what respect very large doses would be deleterious. On these points he would be glad to learn the experience of other practitioners who have largely employed the remedy. He has generally found that the desired effect has resulted after ten-grain doses had been kept up for three or four days, and in cases where the bleeding did not actually cease, it was well under control. In several of those painful cases of hemorrhage from fungous growth, the bleeding was much lessened and the fatal result postponed; in some of his cases he should say that death was due rather to exhaustion and weakening of the general health than to the hemorrhage. He therefore commends this remedy in the cases of hemorrhage to which he has referred, and he prescribes it with confidence, so that its use may be steadily continued until its beneficial action is clearly established.—*Medical and Surgical Reporter.*

Surgical Uses of Collodion.

Mr. Sampson Gamgee writes, in *Birmingham Medical Review:* Collodion is one of those therapeutic agents whose value to the surgeon is admitted, without being adequately appreciated or utilized. Composed of ether, gun-cotton and spirit, collodion is a powerful antiputrescent, and by ready evaporation and contraction it exercises the dual antiphlogistic power of refrigeration and compression. In acute orchitis I know of no plan of treatment so simple, rapid and satisfactory as coating the cord and scrotum with layers of collodion, by the aid of a camel-hair brush previously dipped into it. The sensation is momentarily sharp, the shrinkage rapid, and so the subsidence of the inflammatory process — facts pointed out some thirty years ago, by Bonnafant, but much doubted, and almost forgotten. To swollen parts which cannot be well bandaged, collodion is especially applicable for the compression attending its contraction. I was recently consulted in the case of a good looking boy, considerably disfigured by a red and swollen nose, which became very pale and visibly contracted just after I painted it with successive layers of collodion. I repeated the application three times in the succeeding fortnight, with the effect of reducing the organ to its natural size and color. When the nasal bones are fractured, a **very effective mold for keeping** them immovable, after adjusting them with the fingers, may be thus made: Place over the nose a thin layer of absorbent cotton, soaked in collodion. As it dries, another layer of cotton, and more collodion, taking care that the application extends sufficiently on each side to give buttress-like support. The patient compares the feeling to the application of a firm bandage to the nose, and the bones consolidate effectively under the shield, which may be renewed as it cracks and peels off.

Other cuts than recent ones do well under collodion. A horse-breaker sought my advice for a grazed wound inflicted by a carriage step on the front of his right shin, ten days previously. He had applied water dressing continuously. The surface of the wound had suppurated, and the edges for some distance around were red and tender. I raised the foot, to empty the limb of blood, dried the surface of the sore with absorbent tissue, then brushed it over with collodion and applied a smoothly compressing bandage over one of my pads. The part was easy at once, and after two more dressings, at intervals of four days, cicatrization was perfect, the patient having continued his business of riding and driving without losing an hour.

Proper Method of Trephining.

In trephining for depressed fractures of the skull, always select the *smallest* trephine, since the only object of its use is to make such an opening as will permit the introduction of an elevator. If you desire to elevate and remove comminuted pieces, apply the crown of the trephine upon uninjured bone adjoining and overlapping the *least* depressed portion of the depressed fragments. It is much easier to remove the fragments when the opening is thus made, than when the trephine is applied at the side of the most depressed portion of the fracture.—*Polyclinic.*—*Analectic.*

Resection of the Knee.

Mensing has collected eighty cases of total and three of partial resection of the knee, operated upon at Kiel, and nine operations of removal of a wedge-shaped piece of bone for rectangular anchylosis. Forty eight of these (52.01 per cent.) were discharged well. The average shortening was two and one-half centimeters, and flexion only occurred in two cases; two had good motion; one only slight motion. From thirty-two of these later information was obtained, and in three cases a moderate flexion had taken place; in two a relapse had occurred, followed in one case by a second resection, and in another by amputation.

In thirty-four patients the excision was not perfectly successful (that is, thirty-seven per cent.), fourteen undergoing a subsequent amputation, and twenty having an unhealed sinus at the time the patients left the hospital. Of these twenty the ultimate results of thirteen were obtained: in ten cicatrization took place; three died. Of the fourteen secondary amputations, ten recovered, and two died.

Ten patients who underwent excision at the clinic died recently from the operation, five of pyemia one of Bright's disease, one of general tuberculosis, two of exhaustion, one of hemophilia.

These operations were performed in the years from 1857 to 1883, and the time is divided by the writer into three epochs: First, before the introduction of Listerism and Esmarch's bloodless method; Second, after these were introduced; Third, after the introduction of Neuber's permanent dressing. The mortality in the first period in twenty-one cases was 33.03 per cent.; in the second period, twenty-three cases, was 8.7 per cent.; and in the third period, forty-eight cases, two per cent. The length of time required for healing in the first two periods averaged 129 days; in the third period eighty-nine days.— *Boston Med. and Surg. Journal.*

Malignant Disease of the Testicle Tapped for Hydrocele.

Dr. John B. Roberts presented the following report at a recent meeting of the Philadelphia Pathological Society: This case is clinically interesting because it resembled a hydrocele, and misled me, as well as other surgeons who had previously seen it. When the man came to me, I found a large oval swelling of left side of scrotum, which he gave me to understand had existed for two years. The tumor, for six or eight inches long in the vertical dissection, had a sharply defined upper limit, as does hydrocele of the vaginal tunic, and was indistinctly elastic, as a tense hydrocele. The veins on the surface, however, were well marked, and it looked at the lower part a little as if the subcutaneous tissue was about to suppurate. It was this which gave rise to the pain which induced him to seek medical advice at this time, for he had previously postponed having another surgeon draw off the yellow water which he had been told was in it. I did not at that time try to transmit light through the supposed hydrocele, because it is very often a fallacious test. At least, absence of light transmission does not negative the existence of hydrocele. I accordingly thrust a trocar into it and drew about six fluid ounces of pure coagulable blood through the canula. Reinserting the trocar, I pushed it in various directions, but met only solid tissue and no blood, except when it was pushed in the direction originally taken, then blood flowed in a quite free stream. No marked reaction followed, but this pain and tendency to suppuration was removed. Two weeks later I removed the mass by enucleation, and then found a solid tumor here presented, which is the enlarged and infiltrated testicle. The patient now says that fifteen years ago, when about eighteen years of age, the testicle or scrotum began to grow larger. He is now rapidly convalescing.

Steam After Tracheotomy Operations.

How persistent humanity is in introducing complications in almost every attempt to accomplish any plans which may be undertaken. And even if fortuitous circumstances blend so happily that an individual worker presents the question from the first in the most simple and practical manner, the desire for complication and modification contorts the simplicity of the device and shrouds it with a paraphernalia corresponding to the conventionalities of society as compared with primitive manners. In the after treatment of tracheotomy, carbolic acid, eucalyptol, lime-water, carbonate of soda, etc., have been used, and now Dr. G. W. Gay, in giving the result of his experience, in the Bost. Med. and Surg. Jour., says :

"Next to nourishment, I consider steam to be the most important part of the treatment. It is conducted from the radiator through a rubber tube, and directed upon the neck of the patient. The vapor is warm, moist and does not condense in sufficient quantity to saturate the clothing. Atomized or medicated liquids are not used at present. Lime-water often produced a disagreeable erythema of the face, and thinking that possibly it might act as an irritant to the air passages, pure steam was substituted, and so far it seems to act as favorably as did any of the sprays formerly in vogue.

In all cases the patient received steam half the time, while to the more serious it was constantly supplied. The very great benefit derived from breathing the warm vapor was demonstrated beyond a doubt in many instances. Under its use the secretion would soften, the respiration become easier, the child would become quiet, and fall asleep. The importance of a constant and generous supply of steam cannot be overestimated in this affection.

It would seem as though with a little child's complicated organism with a diphtheritic or croupous affection added and superimposed tracheotomy, that any further complication in the way of drugs should be reduced to a minimum. So it should, only we require to be reminded of it repeatedly.— *Weekly Med. Review.*

Treatment of Acute Abscess.

In many instances of the ordinary acute abscess I have recently had excellent results in treating them for immediate cure. The following example illustrates the course pursued :

A man had an abscess on the external part of the thigh, resulting from a severe fall. There had been a high grade of inflammation, much suffering, and a temperature of 103°. At the time of the operation the temperature was 101°. There was fluctuation, but pus was not very near the surface. The treatment was as follows :

When the patient was fully under the influence of the anesthetic, the parts were thoroughly washed with soap and water and a flesh brush, and then with a douche of corrosive sublimate solution 1 to 500. Then the abscess was opened with a knife, treated with a carbolic solution 1 to 30, the opening being of a size to admit the nozzle of a Davidson syringe. The depth of the abscess cavity was two inches. The pus was forced out by pressure, and when it ceased to flow the nozzle of the syringe, well disinfected, was introduced and the edges of the wound held firmly around it. The cavity was then distended to its fullest capacity, with corrosive sublimate solution 1 to 5,000, the amount of water injected being one pint. Withdrawing the syringe tube, the solution was forced out, with strong and gentle pressure. This injection and hyperdistension was repeated three times, when the water flowed away quite undiscolored. An incision was then made down to the cavity of the abscess, its full length, the incision being six inches long. With tenacula the edges of the wound were held apart, and the entire cavity exposed. During this part of the operation the irrigation with the corrosive sublimate solution, 1 to 2,000, was continued. The internal surface of the abscess was covered with large granulations and shreds and broken down connective tissue.

The process of cleansing the wound was next begun with disinfected hands and instruments. All the shreds of tissue were carefully dissected away, and the granulations were gently scraped off with the curette until a perfectly clean surface was everywhere apparent. Several small vessels were ligated with carbolized ligatures, and the whole surface of the cavity thoroughly irrigated. The wound was closed with the interrupted suture, except at the lower extremity where a small opening was left for drainage, over which was placed a disinfected sponge to absorb the discharge. The external wound and adjacent skin were sprinkled with iodoform; folds of gauze, between which iodoform was sprinkled, were applied around the limb from below the knee to the hip; over these layers a dressing of borated cotton was wrapped about the leg and thigh, and over this was applied a light plaster of Paris dressing, which completed the operation.

On the following day the temperature had fallen to normal, and did not rise again to 100°: the pain entirely ceased; the appetite returned: sleep was sound and undisturbed. The patient stated that from his recovery from the anæsthetic he felt entirely well. The dressing was removed on the eighth day. The wound was entirely closed, and though there was some thickening of the tissue involved by the injury there was no tenderness. He could walk without pain or inconvenience, and there was a rapid subsidence of the swelling of the part.

It is safe to estimate that this man saved at least a month in time by the operation. What was saved in pain, impaired health, and possible dangerous sequelæ, can not be estimated. I have operated for acute abscesses of the neck, back, groin, etc., in a similar manner, and have not failed of rapid and complete recovery without further symptoms.

This operation may extend to furuncles and carbuncles when they have a local origin. The exciting cause is some small necrosed tissue. If this irritant is early and thoroughly removed, and the parts rendered aseptic, the disease will be arrested. Carbuncle of the face, the so-called malignant pustule, has long been treated, and generally the disease is arrested by early incision, filling the wound with spirits of turpentine. The value of this treatment was supposed to lie in the local suppuration induced, but it is more probable that the turpentine acted as an antiseptic. If the surgeon would go a step further, and not only make a free incision through the inflamed tissues, but carefully scrape off, as far as possible, all diseased structures, and render aseptic the surface of the wound by remedies now to be found so efficient, the disease could doubtless be arrested in its incipient stage.

We are evidently on the eve of the adoption of measures for the *prevention* of this formation of pus in a great number of cases where hitherto the practice has been to encourage suppuration as the proper method of cure. Indeed, there is little doubt that the time is at hand when the very presence of pus in the practice of surgery will be evidence of the inefficient use of remedial measures.—*The Æsculapian.*

The Nature and Treatment of Scrofula, from the Standpoint of Recent Investigations Concerning the Influence of Bacilli.

Albrecht defines scrofula, in the terms of Baginsky, as an excessive vulnerability of all the tissues, especially the skin, the mucous membranes, and the general lymphatic system. This peculiarity is combined with an inaptitude for rapid and complete regeneration, from which result the multiplicity and protracted duration of the lesions belonging to the disease. It is not yet settled to what extent the cell life *per se*, or changes in the blood and lymph, operate in this process. Even the question as to the influence of an infectious material cannot be decisively answered, not even after the experimental efforts which have been made with respect to the closely allied process of tuberculosis. After reviewing briefly the investigations (or rather the results of those investigations) of various mycologists with reference to the bacillus of tuberculosis, the author remarks that the decisive method of recognizing the tuberculous character of a substance has been revealed in Koch's discovery. In the further development of this method is to be sought the key to the recognition of the nature of the products of scrofula. Among the recent investigations which bear upon this point the following may be mentioned: Cohnheim and Salomonsen conclude that fungous arthritis, cheesy degeneration of the glands, and cheesy pneumonia are to be regarded as tuberculous in their nature; Schuller observed that tuberculous affections in joints occur after inoculation with cheesy material from scrofulous glands; Kiener and Poulet uniformly obtained general tuberculosis after inoculation with scrofulous material. Similar testimony is borne by other investigators, whose results are published by the author, who asks the pointed question, Will scrofula develop into tuberculosis? The answer to this question is, that while this may be possible, the conceptions of the two conditions must remain distinct. He considers it certain, however, that scrofula furnishes the most favorable foundation for the development of tuberculosis. Two recommendations are made, the utility of which is undeniable: first, that means should be taken to anticipate and prevent scrofula; second, in individuals in whom it already exists, to use such means that tuberculosis cannot result. One means of prevention is to be found in the substitution, in all cases, of animal vaccine for vaccination purposes, in the place of the arm to arm method. Another is the substitution of the bottle for the breast milk in all cases in which the mother or wet nurse is of a scrofulous diathesis. A third is to subject syphilitic parents to a suitable course of antisyphilitic treatment, since the children of such parents, if they escape syphilitic infection, often develop scrofula. In cases in which scrofula already exists, the the plain indications are abundance of pure air and sunlight, cleanliness as to the person, the clothes, and the dwelling apartments, and especially the substitution of nitrogenous for starchy food. Among the former may be mentioned cod-liver oil and various forms of peptone.—*Archives of Ped. from Arch. f. Kinderheilk.*

Examination per Rectum in Coxitis.

This method of examination is recommended by Corin in inflammatory conditions of the hip-joint, as well as of the pelvic bones, as a means of especial value in the period of childhood. Either the dorsal or the knee-elbow position may be chosen, the most important structures in and about the pelvis being easily accessible to the examining finger. The author recommends, however, the dorsal position when the right hip-joint is diseased, and the knee-elbow position when the disease is in the left side. [It seems hardly necessary to direct, as the author does, that the examining finger should be well greased, and slowly introduced into the rectum.] The disengaged hand may be placed upon the abdomen, and may assist the examining finger in confirming its discoveries. Several cases of acetabular disease have been diagnosticated by the author by this means. His conclusion is that all cases of coxitis should be investigated per rectum, but especially those in which resection is to be performed.—*Archives of Pediatrics.*

The Medical Chronicle.

A Monthly Journal for the Practitioner.

GEORGE H. ROHÉ, M. D., Editor.

☞ It is requested that all literary and business communications, books for review, exchanges, etc., be addressed to, and all checks, drafts and post office orders drawn to the order of
Dr. GEORGE H. ROHÉ,
Cor. Greene & Mulberry Sts., - Balto., Md

BALTIMORE, JULY, 1884.

EDITORIAL.

The Administration of Ether by the Rectum.

When, a month or two since, it was announced in some of our great metropolitan weeklies that Monsieur Molliére, of Lyons, had successfully practiced, and recommended the administration of ether by the rectum for the purpose of producing anesthesia, we were disposed to look upon the whole matter as a joke. In the first place, it seemed to us very absurd and irrational that an organ, through which certain vapors and gases, often of unpleasant odor, found their way out of the body, should be used for the purpose of introducing irritant and unpleasant vapors into the body. Especially unscientific did it seem to us that an agent, whose principal effect is upon the nervous centres should be conveyed into the organism at a point as far distant as possible from those centres. Secondly, the name of our Gallic confrére had a very suspicious sound to us. We recalled the fact, which we had learned during our literary studies, that a certain M. Moliére, who also lived in Lyons, somewhere about the middle of the seventeenth century, gained much reputation as a wit by ridiculing the doctors of those days. Can it be, we thought, that the contemporaneous M. Molliére is trying to make game of the learned profession of our own day? In doubt about the matter, we decided to await events, and make no premature announcement in our columns of the new use to which the rectum of man had been put by our Lyonnaise confréie.

The young men who practice surgery in some of the hospitals of New York and other cities took the announcement in all seriousness, however, and forthwith began pumping ether vapor—perhaps sometimes also liquid ether—into the lower bowels of the poor sufferers, whom an inscrutable Providence allows to fall into their hands. It reminded us of the cruelty of the small boy, who, inserting a straw into the rectum of a frog, blows him up, and then throwing him into the water, gleefully watches his ineffectual struggles to reach the bottom. The unfavorable and in one case even fatal results that have already followed these senseless experiments in the hands of some New York surgeons, should warn others from imitating them. The proper way to administer ether vapor is by the respiratory passages. With a proper knowledge of the physiological effects of the anesthetic, and a little ordinary gumption, any physician should be able to anesthetize a patient quickly, safely and completely with pure ether, used in the usual way. Hastily discarding tried and reliable remedies and methods for novel and uncertain ones, is often followed by repentance at leisure.

We advise our readers to stick to the old plan of giving ether. It is cleaner, safer and more efficient.

The American Public Health Association.

The next annual meeting of the American Public Health Association will be held in St. Louis, October 14—17 inclusive. The following matters of interest will be discussed: Hygiene of the Habitations of the Poor; Hygiene of Occupations; School Hygiene; Adulteration of Food; Water Pollution; Disposal of

Sewage by Irrigation or Chemical Action; The Observable Effect upon the Public Health of Official Sanitary Supervision; The Work of Municipal and State Boards of Health.

From the extensive arrangements being made by the local committee, it is believed that this will be the largest and one of the most interesting meetings the association has ever held. Persons desiring to read papers before the association upon any of the subjects above mentioned, are requested to notify the Secretary, Dr. Irving A. Watson, Concord, N. H., at once, and to furnish him an abstract of the paper not later than September 1st. Active and associate members have equal privileges in the presentation and discussion of papers.

CURRENT LITERATURE.

Health Hints for Travelers. By Jno. C. Sundberg, M. D. Philadelphia, D. G. Brinton, 1884.

In this little manual, Dr. Sundberg, who is the most restless rover of our acquaintance, gives a number of valuable hints to all who travel for business, health, or pleasure. Dr. Sundberg's advice is of that practical character which indicates its origin in personal experience. Whether in the jungles of India, on the snow-clad shores of Norway, in the saloon of a trans-atlantic steamer, in a parlor car, on horse-back, or on foot, he always knows the proper thing to do, and tells how to do it in the fewest possible words. Everyone, no matter how extensive his experience, can learn something from this little book. We can cordially recommend it as one of the most valuable books of the year.

Sexual Neurasthenia. Its hygiene, causes, symptoms, and treatment, with a chapter on Diet for the Nervous. By George M. Beard, A. M., M. D., etc. Edited from the Author's Posthumous Manuscript by A. D. Rockwell, A. M., M. D., Fellow of the Academy of Medicine, etc. New York, E. B. Treat, 1884, pp. 270.

The late Dr. George M. Beard was a prolific and aggressive writer upon neurological topics. In this posthumous essay, which is full of his peculiarities of thought and expression, he has stated at length his views upon the cause and treatment of a class of cases familiar to every medical man under various names, and which he classes together under the designation "Sexual Neurasthenia." The book is interesting as the last production of a man of striking force, but adds little to the common stock of knowledge upon the subject.

FLOTSAM.

THE Massachusetts Medical Society has at last decided to admit women to membership.

THE International Congress of Hygiene will hold its sessions at the Hague, August 21 to 27. A number of very important papers and reports are announced. Dr. Stephen Smith, of New York, will deliver an address on *the Maritime Sanitary Service of the United States*.

THOSE enterprising Western publishers, Messrs. J. H. Chambers & Co., of St. Louis, send us the *American Journal of Ophthalmology*, edited by Dr. Adolph Alt, an eminent specialist that city. Among the collaborators we find the names of Drs. Samuel Theopald, of Baltimore, G. Strawbridge, of Philadelphia, F. B. Loring, of Washington, F. C. Hotz, of Chicago, E. Gruening, of New York, O. F. Wadsworth, of Boston, and others of note in the specialty. This is the only American monthly journal devoted to ophthalmology, and from the contents of the number before us as we write, we regard it as worthy of the active support of the profession. The subscription price is $2.50 per year.

TRANSACTIONS

OF THE

AMERICAN

Dermatological Association,

AT THE

SEVENTH ANNUAL MEETING,

HELD AT

LAKE GEORGE N. Y., AUG. 29, 30 and 31, 1883.

OFFICIAL REPORT OF THE PROCEEDINGS BY THE SECRETARY,

Dr. ARTHUR VAN HARLINGEN.

BALTIMORE:
PRESS OF THOMAS & EVANS.
1883.

TABLE OF CONTENTS.

PAGE.

List of Officers for the Year 1882-3.	4
The Treatment of Acne...Dr. H. G. Piffard,	5
General Exfoliative Dermatitis...Dr. J. E. Graham,	8
Impetigo Contagiosa...Dr. H. C. Stelwagon,	12
A Case of Multiple Cachectic Ulceration...Dr. I. E. Atkinson,	14
A Trip to Tracadie...Dr. George H. Fox,	16
Experiments in the Use of Naphtol...Dr. A. Van Harlingen,	18
Paget's Disease, or Malignant Papillary Dermatitis...Dr. S. Sherwell,	19
The Pathogenesis of Drug Eruptions...Dr. P. A. Morrow,	21
Polymorphous Changes Observed in Tubercular Syphilide, Dr. R. W. Taylor,	22
Pseudo-Psoriasis of the Palms...Dr. S. Sherwell,	24
Psoriasis of the Palms...Dr. W. Alexander,	25
A Study of the Coincidence of Syphilitic and Non-Syphilitic Affections of he Skin...Dr. J. N. Hyde,	26
Peculiar Appearance of the Initial Lesion of Syphilis at its Beginning, Dr. R. W. Taylor...	28
Value of a Lotion of Sulphide of Zinc in the Treatment of Lupus Erythematosus...Dr. L. A. Duhring,	29
Report of a Case of Ainhum with Microscopic Examination, Dr. L. A. Duhring,	31
Papillary Disease of the Skin...Dr. W. A. Hardaway,	32
Case of Lymphangioma Cutis...Dr. J. E. Graham,	33
List of Publications and Writings of Members of the Association, between July, 1882 and July, 1883...	35
Report of the Committee on Statistics, Drs. E. Wigglesworth and Jas. C. White.	38
List of Officers for the Year 1883-4...	49

OFFICERS OF THE ASSOCIATION

FOR 1882-3.

PRESIDENT,

Dr. R. W. TAYLOR, New York.

VICE-PRESIDENTS,

Dr. I. E. ATKINSON, Baltimore.

Dr. A. R. ROBINSON, New York.

SECRETARY,

Dr. ARTHUR VAN HARLINGEN, Philadelphia.

TREASURER,

Dr. GEORGE H. ROHÉ, Baltimore.

AMERICAN DERMATOLOGICAL ASSOCIATION.

SEVENTH ANNUAL MEETING,

HELD AT LAKE GEORGE, N. Y.,

AUGUST 29, 30 AND 31, 1883.

FIRST DAY.—Morning Session.

The President, Dr. R. W. Taylor, in a short address, extended a hearty welcome to all the members assembled.

The first paper was read by Dr. H. G. Piffard, of New York, entitled:

THE TREATMENT OF ACNE.

The writer referred to possible causes of acne in gastric, intestinal, uterine disorders, and the necessity of removing such causes. In the treatment of acute acne vulgaris, he recommended the internal use of calcium sulphide, in small doses. Bromide of arsenic in doses of $\frac{1}{100}$ to $\frac{1}{30}$ of a grain was also spoken of as valuable. This is to be administered in alcoholic solution, one per cent. strength.

As to the treatment of the acute papule it should consist in the application of water as hot as can be borne. If there are any pustules they should be punctured.

Soothing applications, ointments of belladonna and stramonium were advised, especially the latter, in the form of the fluid extract made from fresh leaves gathered in the fall, the base of the ointment being benzoated lard or oxide of zinc otntment. In the subacute form the internal treatment may consist in the administration of calcium sulphide—pushed until additional lesions appear, when it should be stopped. Ergot was also of great service.

Complications. . The most troublesome spoken of was comedones, but this yields to but one method of treatment—mechanical—either pressure with the finger-nails or with a key ; or, better with an instrument specially devised for the purpose.

Acne indurata may be regarded as an aggravated form of acne vulgaris. The treatment is generally the same as the latter. In acne indurata striking effects from ergot have been seen.

DISCUSSION.

Dr. Atkinson said that he had failed to get any good results from the use of calcium sulphide. Ergot he had also used and failed to see any benefit follow. The only good results had in his experience followed local applications and attention to any constitutional disturbance.

Dr. VanHarlingen recommended for the treatment of comedones a paste composed of glycerine 3 parts, vinegar 2 parts, and kaolin 4 parts. This has been suggested by Unna, and in most cases seems to be of decided value.

Dr. Alexander had used calcium sulphide in many cases and found it to do good in the pustular variety. In a case of leprosy then under his care, calcium sulphide had no effect in preventing suppuration. In many cases of acne, ergot seemed to diminish the redness, which, however, returned as soon as the remedy was discontinued.

Dr. Sherwell said that he had not had much experience with calcium sulphide, having had sufficiently good results from the use of external applications. In the acute pustular form in the female, where he had noticed exacerbations at the menstrual period, and in the congestive variety he noticed some benefit following the use of oxytocics. He thought he had also some good results with ergot in the male.

Dr. Rohé claimed that there were many conditions that may give rise to dysmenorrhœa and other uterine troubles, which may have connection with cutaneous eruptions, and he could not conceive how one remedy could control them all.

Dr. Sherwell claimed that dysmenorrhœa is generally regarded by authorities as a functional disturbance, but his reasons for the use of ergot were purely empirical. There may be some passive hyperenia of the mucous membrane of the uterus, which reflexly causes the cutaneous eruption, analogous to urticaria following disturbances of the intestinal circulation. He believed the process was reflex, and gave the remedy on empirical grounds, and with good results.

Dr. Piffard claimed that the beneficial results obtained in the treatment of acne did not depend upon the special action of any particular medicinal agent, but, rather upon the amount of irritation an agent, whether given internally or applied externally, was able to create in the lesions.

Dr. Graham asked what the action of calcium sulphide was?

Dr. Piffard answered that it breaks down tissue.

Dr. Graham was inclined to think that it had a disinfectant action.

Dr. Piffard spoke of a case which he brought before the New York Dermatological Association. It was the worst case he ever had seen. There was uterine disorder for which he placed the patient under the charge of a gynecologist. For the treatment of the cutaneous eruption he sent her to Dr. Taylor, who gave her ergot internally, and externally ordered mercurial ointment. After a time she returned to him much improved. He kept up the same treatment, the gynecologist also keeping up the use of pessary, etc., and she got well. The external treatment was kept up only for a short time. The three factors of treatment were: first, external treatment for a short time; second, internal treatment for a long time; third, treatment of the uterine trouble.

Dr. Taylor thought that the point of interest was the more or less comparative importance of local and of constitutional treatment. He thought that the local treatment was of paramount importance and the internal treatment subsidiary. In regard to the relation of uterine disorders to acne, he had nothing to say; the connection between some of these disorders and those of the skin was recognized by everybody. He spoke of other constitutional conditions which stand in some relation to cutaneous disorders. He was unsettled in his opinion regarding the actual relation of these uterine troubles. In the treatment of acne he places great reliance on the use of alkaline salts and diuretics, Rochelle salts one to two drachms, acetate of potash, thirty grains, three times a day in a wine glass of water. In indurated acne he punctures and applies acid nitrate of mercury, one part, to eight of water, to each lesion, immediately afterwards making applications of hot water.

Where there was also rosacea, he had used the following with marked benefit: Chrysarobin one-half drachm to one ounce flexible collodion. This is to be pencilled over the patches. It has the advantage of not coloring the surrounding skin as is the case when chrysarobin is used alone. It necessitates the seclusion of the patient, but it is a successful mode of treatment. As for the internal treatment of indurated acne he had seen good results follow the use of Donovan's solution, pushed to twelve drops three times a day. He has never seen ergot cure a case. It has no effect on the infiltration, it simply relieves hyperæmia.

In the external treatment he also wished to add the mercurial ointment one-half drachm, cosmoline one ounce, and especially the iodide of zinc, five to thirty grains to the ounce of vaseline.

Dr. Stelwagon had seen good results follow the use of a lotion composed of sulphate of zinc, sulphuret of potash, each one drachm to four ounces of water.

Drs. Sherwell and Taylor endorsed the value of the lotion just mentioned.

A paper was then read by Dr. J. E. Graham, of Toronto, entitled:

GENERAL EXFOLIATIVE DERMATITIS.

The writer reported thirty-four cases, eleven terminating fatally, ten recovering entirely, and in the rest the result was not known. In eight cases the disease was acute, recovery taking place in a few weeks, while in twenty-five it was chronic. Four cases came under his own observation; of these, two were acute and two chronic.

He thought that cases of general exfoliative dermatitis were often mistaken for scarlet fever. The special characteristics of the disease were as follows:

1. General hyperemia.
2. General exfoliation of the epidermis.
3. Constitutional symptoms which may end fatally.

The writer agreed with Drs. Baxter and Jamieson that the name, general exfoliative dermatitis, may embrace those cases described under the names pityriasis rubra and pemphigus foliaceus.

Two principal subdivisions may be made—acute and chronic; of the latter there may be two varieties: 1st. Those cases attended with hyperæmia and exfoliation, which may be called dermatitis exfoliativa rubra. 2d. Those cases where exudation and formation of bullæ precedes the exfoliation which may be called dermatitis bullosa et exfoliativa: the former variety including pityriasis rubra, the latter pemphigus foliaceus.

DISCUSSION.

Dr. Hardaway said he had seen one typical case of pityriasis rubra. It was a miner, who insisted that he shed a bandbox full of scales in twenty-four hours, and ascribed the disease to exposure to the alternating hot and cold atmosphere of the mine. There was no moisture. The skin was deeply red from venous congestion. The treatment adopted was that proposed by Dr. Jamieson in the *Edinburgh Medical Journal*. Internally tincture of the chloride of iron, and locally large quantities of cosmoline. Arsenic was given for months without benefit. He thought the iron had done some good. He could report one case of acute exfoliative dermatitis. The patient was a young lady, who recovered in one month, and there was no recurrence; also, a case of a child seven months old.

Another case, which came under his notice, was that of a young lady belonging to a neurotic family. The peculiar feature of the case was after subsidence of the acute attack, the frequent occurrence of hyperæmic spots varying in size from a silver dollar to the palm of a hand. These spots were exceedingly hot, there was no exfoliation and the process had been going on for seven years.

Dr. VanHarlingen thought the speaker had described two varieties of disease, one having the symptoms of pityriasis rubra, the other of extensive exfoliation over larger surfaces, in which the cast of a hand may be shed like a glove. The latter form he thought may sometimes be acute, sometimes chronic.

Dr. Atkinson claimed that it is improper to describe a distinct disease under the name of general exfoliative dermatitis. He spoke of many cases which may be distinctly eczematous in character. Cases of universal eczema with moisture and scaling, also of the many eruptions due to medicinal agents, quinine, etc., have undoubtedly been described under this title. Cases supposed to be recurrent scarlet fever have been found to be due to small doses of quinine. At first there is an erythema, and finally scaling. All these processes may, he thought, be grouped under the head of general exfoliative dermatitis, they being also symptomatic and probably trophoneuroses.

Dr. Morrow thought that the disease is essentially a trophoneurosis, and he had seen excellent results from the use of arsenic.

Dr. Sherwell did think the name was too comprehensive—in that it includes a disease so classically distinct in symptoms, objective and subjective, as pemphigus foliaceous. The name, general exfoliative dermatitis might cover the first variety as mentioned by Dr. Graham.

Dr. Piffard claimed that three distinct diseases had been included under this name—pemphigus foliaceous, pityriasis rubra, and dermatitis exfoliativa. He thought it may sometimes be difficult to differentiate, but there are differences, and they must be recognized.

Dr. Graham was inclined to regard the disease as a trophoneurosis as the general eruption was preceded, in one of the cases presented, by herpes, which is of nervous origin. He thought it was an unsettled question whether it is strictly correct to include pemphigus foliaceous under this head, but he thought it had many features in common with general exfoliative dermatitis. The fact that there is sometimes little and sometimes much fluid exudation, bears little upon the question, according to him, as in pleuritis sicca there is little exudation, yet it is a pleuritis.

Dr. Taylor remarked that there was evidently a necessity for further study and discrimination on this subject. He wished to call attention to two cases, the photographs of which were passed around:

Case I.—A lady, forty-four years of age, a widow, having one child. She was of poor fibre, thin, and, having been born and having lived in Louisville, she suffered from malaria for years, for which she had taken quinine. She was said to have had fifteen attacks of scarlet fever of varying intensity. Having given her fair doses of quinine, after twenty-four hours he found that, after twenty grains had been taken, the patient had a chill. The surface of the body was hot, and the seat of an erythematous eruption much like scarlet fever. There was no sore throat. There was thickening of the palms and soles. Exfoliation followed, in which casts of the hands and feet were shed. He advised her to discontinue the use of quinine. A year later, however, she took some elixir calisaya, which brought out the rash. Then following the advice of a physician, she took some preparation of gentian, which, undoubtedly, contained quinine, and this was followed by the eruption. Five years after her first visit she presented herself again, and cinchonine was prescribed; this also was followed by the eruption, when she went into St. Francis' Hospital. Altogether she had fifteen attacks.

Case II. This was also seen by Drs. Fox, Sherwell, Bronson, Alexander and Morrow. It was under his observation five months, the patient receiving only tonic treatment, so that the cutaneous lesions were allowed to run their course without interruption. The patient was a boy nineteen years of age, with bad family history, lung disease having caused the death of many relatives. In January last he contracted a sore on his penis, and gonorrhœa followed by epididymitis and urethral fistulæ. About two months ago he noticed a slight scaliness on his wrists, which soon extended to his face and chest. The skin felt hard and dry but did not itch. The scaliness soon spread over the whole body. Over the abdomen and chest were the remains of what seemed to be a syphilitic eruption, in the form of flattened tubercles and papules, of a much darker color than the skin in general. The hair of the head was very scanty and the scalp was covered with scales. The patient was much emaciated and presented a marked anæmic appearance, the whole body, especially the abdomen and chest, covered with scales usually of large size, which easily fell off, leaving the skin everywhere decidedly pigmented. The lunulæ of the nails were also affected, being wrinkled and thicker than natural. The patient stated that his bed usually contained a large quantity of scales after he had been in it for some time. The skin was but little thickened and there was not much pruritus, except in the axillæ. There was leucoplakia of the buccal mucous membrane and of the tongue, also fissures at the angles of the mouth. The glandular enlargement was also marked.

These lesions were not of a syphilitic nature. Glandular enlargement is no proof of syphilis, the same existing in eczema and exfoliative dermatitis. It might possibly be some profound change accompanying the syphilitic papule. The subcutaneous tissue was not infiltrated, the lesion being only in the epidermis, which was of a dirty brown color and in a state of farinaceous desquamation. The patient was not subjected to antisyphilitic treatment, the treatment adopted was only dietetic and tonic. The disease was general, but there were some healthy spots on the back and legs. In some places the skin presented an appearance very much like ichthyosis nigra.

(The case is reported in the *Journal of Cutaneous and Venereal Diseases*, Vol. 1, No. 10.)

Dr. Alexander asked whether any good result had followed the use of chrysarobin?

Dr. Taylor answered, "none."

Dr. Piffard suggested the use of jaborandi, one drachm of the fluid extract daily, which had been used by him in one case with decided benefit. He had seen it work wonders in ichthyosis. It should, however, be used with caution, as some individuals will not bear it.

Dr. Fox recommended chaulmoogra oil. Where there is redness and thickening of the skin as in leprosy and other diseases, it may prove of value. He thought it might be used internally together with external inunction.

Dr. H. W. Stelwagon, of Philadelphia, read a paper on

IMPETIGO CONTAGIOSA,

In which he set forth the various theories held by different authorities respecting the disease. From an investigation and thorough examination of the subject, he came to the following conclusions:

1. That impetigo contagiosa is a separate and distinct disease.
2. That is not parasitic.
3. That it has no relation whatever to vaccination.
4. That it is an acute contagious, systemic disease, with cutaneous manifestations, having a definite course and due to a specific virus. The first three conclusions were, he thought, well founded; the fourth was for the present, merely suggestive.

DISCUSSION.

Dr. Hardaway considered it an independent disease, on account of its contagiousness, its other clinical features, and as the author of the paper says, on account of its appearing in epidemics. He had not seen any cases for three or four years. The fact that it occurs in epidemics, was, in his opinion, a strong argument for its independent nature.

Dr. Atkinson felt uncertain about the true character of this disease. In warm weather there seems to be some contagious element in many forms of pustular eruptions.

Dr. Rohé's experience was similar to that of Dr. Hardaway, in that he had not seen any cases for two years. That the pus of contagious impetigo is inoculable he felt convinced, having performed experiments to that effect upon himself. He thought it was also inoculable on healthy individuals, successive generations of pustules becoming weaker. He had found no fungus. He furthermore did not believe that the disease had any relation with vaccinia.

Dr. Fox sustained the question of its inoculability, not dependent upon the character of the soil, but upon the pus. He did not believe it had any connection with vaccination, although one case which he could recall would seem to indicate this. A physician after vaccinating a child put the lancet in his pocket, and from putting his hand in this pocket, and pricking his finger with the lancet, he received a typical vesico-pustular eruption.

Where the lesions already exist pediculosis will cause it to spread by scratching, rupturing vesicles and conveying the contagious element by the nails.

Dr. Graham said he had seen several cases and was inclined to agree with the theory of Dr. Stelwagon.

Dr. Piffard thought that the disease could not be recognized in the porrigo of Willan, but that Naylor and Tilbury Fox had described the disease as we know it to-day. In regard to its connection with vaccination he had seen a series of cases in a certain family, start after vaccination. He thought it of a parasitic nature, that the fungi are to be found in the crust, and that these are of different kinds. He had found a certain special kind, and others which he regarded as accidental. The special fungus, he thought, was the same as that found in vaccinia and not described in connection with any other disease. He asked what method Dr. Stelwagon employed to render the fungi visible.

Dr. Stelwagon used solution of caustic potassa.

Dr. Piffard used the same, also a solution of caustic soda. He thought it was not a self limited disease but might continue several months. He thought that one point in favor of its parasitic nature is the fact that a prompt cure follows the use of a parasiticide.

Dr. Taylor did not think the disease was systemic; as proof, he called attention to the fact that it begins locally, about the face; he had seen sixty cases in one epidemic, and in every case the trouble commenced about the nails or face. In regard to the prodromal symptoms he noticed that the younger the child, the more marked are these symptoms, yet altogether indefinite, and in many cases by close examination they may be excluded. It spreads, he thought, by immediate contagion, and there was one case which he could recall, that of a mother, who, after four weeks exposure to the disease affecting her child, had about the nails vesico-pustules, which were soon transmitted to the parts about the genitals. He thought that the disease first makes its appearance about the mouth and asked whether any one present had seen it otherwise?

Several members had seen it elsewhere.

Dr. Taylor held that it always appears on those parts accessible to the hands. He believed it begins from pus which lodges on the skin. He remembered inoculating a physician, on whom it appeared three days after inoculation.

Dr. Stelwagon asserted that he had seen the disease develop in four or five children in the same family simultaneously.

Dr. Taylor thought that some persons although exposed to the infection, escape.

Dr. Fox offered an objection to the statement made by Dr. Piffard, that the disease is so promptly cured by means of a parasiticide. He had had a number of cases where the cure was not so easily effected.

Dr. Stelwagon expressed the same opinion.

Dr. Piffard held that his treatment cures every lesion, but it may not prevent other lesions from coming out.

Dr. Stelwagon thought that the disease is systemic, in the nature of varicella, variola, etc. He was not fully satisfied, and only advanced it in his paper as a theory. He thought that many cases had been described under acute contagious pemphigus, which were undoubtedly contagious impetigo. He had never seen pediculosis produce impetigo contagiosa. In about 500 microscopic examinations, he found the fungus of Piffard ten times, that of Kaposi three times.

Dr. Hardaway said he had vaccinated many thousands, but had never seen impetigo contagiosa follow.

FIRST DAY.—Evening Session.

A paper on:

A CASE OF MULTIPLE CACHECTIC ULCERATION,

Was read by Dr. I. E. Atkinson, of Baltimore.

A child 28 months old, good personal and family history. Small papules and vesicles appeared upon the dorsal surfaces of the fingers and toes—rapidly followed by deep ulcerations with copious discharge. Ulceration extended upon hands and feet; diarrhœa set in; the patient became weak; later small ulcers appeared on the mucous membrane of cheek, tongue, gums, left angle of mouth, extending rapidly half-way to the ear and nearly to the eye. Ulcers soon formed upon the leg; all the lesions there remained inactive about six weeks; then new lesions appeared on the right fore-finger at the second phalanx. The process caused the tissues literally to melt away so that by the third day the two terminal phalanges were laid bare, separated from their attachment and thrown off. Similar ulcers formed upon the toes and right thumb, but did not advance with rapidity. At end of eighth day the ulcers were dry, pale, covered with membrane-like deposit; patient now very weak; could not stand. Under appropriate treatment got well—lesions left scars.

The case presented close similarity with the affection first described by Simon as "multiple cachectic gangrene." In a case described by Bœck, micrococci of ordinary character were found in the discharges, but were not considered as of etiological importance. For the present it is better to consider the affection as a neurosis, and to adopt provisionally the theory of Weiss, according to which the vaso-motor centre is readily thrown into a condition of hypertonus; that the importance of the symptoms depends upon the dignity of the parts in which the vascular spasm is developed. Contraction of the cutaneous arteries will produce a bloodless condition of the skin. By venous spasm is produced local cyanosis. Similarly by vascular spasm of those portions of the posterior columns standing in functional relation with the skin, will be produced nutritive disturbances of the skin and epidermal structures.

DISCUSSION.

Dr. Van Harlingen called attention to a case that had come under his observation. The patient was a man who had recently suffered amputation of one of his limbs, and soon after the operation showed lesions over the knuckles and on the fore-arm of the right upper extremity. The lesions at first resembling erythema-multiforme later appeared as blackened, smooth sloughs, which were finally cast off. It was a case of spontaneous gangrene of a probably reflex character.

Dr. Taylor detailed in this connection two cases:

1. A child much run down, free from syphilis; its mother pale, thin, and worn. The child had an ulcer on its back, size of a silver quarter dollar. It commenced as a water-blister. The most approved methods of treatment were used, and nevertheless the ulceration extended through the skin down to the fascia and muscle, forming a lesion four inches in length, and two and one-half in breadth. By means of a generous diet, cod-liver oil and iron tonics, the patient was cured.

11. A nervous, sanguineous woman; no child; lesion on fingers, beginning with a bluish, congested condition. There was also a swelling on the nose, upon which was a bulla that broke down, and the surrounding tissue becoming involved the tissue in healing contracted on the cartilage of the nose which appeared as a sharp-pointed prong. The pulp cushion of the fingers was lost. The cure of this case was difficult, and deformity followed. The only etiological point in the case was that the woman had been living largely on buckwheat cakes. Her attention was first called to the disease by the fact that she could no longer thread her needle.

A paper was then read by Dr. G. H. Fox, of New York, on:

A TRIP TO TRACADIE.

The writer described the Hospital for Lepers, at Tracadie, New Brunswick; the character of the cases present, and gave some conclusions which he presented in common with Dr. Graham, who had also recently made a visit to the leper asylum.

The following are the ten propositions submitted as a result of the combined investigations of Drs. Fox and Graham:

1. Leprosy is a constitutional disease, and in certain cases appears to be hereditary.
2. It is, undoubtedly, contagious by inoculation.
3. There is no reason for believing that it is transmitted in any other way.
4. Under certain conditions a person may have leprosy and run no risk of transmitting the disease to others of the same household or community.
5. It is not so liable to be transmitted to others as is syphilis in its early stages. There is no relation between the two diseases.

6. Leprosy is usually a fatal disease ; its average duration being from ten to fifteen years.

7. In rare instances there is a tendency to recovery after the disease has existed for many years.

8. There is no valid reason for pronouncing the disease incurable.

9. Judicious treatment usually improves the condition of the patient and often causes a disappearance of the symptoms.

10. There is ground for the hope that an improved method of treatment will in time effect the cure of leprosy, or at least, that it will arrest and control the disease.

DISCUSSION.

The President suggested that in the discussion members should confine themselves to the following points :

1. Clinical history.
2. Question of heredity.
3. Modes of contagion.
4. Duration.
5. Curability.
6. Treatment.

Dr. Rohé thought that if leprosy spreads by contagion there must be a great difference as to the susceptibility on the part of individuals, and that this difference is a great deal more marked than in any other disease. Cases have occurred where there was contact for years without infection—while others, after contact for a comparatively short time, seemed to acquire the disease.

Dr. Wigglesworth said it was a noticeable fact that physicians or nurses are rarely, if ever affected. His idea was that leprosy while inoculable, is hardly contagious and probably not infectious.

Dr. Graham said, in regard to contagiousness, that he went to Tracadie unbiased in his views, but came back a firm believer. It was, he thought, the only plausible way in which we can explain the manner of its spreading. The history of the settlement bears upon the question. Certain families that came there, were, when they departed from their native place entirely free from the disease, and, after a time several members took the disease. In regard to the question of heredity, there was no case at Tracadie which could furnish any evidence. There seems to be in his opinion, a susceptibility in certain families, while many seem to possess an immunity.

Dr. Hardaway thought it a question of importance to determine, whether leprosy is more inoculable at one time than at another, and also whether the acquired form is more virulent than the hereditary.

Dr. Piffard, contrary to the opinion expressed by Dr. Fox, that physicians were never known to be affected, cited the case of Dr. Boileau, of the island of Mauritius. He agreed with the ten propositions as read by Dr. Fox.

Dr. Wigglesworth spoke of a conversation which he had with Dr. Boeck, of Christiania, who told him of two healthy Norwegians that emigrated to America, and some of whose descendants developed leprosy. Under changed climatic influence, the disease, as developed, seemed to have lost in virulence.

Dr. Piffard was of the opinion that in the case of a child it would be difficult to determine whether the disease is hereditary, or due to inoculation.

The next paper, entitled:

EXPERIMENTS IN THE USE OF NAPHTOL, *

Was read by Dr. A. Van Harlingen, of Philadelphia. The writer detailed at some length the statements of Kaposi, of Vienna, as to the uses of naphtol, adding a running commentary as to his personal experience of the action of this drug in various skin diseases. In scabies naphtol is the best remedy, in the writer's opinion, which has yet been employed. In psoriasis it ranks next to chrysarobin and pyrogallic acid in efficiency, while much more agreeable than those drugs to use. In eczema, except squamous eczema of the scalp, it is of no value. The writer concludes that naphtol has a certain value as a therapeutic agent in skin diseases.

DISCUSSION.

Dr. Fox said that from the time Kaposi first published his views as to the therapeutic value of naphtol, until lately, he had used the agent whenever he had a chance, but felt obliged to say that in his hands it fell short of the value of the preparations of tar. He had used it in

---

* Am. Jour. Med. Sciences, Oct. 1888.

eczema and psoriasis. In eczema of the scalp it did well in the form of a lotion; in other cases of eczema it was of less value, except in eczema ani, where in a five per cent. ointment it acted well. In psoriasis of the face and scalp it was used without benefit, and in these cases he still preferred an ointment composed of the white precipitate. He thought Kaposi claims too much for naphtol and furthermore did not feel inclined to agree with Dr. Van Harlingen that the drug will become a standard remedy in the treatment of cutaneous affections.

Dr. Wigglesworth agreed with the opinion expressed by Dr. Fox, and believed the drug had no advantages over other members of its class, such as carbolic acid, creosote, tar, etc.

Dr. Hardaway had used the drug in eczema and psoriasis; in the latter disease conjointly with chrysophanic acid, but soon surrendered it for the latter. In eczema fissum, however, he found it of value, using it at fifteen per cent. strength.

Dr. Stelwagon was of the opinion that the drug is used in Vienna more especially for scabies, prurigo, etc.

Dr. Piffard said he had never used it, and thought it dangerous.

Dr. Taylor mentioned two cases of scabies, in which he had used it with good results; in psoriasis it was found wanting.

A paper was read by Dr. S. Sherwell, of Brooklyn, on:

PAGET'S DISEASE, OR MALIGNANT PAPILLARY DERMATITIS.

Dr. Sherwell stated that the number of cases which he had been able to find recorded, was twenty-seven, and were as follows:

1.	Sir James Paget, * about	. . . .	15
2.	Dr. Butlin,	. . . . . .	4
3.	Henry Morris,	. . . . . .	2
4.	George Thin,	. . . . . .	2
5.	L. A. Duhring,	. . . . . .	2
6.	S. Sherwell,	. . . . . .	2
			27

---

* 1 St. Bartholomew's Hosp. Rep. 1874, Vol. X, p. 87.
   2 Med. Chirurg. Trans., Jan. 11, 1876.
      "   "   " Jan., 1877, Vol. LX.
   3 "   "   " Dec., 1879.
   4 Brit. Med. Jour., 1831, May 14th.
   5 American Jour. Med. Sciences, July, 1883.

The following were the two cases observed by himself:

Case 1. Mrs. X, æt. 75. Mother of several children; good general health, and family history unusual for longevity and freedom from disease. About ten years ago first noticed weeping around the nipple due, as she has since maintained, to traumatism from attempt at nursing a young child, her grandson. Disease kept extending; its appearance was that of ordinary chronic eczema. When the case was first seen, there was no induration around the edges—nothing but a soggy infiltration; the "melted away" (see Morris) appearance of the nipple was the only remarkable feature; axillary glands were unaffected; no pain, except an occasional burning and sometimes extreme pruritus. It was treated as an eczema, and for a time with good effect, but this was only temporary.

About two months later, the warty growth had commenced, and axillary glands were indurated. There was a burning, smarting sensation; increase of discharge. By degrees the healthy derma was invaded, until the whole anterior half of the thorax became involved; general health continued good. Died in March, 1883, from an attack of idiopathic peritonitis.

Case 2. This has been recorded in the *Journal of Cutaneous and Venereal Diseases*, *March*, 1883, and this is, according to the statement of Dr. Sherwell, the first placed on record in the United States.

Rose N , æt. 49 years. Married; childless; good family history; stout, robust; presented herself January, 1883. Centre of right breast revealed a weeping surface—itching and occasional burning—patch two by three inches. Paget's description was said to cover the case exactly. Ablation was advised, but the patient refused to consent. It was then treated with acid nitrate of mercury, on account of an alterative action which it is believed to possess. The patient made a fair recovery. After three days profound ptyalism set in; at her last visit, there was much scar tissue, but upon site of nipple there was a lesion similar to the old process.

The conclusions were as follows:

1. The subjective symptoms—itching, burning—are those of eczema, and not of ordinary carcinomatous affection—but more marked than those of ordinary eczema.

2. The objective appearances—discharge, crusts, indistinguishable from those of eczema—color of surface perhaps more livid.

3. The "melting away" of the nipple best describes its gradual obliteration, there seeming to be no manifest erosion or ulceration.

4. The retraction of the nipple or tissues beneath not so marked as in ordinary cancer.

5. The "malignant papillary" feature is a very diagnostic point, and would of itself instantly resolve any doubts between it and true eczema.

6. In the first case twelve years elapsed from attack to death, the latter event not seeming in any way connected with the skin lesion. In the second case, considerably over the time mentioned by Paget as certain to bring out epitheliomatous features, (two years) had elapsed.

SECOND DAY.—Morning Session.

A paper entitled :

THE PATHOGENESIS OF DRUG ERUPTIONS,

Was read by Dr. P. A. Morrow, of New York. A synopsis of the paper is as follows :

Cutaneous eruptions follow the absorption and elimination of certain drugs, and may be called an expression of the physiological action of the drugs.

The effect produced depends largely upon individual susceptibility. The effect of the external application of certain drugs may be explained upon purely physical grounds—irritation of the peripheral endings of the nerves and the production of congestion. The intensity of the action depends upon the nature of the drug and duration of contact. The most characteristic feature of drug eruptions is their prompt disappearance after discontinuance of the drug. In the study of these disorders we are embarrassed by our lack of definite knowledge of the physiological action of drugs, also of the idiosyncrasies of individuals. The theory adopted by most authorities is, that drugs, in their elimination through the glands of the skin cause irritation.

Bazin suggested that there was an election, on the part of drugs, for certain elements of the skin. Others claim that the effect is produced by a cumulative action, and that the system must first become saturated. This, however, is not so, as small doses are frequently sufficient to produce marked effects.

In the iodine and bromine eruptions the sebaceous glands are not always involved. The drug is not always found in the lesions.

The theory of Behrend is that of a dynamic action of drugs, independent of their physiological and therapeutic action. According to this theory a mysterious chemical compound is formed. It is a modification of the old humoral theory.

A large proportion of drug eruptions are the result of congestion, and in some cases this is of reflex character. Many that are consecutive to the elimination are produced by irritation of the vasomotor centres. The mental or emotional eruptions depend upon such a cause.

We know that when disturbance of the nutrition of a part occurs, we may have as a result such changes as gangrene, herpes zoster, ulcer of the leg, etc.

It is probable that drugs act in a similar way on the nervous centres. As evidence of such an action, he referred to the symmetry of the eruptions. He then alluded to the idiosyncrasies of individuals, and thought that persons of a cachectic nervous habit were more susceptible to the irritant action of drugs. In conclusion, he added that he believed that the neurotic theory best explained the phenomena of drug eruptions.

Dr. R. W. Taylor then read a paper on :

POLYMORPHOUS CHANGES OBSERVED IN THE NON-ULCERATING TUBERCULAR SYPHILIDE. *

He referred to a case which he had under observation for five months, and which departed from the usual course of development characteristic of the tubercular syphilide in that the lesions became degenerative instead of hypertrophic. The eruption was generally symmetrical, copious, possessing the characteristic of secondary lesions, also deep-seated, a feature of the tertiary, and might, therefore, be called, according to the French, intermediate.

The patient was a male, æt. 47 years. Had a sore on his penis, not attended with bubo ; followed by roseola, mucous patches, which lasted two or three months, when it was cured by treatment.

Then appeared an eruption, symmetrically distributed, and consisting of large, flat, scaly patches, numerous on the anterior and posterior aspect of the trunk. General appearance of lesions that of

---

* " Journal Cutaneous and Venereal Diseases," October 1883, p. 385.

psoriasis. The case was pronounced one of non-ulcerating tubercular syphilide. The centre of the larger patches was atrophic, an appearance of superficial thinning. Where the scales were easily removed a red base was revealed ; where the scales were adherent, removal revealed a moist surface. By the use of vaseline the scales were removed, but appeared again. The lesions then changed, becoming more deeply seated. They increased in size ; became elevated, hypertrophic ; and the tissue assumed a soft colloid character like in lupus. Some of the lesions, however, remained firm, like the ordinary tubercle and of coppery hue.

In the tubercles yellowish puncta appeared, which grew in height, gradually coalesced, forming bullæ as in syphilitic pemphigus. These were of short duration, becoming flattened, ruptured, and in their places were blackish brown crusts, resembling rupia. On the base of the nose and on the cheeks were rupial crusts. Many lesions became hypertrophic ; others were the seat of degeneration with formation of pus.

The changes supposed to go on in such lesions are, first, an increase of the granulation cells in the tubercle ; second, a degeneration ; and third, a profuse proliferation of the epidermis.

A microscopic examination of the scales showed pus. Altogether, the appearances warranted the suspicion that the psoriasis rupioides of McCall Anderson and Fox is a late form of the papillary or tubercular syphilide.

Later the crusts fell off and the spots passed away by absorption. The conclusions drawn from the case were :

1. Its resemblance to psoriasis.
2. The colloid degeneration of some of the tubercles concomitantly with the increase of the granulation tissue in the others.
3. The degeneration of the colloid tissue into pus, and the formation of bullæ.
4. The evidence offered that true bullæ may appear in a syphilitic subject, though they result from degeneration of tissue, rather than from effusion of serum and pus, as occurs, as a rule in simple pemphigus.
5. The development of tubercles having thick, imbricated, conical, epidermal crusts appearing like rupia.
6. In the suggestion offered by these lesions, that perhaps the psoriasis rupioides of authors is more or less dependent upon syphilis.

7. The formation of true rupia crusts from the bullæ above spoken of.

8. The fact that the non-ulcerated tubercular sypilide may be the starting point of severe and extensive gummatous infiltration.

DISCUSSION.

Dr. Hardaway mentioned a case of psoriasis rupioides of McCall Anderson, but certain features proved it to be a case of psoriasis. The lesions were covered with masses of dirty scales, which, being removed, there was revealed a non-ulcerating base. The only departure from ordinary psoriasis was the heaped up conical shape of the mass of scales.

The patient was a female, æt. 26 years. Her mother, æt. 56 years, had an eruption of psoriasis vulgaris.

Dr. Taylor asked whether the history of the father pointed to any hereditary nature of the affection in the patient?

Dr. Hardaway answered, No.

Dr. Atkinson referred to a point of interest in connection with the paper of Dr. Taylor, namely, the evidence it gives to the fact that syphilis may simulate all forms of cutaneous disease.

A paper entitled:

PSEUDO-PSORIASIS OF THE PALMS, *

Was read by Dr. S. Sherwell. The writer included all those lesions invading the structures anatomically analogous to the plantar surfaces. He believed that psoriasis or pseudo-psoriasis of the palms when present, is the result of a comcomitance of a superimposed or congenitally double diathesis, and that when such eruption appears, clinically not to be differentiated from a frank psoriasis in this position, it is to his mind entire proof of a syphilis, "larvata" it may be, or of traceable dyscrasia of some kind. He referred to the clinical fact that the palms are generally exempt in psoriasis vulgaris, while in late syphilis it is common.

In conclusion, he added that he believed the squamous eruption on the palms (excluding eczema, etc.), resembling psoriasis, always had a specific diathesis for its base or one of its bases. He then offered a

---

* See Jour. Cutaneous and Venereal Dis., Oct. 1883.

case as proof of how readily the implantation of syphilis on psoriatic grounds leads to the formation of pseudo-psoriatic efflorescences on the hands.

Mr. X, æt. 35. Robust, stout; presented himself Aug. 6, 1882, with initial lesion on corona; under treatment lesion disappeared. The patient at that time had psoriatic lesions about the elbows, etc. Had had attacks for past eight years, and since first invasion had not been altogether free; never had eruption on palmar or dorsal surfaces of hand. Five weeks subsequent to initial lesion roseola appeared, also pharyngitis, mucous patches, etc.; all disappeared under treatment In January, 1883, patient came with squamous eruption of palms and about the nails. Under treatment it vanished, appeared again, and again was expelled.

The next paper, entitled:

PSORIASIS OF THE PALMS,

Was read by Dr. Alexander, of New York. The writer presented a description of three cases of psoriasis of the palms, in which the closest examination failed to elicit any evidence of the presence of syphilis. (The report was accompanied by photographs.)

DISCUSSION.

Dr. Graham said that during the last two years he had seen two cases of psoriasis of the palms, in each of which there was a peculiar affection of the finger-nails. There was no syphilitic taint traceable. These were the only cases that had come under his notice.

Dr. Morrow regarded psoriasis occurring on the palms, as an exceedingly rare condition. There appeared to him no argument in favor of the non-development of psoriasis on the palms and soles, from any peculiarities of anatomical structure. Psoriasis affects parts where the epidermis is thick, especially the extensor surfaces; on the face and flexor surfaces it was not so liable to occur. Last year he had seen cases where it was upon the palms; in one case, coincident with a generalized eruption, where there was not the slightest evidence of a syphilitic taint. It was a woman, who had had previous attacks of psoriasis. As far as his observation went, psoriasis of the palms without specific basis, though rare, may occur.

Dr. Taylor had seen the three cases of Dr. Alexander; examined them thoroughly, and could find no history of specific trouble. He referred to a case of Dr. Morrow's, in which there was also no syphilitic history.

Psoriasis about the hands, he thought, always begins with the affection of the nails. In most of the cases that he had seen, the nails were affected, and undoubtedly the cause was traumatic. This feature in psoriasis of the palms, should, in his opinion, always be remembered; as it is well, to ascertain the date of appearance of lesion on the body, and also of lesion on the palms; also, where it began on palms. Out of seven cases, one did not begin about the nails. He thought local irritation should be taken into consideration.

Dr. Morrow had seen a case in which it was confined to the palms—there being no affection of the finger nails.

Dr. Sherwell still held to his view. He spoke of the difficulty of proving negative syphilis, and said that congenital trouble was part of his theory. He had seen many cases of almost universal psoriasis, except the palms; then, after the acquisition of syphilis, the affection of the palms appeared. He was prepared to accept the theory that psoriasis was in some way modified by syphilis, so that it appeared upon the palm.

Dr. Taylor thought that in this affection there is a psoriatic tendency over the entire body, and that it will appear on the hands, which have a quasi immunity, if sufficient irritation be applied.

Dr. Alexander recalled a case of generalized psoriatic eruption, in which the palmar lesions disappeared one week after their appearance. The eruption may, therefore, he thought, be evanescent. Lesions may be rare upon the soles and palms, because these parts are subjected to friction, causing rapid tissue change, and resisting disease. Within the last year, he had had four cases of undoubted psoriasis of the palms.

A paper by Dr. James Nevins Hyde, of Chicago, entitled:

A STUDY OF THE CO-INCIDENCE OF SYPHILITIC AND NON-SYPHILITIC AFFECTIONS OF THE SKIN.

Was read by Dr. Wigglesworth.

He spoke of the tendency on the part of practitioners to overestimate the part which syphilis plays in the human system, especially when present with intercurrent affections, where there is a variety and an anomalous character to the symptoms.

The following points, he thought, must be recognized:

1. Syphilis much more resembles other diseases in its career, and its subjection to accidental influences is greater than has been commonly supposed and taught.

2. When preceding, coexisting with or following other pathological conditions, its unity is preserved, and it rarely undergoes itself, or induces in other diseases, such a modification as distinctly changes the type of the resulting symptoms.

In regard to the subject of the coincidence of psoriasis and syphilis, he offered two cases, in which the two affections developed according to their respective natures, each always exhibiting its own special characteristics.

A summary of the facts was as follows:

1. Two patients, affected with generalized psoriasis, become unmistakably syphilitic.

2. At the date of the explosion of syphilis, both patients are seen covered with an abundant psoriatic eruption of a typical aspect.

3. In the former case, the psoriatiform eruption is succeeded by a pustular syphiloderm, irregular in type, anomalous in certain features and erratic in development, modified indeed subsequently by mercurial and other treatment, but not thus made to change its essential features. With this there is no admixture of a psoriatic eruption.

4. As this same progresses the purely syphilitic symptoms gradually give place to those of a purely psoriatic type till the latter preponderate and are finally completely substituted for the former.

5. From first to last, no lesions, no groups, nor series of lesions can be recognized as exhibiting features common to both of the diseases in question.

6. These two forms may be described as, first, typical psoriasis; second, modified syphilis.

7. The modification of the syphilodermata was not in the direction of the psoriasis. If there was a modification, it was in the direction of eczema.

8. It is reasonable to conclude that any prolonged cutaneous affection, one also long treated by external stimulating remedies, would

leave such an impression upon the skin as to somewhat modify its expression of a syphilitic influence.

9. The palms and soles were not invaded; regions where the differential diagnosis between the two diseases in question, has been studied with special care.

10. When the two exist together the value of these diagnostic differences is diminished. These points are the symmetry of the one disease, and relative failure in the other; palmar and plantar involvement; the abundance or reverse, of scales; the size and degree of infiltration of the involved areas; the color of the patches; the appearance of new formation in syphilis, and the well known tendency of psoriasis to invade the regions of the knees and elbows.

SECOND DAY.—Evening Session.

A paper was read by Dr. R. W. Taylor, entitled:

PECULIAR APPEARANCE OF THE INITIAL LESION OF SYPHILIS AT ITS BEGINNING. *

Dr. Taylor spoke of the importance of the early recognition of the initial lesion, and that any new facts to enlighten us are of more than ordinary value.

In the American Journal of Syphilography and Dermatology, July, 1871, he had published a description of the peculiar appearance of the initial lesion on the first day, and wished now to present two additional cases:

Case 1. Mr. M., a Pole, presented himself January 17, 1870, with a lesion on inner aspect of the right lip of the meatus urinarius. The spot was the size of two pin-heads, of silvery appearance, without elevation or fissures. It looked as if cauterized with nitrate of silver. It was evident that the lesion was a change in the superficial epithelium of the part. In four days there was a small amount of induration; in one week it developed into a distinctly indurated small pea-sized nodule. Induration of inguinal glands followed. One week later, the epithelium desquamated, leaving a greyish exulcerated surface with scant secretion. In six weeks appeared roseola, affection of the fauces, general malaise, etc., all of which disappeared under proper treatment.

---

* See New York Med. Record, Sep. 8, 1883.

Case 2. On the 20th of May, 1883, a gentleman consulted him on account of a suspicious connection the night before. His anxiety was so great that he came daily. After twelve days there was to be seen on the dorsum of the glans a spot the size of three small pin-heads, oval, and of a glistening, silvery appearance. It increased in area, at first, but was distinctly confined to the epidermal layer; on the eleventh day, induration of the inguinal glands appeared; on the fifteenth, induration of lesion; twentieth day, typical indurated, sharply defined chancre; July 13th, roseola.

The practical conclusions to be drawn were, that the initial lesion may be a small, unelevated, silvery spot in the mucous membrane, without inflammatory areola. The spot may remain superficial for about two weeks before becoming indurated.

He also called attention to two other appearances of early date; one, the minute, round, slightly excoriated appearance like a superficial erosion of the epithelium with a future course of extension and elevation. Where many such lesions appear, we have the multiple herpetiform chancre of Dubuc; the other early appearance is in the form of a small, slightly elevated papule, having an unbroken surface, the *papule seche* of the French writers.

A paper by Dr. L. A. Duhring, of Philadelphia, entitled:

THE VALUE OF A LOTION OF SULPHIDE OF ZINC IN THE TREATMENT OF LUPUS ERYTHEMATOSUS,

Was read by Dr. Stelwagon. The writer called attention to the value of a certain zinc sulphide lotion in the treatment of the superficial forms of the disease, occurring either in discrete or confluent patches of recent or long duration. The lotion was not recommended as one which would exert a cure in all cases, but it was spoken of as a highly useful remedy. The formula is as follows:

℞
Zinci sulphat.
Potass. sulphuret, aa. ʒ ss
Aq. Rosarum, . f. ℥ iijss
Alcohol, . . . f. ʒ iij

If this strength agrees with the skin, the two active ingredients may be increased to the amount of a drachm each to four ounces of the fluid. The lotion should be shaken well before using, and applied lightly to the part from five to twenty minutes by means of a sponge. Two or three applications are to be made in twenty-four hours.

The writer described the chemistry of the lotion, and referred to three cases, in which, after using various other agents, this lotion afforded a marked improvement.

DISCUSSION.

Dr. Alexander mentioned a case which he had at present under treatment, and which is very obstinate. He had scarified some patches with gratifying result; others were made worse by the operation.

Dr. Sherwell said that he had used the lotion largely for acne, but failed to see how it could be curative in lupus; it may reduce the hyperæmia by acting as an astringent.

Dr. Van Harlingen said that he had had an opportunity of seeing one of the cases mentioned by Dr. Duhring, where the lesion on the face was of the butterfly form, having spots of infiltration at certain points; to which was superadded an extensive acute erythematous condition. The patient was greatly disfigured, and in one week the lotion produced a marked change. The disease was reduced to a few patches. As he understood it, Dr. Duhring referred to the lotion as one of value and not as an invariably a curative agent.

Dr. Wigglesworth thought that lupus erythematosus was an opprobrium to the profession, nothing being so hard to treat. Hebra was right in calling it seborrhœa congestiva. Dr. Fox had advised something which he has used in several cases with good results; it is salicylic acid and chrysarobin. He wished to hear from Dr. Fox on this subject.

Dr. Fox said in regard to the remedy mentioned by Dr. Wigglesworth, that he had used it in certain cases of lupus erythematosus with good results. In one case, however, it acted well on one side of the face, while it aggravated the lesions on the other. In cases of a chronic nature, with little tendency to increase, it acts well. In his experience with this disease, the local application of pure carbolic acid had benefited the greatest number of cases; painted over the part once or twice a week, it produces a rapid cure. It lessens the vascularity.

In three cases, phosphorus was used internally, with good effect, but carbolic acid gave the most gratifying results. The combination of the two remedies may, perhaps, be better.

Dr. Stelwagon remarked that, in a case mentioned by Dr. Duhring, carbolic acid had been used without effect, and that scarification had in one case produced a dermatitis, and aggravation of the disease.

Dr. Piffard claimed that when scarification is performed, it should be complete and thorough, and that dermatitis was necessary. Hardy used locally the biniodide of mercury in such strength as to excite enough inflammation to strangulate the new lupus cells There are, he said, cases on record where lupus erythematosus was cured by an erysipelas.

Dr. Hardaway claimed that he had had success by the use of electrolysis.

A second paper of Dr. L. A. Duhring, entitled:

REPORT OF A CASE OF AINHUM WITH MICROSCOPIC EXAMINATION,

Was read by Dr. Van Harlingen. The writer reported a case which had been sent to him by Dr. G. B. Simpson, of Weston, West Virginia.

The patient, a negro, forty years of age, noticed when ten years old, a furrow in the digito-plantar fold of little toe upon both feet. The toes gradually enlarged, with pain in the furrow. When first seen by the doctor, ten years ago, the toes seemed nearly amputated. Two years ago one toe fell off spontaneously ; the patient insisted upon its being buried. A few months ago the other toe dropped off, and was preserved by the physician and sent for examination.

The father of the patient lost both toes in a similar manner. The mother is at present suffering from the same affection. These facts would seem to indicate an hereditary tendency.

The microscopic examination prepared by Dr. Duhring's assistant, Dr. Henry Wile, may be summarized as follows :

1. Increase in thickness of epidermis.
2. Enlargement and elongation of papillary body.
3. Blood-vessels of papillary body, also peri-vascular spaces dilated and filled with red and white corpuscles.
4. The meshes of the connective tissue of the corium contain larger and smaller clusters of small round cells, which for the most

part immediately surround the blood-vessels. In some places the cells composing these cellular collections have gone on to organization, forming connective tissue.

5. The lower layers of the corium are composed of loosely arranged bundles of connective tissue and smooth muscular tissue, between the bundles of which are variously sized empty spaces.

6. Blood-vessels are everywhere numerous—arteries, capillaries, venules dilated and filled with blood corpuscles, veins for the most part empty.

7. In the walls of the larger arteries there is a noticeable thickening of the media and adventitia, and proliferation of endothelium.

8. Lymphatics distended, but mostly empty.

9. Sweat-glands numerous, but atrophic.

10. About the coils of sweat-glands are numerous fat vesicles and round alveoli filled with lymphoid cells.

11. The tissue attached to the pedicle is composed of connective and yellow elastic tissue closely packed together.

12. The epidermis is observed to descend with step-like processes to the place of attachment.

13. Altogether the general impression obtained from a careful study and comparison of sections is one that would be conveyed by the study of a tissue, which is the seat of a *chronic, inflammatory œdema*.

The cause of the disease is supposed to be a disturbance of the circulation, which was intermittent in its action.

DISCUSSION,

Dr. Sherwell said that he had treated many natives from the West Indies, for various cutaneous disorders, and has heard of an affection called "ring-toe," a species of self mutilation, practiced by the lazy negro. It was his impression that ainhum is the result of willful traumatism, akin if not identical with "ring-toe."

PAPILLARY DISEASE OF THE SKIN.

Dr. Hardaway presented five cases, representing a peculiar papillary disease of the skin :

Case 1. Patient healthy, æt. 12 years. Eruption on left cheek, and dorsum of both hands, discrete, oval, split pea-sized, solid, smooth, painless, peculiar lemon-colored lesions. On pinching them a drop of blood would ooze out.

The following ointment caused them to disappear in two weeks:

℞
    Hydrarg. ammoniat.
    Liq. picis alk. . aa. ʒ i.
    Ungt. petrol, . ℥ i.

There was no relapse.

Case 2. Similar eruption on right arm, also slightly on the thumbs. It had existed several months.

Same treatment.

Case 3. Ten lemon-yellow papules on the forehead near the hair, also had existed several months. It was obstinate, but finally yielded to same treatment.

Case 4. Little boy; eruption on left side of forehead near hair; similar in character to others. Same treatment caused it to disappear.

Case 5. A merchant æt. 35 years. A dozen split pea-sized papules on the back of the neck. They were of a yellowish color, and on being pricked blood issued; they were more closely grouped than in the other cases; some had coalesced.

These cases resembled one another strikingly. In all, the eruption was of a chronic type—dark lemon-yellow color; pseudo-vesicular appearance; varied in size from a grain of wheat to a split pea; solid; no areola; non pedunculated; upon puncture gave exit to a drop of blood; flattened, smooth; had no aperture. It was not xanthoma; left no stain or cicatrix; evidently non-contagious.

DISCUSSION.

Dr. Wigglesworth regarded them as new lesions. Xanthoma tuberosum, he thought, was suggested, but the translucency contraindicated this.

Dr. Atkinson mentioned a case of a young negro woman having an eruption which looked like large vesicles, and on being punctured gave exit to a drop of blood. The patient was not long under observation. He regarded the lesion as papilloma in the sense of wart.

CASE OF LYMPHANGIOMA CUTIS.

Dr. Graham described a case of lymphangioma cutis:

Mrs. L., æt. 21 years. Always enjoyed good health. When five years old, a tumor appeared on the right elbow, which gradually extended upwards and downwards. Present condition as follows: From the shoulder to the wrist on the outer surface is a loose fold of integument, which hangs down. Near the shoulder is a hard nodule. The epidermis is much hypertrophied; near the elbow are deep furrows, and brown pigmentation; near the middle third of the forearm is a large round tumor, and to the touch large dilated vessels are perceptible. The surface of the entire lesion has a soft, velvety feeling. It can be reduced in size by elevation of the part or by compression. (Photographs were shown.)

DISCUSSION.

Dr. Atkinson reported a case almost identical with the one described by Dr. Graham, the lesion being higher up the arm. He thought it differs from dermatolysis in that there is a densely infiltrated condition and enlarged lymphatics. This condition, he argued, was a striking illustration of the inaccuracy of Dr. Formad's views in regard to the formation of tubercles, *i. e.*, that they are formed from an accumulation of cells in the lymph channels, as a result of overcrowded, obstructed lymph channels. If this were the case, we would have tubercles in elephantiasis, dermatolysis and all allied conditions.

Dr. Piffard suggested in regard to treatment the galvano caustic ligature, applied in loops to different parts.

Dr. Sherwell referred to a case of lymphangioma cutis, of a solidifying nature, where the lymphatics are indurated so that the patient, a man, can scarcely move either limbs or body.

Dr. Atkinson thought that a removal of the growth would be followed by a relapse.

THIRD DAY.—Morning Session.

The session was devoted to the examination of microscopic specimens, prepared by Dr. Henry Wile, of Philadelphia, to illustrate the paper of Dr. Duhring, on "Ainhum," also by Dr. Sherwell, to illustrate that on "Paget's Disease, or Malignant Papillary Dermatitis."

APPENDIX.

A List of the Publications and Writings of Members between July, 1882, and July, 1883, compiled from replies to a circular-letter of the President.

ALEXANDER.   Referate.   *Monatshefte fuer Praktische Dermatologie.*

ATKINSON.   Syphiloderma papulosum circinatum.   *Journal of Cutaneous and Venereal Diseases, October, 1882.*

The vesicular and bullous forms of erythema exsudativum multiforme.   *Phila. Med. News, Vol. xli, No. 23, 1882.*

Extra-genital infecting chancre. Clinical lecture on.   *Maryland Med. Jour., Vol. x, No. 1.*

Notes of a case of erythematous lupus complicated by the tubercular syphiloderm.   *Medical Chronicle, June, 1883.*

BULKLEY.   Analysis of 8000 cases of skin disease.   *Archives of Dermatology, October, 1882.*

Clinical illustrations of diseases of the skin.   *Ibid. July and October,* 1882.

Acne atrophica or lupoid acne.   *Jour. Cutaneous and Venereal Diseases, October,* 1882.

Note concerning a convenient method of applying lotions to the hairy scalp.   *Ibid.   February,* 1883.

DUHRING.   Case of sarcomatous, "inflammatory fungoid neoplasm."   *Medical News, January 6, 1883.*

Case of impetigo herpetiformis; recovery.   *Med. News, June 2, 1883.*

Two cases Paget's disease of the nipple.   *Amer. Jour. of the Med. Sci., July,* 1883.

Fox.   Note on the development of tricophytosis cruris (colored plate).   *Jour. Cutaneous and Venereal Diseases, October, 1882.*

The treatment of lupus.   *Phila. Med. News.*

The etiology of urticaria.   *Jour. Cutaneous and Venereal Diseases, January,* 1883.

The treatment of urticaria.   *Ibid.   April,* 1883.

HARDAWAY. Essentials of vaccination. Chicago: Jansen, McClurg & Co. 1882.

Case of pigmented neoplasm of the skin. Read before the American Dermatological Association. *Jour. Cutaneous and Venereal Diseases, January*, 1883.

Acne. *St. Louis Courier of Med., January*, 1883.

Dermatological clinic. Tinea versicolor in a child. Extensive development of tinea circinata. Symptomatic papilloma cutis. Psoriasis rupioides. *Ibid. May*, 1883.

Electricity in the treatment of diseases of the skin. *Ibid. June*, 1883.

HYDE. A clinical study of dermatitis papillaris capillitii. *Journal Cutaneous and Venereal Diseases, Vol.* 1, 1882, *Nos.* 2 *and* 3.

On certain cutaneous affections of the hands. Clinical lecture. *Phila. Med. News, December* 9, 1882.

MORROW. On excision of the chancre as a means of aborting syphilis. *Jour. Cutaneous and Venereal Dis.*

On chrysophanic and pyrogallic acids. *Ibid.*

On the incidental effects of vaccination. *Ibid.*

PIFFARD. Calx sulphurata and its uses in cutaneous, and some other diseases. *Jour. Cutaneous and Venereal Diseases, January*, 1883.

Tricophytosis barbæ. *Illustrated Medicine and Surgery, April*, 1883.

ROBINSON. Erythema diphtheriticum. *Jour. Cutaneous and Venereal Diseases.*

ROHÉ. Two cases of acute general psoriasis following vaccination. *Jour. Cutaneous and Venereal Diseases, October*, 1882, *p.* 11.

The treatment of acute eczema. *Medical Chronicle, February*, 1883, *p.* 169.

ROHÉ. Recent progress in dermatology. *MedicalChronicle, March*, 1883, *p.* 209.

The treatment of the various forms of acne. *Ibid. May*, 1883, *p.* 247.

Hints on the treatment of some parasitic skin diseases. *New York Med. Record, June* 2, 1883.

Pemphigus and the diseases liable to be mistaken for it. *Phila. Med. News, June* 23, 1883.

Review of Hyde on diseases of the skin. *Medical Chronicle, April*, 1883, *p.* 247.

SHERWELL. Report of a case of pellagra. *Jour. Cutaneous and Venereal Diseases, February*, 1883.

Report of a case of Paget's disease of the breast. (Malignant papillary dermatitis of Thin). *Ibid. March*, 1883.

STELWAGON. An unusual case of herpes iris. *Phila. Medical News, October* 14, 1882.

A sebaceous cyst, containing a coil of hair, consisting of two hairs, each several inches in length. *Phila. Medical Times, March* 24, 1883.

An analytical study of two thousand consecutive cases of skin disease. (Dispensary cases for 1880, 1881 and 1882). *Ibid. May* 19, 1883.

Sulphur preparations in acne. *Med. and Surg. Reporter, June* 16, 1883.

TAYLOR. Notes on psoriasis. *Jour. Cutaneous and Venereal Diseases, October*, 1882.

Case of second infection with syphilis. *Ibid. April*, 1883.

Case of hypertrophy of the labia majora. *Ibid. May*, 1883.

Case of dermatitis exfoliativa ; case of keloid following syphilis ; case of pain accompanying the initial lesion of syphilis ; case of gummous bursitis. *Ibid. July*, 1883.

VAN HARLINGEN. Notes on the management of ringworm of the scalp. *Phila. Medical Times, March* 17 *and* 24, 1883.

WHITE. The question of contagion in leprosy. *American Jour. of Med. Sciences, October*, 1882.

The old age of the skin. *Boston Med. and Surg. Journal, November* 23, 1882.

REPORT *of the Committee on Statistics for the Year ending July 1st,* 1883.

TABLE I.

	PRIVATE.	DISPENSARY.	TOTAL.
District 1. Boston................	746	2444	3190
" 2. New York............	755	5929	6684
" 3. Philadelphia..........	...	1376	1376
" 4. Baltimore............	...	623	623
" 5. St. Louis.............	294	156	450
" 6. Chicago..............	1694	1473	3167
" 7. Canada..............	167	181	348
	3656	12182	15838

TABLE II.

Showing the Returns from the respective Districts.

DISEASES.	Private Cases.	Dispensary Cases.	Total No. Cases.	Boston.	New York.	Philadelphia.	Baltimore.	St. Louis.	Chicago.	Canada.
Class I. Disorders of the Glands.										
1. *Of the Sweat Glands.*										
Hyperidrosis	16	21	37	1	27	2	2	1	4	..
Miliaria crystallina	15	44	59	...	12	11	...	3	33	..
Anidrosis	1	3	4	...	...	...	...	...	4	..
Bromidrosis	8	14	22	2	7	1	...	1	11	..
Chromidrosis	1	1	2	...	1	1	...	...	...	..
2. *Of the Sebaceous Glands.*										
Seborrhœa:	24	112	136	65	33	37	...	...	...	1
a. oleosa	33	65	98	2	65	1	...	...	28	2
b. sicca	71	68	139	6	37	23	3	14	56	..
Comedo	65	118	183	22	76	2	2	2	79	..
Cyst:										
a. Milium	6	3	9	2	1	1	...	3	2	..
b. Wen	18	23	41	1	16	3	5	2	14	..
Molluscum sebaceum	10	22	32	2	17	...	...	...	13	..
Diminished secretion	2	1	3	...	3	...	...	...	...	..
Class II. Inflammations.										
Exanthemata	73	99	172	11	38	13	2	...	108	..
Erythema simplex	48	113	161	29	51	3	7	...	62	9
Erythema multiforme	6	15	21	4	17	...	...	...	...	..
a. papulosum	28	108	136	10	77	9	9	...	26	5
b. bullosum	7	15	22	2	3	5	3	5	4	..
c. nodosum	7	14	21	4	6	...	...	...	6	5
Urticaria	70	311	381	70	210	30	6	6	50	9
*Dermatitis:	3	118	121	74	17	28	...	...	...	2
a. traumatica	28	43	71	3	29	6	1	4	28	..
b. venenata	48	74	122	22	33	14	14	1	35	3
c. calorica	20	39	59	5	30	5	1	...	18	..
Erysipelas	43	110	153	13	71	6	4	1	41	17
Furuncle	52	248	300	28	182	26	10	8	39	7
Anthrax	14	16	30	1	15	3	...	2	9	..
Phlegmona diffusa	4	19	23	3	11	...	6	...	3	..
Pustula maligna	...	4	4	...	4	...	...	...	...	..
Herpes:	2	45	47	6	41	...	...	...	...	..
a. facialis	21	60	81	9	14	7	12	...	33	6
b. progenitalis	87	77	164	34	50	2	3	4	68	3

* Indicating affections of this class not properly included under other titles.

TABLE II.—Continued.

Showing the Returns from the respective Districts.

DISEASES.	Private Cases.	Dispensary Cases.	Total No. Cases.	Boston.	New York.	Philadelphia.	Baltimore.	St. Louis.	Chicago.	Canada.
Herpes zoster..	35	170	205	47	79	20	16	5	31	7
Psoriasis	122	419	541	113	250	39	12	12	91	24
Pityriasis rubra..	2	6	8	...	4	...	...	1	...	3
Lichen:	4	5	9	...	7	...	...	...	...	2
a. planus	13	29	42	...	24	5	...	2	11	..
b. ruber	3	8	11	5	5	...	...	...	1	..
Eczema :	213	2400	2613	988	962	478	...	...	143	42
a. erythematosum	161	121	282	3	236	...	...	...	40	3
b. papulosum	61	163	224	2	159	...	...	...	56	7
c. vesiculosum	130	408	538	2	78	...	252	172	24	10
d. madidans	25	27	52	5	23	...	...	...	14	10
e. pustulosum	65	184	249	2	163	...	...	...	72	12
f. rubrum	36	116	152	9	106	...	...	...	33	4
g. squamosum	82	221	303	3	212	...	...	...	68	20
Prurigo	...	7	7	...	7	...	...	...	...	..
Acne	330	737	1067	263	440	86	30	18	207	23
Impetigo	41	130	171	54	50	12	1	2	46	6
Impetigo contagiosa	12	65	77	10	13	35	3	...	14	2
Impetigo herpetiformis	1	2	3	...	2	1	...	...	...	..
Ecthyma	17	73	90	8	28	10	2	2	36	4
Pemphigus	8	20	28	2	11	1	2	1	10	1
Class III. Hæmorrhages.										
Purpura :	...	2	2	2	...	...	...	...	...	..
a. simplex	9	35	44	8	17	5	1	2	9	2
b. hæmorrhagica	2	20	22	...	19	...	...	1	2	..
Class IV. Hypertrophies.										
1. *Of Pigment.*										
Lentigo	9	5	14	4	...	...	...	2	8	..
Chloasma :										
a. locale	29	28	57	13	21	5	2	7	8	1
b. universale	1	1	2	1	1	...	...	...	...	..
2. *Of Epidermal and Papillary Layers.*										
Keratosis:										
a. pilaris	9	6	15	2	3	3	...	2	5	..
b. senilis	8	3	11	7	...	...	...	...	4	..
Callositas	2	9	11	1	6	1	1	...	2	..
Clavus	...	7	7	...	5	2	...	...	...	..
Cornu cutaneum	4	3	7	1	2	...	...	1	3	..
Verruca	60	99	159	45	48	6	5	7	48	..
Verruca necrogenica	...	...	...	...	...	...	...	...	...	..
Xerosis	4	10	14	10	3	...	...	...	1	..
Ichthyosis	13	21	34	2	14	8	2	3	4	1

TABLE II.—Continued.

Showing the Reports from the respective Districts.

DISEASES.	Private Cases.	Dispensary Cases.	Total No. Cases.	Boston.	New York.	Philadelphia.	Baltimore.	St. Louis.	Chicago.	Canada.
Of Nail..................	3	5	8	...	4	2	...	...	2	..
Hirsuties................	54	6	60	25	7	...	...	12	16	..
3. *Of Connective Tissue.*										
Scleroderma.............	1	4	5	1	2	..	...	...	2	..
Sclerema neonatorum.....	...	...	...	...	...	..	...	...	...	..
Morphœa................	..	...	...	.	..	..	...	.	..	..
Elephantiasis Arabum.....	2	3	5	.	2	1	...	1	1	..
Rosacea :...............	46	16	62	4	33	13	..	12	...	..
a. erythematosa.	71	60	131	19	65	3	...	...	38	6
b. hypertrophica..	6	41	47	8	33	...	...	...	6	..
Framboesia..............	..	...	...	...	...	...	...	...	...	..
Class V. Atrophies.										
1. *Of Pigment.*										
Leucoderma..............	7	6	13	...	7	...	...	3	1	2
Albinismus...............	..	..	...	..	..	..	..	..	..	..
Vitiligo.................	11	9	20	3	2	6	...	...	9	..
Canities.................	2	1	3	1	...	...	...	1	1	..
2. *Of Hair.*										
Alopecia.................	71	17	88	37	22	1	1	...	27	..
Alopecia areata...........	44	42	86	25	37	4	1	3	14	2
Alopecia furfuracea.......	47	9	56	46	6	...	...	3	1	..
Atrophia pilorum propria..	4	...	4	...	...	...	...	4	...	..
3. *Of Nail.*	...	3	3	...	1	1	1	...	...	..
4. *Of Cutis.*										
Atrophia senilis...........	1	3	4	...	..	..	...	.	4	..
Atrophia maculosa et striata	...	...	...	...	...	...	...	...	...	..
Class VI. New Growths.										
1. *Of Connective Tissue.*										
Keloid...................	5	15	20	...	9	3	2	2	4	..
Cicatrix..................	2	8	10	...	6	...	2	1	1	..
Fibroma..................	7	12	19	5	7	...	.	3	4	..
Neuroma.................	..	...	...	..	...	..	..	..	..	..
Xantboma................	2	3	5	1	4	...	...	...	...	..
2. *Of Vessels.*										
Angioma.................	27	26	53	11	19	2	2	9	10	..
Angioma pigmentosum et atrophicum	1	3	4	1	3	...	..	...	...	..
Angioma cavernosum.....	3	...	3	...	...	...	...	3	...	..
Lymphangioma	...	5	5	...	4	1	...	...	...	..
3. *Of Granulation Tissue.*										
Rhino-scleroma...........	...	2	2	...	2	...	...	...	...	..
Lupus erythematosus......	19	45	64	15	22	3	1	5	17	1
Lupus vulgaris............	15	46	61	8	34	1	1	...	15	2
Scrofuloderma............	9	84	93	28	45	11	4	1	4	..

TABLE II.—Continued.

Showing the Returns from the respective Districts.

DISEASES.	Private Cases.	Dispensary Cases.	Total No. Cases.	Boston.	New York.	Philadelphia.	Baltimore.	St. Louis.	Chicago.	Canada.
Syphiloderma :	174	791	965	323	237	134			271	
a. erythematosum	31	60	91		61				26	4
b. papulosum	71	182	253		189				56	8
c. pustulosum	106	148	254		59			11	183	1
d. tuberculosum	26	127	153		124				29	
e. gummatosum	121	102	223		106		87		29	1
Lepra :		2	2		1				1	
a. tuberosa		4	4		4					
b. maculosa		2	2		2					
c. anæsthetica		2	2		2					
Carcinoma	20	71	91	10	30	26	14	1	10	
Sarcoma	4	7	11	1	6	1			3	
Class VII. Ulcers	125	605	730	82	385	27	26	11	177	22
Class VIII. Neuroses.										
Hyperæsthesia		1	1	1						
a. Pruritus	57	235	292	52	105	43	25	19	44	4
b. Dermatalgia	2	3	5		2	1			2	
Anæsthesia	2	2	7		1				6	
Class IX. Parasitic Affections.										
1. *Vegetable.*										
Tinea favosa	5	59	64	4	37	6			17	
Tinea trichophytina :	14	24	38	38						
a. circinata	46	132	178	55	77	10	5	5	24	2
b. tonsurans,	25	130	155	34	51	25	6	5	20	14
c. sycosis	40	78	118	22	37	14	10	1	30	4
Tinea versicolor	34	121	155	41	52	15	13	16	18	
2. *Animal.*										
Scabies	34	308	342	96	132	25	2	7	72	8
Pediculosis capillitii	2	236	238	91	72	23	6	7	36	3
Pediculosis corporis	2	204	206	36	95	14	4	1	48	8
Pediculosis pubis	22	31	53	8	11	1			33	

TABLE II.—Concluded.

UNCLASSIFIED.	Private Cases.	Dispensary Cases.	Total No. Cases.	Boston.	New York.	Philadelphia.	Baltimore.	St. Louis.	Chicago.	Canada.
Varicella	1		1	1						
Cheiro-pompholix	2		2	2						
Abscess	7		7	7						
Onychia	3	1	4	3	1					
Lichen tropicus	2	8	10	2	8					
Sycosis, non-parasitica		3	3			3				
Varieties of exfol. dermatitis	3		3					3		
Rodent ulcer	2		2							2
Purpura rheumatica		2	2		2					
" cortic	1		1		1					
Acne, lupoid	1	1	2		2					
Adenitis		4	4		4					
Cætrophia cutis	2		2		2					
Cellulitis		2	2		2					
Dermatitis exfoliativa		3	3		3					
" medicamentosa	1	8	9		9					
" papillaris capillitii		1	1		1					
Dysidrosis	2	3	5		5					
Hydroa		2	2		2					
Leukoplakia	2	1	3		3					
Lichen scrofulosorum		5	5		5					
" strophulus		1	1		1					
Myxomata		2	2		2					
Nævus pilosus		1	1		1					
Paget's disease		1	1		1					
Papilloma		1	1		1					
Paronychia		4	4		4					
Pityriasis maculata et circinata	1		1		1					
Pityriasis rosea	3	2	5		2				3	
" simplex	1	2	3		3					
Pompholix		4	4		4					
Sudamina		1	1		1					
Sycosis	4	29	33		33					
Trichorexis nodosa	1		1		1					
Tylosis		1	1		1					
Unclassified	1	69	70		70					
Syphiloderma, hered		8	8		8					
Epithelioma	10	44	54		54					
	50	214	264	15	238	3		6		2

TABLE III.

Combined Returns of Five Years, 1878–1882.

YEAR.	Boston.	New York.	Philadelphia.	Baltimore.	St. Louis.	Chicago.	Canada.	Dispensary.	Private.	Total.
1878...	11921	1680	777	1092	168	1227	......	13828	3035	16863
1879...	3485	1795	645	......	203	1989	......	5777	2340	8117
1880...	3315	3326	896	663	260	2587	......	8199	2898	11047
1881...	3264	3837	1108	503	264	2100	......	8435	2641	11076
1882...	3212	3231	1451	520	424	2564	112	7960	3554	11514
Total..	25197	13869	4877	2778	1319	10467	112	44199	14418	58617

TABLE IV.

Combined Returns of Five Years, 1878-1882.

DISEASES.	NO. CASES.	% CASES.
Class I. Disorders of the Glands.		
1. Of the Sweat Glands.		
Hyperidrosis	156	.266
Miliaria crystallina	93	.158
Anidrosis	5	.008
Bromidrosis	49	.083
Chromidrosis		
2. Of the Sebaceous Glands.		
Seborrhœa :	1289	2.19
a. oleosa		
b. sicca		
Comedo	692	1.18
Cyst:		
a. Milium	140	.238
b. Wen	28	.047
Molluscum sebaceum	74	.126
Diminished secretion		
Class II, Inflammations.		
Exanthemata	1098	1.87
Erythema simplex	481	.820
Erythema multiforme :	683	1.16
a. papulosum		
b. bullosum		
c. nodosum		
Urticaria	1502	2.54
* Dermatitis:	1167	1.99
a. traumatica		
b. venenata		
c. calorica		
Erysipelas	576	.908
Furuncle	1123	1.91
Anthrax	145	.247
Phlegmona diffusa	152	.259
Pustula maligna	3	.005

* Indicating affections of this class not properly included under other titles.

TABLE IV.—Continued.

Combined Returns of Five Years, 1878-1882.

DISEASES.	NO. CASES.	% CASES.
Herpes:	1077	1.83
a. facialis		
b. progenitalis		
Herpes zoster	807	1.37
Psoriasis	1924	3.28
Pityriasis rubra	16	.027
Lichen:	105	.179
a. planus		
b. ruber		
Eczema:	18525	31.63
a. erythematosum		
b. papulosum		
c. vesiculosum		
d. madidans		
e. pustulosum		
f. rubrum		
g. squamosum		
Prurigo	6	.010
Acne	4157	7.09
Impetigo	821	1.40
Impetigo contagiosa	285	.486
Impetigo herpetiformis	4	.006
Ecthyma	351	.598
Pemphigus	89	.151
Class III. Hæmorrhages.		
Purpura:	272	.463
a. simplex		
b. hæmorrhagica		
Class IV. Hypertrophies.		
1. *Of Pigment.*		
Lentigo	48	.081
Chloasma:		
a. locale	295	.504
b. universale		

TABLE IV.—Continued.

Combined Returns of Five Years, 1878-1882.

DISEASES.	NO. CASES.	º/₀ CASES.
2. *Of Epidermal and Papillary Layers.*		
Keratosis	89	.151
a. pilaris		
b. senilis		
Callositas	39	.066
Clavus	34	.057
Cornu cutaneum	16	.027
Verruca	528	.907
Verruca necrogenica	1	.001
Xerosis	41	.069
Ichthyosis	148	.252
Of Nail	32	.054
Hirsuties	181	.308
3. *Of Connective Tissue.*		
Scleroderma	15	.025
Sclerema neonatorum		
Morphœa	17	.029
Elephantiasis Arabum	35	.059
Rosacea:	562	.958
a. erythematosa		
b. hypertrophica		
Frambœsia	22	.037
Class V. Atrophies.		
1. *Of Pigment.*		
Leucoderma	34	.057
Albinismus	6	.032
Vitiligo	78	.133
Canities	25	.042
2. *Of Hair.*		
Alopecia	483	.823
Alopecia areata	350	.597
Alopecia furfuracea	393	674
Atrophia pilorum propria	10	.017
3. *Of Nail*	23	.039
4. *Of Cutis.*		
Atrophia senilis	5	.008
Atrophia maculosa et striata	17	.029
Class VI. New Growths.		
1. *Of Connective Tissue.*		
Keloid	81	.136
Cicatrix	51	.086
Fibroma	42	.071
Neuroma	8	.013
Xanthoma	42	.071

TABLE IV.—Concluded.

Combined Returns of Five Years, 1878-1882.

DISEASES.	NO. CASES.	º/₀ CASES.
2. *Of Vessels.*		
Angioma	234	.399
Angioma pigmentosum et atrophicum	8	.005
Angioma cavernosum	15	.025
Lymphangioma	8	.013
3. *Of Granulation Tissue.*		
Rhino-scleroma		
Lupus erythematosus	217	.371
Lupus vulgaris	239	.407
Scrofuloderma	256	.436
Syphiloderma:	6304	10.7
a. erythematosum		
b. papulosum		
c. pustulosum		
d. tuberculosum		
e. gummatosum		
Lepra :	19	.032
a. tuberosa		
b. maculosa		
c. anæsthetica		
Carcinoma	401	.684
Sarcoma	16	.027
Class VII. Ulcers	1961	3.34
Class VIII. Neuroses.		
Hyperæsthesia :		
a. Pruritus	1278	2.17
b. Dermatalgia		
Anæsthesia	12	.024
Class IX. Parasitic Affections.		
1. *Vegetable.*		
Tinea favosa	154	.262
Tinea trichophytina.:	1834	3.07
a. circinata		
b. tonsurans		
c. sycosis		
Tinea versicolor	644	1.08
2. *Animal.*		
Scabies	665	1.10
Pediculosis capillitii	1500	2.55
Pediculosis corporis	919	1.56
Pediculosis pubis	227	.387

OFFICERS OF THE ASSOCIATION

FOR 1883-4.

PRESIDENT,

Dr. R. W. TAYLOR, New York.

VICE-PRESIDENTS,

Dr. ARTHUR VAN HARLINGEN, Philadelphia.

Dr. J. E. GRAHAM, Toronto.

SECRETARY,

Dr. W. T. ALEXANDER, New York.

TREASURER,

Dr. GEORGE H. ROHÉ, Baltimore.

www.ingramcontent.com/pod-product-compliance
Lightning Source LLC
Chambersburg PA
CBHW032102230426
43672CB00009B/1614